Approaching Disparities in School Discipline:

Theory, Research, Practice, and Social Change

Anthony Troy Adams
Clark Atlanta University, USA

A volume in the Advances
in Educational Marketing,
Administration, and Leadership
(AEMAL) Book Series

Published in the United States of America by
    IGI Global
    Information Science Reference (an imprint of IGI Global)
    701 E. Chocolate Avenue
    Hershey PA, USA 17033
    Tel: 717-533-8845
    Fax: 717-533-8661
    E-mail: cust@igi-global.com
    Web site: http://www.igi-global.com

Library of Congress Cataloging-in-Publication Data

Names: Adams, Anthony T., 1960- editor.
Title: Approaching disparities in school discipline : theory, research,
    practice, and social change / Anthony T. Adams, editor.
Description: Hershey, PA : Information Science Reference, 2022. | Includes
    bibliographical references and index. | Summary: "This book will be a
    comprehensive resource on school discipline, summarizing current theory,
    describing research methods and analytical approaches, sharing new
    results, discussing school policy, and introducing colleagues from mass
    communication and media communications to the topic"-- Provided by
    publisher.
Identifiers: LCCN 2021060932 (print) | LCCN 2021060933 (ebook) | ISBN
    9781668433591 (hardcover) | ISBN 9781668433607 (paperback) | ISBN
    9781668433614 (ebook)
Subjects: LCSH: School discipline--Social aspects--United States. |
    Educational equalization--United States.
Classification: LCC LB3012.2 .A77 2022 (print) | LCC LB3012.2 (ebook) |
    DDC 371.50973--dc23/eng/20220124
LC record available at https://lccn.loc.gov/2021060932
LC ebook record available at https://lccn.loc.gov/2021060933

This book is published in the IGI Global book series Advances in Educational Marketing,
Administration, and Leadership (AEMAL) (ISSN: 2326-9022; eISSN: 2326-9030)

British Cataloguing in Publication Data
A Cataloguing in Publication record for this book is available from the British Library.

All work contributed to this book is new, previously-unpublished material.
The views expressed in this book are those of the authors, but not necessarily of the publisher.

For electronic access to this publication, please contact: eresources@igi-global.com.

Advances in Educational Marketing, Administration, and Leadership (AEMAL) Book Series

ISSN:2326-9022
EISSN:2326-9030

Editor-in-Chief: Siran Mukerji IGNOU, India Purnendu Tripathi IGNOU, India

MISSION

With more educational institutions entering into public, higher, and professional education, the educational environment has grown increasingly competitive. With this increase in competitiveness has come the need for a greater focus on leadership within the institutions, on administrative handling of educational matters, and on the marketing of the services offered.

The **Advances in Educational Marketing, Administration, & Leadership (AEMAL) Book Series** strives to provide publications that address all these areas and present trending, current research to assist professionals, administrators, and others involved in the education sector in making their decisions.

COVERAGE

- Direct marketing of educational programs
- Marketing Theories within Education
- Academic Administration
- Educational Finance
- Faculty Administration and Management
- Advertising and Promotion of Academic Programs and Institutions
- Educational Leadership
- Technologies and Educational Marketing
- Enrollment Management
- Educational Marketing Campaigns

IGI Global is currently accepting manuscripts for publication within this series. To submit a proposal for a volume in this series, please contact our Acquisition Editors at Acquisitions@igi-global.com or visit: http://www.igi-global.com/publish/.

Titles in this Series

For a list of additional titles in this series, please visit:
http://www.igi-global.com/book-series/advances-educational-marketing-administration-leader-ship/73677

701 East Chocolate Avenue, Hershey, PA 17033, USA
Tel: 717-533-8845 x100 • Fax: 717-533-8661
E-Mail: cust@igi-global.com • www.igi-global.com

In loving memory of Harriett Anita Kerridge, May 9, 1944 – March 3, 2021

EDITORIAL ADVISORY BOARD

Table of Contents

Section 3
Practice

Section 4
Social Change

Chapter 12

Detailed Table of Contents

Section 1
Theory

This collection of chapters examines various theoretical lenses, including Critical Race Theory, Racial Threat Theory, the Racialized Theory of Organizations, and other frameworks to describe and provide a foundation for understanding school discipline disparities.

Chapter 1

Minority students in both urban and suburban school settings within the United States are subject to harsher and more frequent disciplinary actions than their white counterparts. Implicit bias and lack of cultural awareness contribute to a large disparity in discipline referrals for Black males in particular. Through the application of Critical Race Theory and Racial Threat Theory, this chapter examines the historical influences that have created confirmation bias in the education environment as well as the prevalence of zero-tolerance policies that exist in schools with large minority populations. Data gathered from the 2017 Civil Rights Data collection reported to the US Department of Education were used to highlight the discipline trends of six US school districts.

Chapter 2

This chapter explores the concept of implicit racial bias as a significant factor contributing to the disparities between the discipline rates of White and Black students. While overt acts of racism are not as common as they were during other times in

United States' history, implicit or unintentional racial bias still leads to differences in educational opportunities for the nation's students. The chapter begins with an examination of the concept of implicit bias broadly before turning toward implicit racial bias specifically. The chapter continues with a historical overview of the ways in which schooling for Black students has always been controlled by a dominant White society. Next, the researcher presents current data about the inequities in exclusionary discipline practices. The chapter concludes with recommendations for recognizing and addressing implicit bias and the problems it creates.

The concepts of discipline and law are linked together. Laws are often constructed to define what is considered acceptable conduct, and a form of discipline is often used to align unacceptable conduct to those laws. This is especially evident in the K-12 setting. Schools promote their brand of laws or "policies" to allow for an efficient education process with minimal disruption. However, when you are dealing with children who are not in full control of their impulses, disruptions are bound to occur. In the U.S., given the disproportionate sentencing and incarceration rates between whites and minorities, it can be reasonably deduced that the same phenomenon occurs within the K-12 school space as well. In consideration of these discrepancies, and U.S. constitutional concepts such as due process and equal protection are referenced. What exactly are they, and how do they come into play to correct these inequities? How do landmark cases argued in front of the U.S. Supreme Court citing these concepts help to frame what is considered acceptable discipline in the K-12 school space?

Chapter 4

The chapter explores how two geographically distant countries are brought close by their cultural acceptance of corporal punishment (CP) in school. The chapter details that though both societies have formulated several bills engaged in numerous debates over a lengthy period, culture, religion, and politics sustain school CP. The Guyanese argument engages various stakeholders, significantly influenced by the US's "ban" on school CP and the perceived negative results from such "prohibitions." This study assesses the legality, prevalence, theories, and applicable corporal punishment laws in the US and Guyana. The findings suggest that corporal punishment remains legally sanctioned in 19 US states and Guyana. Annually, substantial numbers of children experience corporal punishment at school. Legal, political, educational, and familial institutions endorsed such use.

Section 2
Research

Chapters 5-6 provide current research on school discipline.

Chapter 5

Jennifer Wyatt Bourgeois, Texas Southern University, USA
Melissa Kwende, Texas Southern University, USA
Howard Henderson, Texas Southern University, USA

This chapter will analyze school disciplinary actions across large metropolitan school districts. In recent decades, K-12 school disciplinary practices have garnered national attention from researchers, policymakers, and educators. Racial disparity among school discipline raises serious questions about continued violations of the 1954 Brown vs. Board of Education decision. The purpose of the chapter is to provide a series of evidence-supported recommendations for the dismantling of the school-to-prison pipeline. The current chapter will examine the discipline records for the 2016-2017 academic school year in 19 independent school districts to identify the equitable assignment of suspensions and expulsions. Disparity ratio analysis will help us understand the relationship between race, ethnicity, and school suspension. The findings will be utilized to guide policy recommendations. The results will provide an evidence-based understanding of racial disparity in school suspensions.

Chapter 6

Melissa F. Kwende, Texas Southern University, USA
Jennifer Wyatt Bourgeois, Texas Southern University, USA
Howard Henderson, Texas Southern University, USA
Julian Scott, Texas Southern University, USA

This chapter will examine the disproportionate rate of minority school suspensions relative to race/ethnicity, gender, socioeconomic status, grade level, and school population size. Although Black students account for 20% of the school population for this chapter's study, the rate of in-school discipline for Black students far exceeded the rates for White and Hispanic students. Notably, the authors find that race, gender, socioeconomic status, and grade level are correlated with the disproportionate disciplinary practices imposed upon minority students regardless of grade level. In this chapter, the authors review the previous research on race, gender, poverty, grade level, and school discipline before laying out their methodological approach for understanding suspension disparities. After analysis, they conclude with recommendations for improvement.

Section 3
Practice

Chapters 7-8 offer creative alternative approaches to exclusionary discipline.

Chapter 7

 Kisha Solomon, Independent Researcher, USA

Storytelling is an effective technique for resolving disputes and conflict while preserving relationships, self-image, and cultural standards. With increased access to the internet and social media, digital storytelling has become instrumental in spurring awareness and change in areas of social injustice and inequality. This chapter briefly examines the science and culture of storytelling and explores the use of digital storytelling in multiple contexts. The author establishes evidence-based support for the use of storytelling and/or digital storytelling 1) to mitigate educator bias in school discipline policy and practices; 2) to counteract and/or reduce negative psychological, emotional, and cultural impacts of excessive or disparate disciplinary practices; 3) to increase cross-sector awareness, advocacy, and engagement on exclusionary discipline issues. The author also proposes a counter-storytelling method for enhanced qualitative and quantitative data-gathering in school discipline cases.

Chapter 8

 Thelma Laredo Clark, Baylor University, USA
 Brandi R. Ray, Baylor University, USA
 Elizabeth Anne Murray, Baylor University, USA

Exclusionary discipline practices are continuously pushing economically disadvantaged students out of their traditional home campuses instead of rehabilitating them with the ability to become productive members of their communities. This chapter explores the development of exclusionary discipline consequences and the known outcomes of these consequences on economically disadvantaged students. The chapter provides background information regarding the initial appeal of exclusionary discipline practices followed by the subsequent harm it created for certain groups of students. The chapter identifies the possibilities for decreasing the use of exclusionary discipline by adopting strategies like PBIS and restorative justice practices. The chapter closes with a discussion of the importance of schools moving away from exclusionary discipline practices. The authors argue transparency from school leaders with school community members is essential for the initial and continued success of restorative practices and the curbing of the damage of exclusionary consequences for students.

Section 4
Social Change

Chapters 9-12 approach school disciplinary disparities from a social change perspective. These chapters offer innovative approaches and strategies for combatting school discipline disparities. The chapters sought guidance from teachers and practitioners regarding their lived experiences and ideas for approaching school discipline disparities.

Across the nation, various movements have persistently called for the removal of punitive practices in school; this includes removing law enforcement officers (LEOs) and school resource officers (SROs) and prioritizing funding toward student support services. This chapter brings attention to the role of school administrators and how they can leverage and support school counselors to address disparities in school discipline that impact racially minoritized youth. The authors draw on the theory of racialized organizations to demonstrate how schools are a racialized space, as individual agency is constrained or enabled by their social position within the organization, and how schools further reproduce inequity through their unequal distribution of resources. This chapter offers some practical approaches to reveal how school administrators can leverage school counselors to dismantle disparities in school discipline and prioritize practices of care.

Punitive disciplinary policies in schools have drastic effects on student performance and success among minority students. These disciplinary policies have a direct impact on the school-to-prison pipeline issue in America. In recent years, restorative justice practices have been implemented in schools to replace punitive disciplinary policies like the zero-tolerance policy. However, to truly see the benefits of restorative justice practices in schools, there needs to be an increased awareness of its principles and benefits. This study examines how restorative justice discourse on Twitter can build an agenda for increased awareness of restorative justice practices in schools and policy changes regarding punitive discipline practices.

This chapter is intended to help others seeking answers to the disciplinary disparities that limit opportunities for communities and students of color. The chapter begins with a grounding in the historical context, then identifies current issues in discipline disparities, and concludes with a call for transformational change in public education. Education significantly sets the path for individuals; likewise, it affects the course of society in crucial ways. Disparities in educational experiences have compounding effects. Discipline disparities in K-12 schools are particularly impactful.

This chapter asserts that too much commentary has been given to school disciplinary disparities with few remedies for mitigating the problem. The time has come to move from courageous to unapologetic conversations about disciplinary disparities. Data furnished by the U.S. Department of Education, Office of Civil Rights, for the school year 2017-18 estimates that 11,205,797 youths missed school days from our nation's public schools due to out-of-school suspensions. The average school year is roughly 182 days. Thusly, 61,570 students per day missed invaluable instructional time due to out-of-school suspensions. Black/students of color, males, and students with special education identification are especially vulnerable. This chapter summarizes the extant literature; discusses the core issues, controversies, and problems; highlights the correlates associated with school disciplinary disparities; and proposes several unapologetic and radical recommendations for reducing disparities.

Preface

This book addresses one of the most widespread and intractable problems in the history of 21ˢᵗ Century public education – disparities in school discipline. The problem is as pervasive as Jim Crow laws of the past. School disciplinary disparities topple the scales of justice and fairness, homogenize public education demographics, and deprive Black and Brown children of their inalienable rights to public education.

Disparities in school discipline refers to the disparate rate at which Black, minority, and students with IDEA designation are excluded from school. The effects of exclusion include: the obvious loss of instructional time; grade retention and the costs associated with grade retention (Losen and Martinez, 2020); stop-outs and drop-outs (Chu & Ready, 2018; Hinze-Pifer & Sartain, 2018); decreased odds of college attendance (Brazil, 2022); and, increased likelihood of negative experiences related to the school-to-prison pipeline and contact with the juvenile and/or criminal justice system (Dutil, 2020; Morgan, 2021; Novak & Fagan, 2021; Novak, 2019; Arredondo et. al., 2012; Gonzalez, 2012).

In the 1830s Horace Mann advocated for a public education that would benefit an entire nation by preparing children to become literate, responsible, and productive citizens. Common schools (sometimes referred to as universal education) would prepare young people for civic responsibility, helping them transition into their adult social roles and the world of work and labor. Education would also provide the seeds for moral development congruent with American values. Proponents of common schools promoted the idea that universal education could eradicate poverty, crime, and other social problems.

Mann's idea of public education becoming universally accessible was closer to becoming realized, in part, because of Lincoln's Emancipation Proclamation of 1863, ordering all enslaved individuals freedom. However, Jim Crow laws, lasting nearly 100 years, would thwart Mann's vision. It was not until Brown v. Board of Education's (1954) reversal of Plessy v. Ferguson's (1896), institutionalized discriminatory practices, which would revitalize the idea of U.S. universal schooling. Brown offered an illusion of accessibility to students regardless of racial/ethnicity identity, however

Separatist ideology and Jim Crow laws nearly interrupted public education's mission and posed a threat to democracy. Brown v Board of Education and other important federal mandates helped place public education back on track. The author is reminded that a prevailing lag time exists between federally-mandated court decisions and the actual enforcement of laws taking effect (e.g., Lincoln's Emancipation Proclamation on January 1, 1863 and full enforcement June 19, 1865; Brown v Board of Education, 1954 and enforcement of the legal doctrine, Little Rock 9, 1957, three years later), altogether these legal mandates 'appeared" to open doors for the prospects of public education.

Despite Brown v. Board of Education and a litany of legal cases aimed at dismantling discrimination in education, housing, and in labor; equality has been under siege by status quo state and local policies. Today, zero tolerance policies and implicit bias reproduce disproportionalities in school discipline. These policies and practices contribute to inequities in educational opportunity. Students who are unfairly and systematically removed from our nation's schools undermines our country's principles of life, liberty, and pursuit of happiness set forth in the U.S. Declaration of Independence, and ultimately threatens our democracy.

School disciplinary disparities K-12 has reached epoch proportions in the United States. School disciplinary disparities threaten public education and access to educational opportunities. Students are being excluded (suspended, expelled, and transferred for disciplinary reasons) from our nation's public schools in unprecedented numbers. The country currently struggles with systemic and structural racism, political upheaval, and a pandemic that serves to further polarize political and ideological groups.

Two reports from the Department of Education Office of Civil Rights (U.S. Department of Education Office of Civil Rights, 2021$_a$, 2014$_b$) tell a disheartening story about U.S. schools and discipline. First, school year 2017-2018 describes the intersectionality between disciplinary exclusion by race, sex, and IDEA identification. The alarmingly high rate of exclusion convey that:

- 11,205,797 total school days were missed due to out-of-school suspensions
- Black students (accounting for 15.1 percent of total enrollment) were expelled at a rate twice their proportion in the population at 38.8, with educational services, and 33.3% without educational services.
- Black students represented 28.7% of all students referred to law enforcement officials.
- Boys accounted for 51.4% of the total student enrollment and received nearly 70 percent (69.5%) of the in-school suspensions and 70 percent of the out-of-school suspensions.

- Black students served under IDEA represented 2.3 percent of the total student enrollment, and were nearly four times as likely to be referred to law enforcement.

A second report for school year 2011-2012 combined with the 2017-2018 data reveals that over 14.5 million students were excluded from school during two years alone. During the 2011-2012 school year, 3.45 million children were removed for disciplinary reasons. Another 11,205,797 students were excluded from school through out-of-school suspensions during the 2017-2018 campaign (June 2021). Most daunting is that disciplinary exclusion has increased at a rate of 224 percent from 2012 to 2018. Even more staggering is if one considers that a typical school year is 182 days, over 61 thousand students per day were excluded from schools in the 2017-2018 school year (61,570 = 11,205,797/182). Compounding matters is that Black and students of color, K-12, have experienced exclusion (e.g., suspension, expulsion, disciplinary transfers) and denied regular access to public education in the nation's schools at rates two and five times greater than their White peers (Anderson & Ritter, 2020; Williams et al., 2020).

Parallels Between the New Jim Crow, Mass Incarceration, and Exclusionary Discipline

Parallels between Diane Alexander's (2010) *mass incarceration* and exclusionary discipline can be drawn. Alexander describes how mass incarceration has become the New Jim Crow creating a *racial caste* system. Alexander defines *racial caste* as a racial group locked into an inferior position by law and custom (p. 12). Mass incarceration functions, as did pre-Civil War Slavery and the post-Civil War Jim Crow; it

Is a system that locks people not only behind actual bars in actual prisons, but also behind virtual bars and virtual walls—walls that are invisible to the naked eye but function nearly as effectively as Jim Crow laws once did at locking people of color into a permanent second-class citizenship. The term mass incarceration refers not only to the criminal justice system but also to the larger web of laws, rules, policies, and customs that control those labeled criminals both in and out of prison. Once released, former prisoners enter a hidden underworld of legalized discrimination and permanent social exclusion.

Mass incarceration and disciplinary exclusion share at least five similarities. First, neither incarceration nor disciplinary exclusion has proven effective. Theoretically, punishment functions include deterrence, rehabilitation, and incapacitation. Jail and prison time do not deter, nor do they rehabilitate. A team of researchers led by Harding from the University of California, the University of Michigan, Kaiser Permanente Colorado Institute for Health Research, the State University of New York and the University of Colorado found evidence that incarceration among serious offenders does not prevent them from committing future crime (Harding et al., 2019; Galbiati & Drago, 2018; Cullen, Jonson, & Nagin, 2011). Related, suspensions and expulsions have not made schools safer. Students who are suspended or expelled are more likely to experience negative outcomes. These include grade retention, becoming high school dropouts, arrest and contact with law enforcement officials, and incarceration (Fabelo et al., 2011). Mass incarceration and disciplinary exclusion are fallacies. Neither incarceration nor exclusion deter future deviance or rehabilitates offenders, or improve life's chances.

Second, both felons and students excluded for disciplinary reasons are denied services. Felons, for example, lose food stamps, social security, educational assistance, and other public benefits. Students by contrast lose invaluable instructional time, counseling services, library privileges, free and/or reduced priced lunches; many of which are important for scholastic growth and positive educational outcomes.

A third commonality that felons and students removed from school share is they are labeled. Labeling theory finds its origins in the work of French sociologist Emile Durkheim (1897). Durkheim argued that crime, from a societal perspective, it not so much a matter of violating a penal code, but rather an act against society. Labels affect how individuals perceive themselves and how others perceive them. Among felons, members of society may hold negative perceptions that discolor or devalue a felon's worth. Consequently felons are viewed with suspicion and characterized as untrustworthy, unreliable, and potentially dangerous. For students, labeling can trigger a processes leading to greater engagement in asocial misbehavior (Liberman et al., 2014), including repeat offenses, associations with individuals involved in aberrant activities, and time spent without adult supervision.

Fourth, felons may have a greater propensity to commit future crimes because of difficulties associated with re-acclimation to society (e.g., finding employment, housing, etc.). Students excluded from school are more likely to be removed from school multiple times (Novak & Fagan, 2021).

A fifth similarity between felons and students excluded from school is that they are reduced to second-class citizenship. Felons may forfeit their right to vote and participate in the democratic process. For example, in nine states (Alabama, Arizona, Delaware, Florida, Iowa, Kentucky, Mississippi, Tennessee, and Wyoming) felons cannot hold public office, or serve on jury duty. Similarly, students are banished from school property. They cannot attend after school programs, participate or attend sporting events, or socials during their disciplinary exclusion. Summarily, both systems of behavioral correction fail to rehabilitate, reduce individual or collective recidivism, and possess a litany of negative and unintended consequences.

Is help on the way? The federal government is promoting initiatives to close the school discipline disparity gap. The Biden-Harris administration is playing an eminent role through the appendages of the Office of Civil Rights and the Department of Justice's Civil Rights Division. At its convening, "Brown 67 Years Later: Examining Disparities in School Discipline and the Pursuit of Safe and Inclusive Schools (May 11, 2021)," efforts were made to galvanize all stakeholders in meaningful dialogue to drive policy and to identify needed technical and other important resources to positively influence school climate and the administration of discipline.

Additionally, the U.S. Department of education (DOE) has stalwartly provided a myriad of school climate and discipline resources. From training modules on bullying prevention, creating safe and respectful classroom environments, to dealing with students with disabilities that interfere with classroom instruction, and school discipline courses for school and community leaders, to overall school safety. DOE has entered innumerous consent decrees and settlement agreements with school districts to improve their disciplinary system and reduce reliance on exclusion, so that all students receive equitable treatment and gain full access to educational opportunities. DOE has also provided policy guidelines, guides & brochures, Webinars, and access to surveys and technical assistance centers and regional Civil Rights Offices to state departments and local school districts. An unanswered question remains: What more can the federal government do to eliminate school discipline disparities?

Individual states are exploring measures to reduce school discipline disparities too. And while states make earnest efforts to address exclusionary disparities, the topic has become highly politicized with Obama-era guidance (Guidance document, 2014) supporters on one side, urging districts to reduce reliance on exclusionary discipline, and Trump-rescinding proponents on the other, contending that by reducing its use is associated with decreased school safety. Nevertheless, states like California, Massachusetts, and Minnesota are collecting disaggregated school suspension data, analyzing the information, and proposing and administering policies and practices to reduce exclusionary discipline. California, for example, placed a ban on suspension for disruptions/defiance in grades K-3 to K-8; called for greater state oversight on school districts with high rates of lost instruction; and, strive to work discipline into the state's accountability infrastructure, among other key policy recommendations (The Center for Civil Rights Remedies at The Civil Rights Project, "Is California Doing Enough to Close the School Discipline Gap?, Daniel J. Losen & Paul Martinez, June 22, 2022). Similarly, the state of Illinois amended its school code to include intensive data collection and reporting to combat disciplinary disproportionalities.

Public educations operates under a decentralized system. State departments of education and local school districts have the authority to set school policies, and school discipline, more specifically. More must be done to reduce and limit the use of exclusionary discipline. This book weaves together current theory and research on school discipline disparities, but it also discusses current developments and practices in the field and explores ways to affect social change.

ORGANIZATION OF THE BOOK

Theory, Research, Practice, and Social Change

This book is organized into twelve chapters. Chapters 1-4 embrace theory. The collection of chapters examines various theoretical lenses, including Critical Race Theory, Racial Threat Theory, the Racialized Theory of Organizations, and other frameworks to describe and provide a foundation for understanding school discipline disparities. Chapters 5-6 provide current research on school discipline. Chapters 7-8 offer creative alternative approaches to exclusionary discipline. Chapters 9-12 approach school disciplinary disparities from a social change perspective. These chapters offer innovative approaches and strategies for combatting school discipline disparities. The chapters sought guidance from teachers and practitioners regarding their lived experiences and ideas for approaching school discipline disparities. Scholars in the fields of communications, social work, and sociology contributed their thoughts to taking on school discipline disparities. Multidimensional lenses were employed to address lofty questions. For example, how can we invest time, money, and resources into reducing the use of exclusion from a social change perspective? How can social change agents arm themselves to battle codified traditions, entrenched practices, social structures, hierarchies, and status quo to promote change? What can we do differently to stop the hemorrhaging and ameliorate or eradicate the use of disciplinary exclusion and disciplinary disparities? A description of each of the chapters follows:

Chapter 1 explores the theoretical underpinnings of cultural bias and its relationship to discipline disparity. Integrating both critical race theory and racial threat theory, the author contends that America's views of brown-skinned students is deeply embedded in a pervasive negative narrative that tarnishes teachers' perceptions of Black and Hispanic students. The author insists that breaking this vicious cycle requires in-service training and augmentations to status-quo curriculum requiring cultural awareness and sensitivity.

Chapter 2 explores the nuances of implicit bias and its relationship to school disciplinary disparities. The author purports that implicit bias is rooted in racism since public education's inception. Several definitions of implicit bias are provided. The extant literature conveys the concept's multidimensional aspects (e.g., cognition, attitudes, and stereotypes). Explicit cultural sensitivity training is needed for teachers, the administration of Implicit Association Test, and careful attention directed at *situations.*

Chapter 3 offers a historical excavation of Due Process, dating back to the Magna Carta. Theories of punishment are explored and their conceptual relationship to school discipline is discussed. Second, the chapter places school discipline in a legal context, tracing the developments of legal history from the Magna Carta to 1776. Third, the chapter describes how a legal analysis of U.S. Constitutional provisions could be a mechanism for combating school discipline disparities.

Chapter 4 provides an international comparison on the use of corporal punishment. The author describes how two geographically distant and normatively divergent countries are brought close by their cultural acceptance of corporal punishment. Both societies have passed bills and engaged in long-standing debates over its praxis. Culture, religion, and politics sustain corporal punishment's use. The legalities, prevalence, theories, and applicable corporal punishment laws in the US and Guyana are compared. Corporal punishment remains legally sanctioned in nineteen US states and Guyana.

Research

Chapter 5 describes research findings from a study using state-level data collected from the Texas Education Agency, Harris County Independent School Districts. The authors found that Black students were more likely to be removed from classrooms due to disciplinary reasons, and the largest school district generated the highest disparity ratio of 5.52 per 100 students. The authors state that future studies must disaggregate data, mandate cultural awareness training among teachers, and foster community-to-school partnerships among other findings.

Chapter 6 examines the empirical relationship between school discipline disparities and race. Using a convenience sample of two hundred sixty-two students from a small rural Texas school district, grades 3 through 12, the authors find that Black students' rate of suspension are disproportionately greater than White and Hispanic students. The authors' findings support the claim that zero tolerance policies contribute to school disciplinary disparities and is consistent with the expanding literature.

Practice

Chapter 7 provides a refreshingly unique approach for combatting school discipline disproportionality and social inequality. The author discusses the ancient practice and art of storytelling combined with digitization, making this formidable method for giving students agency. Storytelling can teach students poise, self-restraint, and improve listening and communicative skills. The author demonstrates how storytelling has crossover elements with conflict resolution. Digital storytelling is linguistic, educative, and facilitates negotiated transactions.

Chapter 8 discusses the promise of restorative discipline and positive behavior interventions for decreasing the use of exclusionary discipline. The benefits of restorative approaches include student engagement, building a stronger school community, and helping students reflect on their attitudinal and behavioral experiences. The author cements that interventions will only work to the extent that the broader school community, faculty and staff, and parents and students are committed to the success of these interventions.

Social Change

Chapter 9 raises a provocative question. Why do some schools have a greater presence of security, police, and resource officers on campus than counselors? The authors argue that the very nature of security and police presence on school campus erodes the very fabric of the school organization. The author recommends that schools gravitate towards a culture of care. Using racialized organizational theory, the authors maintain that school administrators must build partnerships with school support staff, including counselors.

Chapter 10 offers an invigoratingly new approach for targeting school disciplinary disparities. Through the aperture of a public relations approach, the author insists that restorative justice approaches combined with public relations and media campaigns have a real shot at influencing individuals' behaviors and reducing dependency on exclusionary discipline. The author strenuously recommends increasing media messaging about school discipline disparities and discusses benefits gained by restorative justice programs.

Chapter 11 discusses the detrimental effects of the school-to-prison pipeline and the need for more school counselors. The negative effects of law enforcement officials (LEOs) and school resource officials (SROs) is tantamount to a police state, and their presence on campus is associated with emotional distress among students, symptoms of depression, racism-induced trauma among other emotional, psychological, and social stressors. Twenty-First Century school counselors are prepared to assist students with their emotional and psychological wellbeing, and collaboration with students, parents, teachers, administrators and communities.

Chapter 12 takes a look at the discourse on disparities in school discipline. The chapter argues that the problem of disciplinary disparities has been an ongoing saga for over five decades; the rhetoric has run rampant and the solutions appear distant.

The author calls for more radical approaches to ameliorating school disciplinary disparities, including greater nationwide exposure to the issue, school and district-level leaderboards, disciplinary report cards, grassroots initiatives, and engaged scholars as instruments of change.

Anthony Troy Adams
Clark Atlanta University, USA

REFERENCES

Alexander, M. (2010). *The new jim crow: Mass incarceration in the age of colorblindness*. The New Press.

Anderson, K. P., & Ritter, G. W. (2020). Do School Discipline Policies Treat Students Fairly? Evidence from Arkansas. *Educational Policy, 34*(5), 707–734. doi:10.1177/0895904818802085

Arredondo, M., Williams, N., & Convey, M. (2012). The School-to-Prison Pipeline: Pathways from schools to juvenile justice. In *Discipline Disparities: A Research-to-Practice Collaborative*. The Equity Project at Indiana University.

Brazil, B. (2022, Feb. 9). School discipline causes lasting, harmful impact on Black students, study finds. *Daily Pilot*. https://www.latimes.com/socal/daily-pilot/entertainment/story/2022-02-09/school-discipline-causes-lasting-harmful-impact-on-black-students-study-finds

Chu, E. M., & Ready, D. D. (2018). Exclusion and urban public high schools: Short- and long-term consequences of school suspension. *American Journal of Education, 124*(4), 479–509. doi:10.1086/698454

Cullen, F. T., Jonson, C. L., & Nagin, D. S. (2011). Prisons do not reduce recidivism: The high cost of ignoring science. *The Prison Journal, 91*(3), 48–65. doi:10.1177/0032885511415224

Dutil, S. (2020). Dismantling the school-to-prison pipeline: A trauma-informed, critical race perspective on school discipline. *Children & Schools, 42*(3), 171–178. doi:10.1093/cs/cdaa016

Fabelo, T., Thompson, M. D., Plotkin, M., Carmichael, D., Marchbanks, M. P. III, & Booth, E. A. (2011). *Breaking schools' rules: A statewide study of how school discipline relates to students' success and juvenile justice involvement. New York, NY, and College Station*. Council of State Governments Justice Center and Texas A&M University Public Policy Research Institute. https://www.ojp.gov/ncjrs/virtual-library/abstracts/breaking-schools-rules-statewide-study-how-school-discipline-0

Gaibiati, R. & Drago, F. (2018). *Deterrent effect of imprisonment*. doi:10.1007/978-1-4614-5690-2_407

Gonzalez, T. (2012). Keeping kids in schools: Restorative justice, punitive Discipline, and the school to prison pipeline. *Journal of Law & Education, 41*(2), 281–335.

Harding, D. J., Morenoff, J. D., Nguyen, A. P., Bushway, S. D., & Binswanger, I. A. (2019). A natural experiment study of the effects of imprisonment on violence in the community. *Nature Human Behaviour, 3*(7), 671–677. Advance online publication. doi:10.103841562-019-0604-8 PMID:31086334

Hinze-Pifer, R., & Sartain, L. (2018). Rethinking universal suspension for severe student behavior. *Peabody Journal of Education, 93*(2), 228–243. doi:10.1080/0161956X.2018.1435051

Liberman, A. M., Kirk, D. S., & Kideuk, K. (2014). Labeling effects of first juvenile arrests: Secondary deviance and secondary sanctioning. *Criminology, 4*(3), 1–26. doi:10.1111/1745-9125.12039

Losen, D. J., & Martinez, P. (2020). *Lost opportunities: How disparate school discipline continues to drive differences in the opportunity to learn*. Learning Policy Institute, Center for Civil Rights Remedies at the Civil Rights Project, UCLA.

Morgan, H. (2021). Restorative justice and the school-to-prison pipeline: A review of existing literature. *Education Sciences, 11*(4), 159. doi:10.3390/educsci11040159

Novak, A. (2019). The school-to-prison pipeline: An examination of the association between suspension and justice system involvement. *Criminal Justice and Behavior, 46*(8), 1165–1180. doi:10.1177/0093854819846917

Novak, A., & Fagan, A. (2022). Expanding research on the school-to-prison pipeline: Examining the relationships between Suspension, expulsion, and recidivism among justice-involved youth. *Crime and Delinquency, 68*(1), 3–27. doi:10.1177/0011128721999334

U.S. Department of Education Office of Civil Rights. (2014). *Civil rights data collection data snapshot: School discipline*. Retrieved from https://www2.ed.gov/about/offices/list/ocr/docs/crdc-discipline-snapshot.pdf

U.S. Department of Education Office of Civil Rights. (2021). *An overview of exclusionary discipline practices in public school for the 2017-18 school year.* Retrieved from https:// www2.ed.gov/ about/offices/list/ocr/docs/crdc-exclusionary-school-discipline.pdf

Williams, J. A., Johnson, J. N., Dangerfield-Persky, F., & Mayakis, C. G. (2020). Does employing more novice teachers predict higher suspensions for black students? A Hierarchical Multiple Regression Analysis. *The Journal of Negro Education*, *89*, 448–458. https://www.jstor.org/stable/10.7709/jnegroeducation.89.4.0448

Section 1
Theory

This collection of chapters examines various theoretical lenses, including Critical Race Theory, Racial Threat Theory, the Racialized Theory of Organizations, and other frameworks to describe and provide a foundation for understanding school discipline disparities.

Chapter 1
Cultural Bias and Its Implications for Discipline Disparity

Wilsando Seegars
Independent Researcher, USA

ABSTRACT

Minority students in both urban and suburban school settings within the United States are subject to harsher and more frequent disciplinary actions than their white counterparts. Implicit bias and lack of cultural awareness contribute to a large disparity in discipline referrals for Black males in particular. Through the application of Critical Race Theory and Racial Threat Theory, this chapter examines the historical influences that have created confirmation bias in the education environment as well as the prevalence of zero-tolerance policies that exist in schools with large minority populations. Data gathered from the 2017 Civil Rights Data collection reported to the US Department of Education were used to highlight the discipline trends of six US school districts.

INTRODUCTION

What do Krunk dancing, Hip-Hop culture, playing the dozens, comedy, slam poetry and athletic competition all have in common? Aside from them being outlets of creative expression, major business industries, and associations of youth culture, they are all forms of cultural expression that are rooted in competition and domination. If you are an educator working with minority youth ages 5 to 18 and you do not know what these things are you are operating from a cultural deficit that may harm

DOI: 10.4018/978-1-6684-3359-1.ch001

your relationship with students before you ever get started. This chapter identifies the ways in which discipline disparities can be attributed to cultural ignorance, prejudice, power struggles, and implicit bias.

In order to adequately and effectively address the biases that exist for many educators who find themselves working with an ever-changing demographic, it is necessary to identify the genesis of these biases and the ways in which they play out in the school environment. It is not enough to simply be able to recognize the bias, educators must be able to create solutions so that favorable outcomes for all students are achieved through an equitable lens.

The goal of this chapter is to offer insight into several commonly overlooked cultural subtleties that can lead to misinterpretations of student behavior and academic marginalization. Such consequences whose origins can be found in confirmation bias and Racial Threat Theory may ultimately end in damaged relationships between teachers and students.

Although there is no easy path to eliminating implicit bias,there are ways for educators to become more knowledgeable of what their biases are, where they may have begun, and how they impact students. The historical references in this chapter allow educators to examine their pedagogical practices when and where these biases interject into their learning community. By applying the strategies learned in this chapter educators will not only grow personally, they will gain insight into adapting best practices for students that will help eliminate cultural discipline disparities in classrooms throughout the United States.

As a dean of students, this author has first-hand experience in how cultural deficits can lead to misinterpretations of student actions, consequently creating missed opportunities, frequent referrals and punitive actions for minor offences. This author has seen positive gains in student behavior and efforts when students perceive the goal of redirection is not to send them home for every infraction. Prioritizing empathy over apathy should be the priority when interacting with student referrals. Seeking to understand students' actions allows for growth and reflection that results in an environment that fosters self-efficacy. Viewing discipline referrals through an equitable lens versus relying solely on zero-tolerance policies has led to reduced infractions and a boost in both student confidence and morale. As such, helping educators reflect on their practices and evolve to best serve students of all backgrounds is the priority that drives this research.

OVERVIEW

False narratives have plagued American society since its inception. This has recently been demonstrated in debates regarding use of Critical Race Theory (CRT)-originally a law scholar theory "aimed to reexamine the terms by which race and racism have been negotiated in American consciousness"-to teach American history in public schools (Crenshaw, Gortanda, Pellar, & Thomas, 2018). Such debates have become so politicized that the value behind its construct has been lost, "Despite its academic origins, Critical Race Theory no longer lives in the university. Nearly every invocation of the term, favorable or not, is now in the zeitgeist. It is the problem with having your theory go mainstream: Prominent people have interpreted and emphasized aspects of this scholarship and disseminated their versions to the public, who in turn do their own interpreting as they go (Eduardo, 2021, para. 6)." This has led to an environment in which many Americans are reticent of having dialogue with minorities surrounding the recognition and acceptance of their bias. This reluctance to reflect on said bias has contributed to many Americans having a social cultural disconnect, particularly in the field of education. Although there are opposing perspectives for its value, this author's application of CRT reflects the sentiment that race plays an integral part in the mechanisms of American society. Whether stated or not, race contributes to the disparity seen in school discipline outcomes. Similar to how society cannot ignore the application of CRT as it pertains to the over representation of Black males in US prisons, society can ill afford to overlook the massive representation of students of color receiving the majority percentage for out of school suspensions and overall school discipline.

The counterpart to Critical Race Theory, for the sake of this chapter is Racial Threat Theory (RTT). Founded by three sociologists—Herbert Blumer, Hubert Blalock, and Robert Blauner, it played a critical role in setting the foundation for analyzing the 1960's civil rights movement by introducing the concept of fear into the racial discussion. Its assertion 'was "large or growing minority group [s] may be perceived by [the] dominant group as a potential threat to their economic or political privilege, which can lead to increased efforts at controlling the threatening population' (Stults and Swagar, 208, p. 147, as reported in Smith, 2021). Adding RTT to the discussion on racial implicit bias in school discipline is a natural fit when examining its premise centered around "providing criminology with an illustrative framework for understanding social control" (Smith, 2021, para 1).

California Law Review defines implicit bias it as:

An aspect of the new science of unconscious processes that have substantial bearing on discrimination law…theories of implicit bias contract with the 'naive' psychological conception of social behavior which views human actors as being guided solely by their explicit beliefs and their conscious intentions to act. In contrast, the science of implicit cognition suggest that actors do not always have conscious, intentional control over the processes of social perception, impression formation, and judgment that motivate their actions (Greenwald and Krieger, 2006, p. 946).

Bias is considered to be a normal part of the social construct when taking into consideration that members of our society all come to the proverbial table with their own set of experiences, influences and opinions. However, bias begins to become dangerous when combined with unchecked power, prejudice and ignorance. Implicit bias can then have lasting consequences that are injurious to its victims and create false narratives for its perpetrators.

Mainstream America having social cultural disconnections created from false narratives has played a key role in causing discriminatory practices in education bred from the fertile soil of ignorance. This ignorance persists not because differing perspectives of historical context are not readily available but because, despite multiple perspectives being available, the one that prevails generally comes from the mainstream perspective. In public education, this has led to many minority students being treated, educated and disciplined with unfavorable outcomes. A litany of research regarding the prevalence of such disparaging treatment are ascribed to post slavery civil unrest, but it is the observation of this author that its current impetus can be found in more contemporary historical context.

When taught by a non-minority teacher, minority children often walk into the classroom wearing the antiquated suit of racial stereotypes that foster subconscious inconsistencies in behavioral and academic expectations from teachers. The following historical context offers insight into what may have contributed to the common implicit biases this author has observed as a colleague to non-minority teachers in both urban and suburban school settings. While the cause and effect of America's war on drugs and its ongoing love-hate relationship with Hip-Hop is not an exhaustive explanation for the prevailing minority biases, its analysis offers a commonly overlooked perspective into what could be a sleeper cell in the subconscious of White America.

CHANGING FACE OF DRUG USAGE & DISTRIBUTION

Despite the tendency of the media to focus on recreational drug usage in African American and Latino communities, drugs have been a part of the American social landscape since its founding. The country's most addictive and lucrative unauthorized drugs have been in play dating back to the seventeenth through twentieth centuries (Palmera, 2012). Marijuana farms can be traced back to the Jamestown settlers and were an economic boom before the Civil War (Palmera, 2012). Cocaine's origins can be found in the medical field of the late 1800's. Early versions of its usage promoted it as a *cure-all* tonic deemed safe enough for usage in the formula of Coca Cola and cleared by the Surgeon General of the United States Army to be used for medical purposes (Palmera 2013). Heroin surfaced as a counter drug to combat morphine used during the American Civil War to eliminate pain inflicted upon soldiers during combat (Palmera, 2012). Crack Cocaine introduced an affordable blue-collar drug for working class citizens (Palmera, 2012). It sold at an affordable price and consumers achieved a premium *high*.

The social identification of the drugs shifted from its origins as it became more affordable for workers not identified as White, middle and upper class. For instance, opiates were used by middle- and upper-class women to cure "female problems." Before the American Civil War up until the 1930's marijuana was sold medicinally in pharmacies and general stores. However, after the Mexican Revolution of 1910 Mexican immigrants introduced marijuana as a recreational drug into the US (Frontline, n.d.). The xenophobia associated with Mexican immigration in the era of the 1930's Great Depression (Frontline, n.d.), combined with the paranoia created by Louis J. Gasnier's movie *Reefer Madness*, led to marijuana being associated with violence and unwanted immigrants (Boeri, n.d.). Cocaine was linked to White elitism from its conception. It started in Europe as a medical drug but became associated with Hollywood and could be seen being openly used in the silent movies of the late 19th through early 20th century (Palmera, 2012). It was so coveted by the White community that Coca Cola was originally sold only at racially segregated fountain shops (History, 2018). As its lure expanded beyond the White, middle- and upper-class communities, the first antagonists to its storyline were being strategically crafted.

The Harrison Narcotics Act of 1914 was one of the nation's first narcotics laws. Publicly its passing focused mainly on outlawing "coca and opium products" (History, 2018), but socially its passing gave birth to one of the nation's first on-going drug-associated smear campaigns on communities of color, with the most substantial impact being the Black community. The following quotes reflect the ideology of the social political landscape during the time of its inception:

Most of the attacks upon White women of the south are the direct result of the cocaine-crazed Negro brain,' Testified one doctor, in [a] congressional hearing aimed at drumming up support for the proposed act (Szalavitz, 2017).

The use of coke is probably much more widely spread among Negroes than among whites. Heaven dust, they call it. Its use by Negro field hands in the South has spread with appalling swiftness and results. There is very little doubt that every Jew peddler in the South carries the stuff, although many states have lately made its sale a felony [Dr. J. Leonard Corning – 1908] (Abramsky, 2002).

There were certainly concerns about addiction linked to over-the-counter sale of drugs like cocaine and opium—but this was not the focus of the debate over the law. In the early 1900s, the typical opiate addict was a white housewife who bought her drugs ostensibly as medicine, and yet the media spotlight mainly fell on black and Chinese men (Szalavitz, 2017).

Fear and hatred of the Chinese workers who built the transcontinental railroads and were later seen as threats to American workers also played a role. Journalists and editors stoked fears that opium allowed or encouraged "Chinamen" to rape or seduce white women. Indeed, the same doctor who testified to Congress that cocaine led blacks to sexually assault white women also told the legislators and press that, 'In Chinatown, in the city of Philadelphia, there are enormous quantities of opium consumed and it is quite common, gentlemen, for these Chinese, or 'Chinks' as they are called, to have as a concubine, a white woman' (Szalavitz, 2017).

Although the campaign's racist propaganda did not limit itself to one specific subgroup, the outcome of its slanderous depictions added yet another layer of deeply rooted mistrust and disdain towards the Black community. This mistrust continues to resonate in the minds of many and is no longer limited to the White community. The success of its smear campaign has grown tentacles that reach across all spectrums of American life. Ironically, this also includes influencing subgroups, once identified as co-corruptive conspirators of America's White purity, into being partners that help support oppression.

Despite drugs being a part of America's narrative since the colonial era, historically its production and distribution were generally controlled by adults. Youth may have had access to minor drugs like marijuana due to their proximity to an adult user. Such access may have led to experimentation with more addictive drugs such as heroin. However, the access to the drug's production and distribution flowed through adult control. Originally, adult control was the rule of thumb and the general practice of illegal drug sales up until 1978 when a movement starting in Detroit, Michigan would cause a major shift in the face and image of who and what a drug dealer looks like in the minds of the American public.

In 1978, Young Boys Incorporated (YBI), started as a local heroin and crack cocaine drug cartel in Detroit, Michigan. What made it unique among existing urban cartels is in its namesake. The founders of YBI, were able to identify and exploit a loophole in drug sentencing laws (Flanagan, 1982). By changing the age of its runners from young adults 18 and older to kids 11 to 17, they could not only avoid having runners face serious prison time, young runners could avoid having lasting impacts on their records because at 18 a juvenile record could be sealed or expunged (Tiegen, 2016). This blueprint quickly spread across the country into every crevice where illegal drugs were sold. Once again, the face for this menace to society would emerge as a person of color, except this time the visual depiction would not be an adult Latino or Black male, it would be their children.

FAR REACHING TENTACLES OF HIP-HOP

As the YBI was changing the drug game in Detroit, conterminously from 1973 through 1979 in Bronx, New York an artistic shift was taking place being driven by youth expression. Birthed as a hybrid from Latino, Caribbean, and African American cultures and driven by the economic cuts to school funding for the arts, its form of expression was not limited to one art genre. Instead, it crossed several genres such as dance, visual, poetic expression, fashion, and music (Pirani, 2017). There were common undercurrents that ran through this new tidal wave of art along with vivid depictions of America reflected through a different lens.

More specifically, Hip-Hop-as the culture came to be named-embraced and glamorized everything about urban culture, from its heroes to its sheroes, including its scholars as well as its gangsters and hustlers (Kitwana, 2002). In doing so, it not only glamorized and martyred contributors that mainstream America portrayed as criminals and social outcasts, it rewrote their narratives and highlighted the relatability of their struggles to its consumers in ways previous forms of urban art had failed to embrace. Hip-Hop did not come into existence for the purpose of making people outside of its spectrum comfortable, it came with an attitude that amplified James Brown's 1968 classic, *Say It Loud: I'm Black and I'm Proud* with an unapologetic rejection of traditional mainstream American values, "It don't make sense, goin' to heaven with the goodie-goodies Dressed in white, I like black Timbs and black hoodies (Notorious B.I.G, 1994)."

The Hip-Hop Generation, a majority Latino and African American subgroup of Generation X-was born between 1965 and 1980 (CNN, 2021), went against the tide of the Baby Boomer Civil Rights generation-1946 – 1964 (CNN, 2021). They did not see or embrace the world through the lens of their parents and grandparents that held on to the idea of working in manufacturing companies that paid an affordable living wage and offered pensions for worker loyalty. Instead, they internalized the struggles of Generation X seeing US manufacturing jobs leave for cheaper labor abroad as a nail being placed in their economic coffins and knew from previous historical context that if White America was suffering then surely people of color-specifically urban minorities of the generation- were destined to suffer graver hardships: "When White Folks Catch a Cold, Black Folks Get Pneumonia, (Fulwood, 2015)."

Consequently, instead of waiting for yet another piece Civil Rights legislation to come along and potentially dole out selective branches of fair access to the American Dream, The Hip-Hop Generation opted to embrace Malcolm X's motto of "By Any Means Necessary" as their declaration for self-love, self-reliance, and self-respect. This was a far different chant and mindset than the bellowing words of Dr. Martin Luther King's "We Shall Overcome," sung during Civil Rights protests at the time of the Hip-Hop Generation's birth in 1965. Whereas many from the Baby Boom

Generation "placed family, spirituality, social responsibility, and [cultural] pride at the center of their identity…They, like their parents before them, looked to their elders for values and identity. The core set of values shared by a large segment of the Hip-hop generation-Black America's Generation X- stand in contrast to our parents' worldview. For the most part we have turned to ourselves, our peers, global images and products, and the new realities we face for guidance (Kitwana, 2002)." The embrace of Malcolm's motto also reshaped the collective mindset of the generation's social, political, and economic outlook for how to gain acceptance and access to the American dream: "Like our white peers, [we] are more likely than our parents' generation to be obsessed with our careers and getting rich quick. For us achieving wealth, by any means necessary, is more important than most anything else, hence our obsession with materialistic and consumer trappings of financial success (Kitwana, 2002)."

Hip-Hop culture did not hide its contempt for social and political disparity, "Intensifying social issues related to police brutality, poverty, incarceration, oppression and unemployment became the prime influencers of Hip-Hop's birth" (Pirani, 2017). However, it also used its voice to tell stories of hustling, street life, drugs, and promiscuity. Many of its artists became wealthy by depicting their lived experiences through their art, while others came to see the economic value in crafting false narratives through pseudo imagined characters that were packaged and sold to the masses as the true representation of their urban experiences. Tracy "Ice-T" Marrow, known for being one the founding fathers of the *gangsta* rap style of Hip-Hop culture states, "I couldn't possibly have lived all the things that Ice-T on the records lived. I did what I called 'faction.' It was like factual situations — not always from me — put into fictional settings. That way I could create these great adventures and these great stories" (Century, 2011). Regardless, the realness and relatability of the stories told, coupled with the generations unapologetic, by any means necessary mindset combined to create strong cultural ties driven by its youthful energy and general swagger.

When popular icons of the Hip-Hop generation such as NBA superstar Allen Iverson, boxing heavyweight Mike Tyson and comedian Chris Rock chose to embrace its energy and mindset instead of shunning it, their global influence then played a role in developing the mainstream's image of youth associated with the culture. For many, these icons embracing the culture only added fuel to their disdain. In part, due to their unapologetic swagger and dominance at the height of their careers, and for others because they clearly dressed and behaved differently than Black entertainers that preceded them. As rappers began to have major crossover appeal from music to acting, Hollywood began producing movies that highlighted them as leads in a series of movies depicting urban experiences with drug, gang and prison backgrounds.

Ultimately, as a result, an over glamorized portrayal of the urban experience evolved and saturated the consciousness of White America.

With the appeal of the culture growing, it soon moved from being viewed as a trendy and gimmicky minor culture into the mainstream. This eventually led to suburban White youth being influenced by the culture. Cornell West described Hip-Hop's sphere of influence on the world, and more specifically on White suburban youth as, "The Afro-Americanization of white youth" (West, 1993, as reported in Kitwana, 2002, p. 10).

As with previous calculated attacks on minority communities when the mass media was released on Hip-Hop culture seemingly with the intended purpose of once again looking for a scapegoat for any and all problems associated with setbacks in the country. This time, unlike in 1914, it had the lyrics, videos, and art associated with Hip-Hop culture as prime evidence for its revised version of what a menace to American society looks and behaves like: "Robbin' and stealing, then led to killin', making a living off the {expletive} drug dealing. . . . Try me, die instantly, yeah a couple of shots is all it takes" (Junior M.A.F.I.A. as quoted in Kurtz, 1996, para 9).

The smear campaign became politicized starting in 1989 with the attacks on gangsta rap pioneers such as Niggas Wit Attitudes (NWA) and ICE T, as well as the fast-paced, rump shaking, heavy bass music of Luther Campell and his 2 Live Crew group members (Hudson, 2009). The mooting over the culture's value and impact on America's youth reached its pinnacle in the 1990s when former Secretary of Education, William J. Benett-under President Ronald Regan-helped lead the political charge on characterizing the parts of the culture as unscrupulous. Bennett, Congressman Joseph Lieberman, Congressman Sam Nunn, and C. DeLores Tucker of the National Political Congress of Black Women targeted Sony, PolyGram, Thorn EMI, Bertelsmann Music Group, Time Warner and other corporations that profited from its sales and marketing, "These companies are profiting from the pollution of our culture and poisoning the minds of our children (Kurtz, 1996)."

THE IMPACT OF THE WAR ON DRUGS AND HIP HOP ON SCHOOL DISCIPLINE OUTCOMES

The combined influence of negative stereotypes of Hip-Hop culture and presumed character traits that accompany the youths that mimic the generation's style have created a dangerous cocktail for urban youth as they try to navigate the waters outside of their traditional dwellings. In the 2010 census, for the first time in American History, 50% of African Africans lived in the inner and outer suburbs (McGowen, 2020). As citizens, African Americans have the right to reside in any part of the country they can afford to live. However, because of many stereotypes associated with Black culture, many of the youth leaving the urban setting and moving into the suburbs are facing implicit and confirmation biases that are having a significant impact on their education experience. These biases have roots, but many are unaware of their origins. As described in the history of America's love affair with drugs and the birth of the Hip-Hop Generation-which now spans an age range from 66 to 37-the children and grandchildren of the Hip-Hop Generation are now in the suburbs of America bringing with them the swagger, values, and attitude of their parents and grandparents. For many suburban educators this is a teaching experience that poses a threat to what some may see as their version of equal access to an equitable education. For others it poses a problem due to not feeling comfortable in being able to connect and relate to this new influx of students, thus creating a negative experience for the teacher and the student. Consider the following scenarios as examples of the ways in which cultural awareness can be a useful tool for educators.

Scenario One

Joseph is a new student to the school. He has been assigned to ride bus 144, which happens to be the bus Antonio rides. When Joseph enters the bus to be seated, he hears Antonio in the back of the bus bragging in a rhythm about how he destroyed Raheem in a one-on-one basketball game. Being new, he simply just listens, but he likes the way Antonio puts his words together. Not being afraid to push limits, or buttons, Antonio turns towards Joseph and happens to point at him to put the final punchline on his final verse of rhyme. The kids on the bus are amazed at Antonio's creativity and cleverness to add Joseph to the conversation and they go crazy with excitement as Antonio continues to provide rhythmic entertainment for the remainder of the ride.

Having heard himself being mentioned, having seen the kid's reaction, not being shy, and wanting to make new friends, Joseph quickly responds to Antonio's words with a rhyme of his own. Surprised by Joseph's response, the students get louder with excitement and the battle of words begins.

The bus driver listens attentively but does not interrupt as long as everyone remains seated. When they arrive at the building the driver makes a comment that Antonio may have met his match and how he might have to give up his self-proclaimed title. Determined to not lose his title, or respect, Antonio shakes Joseph's hand and welcomes him to the school. As they enter, Antonio reminds Joseph that the battle is not over and how he will see him at lunch. When they enter lunch and crowds begin to gather to hear what is being said between the two wordsmiths, a teacher sees the crowd gathering, listens to what is being said, and makes the determination that they are being disrespectful towards one another. Thus, both students are reprimanded for their behavior, which may ultimately lead to behavior referrals and more stringent outcomes.

What is the breakdown that led to this outcome?

An inability to relate to students culturally can lead to inaccurate interpretations of student behaviors and abilities. For example, if you are not aware of the aggression associated with rapping, when you see students banging on the table to create a cypher for the next greatest MCs you might assume when the battlers begin to stare at one another and speak with hostile certainty about all the destructive things they are planning to do towards the person in front of them, along with talking astringently about their mother and loved ones, while the crowd stands around seemingly getting worked-up and egging-on the verbal assault that there is surely going to be an altercation. Therefore, leaving you the self-proclaimed mediator no choice but to intervene with a variety of misguided corrective disciplinary actions that may include phone calls home, verbal redress in front of the student's peers, student teacher conference, after school detention, and even sending the verbal assassin to the office for larger disciplinary consequences. However, what you failed to understand is that the witnessed aggression is part of a cultural expression that calls for aggrandizement as well as for perceived weaknesses to be verbally exploited in order to dominate an opponent. This small misstep could lead to mistrust from students, as well as damage relations that will take time to amend. In addition, this lack of cultural awareness could feed pre-existing biases related to a student's ability to have a good relationship with others and potentially limit them to having access to all available resources.

Scenario Two

Sarah moved to the suburbs from the local major city. She likes the quietness of the neighborhood, the resources at the local library, and the idea that lunch at school comes with a variety of options unknown to her in her previous district. In her former community she was surrounded by family and friends scattered throughout every corner of the city. In her new community she has family her age, but she hardly sees them because they are in different schools. Being from a large family with plenty of personality types that believe in challenging one another with intellect and wit, Sarah has learned to hold her own to keep her cousins and siblings from thinking she is too sensitive to take a joke. In fact, in her family she has learned that wit can be used as a sword and shield to back people off of you if you know when and how to use it. Over the years of fine tuning her skills, her motto has become "Come at them before they come at you."

In her new environment, Sarah feels the reading materials offered in English/Language Arts (ELA) often lack cultural connection and that the things intended to be funny go unnoticed by everyone except a few. It was through noticing the few students laughing at the same things as her that Sarah first began to mentally separate the class into the "boring" and the "live" categories.

In Sarah's mind, the boring seemed out of touch, while the live seemed relatable. The things that the boring saw as funny, Sarah saw as dry, and the things Sarah and the live saw as funny, the boring were often unaffected. The boring-including the teacher- seemed to be in the majority while the live were the minority.

Ultimately, Sarah and her newfound compadres began to gravitate towards one another and could be seen sitting in class laughing about topics they found in the literature, on-line, or television. They would make cultural references that kept them laughing through the day. Eventually, they began to make references toward the favorable and unfavorable traits of various sources and seemed extremely comfortable talking about one another with an intensity that seemed offensive. When they talked about one another, not only did it start to seem personal, it seemed that everyone in the group was starting to target one specific person and always telling the person to stop being sensitive. Even as the students were laughing and pointing towards him, he would laugh too and point back at them.

In the meantime, the teacher, having seen enough of what she/he considers disruptive horseplay, and wanting to maintain a highly rated management style in his/her classroom, as well as ensure that no student feels attacked, decides to separate the group. The students try to explain to the teacher that it is just jokes but the teacher is not amused and feels allowing the behavior has immense potential to lead to a fight.

CULTURAL AWARENESS DEFICITS CAN BE COSTLY

Ponder the potential consequences of the actions in the previous scenarios. What has the teacher done that might lead to discipline issues starting to occur? The teacher's inability to recognize differences in cultural social dynamics fostered an environment where students could not be themselves and thus felt punished or ostracized for not practicing the same cultural social etiquette as the majority within their learning environment. There is a difference between teasing, playing the dozens, and being intentionally cruel. Educators that instruct students outside of the ethnic group should make every effort to become familiar with the social nuances of the racial and ethnic populations they serve.

Another example of a possible misread can be found in comedy. What we laugh at and how we laugh plays a significant role in what we take serious about our day-to-day lives as well as what we use as tools to prepare us to maneuver through the rollercoasters of life without breaking our spirit. Some cultures have forbidden topics that are not to be played with (especially by outsiders of the culture). Others may have a more open-book policy on topics that can be approached. This helps those associated with the culture remember to laugh not only at one another but at life. In learning to do so you also learn not to take yourself or life too seriously. Therefore, if you are not culturally aware of the population you serve, when you hear banter that you deem as too personal your inability to relate can be costly towards outcomes for students. Failure to do so could lead to misinterpreting actions as being cruel, maladjusted, and therefore lacking the maturity necessary to enroll in higher level courses that require collaboration and self-pacing.

It is also important to note that some students may attempt to make what is potentially an uncomfortable environment feel more tolerable by bringing familiar elements into that environment. Bringing elements of their home and culture with them make it more palatable. For example, students that may move from the inner-city or spend a lot of time in the inner-city may bring familiar coping strategies with them (e.g. speaking louder when conversing to keep from being spoken over) to environments where they are the minority. This can mean that when teachers separate students to encourage diversity the separation is seen more as a punishment and less as an attempt to be more inclusive.

Speaking tone and cultural approaches to communication help demonstrate how we are taught to express and share our thoughts with the world. While some cultures prefer to avoid direct approaches to conflict resolution, others are taught that to be direct is to eliminate all possibilities for misunderstandings. Each of these cultural subtleties offer an opportunity for educators to reflect on current attitudes as well as develop awareness of certain social and cultural practices that may be unfamiliar in their daily lives yet an integral part of the lives of their students.

Implicit and confirmation bias created from drug and Hip-Hop cultural influences have led to harsher discipline outcomes amongst students of color nationwide. 'Zero Tolerance' discipline policies adopted in the 1980s have been slated as prison pipelines for minority youth. These policies were formed concurrently as the poster child images of drug dealers were being transformed into the faces of African American and Latino youth along with Hip-Hop culture expanding its sphere of influence. For minority communities the implementation of zero tolerance policies has sparked the evolution of a new civil rights battleground, "school discipline has emerged as an imperative in the quest for civil rights in education post-Brown" (Triplett, Allen, & Lewis, 2014).

This call to arms merits traction, especially when considering the research of North Carolina University scholars Nicholas P. Triplett, Ayana Allen, and Chance W. Lewis's article entitled *Zero Tolerance, School Shootings, and the Post-Brown Quest for Equity in Discipline Policy: An Examination of How Urban Minorities Are Punished for White Suburban Violence.*

In their article, published in the Journal of Negro Education, the scholars posit that during the 90's, what the media presented as a disturbing trend of mass school shootings in relatively obscure, rural locations throughout the US served to intensify the propagation of Zero Tolerance in urban school settings. The article states that according to their research "...48 non-collegiate shootings occurred between 1990 and 1999; ... seven prominent rampage-style shootings occurred between the years 1996-1999." Notably, these mass school shootings were not prevalent in the inner-city schools which then bore the brunt of the reflexive policy changes.

Despite there being no empirical evidence substantiating the fears of the general public that school violence was on the rise, these shootings led to a somewhat panic driven support for the need to expand Zero-Tolerance. The Gun-Free Schools Act of 1994 made it mandatory that students in possession of Firearms be expelled for a minimum of one year and subsequent zero tolerance policies extended to weapons of any sort, possession and use of drugs, tobacco and alcohol as well as objectively and subjectively defined acts of violence. According to the article, the results of such policies are that "a nation of urban minority students have been punished for the actions of a small number of predominantly White suburban/rural gunmen."

Reflected in their research are statistics that strongly identify the discipline disparities that may result from implicit bias. The authors highlight that "Principals of schools with 50% or more minority enrollment also reported the highest prevalence of zero tolerance (U.S. Department of Education, 1997, as reported in Triplett et, 2011). Moreover, high minority schools are more likely to use punitive disciplinary responses in dealing with misbehavior to the exclusion of milder discipline alternatives" (McFadden et al., 1992; Welch & Payne, 2010, as reported in Triplett et al, 2014, p. 355).

After gathering and analyzing information for the 2017 Civil Rights Data collection reported to the US Department of Education, this author highlighted the discipline trends of 6 US school districts from varying locations-including areas historically not known for African Americans to reside- and found further evidence to support the claim of implicit bias.

The graph below shows that twenty years later the trend remains in-tact, thus reflecting that schools with 50% or more of minorities continue to carry high disciplinary outcomes amongst students of color. Also reflected in the data is the confirmation that regardless of overall percentage population for any given community

African American students consistently carry the highest discipline percentages for any racial population wherever they reside.

Results from the three largest race contributors represented in the 2017 suspension data reflect that in the United States out of 2,508,595 students with at least one out of school suspension, students of color constituted 64.7% of the suspensions with 36.8% being Black. Black males were disproportionality suspended among all subgroups (24%) while Black females were most likely to be suspended with a frequency of 12.8%. Whites were the second largest group with 31.6%. White males carried an overall number of 24% while White females added 7.6% but were not the lowest subgroup. Hispanics were the third largest group with 20.9%. Hispanic males comprised 14.7% and Hispanic females adding 6.1% making them the smallest group of the majority. Combined, males of color comprised 43.7% of students with at least one of school suspension and females of color made up 21% (Dept of Ed, 2021). [**Note**: It is important to point out that according to US Census data, of the total 76.3% White population, 16.2% identified as being of Hispanic or Latin origins.]

Table 1 reveals that 5% of the overall US student population of 49.5 million received at least one out of school suspension. Regardless of the region, the size of the school district, or the percentage of people of color in the region, Black students were disproportionately suspended at a higher percentage of their overall population. With the exception of Asian students, data from Table 1 affirms the superfluous rates of suspension amongst all students of color when compared to White students. In several instances, the data reveals that communities of color more than doubled the US suspension percentage.

Such discrepancies in the discipline outcomes emphasize the problem with allowing implicit and confirmation bias to go unchallenged. Although it is hard to pinpoint the exact moment and time the seeds of bias are planted, being able to identify and isolate crucial moments within a generation's timeline allows for a deeper understanding regarding what may appear to be unrelated separate occurrences. The birth of Hip-Hop culture combined with the expansion of the drug culture heavily influencing the urban culture in the 80s and 90s have had a tremendous impact on the social lens of White America. Whereby communities of color have long faced the two-faced bias of mainstream America's cultural meniscus. The Black community continues to be its main antagonist. With the majority of Blacks no longer residing in the inner city, removing and identifying the origins of some of the dominant implicit and confirmation biases will allow for honest reflection as well as improved opportunities for equal access to academic rigor.

Table 1. % = At Least 1 out of school suspension (one and multiple suspensions combined) 2017 School Year

Race & Gender:	US	New Mexico	Utah	Illinois Suburb	Maine	Ohio	North Carolina
All Students	5.1%	6.7%	1.4%	1.2%	9.1%	4.7%	6.6%
Black	12.3%	10.8	3.3%	4.3%	21.2%	8.4%	12.2%
White	3.4%	4.5%	1%	1.1%	8.8%	8.8%	2.3
Hispanic	3.9%	7.5%	1.7%	1.9%	10.6%	10.6%	4.3%
Asian	1%	2.3%	.5%	.3%	4.3%	.6%	1.5%
2 or More	5.5%	6.7%	1.2%	1.7%	6.4%	7.6%	5.9%
Hawaiian or Other	4.9%	5%	2.4%	0	0%	0%	2.4%
Students of Color	6.2%	7.3%	1.7%	1.4%	10%	7%	8.2
Am. Indian or Alaskan	6.9%	5.8%	2.7	2.2%	20.4%	0%	8.3%
Male	BM 12.3% WM 3.4% HM 3.9% St of C 6.2% A. In 9.3%	BM 10.8% WM 4.5% HM 7.5% St of C 7.3% A. In 8%	BM 4.6% WM 1.6% HM 2.3% St of C 2.4% A. In 1.5%	BM 4.3% WM 1.1% HM 1.9% St of C 1.4% A. In 4%	BM 40% WM 12.5% HM 12.7% St of C 16% A. In 22.7%	BM 9.3% WM 12.5% HM 12.7% St of C 12.3% A. In 0%	BM 15.8% WM 2.3% HM 5.8% St of C 10.7% A. In 8.5%
Female	BF 8.7% WF 1.7% HF 2.3 St of C 4.1% A. In 4.4%	BF 7.8% WF 2.6% HF 5% St of C 4.8% A. In 3.6%	BF 2% WF .3% HF 1% St of C 1.1% A. In 4.1%	BF 2.6% WF .5% HF 1.1% St of C .8% A. In 0	BF 6.7% WF 5.1% HF 8.2% St of C 5.5% A. In 18.5%	BF 7.6% WF 5.1% HF 8.1% St of C 3.6% A. In 0	BF 8.5% WF 1.2% HF 2.8% St of C 5.7% A. In 8%

SOLUTIONS AND RECOMMENDATIONS

In order for minority students-especially Black students being taught by culturally unaware teachers-to get the most from their school experience, training and growth must be encouraged by all stakeholders. Boards of Education, district and building leaders, as well as teachers need to begin looking for ways to implement the next steps listed below.

With the migration of students of color moving from inner city settings into the inner and outer suburbs it is vital for them to enter into a learning environment that welcomes diversity and is structured to help all students have success. Making false assumptions based on bias sets a tone for a negative student experience. It also impedes educators from being able to see the full potential of their students or develop nurturing relationships. Triplett et al assert that "Because minority students can constitute a threat to the cultural hegemony of predominantly White teachers and school personnel, RTT also informs the understanding of how cultural differences (in communication, social behavior, hairstyles, dress, demeanor, etc.) contribute to the disproportionate application of exclusionary discipline" (Fenning & Rose, 2007; Ferguson, 2001; Gay, 2006; Rocque & Paternoster, 2011; Skiba et al., 2002, as reported in Triplett et al, 2014). Upon arrival into a district new students should complete objective assessments that measure strengths and deficiencies. The outcomes of the assessments should be used for data supported class enrollment versus subjective placement that may come as a result of Racial Threat Theory (RTT) assumptions. Improper placement can lead to behavior issues stemming from boredom which can lead to students having too much down time to socialize or being off task. Ultimately, this could lead to manageable disciplinary avoidances. Inversely, students placed in classes that are too challenging may exude similar actions that can lead to students feeling their teachers do not care therefore starting a breakdown that could lead to discipline disparity.

Recognizing family values regarding education can help eliminate false inferences that success looks the same for every culture. Whereby a college preparatory education has value for students that want to attend four-year universities, some families feel success can be found in the trades as well as through attending community college to obtain a two-year Associate Degree, while others may be happy knowing students will graduate from high school. In general, each generation wants the next generation to exceed their levels of success. However, assuming success looks the same for all families could lead to minority students feeling their view of the world is unaccepted. Feeling unaccepted could lead to misinterpretations of teacher's intent and forge a negative relationship to cultivate discipline imbalance.

RECOMMENDATIONS

Curricula sets a precedent for what a district values and considers relevant for its education outcomes. Culturally relevant information can play a key role in keeping students engaged as learners and allowing them to see themselves and their culture as relevant to the overall success of the country and humanity. Failure to have diversity properly exemplified in a district's curricula exudes a sentiment of irrelevance for the excluded cultures. Constantly depicting one side of historical text can create an inaccurate representation of historical facts leading to a superiority complex amongst the dominant group and an inferiority complex amongst the underrepresented minority. This could have the unintended consequence of alienation. It can also fester a dislike of the majority for failing to be more inclusive. Therefore, leading minority students to rebel against what is taught as well as disconnect by acting out against the teacher and the learning environment.

Diversity in staff plays a key role in helping bring different perspectives to problems that occur within the learning environment. The 2010 census revealed more than 50% of African Americans reside in the suburbs. It is imperative to have the workforce represent the diversity of the students taught. Since policies and procedures for public school districts are top driven, it is also important to diversify the school board so that varying perspectives are considered when policies are created. This will allow all stakeholders to know they have a voice and someone that can relate to them culturally at every level from the building level to the board. Maintaining homogenous leadership and teaching staff in a culturally diverse learning community can be interpreted by minority students as those educators that look like them are not welcomed. Based on this author's observations and experience as a classroom teacher and dean this, in turn, can impact the attitude of students towards teachers and set a tone for a breakdown in communication.

This author suggests professional training should not be voluntary. There should be a system in place for checking to make sure learning is applied and implemented. At the basic level, there should be implicit bias training taken through the district's training professional development system or Global Compliance Network (GCN) courses that districts require educators to take annually. Leadership should require the entire staff to study and discuss culturally diverse books and materials and implement them into lesson plans. Failure to do so would result in evaluation outcomes that reflect negatively on professional and pedagogical best practices. Lack of accountability tends to support a system of bias.

Teachers entering the profession should be required to take classes on diversity as well as fulfill their student pre-service experience in locations that offer access and exposure to a diverse student population. This will allow new educators to become more attuned to the importance of diversification in their planning and begin to phase out antiquated practices that are not multicultural in nature.

CONCLUSION

The ways in which we are socialized to think about and interact with different races have origins. Media representation, family upbringing, and communal ties all combine to inform our knowledge base and perceptions. This is at the foundation of how implicit biases are formed. Biases in education are cankerous cancers contributing to discipline outcomes that are unfavorably disproportionate for students of color-more specifically African American students. Two catalysts that have fed the subconscious of the United States mainstream ideology towards Hispanic and Black youth are the media's portrayal of Hip-Hop culture and its forced matrimony to drug, gang, and prison cultures. With the increased migration of people of color moving away from urban hubs, culture conflicts are occurring in the unfamiliar territory of America's suburbs. Once viewed as the exclusive bedrock of White America, these cultural clashes are creating a new civil-rights battle ground for education fairness and equal access.

If the societal goal is to progress towards equity on all frontiers, examining strategies for improving cultural competence-particularly in education-remains at an all-time high. When eliminating bias is an intentional objective, society wins. Students of all races get to know they are valued, even if they come with an unfamiliar perspective; educators get the opportunity to expand positively upon their sphere of influence by making valued connections with all students. Discriminatory practices-implied or intentional- have long plagued and shackled American society, hindering its goal of getting the most out of all of its citizens. Suggestions made in this research serve as fuel for districts, educators, parents, students, and laypeople to better understand the issue of bias and begin to do the work necessary for its eradication.

ACKNOWLEDGMENT

This research received no specific grant from any funding agency in the public, commercial, or not-for-profit sectors.

The author would like to thank Angela Hancock Bridges for her relentless voice in helping shape the outcome of this work. She served as contributing researcher and editor. Her contributions are truly valued and appreciated.

REFERENCES

Abramsky, S. (2011). *Hard Time Blues* [Ebook version]. Retrieved from https://www.google.com/books/edition/Hard_Time_Blues/dWVZkEDrLAgC

Bakari, K. (2002). *The Hip Hop Generation*. BasicCivitas Books.

Boeri, M. (2018, January 19). *Re-Criminalizing Cannabis Is Worse Than 1930s 'Refer Madness.'* The Conversation. https://theconversation.com/re-criminalizing-cannabis-is-worse-than-1930s-reefer-madness-89821

Casa Palmera Staff. (2012, October 3). *The History of Illegal Drugs in America.* https://casapalmera.com/blog/the-history-of-illegal-drugs-in-america/

CNN Editorial Research. (2021, August 19). *American Generation Fast Facts.* CNN. https://www.cnn.com/2013/11/06/us/baby-boomer-generation-fast-facts/index.html

Conan, N. (Host). (2011, April 11). *Talk of The Nation* [Audio podcast]. NPR. https://www.npr.org/2011/04/27/135771115/ice-t-from-cop-killer-to-law-order

Crenshaw, K., Gotanda, N., Peller, G., & Thomas, K. (1996). *Critical Race Theory.* Academic Press.

Eduardo, A. (2021, June 16). *Stop Telling Critical Race Theory's Critics We Don't Know What It Is | Opinion.* https://www.newsweek.com/stop-telling-critical-race-theorys-critics-we-dont-know-what-it-opinion-1600535

Flannagan, B. (1982). Kids Selling Heroin. *The Detroit News.* https://policing.umhistorylabs.lsa.umich.edu/s/crackdowndetroit/page/young-boys-incorporated

Fulwood, S. (2015, January 28). *When White Folks Catch a Cold, Black Folks Get Pneumonia.* Center for American Progress. https://www.americanprogress.org/article/when-whites-folks-catch-a-cold-black-folks-get-pneumonia/

Greenwald, A., & Hamilton Kreiger, L. (2006). Implicit Bias: Scientific Foundations. *California Law Review, 94*(4), 946. doi:10.2307/20439056

Hall, R., & Wallace, C. (1994). *Suicidal Thoughts. On Ready To Die* [CD]. Bad Boy Records.

History.com Editors. (2018, August 21). *Cocaine.* https://www.history.com/topics/crime/history-of-cocaine

Hudson, D. (2009). *Rap Music and The First Amendment.* The First Amendment Constitution. https://www.mtsu.edu/first-amendment/article/1582/rap-music-and-the-first-amendment

Kurtz, H. (1996, May 30). Benette Renews Attacks On Rap Lyrics. *The Washington Post.* https://www.washingtonpost.com/archive/lifestyle/1996/05/30/bennett-renews-attack-on-rap-lyrics/2bcb1b9e-a5d0-4564-acf3-b2fa7516d7e8/

Pirani, F. (2017, August 11). 44 years ago, hip-hop was born – 7 things you never knew about hip-hop's history in America. *The Atlanta Journal Constitution*. https://www.ajc.com/news/national/years-ago-hip-hop-was-born-things-you-never-knew-about-hip-hop-history-america/8Hcx5Mbf6F3RANDUilWMKJ/

Public Broadcast System. (n.d.). *Marijuana Timeline*. Frontline. https://www.pbs.org/wgbh/pages/frontline/shows/dope/etc/cron.html

Smith, J. (2021). Racial Threat and Crime Control: Integrating Theory on Race and Extending its Application. *Critical Criminology*, *29*(2), 253–271. doi:10.100710612-019-09485-1

Sullivan, J. (2011, October 10). *Black America is Moving to The South–and to the 'Burbs. What it Means?* Colorline. https://www.colorlines.com/articles/black-america-moving-south-and-burbs-whats-it-mean

Szalavitz, M. (2017, June 14). *One Hundred Years Ago, Prohibition Began in Earnest-And We're Still Paying For It*. https://psmag.com/social-justice/one-hundred-years-ago-prohibition-began-earnest-still-paying-97243

Tiegen, A. (2016, July). *Automatically Sealing or Expunging Juvenile Records*. National Conference of State Legislatures. https://www.ncsl.org/research/civil-and-criminal-justice/automatically-sealing-or-expunging-juvenile-records.aspx

Triplett, N., Allen, A., & Lewis, C. (2014). Zero Tolerance, School Shootings, and the Post-Brown Quest for Equity in Discipline Policy: An Examination of How Urban Minorities are Punished for White Suburban Violence. *The Journal of Negro Education*, *83*(3), 352–370. doi:10.7709/jnegroeducation.83.3.0352

U.S. Department of Education, Data, Civil Rights Collection Data. (2017). *School/District/State Comparison Report: At least one out-of-school suspension, Albuquerque, Bangor, Charlotte-Mecklenburg, Gahanna-Jefferson, Indian Prairie, Salt Lake City*. https://ocrdata.ed.gov/dataanalysistools/comparisongraphsanddatareport

KEY TERMS AND DEFINITIONS

Confirmation Bias: The predilection to seek out information that confirms or supports one's own beliefs or values.

Critical Race Theory (CRT): An academic theory that suggests that all aspects of policy, law and curriculum should be examined through a racial lens to ascertain the ways in which race plays a role in the interpretation, application, and impact of their governance.

Implicit Bias: Internalized prejudices based on deeply held beliefs, ideas, or values that operate in the subconscious.

Inner Suburbs: Suburban communities that border or exist within a five-to-ten-mile radius outside of a large city.

Krunk Dancing: An urban dance style within Hip-Hop culture that expresses aggression, creativity, grace and warriorism. It is generally expressed in a competitive environment and is characterized by sharp, distinctive movements performed at an alternating pace.

Outer Suburbs: Suburban communities that are located beyond ten miles from a city.

Playing the Dozens: Verbal competition that uses comedic insults with the goal to exploit emotional weaknesses until all but one of the competitors resigns from the game.

Racial Threat Theory (RTT): A theory in which the dominant culture perceives the accomplishments and attainment of success by a minority group as constituting a loss or threat to the majority's power.

Slam Poetry: Competitive poetry where the goal is to use figurative language, tone, mood, and storytelling to defeat your opponent.

Tagging: Creating graffiti art images generally by using aerosol spray paint.

Zero Tolerance: Judicial and education discipline policies with predetermined outcomes that are generally applied with no subjectivity or individual case-by case consideration for offences.

Chapter 2
Understanding the Relationship Between White Teacher Implicit Bias and Black Student Academic Disparities and High Discipline Rates

Renalda Pamela Yeung
Independent Researcher, USA

ABSTRACT

This chapter explores the concept of implicit racial bias as a significant factor contributing to the disparities between the discipline rates of White and Black students. While overt acts of racism are not as common as they were during other times in United States' history, implicit or unintentional racial bias still leads to differences in educational opportunities for the nation's students. The chapter begins with an examination of the concept of implicit bias broadly before turning toward implicit racial bias specifically. The chapter continues with a historical overview of the ways in which schooling for Black students has always been controlled by a dominant White society. Next, the researcher presents current data about the inequities in exclusionary discipline practices. The chapter concludes with recommendations for recognizing and addressing implicit bias and the problems it creates.

INTRODUCTION

In the United States of America, families often link the attainment of a quality education

DOI: 10.4018/978-1-6684-3359-1.ch002

with the American dream (Noguera, 2003). Parents hope that their children gain equitable access to learning opportunities so that they might succeed academically and socially. Unfortunately, equitable opportunities are not always available; differences in educational experiences exist. Over the course of the last few decades legislators have mandated countless policies to hold schools accountable for the success of their students, but even when schools have ample funding, rigorous curricula, and quality facilities, inequities still appear (Losen, 2014a). These inequities are often visible when comparing outcomes across multiple schools or districts, but they also occur internally within individual schools. For example, two children attending the same school can have vastly different educational experiences, though on paper it would seem all things were equal. While these differences may be traced to a range of causes and effects, of particular concern is the link between implicit racial bias and the disproportionality of school disciplinary practices between White students and their Black peers.

Existing research demonstrates that implicit bias is endemic in society, and the nation's K–12 educational settings are not immune to this problem (Cameron et al., 2010; Chin et al., 2020; Greenwald & Banaji, 1995). Teachers' implicit racial biases negatively affect all students' educational outcomes (Chin et al., 2020; Quinn, 2017; Warikoo et al., 2020) and severely impact Black students in particular. Because of implicit bias, White teachers can see Black students as disobedient, disruptive, or defiant and consequently Black students are more likely to be suspended than their White peers (Anyon et al., 2014; Losen, 2014). Even for minor misbehaviors, Black students often receive harsher punishments. When White teachers discipline Black students, the outcome of those students' experience is often significantly different than those of their White counterparts (Chin et al., 2020; Fay, 2018).

The disciplinary disparity can be detrimental to Black students' psyches and negatively impact their futures. The effects of these disciplinary practices exacerbate the academic demise of Black students but also extends beyond the academic setting (Riddle & Sinclair, 2019). These disciplinary actions put Black students at a higher risk for negative consequences within the school system such as in-school and out-of-school suspension, but furthermore, offenses at school are often linked with the criminal justice system leading Black students to have earlier contact with that system (Riddle & Sinclair, 2019; Vavrus, 2008).

While the problem of implicit bias in K–12 schools is current, it is rooted in the systemic racism that was present at the dawn of this country and ever-present in the history of the country's educational establishments. The story of education in the United States is inextricably linked with the practice of a dominant White society disciplining Black bodies. These practices and their effects were easier to see in the days of slavery and Jim Crow, and although they are less visible when carried out through implicit bias, their impact is still damaging. Though legally, Black students are supposed to have the same education as their White peers, implicit bias lingers in today's modern educational institutions. There is an urgent need in school districts across the country to address racism and implicit bias that influence high discipline numbers among Black students.

This chapter explores the concept of implicit racial bias as it relates to disciplinary disparities in K–12 educational settings in the United States. The chapter begins with a short definition of the concept of implicit bias, specifically implicit racial bias. Next, the discussion continues with a presentation of current data demonstrating the realities of the disciplinary disparities associated with White teachers' implicit racial bias as well as the negative effects of the disciplinary practices. The chapter continues with a discussion of how current implicit racial bias is rooted in the systemic injustices that have plagued formal education in the United States since the days of slavery. The chapter closes with a look to what can be done to recognize and address the problem of implicit bias in our educational settings.

IMPLICIT BIAS DEFINED AND EXPLAINED

Implicit bias or more broadly, implicit social cognition, is a term introduced by social psychologists Greenwald and Banaji to describe the process of an unconscious reaction to a particular social stimulus, "an indirect, unconscious, or implicit mode of operation for attitudes and stereotypes" (1995, p. 4). They explain that their work supported Gaertner and Dovidio's (1986) concept of aversive racism, "defined as a conflict 'between feelings and beliefs associated with a sincerely egalitarian value system and unacknowledged negative feelings about Blacks' (p. 62)" (Greenwald & Banaji, 1995). Both concepts, "implicit bias" and "aversive racism," recognize the possibility for a person to unknowingly act against what they believe.

Implicit bias occurs through the cognitive processing of unconscious awareness (Staats, 2016). Components such as one's worldview, environment, culture, and ethnicity fuel this bias (Berberena & Wirzberger, 2021). Implicit bias consists of three dimensions: implicit cognition, implicit attitudes, and implicit stereotypes (Greenwald & Banaji, 1995; Greenwald & Krieger, 2006). Implicit cognition is a hidden, unconscious process that helps individuals understand the world in a way not expressed through words (JIN, 2015). Implicit attitude, the second dimension of implicit bias, represents "the tendency to like or dislike, or to act favorably or unfavorably toward, someone or something" (Greenwald & Krieger, 2006, p. 4). The third dimension of implicit bias, implicit stereotype, is also referred to as "social stereotype" and is interpreted as the "mental association between a social group or category or trait" that may be favorable or unfavorable in nature (Greenwald & Krieger, 2006, p. 5). These social stereotypes may be based on gender, sexual orientation, religion, race, or ethnicity, but the research shows that implicit bias operates without conscious intent (Greenwald & Banaji, 1995; Greenwald & Krieger, 2006; Hoffman, 2014).

As opposed to direct and explicit bias, implicit bias is problematic because it occurs within one's unconscious mind, making it more difficult to recognize. As Omrod (2017) explained, implicit bias is a problem that affects the unconscious mind and generates negative behavior from a person's cognitive values and beliefs. This behavior is a threat because it creates unintentional stereotypes, attitudes, and discriminatory outcomes that affect the non-dominant races while manifesting visible cultural biases and economic, social, or racial gaps (Greenwald & Krieger, 2006). These biases permeate society, communities, and schools (Greenwald & Krieger, 2006). Implicit bias is challenging to address because while it is rooted in one's unconscious mind, it can become more pronounced when the individual's biased behaviors are not corrected.

Implicit racial bias entails the unconscious or unaware intentions or actions taken against an individual based solely on their race (Greenwald & Krieger, 2006; Nosek, 2007; Nosek et al., 2002). Implicit racial bias creates unconscious cognitive categories in the brain based on learned behavior from the environment (Eberhardt, 2019). Further, researchers argue that implicit bias may be the primary source of racial inequality (Carbado & Roithmayr, 2014). One place those inequalities play out is within the school system of education where implicit racial bias creates unconscious prejudices towards certain groups of students.

When teachers may be unintentionally favoring one group of students and showing disfavor to another, the discrepancies between them grow. Recognizing this issue within our schools, The National Educational Association's (NEA) Center for Social Justice put out a statement pledging to "leverage the power and collective voice of our members to end the systemic patterns of racial inequity and injustice that affect our Association, schools, students and education communities" (Center for Social Justice, 2021, para. 1). In the resources, the NEA describe implicit bias as "the attitudes or stereotypes that affect our understanding, actions, and decisions in an unconscious manner" (Center for Social Justice, 2021, para. 3). For example, implicit racial bias can influence how White teachers see and treat non-White students, even when the teachers believe they behave fairly and objectively. Black boys especially, are dehumanized (and even associated with ape-like features), seen as older than their White counterparts, and treated as older when encountering authorities (Goff et al., 2014). These implicit biases may lead teachers to hold disparate expectations of their students (positively and negatively) based upon a student's position in a particular racial or ethnic group. White teachers' perceptions could lead them to label Black students as "troublemakers," warranting more punishment than White students (Okonofua & Eberhardt, 2015; Staats et al., 2016). Though White teachers may consciously intend to discipline all students equally, the perceptions they have of Black students as "troublemakers" could lead them to dole out more severe punishments unintentionally and unconsciously to Black students than to White students. Still, they are primarily oblivious of the decisions and actions that affect Black students because of unconscious prejudices (Woods, 2018). While implicit bias manifests in various ways in and out of educational settings, recent data from the Department of Education's Civil Rights Data Collection (CRDC) highlights the disproportionate impact of bias in school discipline as made evident by an overrepresentation of Black students receiving punitive disciplinary actions.

BACKGROUND: THE ROOTS OF IMPLICIT BIAS IN THE HISTORY OF EDUCATION IN THE UNITED STATES

The education and discipline of Black students has always been rooted in inequity. Systemic racism is associated with the history of the United States, where education for Blacks was originally limited to Whites' needs. The modern problems with implicit racial bias have their roots in the first educational policies pertaining to Blacks in the United States. Beginning around 1735–1750, these first racist educational policies were deliberate and well-planned slave exclusion schemes ensuring that no Black persons would obtain an education in Colonial America (Wood, 2007). Whites systematically restricted the communication and learning of the enslaved people by denying them the opportunity to read or write and establishing severe consequences—even death—for any Black person caught pursuing an education (Logue, 1981). While this history tells of the physical abuse endured by enslaved people at the hands of White people, it also speaks of the importance of formal education and the connection between Black education and discipline.

From its inception, the United States of America was established as a country for White Anglo-Saxon citizens. The founders did not include Black people in their plans for growing America's citizens. Even Noah Webster, creator of the Webster dictionary, did not feel compelled to write the truths of Black Americans or their history when writing the history of the United States. When eventually persuaded to include Black people in the history, Webster's comments were in line with the derogatory and racist beliefs held by the majority of those in power (Aiséirithe & Yacovone, 2016). While folks like Webster did not see a place for Black people as anything more than property, there were some White people who recognized the horrors of slavery. As one rich, White, aristocrat, antislavery purist, orator said, "Freedom is only an installment of the debt we owe the Negro" (Aiséirithe & Yacovone, 2016, p. 4). With progressive attitudes like this one, the legal, formal education of Black people in America began to take shape as the nation divided.

With the advent of the Emancipation Proclamation and the end of the Civil War, education for Blacks in America became possible, but in these early days, the concept of a public-school education did not exist, even for White students. Black schools were legal, but they lacked the resources and wealthy alumni funding that White schools had. Black schools depended on support from religious institutions. While the religiously affiliated schools offered Black students the education they had been denied, the mission of these schools was less about educating the populous and more about saving souls. Again, education for Black students served as a way of disciplining them to act in a way that was deemed appropriate by a dominant White society (Kendi, 2016).

Eventually, as public schools became the norm for White students in the United States, the government took steps to create public schools for Black students as well. While *Plessy vs. Ferguson* passed in 1896, allowing for legal segregation, it did not provide equal treatment for Blacks under the law (Gasman, 2009). The ruling prohibited denying "equal protection of the laws" to any person within their jurisdiction (Legal Information Institute, 2018) if it is not followed (Fourteenth Amendment). However, this law segregated Black schools, denying Black students the right to an equal and equitable education.

On paper, Black students earned both the right and the path to a formal education from kindergarten through high school, but the segregated education they were offered was sub-standard or worse (Noguera, 2003). Black schools and White schools were separate, but they were far from equal. Black teachers working in Black schools could not offer Black students a curriculum as strong as the ones White students received because they were working with inferior resources and the Black teachers themselves had not had the benefit of a strong education (Lindsay & Hart, 2017). Black public schools were underfunded, and Black teachers were paid less than the White public school teachers (Kendi, 2016). As Black teachers exited the school systems, Black students lost caring advocates who were members of their own communities (Young, 2016). Furthermore, without Black teachers to help mediate, White teachers often promoted racial stereotypes and showed bias. Many White teachers working in Black schools were racist and used their authority in the classroom to devalue and dehumanize the Black students (Goff et al., 2014). The inferior education offered Black students ensured they would remain in inferior positions in society (Woodson, 2017).

As the 20th century continued, segregation in the United States escalated because of ingrained racism and systemic division between Blacks and Whites (Feagin, 2013; Wise, 2021). Two types of racist arguments drove these racial disparities. First, assimilationism stripped Black youth of their culture, separating them from their parents and making them adapt to Anglo-Saxon culture instead of their own (Little, 2018). Second, segregationism introduced policies and laws meant to marginalize and control Black lives. In the case of *Brown v. Board of Education of Topeka* (347 U.S. 483), segregation in K–12 schools was declared unconstitutional (Cook, 2003; Goldstone, 2021) thus ending the *Plessy v. Ferguson* "separate but equal" dogma. At the same time, however, the legislation created another problem whereby the integration of the Black students into White schools affected the racial makeup of the education workforce and impacted job opportunities for Black educators (Gladwell, 2019; Goldstone, 2021; NAACP et al., 2014). As districts scrambled to bus students from the Black communities to schools staffed by White teachers, affording Blacks access to the same educational opportunities (Will, 2019), Black educators were effectively eliminated. The effect of this unexpected consequence is still evident in today's schools where only 7% of public-school teachers and 11% of public-school principals are Black (Ramsey, 2008; Will, 2019).

When Black students, White students, and White teachers lose the opportunity to work with Black educators, implicit racial bias can grow. Black students don't see professionals who look like them working in schools, and White teachers and students lose the opportunity to engage with diverse points of view (Will, 2019). Furthermore, when Black educators were forced out of the school system, America's schools lost most of their adult advocates for Black students. Without Black teachers pushing for diverse curriculum, Black and White students missed opportunities to learn about the lives of Black people before and after they were enslaved in America. The White Eurocentric approach to education had little room for Blackness or Brown-ness. However, the curriculum was not the only part of education that suffered when Black teachers were forced out of the profession. White teachers continued to dehumanize Black students by comparing both their academic and behavioral expectations to White students (Goff et al., 2014). White teachers' education courses used White students as the standard, rather than recognizing and appreciating the diversity of Black students, they saw them from a deficit perspective because of their different features and the color of their skin. Black discipline numbers increased (Douglas et al., 2008) due to the poor relationship between Black students and White teachers in school systems. Since then, racism and implicit bias have run through institutions of education benefitting White teachers who unconsciously maintain the status quo to stay in power rather than using their power to reduce racism and implicit bias negatively impacting Black students (Martin & Baxter, 2001).

In colleges of education, White theories from Vygotsky, Dewey, Maslow, Erikson and Piaget dominated the curriculum, and theories from Black scholars like W.E.B Dubois, Carter G. Woodson, Booker T. Washington, and Nathan Hare were absent (Muhammad et al., 2020). According to Muhammad (2020) omitting materials from Mary McCloud Bethune, Anna Julia Copper, Clara Muhammad, Nannie Helen Burroughs, Fanny Jackson Coppin, Ella Baker, and Ida B. Wells distorts the history of Black Americans and their experiences.

The snapshot of history presented here is but the tip of the proverbial iceberg showing the connection between White disciplinary measures and the history of education for Black people in America. When the White person's history is continuously held up as the standard, disproportionalities and disparities inevitably occur for non-White people. This occurs in all aspects of a non-White person 's life such as with healthcare, real estate, banking, and the criminal justice, but it is perhaps most evident in education. For White Americans, education has always served as a means of progress and betterment, but for Black Americans, education began with the risk of death and continues to be plagued with prejudice, inequity, and submission to a hegemonic Eurocentric curriculum. Throughout the United States' history, racism and discrimination yielded policies that continue to feed inequalities in school systems and contribute to educational disparities. Although subtleties of aversive racism and implicit bias have largely replaced overt racism and discrimination, these problems still fuel the mistreatment of Black people and cement further institutionalized racism in schools in both academics and disciplinary measures (Gaertner & Dovidio, 1986; John F Dovidio & Samuel L Gaertner, 2000).

Overall, schools are making strides away from punitive and exclusionary disciplinary practices, yet certain groups like Black students and students with learning and emotional disabilities are still overrepresented in the statistics of expulsions and suspensions (Pufall-Jones et al., 2018). Change cannot occur without recognizing all that contributes to the disproportionate realities of these discipline practices. As Carter et al. (2017) succinctly explained, "addressing racial disparities requires addressing race" (p. 218). For progress to happen, this history cannot be ignored. White teachers need to be ready to reject racist attitudes, stereotypical behaviors and social structures that maintain the "hierarchical racial identity structure," the model of White racial identity (Martin & Baxter, 2001, p. 7).

IMPLICIT BIAS DISPROPORTIONALTIES

Recognizing that implicit racial bias exists in America today is a big step on the path to helping schools achieve fair disciplinary outcomes. Though American educators may profess and believe that no single group of students is more prone than another to break school rules, recent data tell a different story. Part of dealing with the disciplinary disproportionalities plaguing American schools is understanding that these practices may occur without conscious knowledge or mal intent. As explained by the American Values Institute, "Because so many of our actions are a result of our unconscious associations, implicit bias can result in behaviors that are contrary to our conscious values" (Godsil & Johnson, 2013, p. 8). Therefore, it is difficult for

White teachers who maintain a belief that all people are created equal to see how they can still fall prey to the damaging effects of implicit racial bias.

The nation made progress in exclusionary discipline practices during the Obama administration when in 2014 the Departments of Education and Justice created guidance for schools aimed at promoting nondiscriminatory discipline measures. Specifically, this guidance sought to protect better students with disabilities and students of color from discriminatory disciplinary practices. While this guidance package was not policy, it did offer guiding principles and three priorities from which policy and legislation could be created. The third priority offered by the guiding principles stated that schools should seek to "ensure fairness, equity, and continuous improvement" (U.S. Department of Education, 2014, p. 16). The improvement of discipline includes providing educators with the tools or resources needed to discipline disruptive behavior consistent and fair and providing alternative when suspending or expelling students. Reports from the Civil Rights Data Collection (CRDC), however, show that inequity still persists. Furthermore, the Trump administration issued a "Dear Colleague" letter rescinding the 2014 guidance on the Nondiscriminatory Administration of School Discipline.

If all students were treated equally, then in an ideal world's data set, the number of disciplinary punishments should trend exactly with the demographic make-up of the students. Meaning, more directly, that if 50% of a school's students were Black then 50% of the disciplinary infractions given by that school would be to Black students. Any variances from a trend up or down equates an under or overrepresentation of a particular student group. Again, assuming that all men are created equal, any variances would suggest unequal treatment—explained perhaps by implicit bias on the part of the teachers and administrators. Unfortunately, recent data demonstrate that Black students are grossly overrepresented as recipients of school disciplinary measures. Using data from the CRDC, the U.S. Department of Education website states, "Black students are suspended and expelled at a rate three times greater than white students, while students with disabilities are twice as likely to receive an out-of-school suspension as their non-disabled peers" (U.S. Department of Education, 2017, para. 1).

According to the recent data from the Civil Rights Data Collection (2021), implicit bias contributes to racial disproportionality exhibited in the overrepresentation of certain groups of students receiving both in-school suspensions (ISS) and out-of-school suspensions (OSS). When over-assigned, these disciplinary measures make equitable access to learning difficult for many students—particularly male students of color and students of color with learning differences. The CRDC national data show disproportionality in that the 2017–2018 schoolyear, boys accounted for 51.4% of all K–12 public school students but represented 70.5% of expelled students with an overrepresentation of expelled students of 19.1% (U.S. Department of Education,

2021). Black students only make up 15.1% of the total number of students in the United States but make up 38.2% of the total number of students receiving one or more out-of-school suspension in 2017–2018, an overrepresentation of 23.1%. These statistics show an overrepresentation of male students and of Black students in general, but when controlling for Black male students, the numbers are even more severe. Black male students represent only 15% of the total male student population, but 35.4% of population of male students receiving one or more out-of-school suspensions, an overrepresentation of over 20%. Conversely, while approximately 47.5% of male students are White, only 35% of male students receiving one or more out-of-school suspensions are White, an underrepresentation of 12.5%. These numbers mean that for disciplinary rates to be equitable for Black and White male students, a difference of over 30% needs to be accounted for. While the expulsion of Black male students is a significant problem, it is not the only statistic showing overrepresentation and inequitable learning opportunities. Controlling for gender and race also shows that Black female students' in-school suspension (ISS) rate is 70% higher, and out-of-school suspension (OSS) rate is over 30% higher than the White female students (United States Government Accountability Office, 2018). These national statistics show a difference in opportunities stemming from bias in disciplinary rates, yet at the state and individual school district level rates are even more skewed.

Georgia has one of the harshest discipline and suspension processes where Black students are disciplined disproportionately higher and harsher than their White peers (Downey, 2017, para. 6). Consequently, the numbers of incarcerations, of which 57.6% are non-white, mirrors the number of disciplines in schools at 54% suspensions. Of the almost 1.7 million students enrolled in Georgia schools, Blacks accounted for 37% of the total student population compared to White students who made up 43%, a difference of roughly 6% (Downey, 2014, para. 2). When looking at disciplinary rates for these groups of students, White students would be expected to have a discipline rate of approximately 6% more than their Black peers. Even though the Black students did not make up the majority of total student population, they accounted for 57% of expelled students compared to 31% for White students. That is a difference of 20% and an overrepresentation of 26%. The trend follows for out-of-school suspensions with 67% of the total number being doled out to Black students and 21% to their White counterparts (Downey, 2014). These numbers show an overrepresentation of 52%. The trends shown in the data from Georgia manifest throughout the United States when it comes to high discipline rates among Black students when looking at specific districts. These statistics show that this problem of implicit bias cannot be isolated to urban areas or the South, but is nationwide.

Furthermore, the exclusionary disciplinary disparities begin as early as the preschool years. Statistics from the CRDC show that for the 2017–2018 schoolyear, of the nearly 1.5 million students in public preschools, approximately 18% were African American. Of those preschool students, 2822 received one or more out of school suspension. All things equal, that means that 18% should be African American students, or just over 500 students, yet the number of African American preschoolers who received one or more out-of-school suspension was 1223, or roughly 43.3%, an overrepresentation of 25%. When the disciplinary odds are stacked against a child before they even get to kindergarten, the health of the nation's educational system is in bad shape (U.S. Department of Education, 2021). Young Black students are experiencing trauma in their primitive years where teachers with implicit racial bias are correcting their behavior subjectively using disrespect, disobedience, and disruption as their guide to discipline. The deleterious effects of suspensions and expulsions have lasting effects in their future lives such as unequal access to healthcare, unequal access to higher education, and being denied job opportunities (Thigpen, 2019).

The skewed disciplinary rates are concerning on their own but disciplinary actions at school have consequences that extend beyond classroom and into the criminal justice system (Hirschfield, 2018). Gregory (2017) determined that the out-of-school suspensions can equal up to six percent of missed instructional time if these students are not immediately placed in an alternative education setting. Students who miss instructional time are further at risk of dropping out of school. Writing about disproportionate minority contact (DMC) with the criminal justice system, Hirschfield (2018) explains, "African American students face a higher risk of disciplinary transfer to an alternative school" and alternative schools have relationships with the police departments that mainstream schools do not have (p. 14). Further, as Hirschfield (2018) notes, being sent to out-of-school suspension can violate the terms for students completing juvenile probationary periods, further cementing the link between school discipline and the criminal justice system. When a student is on probation, part of the terms for the probation is that they are attending school, but if they are not sent to OOS, it violates the terms of their probation. While increased contact with the criminal justice system is damaging, so are the other effects of time spent out of the classroom such as the high cost associated with incarcerations and lost income over the student's lifetime and removing these students from school and their families undermine the capability of their community.

Disciplinary racial disproportionalities are clearly happening across the nation, but what contributes to the differences in the numbers is not as clearly understood. While schools appear to be moving away from zero-tolerance policies and toward programs that offer restorative behavioral actions rather than exclusionary discipline policies, research shows that harsher punishments are still being given by administrators and teachers who feel threatened by Black students' "misbehavior" (Losen & Gillespie,

2012). These policies did not make a significant impact in reducing the misbehavior these students were accused of (Payne & Welch, 2015).

One possible association for the continuous disproportionate discipline is cultural conflict—a biproduct of implicit bias. Even before teachers interact with their students, they may be unconsciously predisposed to treat students who belong to other cultural groups differently than students belonging to their own cultural group—not with malintent, but implicit bias. These teachers are less prepared to educate diverse, multicultural students (Gay, 2002). The impact of cultural conflict surfaces in the pedagogical aspects of the classroom, but the social aspects as well. White teachers who do not always understand cultural differences among their students tend to have low expectations for Black students (Gentrup et al., 2020; Jussim & Harber, 2005). As Milner (2010) explained, "students of color are often misunderstood, exploited, abused, and targeted for not being acquainted with cultural norms different from their own" (p. 123). Cultural conflicts occur where the teachers assume power in their classroom and discipline Black students using White students as the yardstick for measuring disruptiveness, disobedience, and disrespect. With sufficient training in diversity, Milner argues, teachers can learn to recognize how dominance creates power imbalances in the classroom and begin to have a more diverse understanding of concepts such as color blindness, deficit thinking, and meritocracy. Teachers lacking preparation in diversity education unintentionally continue with the same systemic habits of implicit racism and discrimination, lowering the expectations and contributing to opportunity gaps for Black students (Milner IV, 2010). White teachers with implicit bias need to understand that teachers' interpretations of a situation affect students long-term. Discipline infractions of disruptiveness, disobedience, and disrespect are subjective characteristics of implicit bias—and that are "problems" from the beholder's eye or teacher's perspective (Staats et al., 2016). This lack of understanding can be attributed to implicit bias, negatively impacting the Black students early on and widening the educational disparity gap as students' progress through their academic careers.

Unfortunately, when the CRDC releases data on student discipline, the conversation inevitably turns to students as the problem rather than disciplinary practices. The statistics on suspensions and expulsions are important, but they do not capture the whole phenomenon. White teachers with implicit bias continue to discriminate and sustain power in decisions of discipline against Black students (Kendi, 2016; Woods, 2018) and contribute to disparities of achievement (Jussim & Harber, 2005). For many Black students, their teachers' behavior results in a self-fulfilling prophecy where implicitly held low expectations of Black students lead to low achievement (de Boer et al., 2010; Staats et al., 2016).

Over the last century, racism and discrimination shifted in tone and behavior, moving away from overt acts to implicit racial bias. However, through implicit racial bias, stereotypes and misinformation against the Black race continue to devalue Black culture (Tatum, 1997). Color lines have not moved; despite the multicultural growth the divide among races persists. The majority of the White students does little to socially include the minority nonwhite student groups (Tatum, 1997). More than a risk to Black culture, this learned antagonism against their heritage leads to the dehumanization of Blacks (Woodson, 2017), and as Owusu-Bempah (2017) explained, for Black students, dehumanization is due in part to educational policies and regulations implemented by White teachers for centuries. Progress is possible, but where implicit bias is involved, White teachers must look back to grow in understanding of Black education in the United States to take steps moving forward.

RECOMMENDATIONS FOR RECOGNIZING AND ADDRESSING IMPLICIT RACIAL BIAS IN SCHOOLS

America's existing school system rests on a longstanding structure that has never been able to serve all students equally or equitably. Although overt expressions of racism are fewer today than in the era of Jim Crow, the systemic racism continues to benefit White individuals while disadvantaging Blacks (Tatum, 1997). Education in the United States still lacks social justice, empathy, equity, and culturally relevant teachings for many of its Black students. People have learned to celebrate diversity in their explicit values, but racial implicit bias surfaces in everyday actions (Chin et al., 2020; Ladson-Billings, 2014) (Ladson-Billings, 2014). Subtle manifestations of bias persist when expressing unintentional verbal gestures or nonverbal expressions rooted in one's unconsciousness (Dovidio et al., 2018). As Staats (2016) explained, "even well-intentioned individuals can act in ways that produce inequitable outcomes for different groups" (p. 30). Therefore, to reduce implicit bias, one must first recognize that they can be acting in ways that uphold the racist system even when outwardly, they disavow racism.

As described earlier, studies continually show that White teachers are biased to see Black students as disobedient, disruptive, or defiant (Anyon et al., 2014; Losen, 2014), particularly when disciplining (Chin et al., 2020). Research also shows, however, that change is possible and teachers can learn to mitigate implicit racial bias (Landsman & Lewis, 2006). Educational researchers have long applauded the work of Gloria Ladson-Billings (2014) and others who have developed strategies for supporting a culturally relevant pedagogical approach. However, in order for these approaches to take effect, educators themselves must be convinced of and admit to the role implicit racial bias has in the continual inequities that plague our schools and in their own interactions. Since implicit bias is a cognitive process that functions in the unconscious mind, most individuals, including White teachers, are not aware of their personal yet negative racially biased tendencies. Therefore, implicit racial bias creates a challenge to self-correct without proper professional development, guidance, and evidence to demonstrate existing thought patterns. Teachers cannot know to fix something they do not know or see as broken.

To address implicit racial bias and the disproportionate exclusionary discipline practices it encourages, first, teachers must learn to recognize and address their own implicit racial biases. Professional development programs that promote cultural relevance can help with this but only if teachers first see their bias (Vavrus, 2015). Second, teachers and schools need to seek out alternatives for exclusionary discipline measures and instead incorporate more restorative approaches to handing infractions at school (Schneider, 2021). Hirschfield (2018) describes these two approaches or processes as happening individually at micro-level and more broadly within schools and districts at the macro-level. Both processes are important and necessary, but unless teachers recognize their own implicit bias at the micro-level, they are not likely to benefit from macro-level diversity education or to embrace the restorative approaches to discipline. Teachers who recognize their behavior is from stereotyping and not from experience become aware of the impact it makes on Black students and begin to change their behavior. It is at this crossroad that the White teacher can move forward or not.

Other ways teachers can mitigate implicit bias in education include using the Implicit Association Test (IAT) and working to diversify their peer groups Staats (2016).

The Implicit Association Test measures how the brain unconsciously makes associations about different groups (Greenwald et al., 1998). While this test is vetted by researchers (Warikoo et al., 2020) and free to take online, it may be unknown to many schools and teachers and also difficult to understand. The IAT measures implicit bias using generic examples, but teachers need to recognize how their own implicit bias plays out in their classrooms. The IAT also shows anti-Black bias and skin-tone discriminations (Warikoo et al., 2020). Staats (2016) explained that simply showing teachers the data about discipline can help localize the effects of implicit racial bias by allowing teachers to see for themselves the disparities that trend in the statistics. Another recommendation Staats offered was for teachers to seek out "counter-stereotypical exemplars" or "to know people who differ from [them] on a real, personal level" (Staats, 2016, p. 36). This is particularly important because as İnan-Kaya and Rubie-Davies (2021) found in their study, when implicit bias occurs, teachers are "not reacting to the behaviour itself, but to the doer" (p. 10). When teachers can make connections with their students and with other members of their students' communities, they respond to individuals rather than stereotypes (Godsil & Johnson, 2013). Implicit bias feeds on negative experiences, but can be decreased by repeated exposure to positive images (Kang, 2012; Pinkston, 2015, Staats, 2016).

In addition to the strategies mentioned above, researchers suggest that teachers should learn to pay attention to the setting in which exclusionary discipline practices occur (Dasgupta & Greenwald, 2001). Staats (2016) suggested that teachers can reduce implicit bias in the classroom actions by "taking enough time to carefully process a situation before making a decision" (p. 37). İnan-Kaya and Rubie-Davies (2021) echo this recommendation explaining that teachers do not plan out their responses to student disciplinary actions the way they plan out their lessons. Actions that happen at an unconscious level, like "the nonverbal channels, such as body language, voice intonations, and facial expressions ... are less easily controlled" (p. 2). Teachers do not set to out to discriminate against their students. Yet there are White teachers who have chronic stress and fatigue and work in poor working conditions with high competing demands. These factors compound and can trigger stereotypical behavior or implicit racial bias (Marcucci, 2020). Warikoo et al. (2016) points out that "teachers tend to work under conditions that heighten the negative impact of implicit associations, potentially increasing their impact in the classroom" (p. 510). A study on the impact of empathy intervention validates that racial implicit bias can be reduced through self-awareness of implicit bias (Whitford & Emerson, 2019). Furthermore, the lasting impact of the disciplinary gap Gregory and Mosely (2004) cannot be underestimated or ignored.

One way of reducing implicit bias and closing the achievement gap is by implementing culturally responsive teaching practices in schools. This process begins by holding Multicultural Relevance Professional Development training and focusing on moving away from traditional instruction and incorporating culturally responsive teaching methods that respond to the diversity of the students in the classroom (2015). Vavrus (2015) found that implementing extensive Multicultural Relevance Professional Development training reduces implicit bias so that Black students are more likely to succeed. A teacher's in-service training should include practicing acquired skills under guided supervision while observing students, identifying economic disparities, and preparing resolutions in the student's teaching curriculum (Gay, 2002; Landsman & Lewis, 2006). Teachers need to transform curriculum "to include analyses that focus on the complexity, purpose, significance, and authenticity of the narrative texts, role models, and authorial sources used in the instructional materials" Guy (2002, p. 108).

After intensive and sustained development hours, teachers who invest in these teaching practices and classroom culture development training are able to change their behavior (Supovitz & Turner, 2000). However, getting teachers to the point where implicit bias does not contribute to disproportionate disciplinary statistics, requires more than the occasional after-school session on diversity. The extent of or hours spent in the development training makes a difference, according to Supovitz and Turner (2000). Supovitz and Turner (2000) validate that teachers' behavior change after 80 hours, while the investigative shift in culture is after 160 hours of development training.

Progress in reducing the disciplinary gap can be made at the macro-level through extensive multicultural relevance professional development and restorative approaches to discipline, but for training to be successful, individual teachers need to recognize their own biases at the micro-level. According to Landsman and Lewis (2006), there needs to be academic achievement, cultural competency, equity, and equality. In addition, all school materials should contain multicultural content based on ethnic experiences and not just during their ethnic celebration day or month. To create more equitable opportunities for all students, educational researchers need to learn more about implicit bias in order to better support teacher education and professional development programs with practices rooted in culturally relevant pedagogy and culturally appropriate training (Landsman & Lewis, 2006).

In addition to reducing implicit bias in teachers and administrators, school districts can begin to mitigate school disparities, disproportionalities, and other disciplinary gaps by changing their approach to discipline and encouraging restorative rather than punitive practices. Instead of punishment, students need positive motivation for behavioral change (Cartledge & Kourea, 2008). Punitive discipline and zero-tolerance policies are associated with an escalation in negative discipline and make students think their lives are disposable (Welch & Payne, 2010). Restorative practice should not be perceived as a tool to reduce disciplinary data but to transform education with the goal to attain successful outcomes for Black and other low income students in education (Ferlazzo, 2016).

Educational organizations are taking steps to address punitive disciplinary practices, but this cannot be where the change begins and ends. Responding to the recent National Association of School Psychologists (NASP) Framework for Effective Discipline, Sevon et al. (2021) explained that the focus on student behavior is not enough. Rather, they expressed, the harm caused by implicit bias in school discipline cannot be overstated: We cannot address the inequitable consequences of school discipline, as policy or as it is enacted by individuals, without attending to the racism and bias intrinsic to these problems (para 1, under Revisiting the Framework).

Non-Black teachers' implicit bias allows the cycles of racism and aversive racism to continue to exist even though the policy measures like the Framework promote the prevention of exclusionary disciplinary practices (Sevon et al., 2021). If followed correctly, the framework can produce a positive outcome, but the Framework operates at a macro-level. The NASP Framework is a useful tool able to equip teachers with the practices they need to respond more positively to disciplinary infractions. However, it is possible for teachers to circumvent the NASP Framework, use its tools, and still not change their own beliefs because they did not learn how to identify their own implicit bias (Hirschfield, 2018). The failure of non-Black teachers to recognize that their concept of racial implicit bias and stereotyping against Black students is directly associated with the disparities in achievement gaps and missed opportunities for academic excellence that their White counterparts receive. Part of the problem, according to Sevon et al. (2021) is that policies like the NASP Framework rely on vague language and generalities to discuss the adverse consequences of negative disciplinary practices placed upon Black students and other minorities like LatinX and indigenous persons. Unless major organizations like NASP and NEA can model in their policies language that recognizes and addresses the specific systemic disparities that continue to shape disciplinary practices, the teachers cannot be expected to adopt that language themselves. Teachers should be held accountable at the individual level, but to best address the problem change needs to span from the macro to the micro level. Teachers are put in position of power therefor need to understand how to address challenging or problematic student behavior.

When helping teachers to recognize implicit bias, they should not be singled out or labeled as the only group plagued with this problem. Although the focus of this chapter is on White teachers' implicit racial bias, teachers as a category of professionals, are just as likely as other professionals to exhibit bias. According to research from Starck et al. (2020), when tested, "teachers held levels of implicit bias, explicit bias, … and symbolic racism that were not statistically different from the levels of nonteachers" (p. 279). Recognizing this is important when looking for ways of reducing bias, because schools and teachers can learn from other fields that are also implementing strategies to combat implicit bias such as the medical field (Sukhera & Watling, 2018), social services (Wong & Vinsky, 2021), and the criminal justice system (Kang, 2012). These fields offer additional avenues for research that may be generalizable to educational research. For example, Sukhera (2018) described a successful health education framework with features of a creation of a safe and nonthreatening learning context. Adapting insights from these other fields allows educators to combat implicit racial bias with strategies that have been deemed successful. In doing so, they can increase in their knowledge of their own implicit bias and recognize how implicit biases influence their behavior and student outcomes.

FUTURE RESEARCH DIRECTIONS

Schools in the United States have an urgent need to address racism and implicit bias influencing high disciplinary referral numbers among Black students. Unfortunately, the typical K–12 teacher may not be familiar with implicit bias, and furthermore, likely does not have time to read extensive literature on how to combat implicit bias. Therefore, it is the academy's responsibility to work with the public to bring about awareness and offer strategies for reducing implicit racial bias and mitigating disproportionate school discipline practices. Discrimination is easy to recognize in the numbers, but where implicit racial bias is involved, less visible in the beliefs of the teachers and administrators.

Schools are working to implement multicultural relevance teaching strategies, restorative justice programs, and professional development. All these improvements are important and forward progress, but in order for them to be more effective, teachers still need to recognize their implicit bias. White teachers' implicit bias is of high interest because it influences disciplinary measures against Black students, perpetuating educational gap disparities. While the research explored above underscores how important it is for teacher to address their implicit bias, a gap exists qualitatively exploring how lived experiences contribute to White teachers' implicit bias in the classroom and how it affects the treatment of their Black students. Understanding more about this phenomenon can better support the teachers' efforts to recognize their own implicit bias. In particular, the primary author is embarking on a study examining the use of an implicit bias framework that includes the creation of a safe and nonthreatening learning environment where teachers can increase one's implicit bias knowledge and self-awareness prior to Multicultural Relevance Professional Development training.

CONCLUSION

The statistics and research shared in this chapter repeatedly showed the disproportionately high disciplinary rates for Black students and the damaging consequences those disciplinary assignments create. Through the continual use of exclusionary discipline measures, the nation's schools constantly place the blame for these behaviors solely on the students. The legacy of formal education for Black students in the United States, however, shows a more complete picture of the ways in which learning for Black Americans has always been tied to discipline at the hands of a dominant White authority. The overrepresentation of Black students assigned exclusionary discipline measures in today's schools carries with it this racist history. Progress demands reckoning with not only the overt racism that still exists in many non-Black places, but also the damage created through implicit racial bias. In order to create equitable educational experiences for all students in the United States, White teachers must recognize that they hold a higher responsibility to correct the wrong that has been ongoing over centuries. It is paramount that teachers reflect about their susceptibility to negative racial beliefs (Gregory & Roberts, 2017; Gibson, 2021) and begin to change their mindset with nurturing positive beliefs that will erase the "invisible barriers to opportunity" for Black students (Staats, 2016,

p. 33). White teachers need to not only acknowledge that implicit bias is harmful to Black students, but also work to address how their biases shape their conscious behavior. This work begins with awareness of implicit racial bias, but must continue by making the changes in pedagogical practice required to reduce high discipline rates and improve the educational experiences of these students.

ACKNOWLEDGMENT

The researcher would like to acknowledge Dr. Laila Y. Sanguras, Dr. Nicholas R. Werse, and Dr. Elizabeth Anne Murray for the editorial assistance and early feedback they provided during the development of this chapter.

REFERENCES

Aiséirithe, A. J., & Yacovone, D. (2016). *Wendell Phillips, social justice, and the power of the past.* Louisiana State University Press.

Anyon, Y., Jenson, J. M., Altschul, I., Farrar, J., McQueen, J., Greer, E., Downing, B., & Simmons, J. (2014). The persistent effect of race and the promise of alternatives to suspension in school discipline outcomes. *Children and Youth Services Review*, *44*, 379–386. doi:10.1016/j.childyouth.2014.06.025

Berberena, T., & Wirzberger, M. (2021). *Bringing Thiagi to the classroom: Reducing stereotype-threat by promoting reflection in CRT* [Conference paper]. EARLI Conference.

Cameron, C. D., Payne, B. K., & Knobe, J. (2010). Do theories of implicit race bias change moral judgments? *Social Justice Research*, *23*(4), 272–289. doi:10.100711211-010-0118-z

Carbado, D. W., & Roithmayr, D. (2014). Critical race theory meets social science. *Annual Review of Law and Social Science*, *10*(1), 149–167. doi:10.1146/annurev-lawsocsci-110413-030928

Carter, P. L., Skiba, R., Arredondo, M. I., & Pollock, M. (2017). You can't fix what you don't look at: Acknowledging race in addressing racial discipline disparities. *Urban Education*, *52*(2), 207–235. doi:10.1177/0042085916660350

Cartledge, G., & Kourea, L. (2008). Culturally responsive classrooms for culturally diverse students with and at risk for disabilities. *Exceptional Children*, *74*(3), 351–371. doi:10.1177/001440290807400305

Center for Social Justice. (2021). *Implicit bias, microaggressions, and stereotypes resources.* NEA. https://www.nea.org/resource-library/implicit-bias-microaggressions-and-stereotypes-resources

Chin, M. J., Quinn, D. M., Dhaliwal, T. K., & Lovison, V. S. (2020). Bias in the air: A nationwide exploration of teachers' implicit racial attitudes, aggregate bias, and student outcomes. *Educational Researcher, 49*(8), 566–578. doi:10.3102/0013189X20937240

Civil Rights Data Collection. (2021). https://ocrdata.ed.gov/

Cook, T. E. (2003). *Separation, assimilation, or accommodation: Contrasting ethnic minority policies: contrasting ethnic minority policies.* ABC-CLIO.

Dasgupta, N., & Greenwald, A. (2001). On the malleability of automatic attitudes: Combating automatic prejudice with images of admired and disliked individuals. *Journal of Personality and Social Psychology, 81*(5), 800–814. doi:10.1037/0022-3514.81.5.800 PMID:11708558

de Boer, H., Bosker, R. J., & van der Werf, M. P. C. (2010). Sustainability of teacher expectation bias effects on long-term student performance. *Journal of Educational Psychology, 102*(1), 168–179. doi:10.1037/a0017289

Devine, D., Savage, M., & Ingram, N. (2012). White middle-class identities and urban schooling. *British Journal of Sociology of Education, 33*(2), 303–314. doi:10.1080/01425692.2012.649843

Douglas, B., Lewis, C. W., Douglas, A., Scott, M. E., & Garrison-Wade, D. (2008). The impact of White teachers on the academic achievement of Black students. *Educational Foundations, 22*(1–2), 47–62.

Dovidio, J. F., & Gaertner, S. L. (2000). Aversive racism and selection decisions: 1989 and 1999. *Psychological Science, 11*(4), 315–319. doi:10.1111/1467-9280.00262 PMID:11273391

Dovidio, J. F., Pearson, A. R., & Penner, L. A. (2018). Aversive racism, implicit bias, and microaggressions. In G. C. Torino, D. P. Rivera, C. M. Capodilupo, K. L. Nadal, & D. W. Sue (Eds.), *Microaggression theory* (pp. 16–31). John Wiley & Sons., doi:10.1002/9781119466642.ch2

Downey, M. (2014). Do schools suspend too many students of color? Divisive discipline. *The Atlanta Journal-Constitution*, p. A12.

Downey, M. (2017, December 27). Research shows black students punished more severely. Why don't schools believe it and fix it? *The Atlanta Journal-Constitution.*

Eberhardt, J. L. (2019). *Biased: Uncovering the hidden prejudice that shapes what we see, think, and do.* Penguin.

Fay, L. (2018, August 14). *The state of America's student-teacher racial gap: Our public school system has been majority-minority for years, but 80 percent of teachers are still white.* https://www.the74million.org/article/the-state-of-americas-student-teacher-racial-gap-our-public-school-system-has-been-majority-minority-for-years-but-80-percent-of-teachers-are-still-white/

Feagin, J. (2013). *Systemic racism: A theory of oppression.* Routledge. doi:10.4324/9781315880938

Ferlazzo, L. (2016, February 6). Response: How to practice restorative justice in schools. *Education Week.* https://www.edweek.org/teaching-learning/opinion-response-how-to-practice-restorative-justice-in-schools/2016/02

Gaertner, S. L., & Dovidio, J. F. (1986). The aversive form of racism. In J. F. Dovidio & S. L. Gaertner (Eds.), *Prejudice, discrimination, and racism* (pp. 61–89). Academic Press.

Gasman, M. (2009). Minority serving colleges deserve more respect. *The Chronicle of Higher Education.* https://www.chronicle.com/article/minority-serving-colleges-deserve-more-respect/

Gay, G. (2002). Preparing for culturally responsive teaching. *Journal of Teacher Education, 53*(2), 106–116. doi:10.1177/0022487102053002003

Gentrup, S., Lorenz, G., Kristen, C., & Kogan, I. (2020). Self-fulfilling prophecies in the classroom: Teacher expectations, teacher feedback and student achievement. *Learning and Instruction, 66,* 101296. doi:10.1016/j.learninstruc.2019.101296

Gladwell, M. (2019). *Revisionist history podcast.* http://revisionisthistory.com/

Godsil, R. D., & Johnson, A. M. (2013). *Transforming perception: Black men and boys* [Executive Summary]. Perception Institute. https://perception.org/publications/transforming-perception/

Goff, P. A., Jackson, M. C., Di Leone, B. A. L., Culotta, C. M., & DiTomasso, N. A. (2014). The essence of innocence: Consequences of dehumanizing black children. *Journal of Personality and Social Psychology, 106*(4), 526–545. doi:10.1037/a0035663 PMID:24564373

Goldstone, L. (2021). *Separate no more: The long road to Brown v. Board of Education.* Scholastic.

Greenwald, A. G., & Banaji, M. R. (1995). Implicit social cognition: Attitudes, self-esteem, and stereotypes. *Psychological Review*, *102*(1), 4–27. doi:10.1037/0033-295X.102.1.4 PMID:7878162

Greenwald, A. G., & Krieger, L. H. (2006). Implicit bias: Scientific foundations. *California Law Review*, *94*(4), 945–967. doi:10.2307/20439056

Greenwald, A. G., McGhee, D. E., & Schwartz, J. L. K. (1998). Measuring individual differences in implicit cognition: The implicit association test. *Journal of Personality and Social Psychology*, *74*(6), 1464–1480. doi:10.1037/0022-3514.74.6.1464 PMID:9654756

Gregory, A., & Mosely, P. M. (2004). The discipline gap: Teachers' view on the over-representation of African American students in the discipline system. *Equity & Excellence in Education*, *37*(1), 18–30. doi:10.1080/10665680490429280

Gregory, A., & Roberts, G. (2017). Teacher beliefs and the overrepresentation of black students in classroom discipline. *Theory into Practice*, *56*(3), 187–194. doi: 10.1080/00405841.2017.1336035

Hirschfield, P. J. (2018a). The role of schools in sustaining juvenile justice system inequality. *The Future of Children*, *28*(1), 11–35. doi:10.1353/foc.2018.0001

Hirschfield, P. J. (2018b). The role of schools in sustaining juvenile justice system inequality. *The Future of Children*, *28*(1), 11–36. doi:10.1353/foc.2018.0001

Hoffman, S. (2014). Zero benefit: Estimating the effect of zero-tolerance discipline policies on racial disparities in school discipline. *Educational Policy*, *28*(1), 69–95. doi:10.1177/0895904812453999

İnan-Kaya, G., & Rubie-Davies, C. M. (2021). Teacher classroom interactions and behaviours: Indications of bias. *Learning and Instruction*, *78*, 101516. doi:10.1016/j.learninstruc.2021.101516

Jin, Z. (Ed.). (2015). Exploring implicit cognition: Learning, memory, and social cognitive processes. IGI Global. doi:10.4018/978-1-4666-6599-6

Jussim, L., & Harber, K. D. (2005). Teacher expectations and self-fulfilling prophecies: Knowns and unknowns, resolved and unresolved controversies. *Personality and Social Psychology Review*, *9*(2), 131–155. doi:10.120715327957pspr0902_3 PMID:15869379

Kang, J. (2012). Implicit bias in the courtroom. *University of California Los Angeles Law Review.* https://www.uclalawreview.org/implicit-bias-in-the-courtroom-2/

Kendi, I. X. (2016). *Stamped from the beginning: The definitive history of racist ideas in America*. Public Affairs.

Ladson-Billings, G. (2014). Culturally relevant pedagogy 2.0: A.K.A. the remix. *Harvard Educational Review, 84*(1), 74–84. doi:10.17763/haer.84.1.p2rj131485484751

Landsman, J., & Lewis, W. (2006). *White teachers/diverse classrooms*. Stylus Publishing.

Legal Information Institute. (2018). *Separate But Equal*. https://www.law.cornell.edu/wex/separate_but_equal

Lindsay, C. A., & Hart, C. M. D. (2017). Exposure to same-race teachers and student disciplinary outcomes for Black students in North Carolina. *Educational Evaluation and Policy Analysis, 39*(3), 485–510. doi:10.3102/0162373717693109

Locke, A., Washington, L. W., Knollenberg, F., Berryman, C. K., Parks, G., Margold, N., Roosevelt, E., Houston, C. H., Marshall, T., & Johnson, L. (2014, October 10). *The Civil Rights Act of 1964: A long struggle for freedom: The Segregation Era (1900–1939)*. Library of Congress. https://www.loc.gov/exhibits/civil-rights-act/segregation-era.html

Logue, C. M. (1981). Transcending coercion: The communicative strategies of Black slaves on antebellum plantations. *The Quarterly Journal of Speech, 67*(1), 31–46. doi:10.1080/00335638109383549

Losen, D. J. (2014). *Closing the school discipline gap: Equitable remedies for excessive exclusion*. Teachers College Press.

Losen, D. J., & Gillespie, J. (2012). *Opportunities suspended: The disparate impact of disciplinary exclusion from school*. The Civil Rights Project. https://escholarship.org/uc/item/3g36n0c3

Marcucci, O. (2020). Implicit bias in the era of social desirability: Understanding antiblackness in rehabilitative and punitive school discipline. *Urban Review: Issues and Ideas in Public Education, 52*(1), 47–74. doi:10.100711256-019-00512-7

Martin, P. S., & Baxter, A. G. (2001). *Mentoring African American middle school students: Applying principles of antiracism education to the problem of closing the Black-White achievement gap* [Conference Paper]. Annual National Conference of the National Association of African American Studies and the National Association of Hispanic and Latino Studies, Houston, TX. https://eric.ed.gov/?id=ED455352

Milner, H. R. IV. (2010). What does teacher education have to do with teaching? Implications for diversity studies. *Journal of Teacher Education, 61*(1/2), 118–131. doi:10.1177/0022487109347670

Muhammad, G. E., Dunmeyer, A., Starks, F. D., & Sealey-Ruiz, Y. (2020). Historical voices for contemporary times: Learning from Black women educational theorists to redesign teaching and teacher education. *Theory into Practice, 59*(4), 419–428. doi:10.1080/00405841.2020.1773185

Noguera, P. (2003). *City schools and the American dream: Reclaiming the promise of public education.* Teachers College Press.

Nosek, B. (2007). Implicit–explicit relations. *Current Directions in Psychological Science, 16*(2), 65–69. doi:10.1111/j.1467-8721.2007.00477.x

Nosek, B. A., Banaji, M. R., & Greenwald, A. G. (2002). Harvesting implicit group attitudes and beliefs from a demonstration web site. *Group Dynamics, 6*(1), 101–115. doi:10.1037/1089-2699.6.1.101

O'Bryant, S. (2018, March 22). *Five strategies for advancing racial equity in public education.* Education Pioneers. https://www.educationpioneers.org/blog/five-strategies-advancing-racial-equity-public-education

Okonofua, J. A., & Eberhardt, J. L. (2015). Two strikes: Race and the disciplining of young students. *Psychological Science, 26*(5), 617–624. doi:10.1177/0956797615570365 PMID:25854276

Ormrod, J. E. (2017). *How we think and learn: Theoretical perspectives and practical implications.* Cambridge University Press. doi:10.1017/9781316691458

Owusu-Bempah, A. (2017). Race and policing in historical context: Dehumanization and the policing of Black people in the 21st century. *Theoretical Criminology, 21*(1), 23–34. doi:10.1177/1362480616677493

Payne, A. A., & Welch, K. (2015). Restorative justice in schools: The influence of race on restorative discipline. *Youth & Society, 47*(4), 539–564. doi:10.1177/0044118X12473125

Pinkston, K. (2015). The Black-White malleability gap in implicit racial evaluations: A nationally representative study. *The Journal of Social Psychology, 155*(3), 189–203. doi:10.1080/00224545.2014.987200 PMID:25492224

Pufall-Jones, E., Margolius, M., Rollock, M., Yan, T. C., Cole, M., & Zaff, J. (2018). *Disciplined and disconnected: How students experience exclusionary discipline in Minnesota and the promise of non-exclusionary alternatives.* GradNation. https://gradnation.americaspromise.org//report/disciplined-and-disconnected

Quinn, D. J. (2017). School discipline disparities: Lessons and suggestions. *Mid-Western Educational Researcher*, *29*(3), 291–298.

Ramsey, S. (2008). *The troubled history of American education after the brown decision.* The American Historian. https://www.oah.org/tah/issues/2017/february/the-troubled-history-of-american-education-after-the-brown-decision/

Riddle, T., & Sinclair, S. (2019). Racial disparities in school-based disciplinary actions are associated with county-level rates of racial bias. *Proceedings of the National Academy of Sciences of the United States of America*, *116*(17), 8255–8260. doi:10.1073/pnas.1808307116 PMID:30940747

Sevon, M. A., Levi-Nielsen, S., & Tobin, R. M. (2021). Addressing racism and implicit bias—Part 1: A response to the framework for effective discipline. *Communique, 49*(5), 10–12.

Staats, C. (2016). Understanding implicit bias: What educators should know. *American Educator*, *39*(4), 29–43.

Staats, C., Capatosto, K., Wright, R., & Jackson, V. (2016). *2016 state of the science: Implicit bias review.* Kirwan Institute for the Study of Race and Ethnicity. https://kirwaninstitute.osu.edu/research/2016-state-science-implicit-bias-review

Sukhera, J., & Watling, C. (2018). A framework for integrating implicit bias recognition into health professions education. *Academic Medicine*, *93*(1), 35–40. doi:10.1097/ACM.0000000000001819 PMID:28658015

Supovitz, J. A., & Turner, H. M. (2000). The effects of professional development on science teaching practices and classroom culture. *Journal of Research in Science Teaching*, *37*(9), 963–980. doi:10.1002/1098-2736(200011)37:9<963::AID-TEA6>3.0.CO;2-0

Tatum, B. D. (1997). *Why are all the Black kids sitting together in the cafeteria? And other conversations about race.* BasicBooks.

Thigpen, K. (2019). *Understanding and dealing with racial trauma* [Excerpted and adapted from the book]. https://hr.baruch.cuny.edu/wp-content/uploads/sites/22/2021/04/EAP-Understanding-and-Dealing-with-Racial-Trauma.pdf

United States Government Accountability Office. (2018). *K-12 education: Discipline disparities for black students, boys, and students with disabilities* (Report to Congressional Requestors GAO-18-258; p. 98). United States Government Accountability Office. https://www.gao.gov/products/GAO-18-258

U.S. Department of Education. (2014). *Guiding principles resource guide for improving school climate and discipline.* https://www2.ed.gov/policy/gen/guid/school-discipline/guiding-principles.pdf

U.S. Department of Education. (2017, January 4). *School climate and discipline* [Laws and Guidance: School guidance and Discipline]. https://www2.ed.gov/policy/gen/guid/school-discipline/index.html

U.S. Department of Education. (2021). *An overview of exclusionary discipline practices in public schools for the 2017-18 school year.* https://www2.ed.gov/about/offices/list/ocr/docs/crdc-exclusionary-school-discipline.pdf

Vavrus, M. (2008). Culturally responsive teaching. In T. L. Good (Ed.), 21st century education: A reference handbook (pp.49–57). Sage. doi:10.4135/9781412964012.n56

Vavrus, M. (2015). *Diversity & education: A critical multicultural approach.* Teachers College Press.

Warikoo, J., Starck, J., Sinclair, S., & Riddle, T. (2020). Teachers are people too: Examining the racial bias of teachers compared to other American adults. *Educational Researcher*, *49*(4). https://journals.sagepub.com/doi/full/10.3102/0013189X20912758

Welch, K., & Payne, A. A. (2010). Racial threat and punitive school discipline. *Social Problems*, *57*(1), 25–48. doi:10.1525p.2010.57.1.25

Whitford, D. K., & Emerson, A. M. (2019). Empathy intervention to reduce implicit bias in pre-service teachers. *Psychological Reports*, *122*(2), 670–688. doi:10.1177/0033294118767435 PMID:29621945

Will, M. (2019, May 15). 65 years after "Brown v. Board," where are all the Black educators? *Education Week.* https://www.edweek.org/policy-politics/65-years-after-brown-v-board-where-are-all-the-black-educators/2019/05

Wise, T. (2021). Justice is a verb: Understanding and undoing systemic racism in education. *Schools: Studies in Education*, *18*(1), 107–130. doi:10.1086/713614

Wong, Y.-L. R., & Vinsky, J. (2021). Beyond implicit bias: Embodied cognition, mindfulness, and critical reflective practice in social work. *Australian Social Work*, *74*(2), 186–197. doi:10.1080/0312407X.2020.1850816

Wood, B. (2007). *Slavery in colonial Georgia, 1730-1775*. University of Georgia Press.

Woods, T. P. (2018). The implicit bias of implicit bias theory. *Drexel Law Review*, *10*(3), 631–672.

Woodson, C. G. (2017). *The mis-education of the Negro*. ReadaClassic.com.

Young, Y. (2016). Teachers' implicit bias against black students starts in preschool, study finds. *The Guardian*. https://www.theguardian.com/world/2016/oct/04/black-students-teachers-implicit-racial-bias-preschool-study

ADDITIONAL READING

Carter, P. L., Skiba, R., Arredondo, M. I., & Pollock, M. (2017). You can't fix what you don't look at: Acknowledging race in addressing racial discipline disparities. *Urban Education*, *52*(2), 207–235. doi:10.1177/0042085916660350

Civil Rights Data Collection. (2021). https://ocrdata.ed.gov/

Dovidio, J. F., Pearson, A. R., & Penner, L. A. (2018). Aversive racism, implicit bias, and microaggressions. In G. C. Torino, D. P. Rivera, C. M. Capodilupo, K. L. Nadal, & D. W. Sue (Eds.), *Microaggression theory* (pp. 16–31). John Wiley & Sons. doi:10.1002/9781119466642.ch2

Godsil, R. D., & Johnson, A. M. (2013). *Transforming perception: Black men and boys* [Executive Summary]. Perception Institute. https://perception.org/publications/transforming-perception/

Kendi, I. X. (2016). *Stamped from the beginning: The definitive history of racist ideas in America*. Public Affairs.

Ladson-Billings, G. (2014). Culturally relevant pedagogy 2.0: A.K.A. the remix. *Harvard Educational Review*, *84*(1), 74–84. doi:10.17763/haer.84.1.p2rj131485484751

Staats, C. (2016). Understanding implicit bias: What educators should know. *American Educator*, *39*(4), 1–29.

Sukhera, J., & Watling, C. (2018). A framework for integrating implicit bias recognition into health professions education. *Academic Medicine*, *93*(1), 35–40. doi:10.1097/ACM.0000000000001819 PMID:28658015

Tatum, B. D. (2017). *Why are all the Black kids sitting together in the cafeteria?: And other conversations about race*. Basic Books.

Vavrus, M. J. (2015). *Diversity & education: A critical multicultural approach.* Teachers College Press.

KEY TERMS AND DEFINITIONS

Aversive Racism: A phenomenon of "bias without intention" where a person may celebrate diversity, but also unintentionally hold onto negative feelings and beliefs about a minority group of people (Gaertner & Dovidio, 1986).

Black/Black Americans: Black Americans are a diverse group of people that identify as Black. They come from different background cultures, ethnicities, and nationalities, but share the same characteristics that include their race, color or complexion of their skin, and their lineage to Africa (Tamir, 2021).

Equality: Providing an opportunity for everyone to have equal treatment despite their race, color, creed, or religion (O'Bryant, 2018).

Equity: Creating a level "playing field" by recognizing that advantages and disadvantages exist making it difficult for equal treatment to be truly fair for poor, underserved, powerless and vulnerable groups or individuals.

Exclusionary Discipline Practices: Disciplinary practices that exclude students from their home school classroom either by excluding them from instruction during school hours through placement in an in-school suspension, out-of-school suspension, or expulsion (U.S. Department of Education, 2021).

Implicit Racial Bias: A significant causal factor that affects the unconscious mind and generates negative behavior from a person's cognitive values and beliefs. This behavior creates unintentional stereotypes, attitudes, and discriminatory outcomes that affect the non-dominant races while manifesting visible cultural biases and economic, social, or racial gaps (Chin et al., 2020; Greenwald & Krieger, 2006; Ormrod, 2017).

Multicultural Relevance: A concept stressing the importance of weaving information about diverse cultures, along with their ethnicity and beliefs, into the curriculum to enrich the educational system (Gay, 2002).

Restorative Justice: Processes designed for criminal justice systems used in the school system to keep large number of Black students in school by working to repair or rehabilitate the student's negative behavior rather than giving them exclusionary discipline measures (Payne & Welch, 2015).

Stereotype: A bias idea or image that one has against a person or group based on an aspect of their identity such as race, gender, or religion. This behavior can go against the person's core principles of not being prejudiced (Devine et al., 2012).

Zero-Tolerance: Extreme disciplinary punishments that administrators assign immediately after one infraction. These policies contribute greatly to the school to prison pipeline process that disproportionately impacts Black students resulting in long-lasting educational gaps (Greenwald & Banaji, 1995).

Chapter 3
Discipline:
A Legal Perspective

Herman R. Moncure
Law Offices of Pyke & Associates, P.C., USA

ABSTRACT

The concepts of discipline and law are linked together. Laws are often constructed to define what is considered acceptable conduct, and a form of discipline is often used to align unacceptable conduct to those laws. This is especially evident in the K-12 setting. Schools promote their brand of laws or "policies" to allow for an efficient education process with minimal disruption. However, when you are dealing with children who are not in full control of their impulses, disruptions are bound to occur. In the U.S., given the disproportionate sentencing and incarceration rates between whites and minorities, it can be reasonably deduced that the same phenomenon occurs within the K-12 school space as well. In consideration of these discrepancies, and U.S. constitutional concepts such as due process and equal protection are referenced. What exactly are they, and how do they come into play to correct these inequities? How do landmark cases argued in front of the U.S. Supreme Court citing these concepts help to frame what is considered acceptable discipline in the K-12 school space?

K-12 SCHOOL DISCIPLINE: A LEGAL PERSPECTIVE

This chapter explores theories of punishment and their relationship to school discipline. First, school discipline is placed in a legal context; the author traces legal history from the Magna Carta to 1776 to demonstrate how the idea of "Due Process" became etched into the fabric of the U.S. Constitution. Second, this chapter

DOI: 10.4018/978-1-6684-3359-1.ch003

illustrates how a legal analysis of U.S. Constitutional provisions can be a mechanism for combating school discipline disparities. Specifically, Due Process and the Equal Protection Clauses of the United States Constitution can be instruments of social change to mitigate school discipline disparities helping to shape the current K-12 school discipline landscape and how they can alter school policies and eliminate practices responsible for school discipline disparities. The following section examines two essential theories of punishment related to school discipline.

THEORIES OF PUNISHMENT

There are multiple purposes used to justify the use of punishment (Young,1983). The main functions of punishment are cited below. They include:

1. Education. The teaching of the general public what is acceptable (or unacceptable) behavior by openly punishing an offender for their wrongdoings.
2. General Deterrence. The effect of a particular punishment on the public to deter others from committing the same or similar offense.
3. Specific Deterrence. The effect of a particular punishment on the individual offender to deter future similar (or the same) offenses.
4. Rehabilitation. The reformation of an offender's behavior through personal development to prevent the offender from committing future offensive acts.
5. Retribution. The punishment of a wrongdoer for committing the offense, i.e., "an eye for an eye."

There are also two prevailing theories regarding punishment in the U.S. The first is the retributive theory, and the other is the utilitarian theory (Young, 1983). Although these theories of punishment are mainly from the viewpoint of criminality, they form the basis for punishment in schools across the United States.

Retributive Theory

The retributive theory's main concern is that individuals are punished for their illegal acts. It is often considered backward-looking, it fails to consider the future ramifications of the punishment, and it only respects the past transgressions of the individual offender (Young, 1983). Retributive theory gives very little (if any) consideration to the reduction of similar offenses committed in the future, nor does it consider whether the public has been educated through the punishment levied on the offender. Retributive theory's main preoccupation is with the offense committed and the sentence. The penalty should be in proportion to the offense. Retribution theory is often referred to as the "eye for an eye" approach. Some Zero Tolerance punishments (to be discussed later in the chapter) that are levied are rooted in retribution, e.g., a student eating a pastry into the shape of a gun and being suspended for it.

Utilitarian Theory

The utilitarian theory focuses on the benefits of punishment to society as a whole. This form of punishment is broadly regarded as serving the "greatest good to society" (Young, 1983). It is often considered forward-looking, and it attempts to protect the community by deterring future wrongdoings. The purposes of deterrence (general and specific), education, and rehabilitation are all considerations utilized under this theory. For instance, if suspending a student for their wrongful act to deter future wrongful acts is for the "greater good," it would be considered utilitarian. Also, using students caught vandalizing the school to clean debris from school hallways to educate others not to commit similar crimes would be utilitarian. Finally, administering after-school detention to rehabilitate truant students would be utilitarian.

Punishment in the K-12 School Setting

In theory, most punishment occurring in U.S. K-12 settings is utilitarian-based. The punishment given for an offense is often forward-looking to prevent future offenses by either the offending student or the student population at large, rehabilitate the offending student, or teach students acceptable (or unacceptable) forms of behavior. However, whether or not school discipline has served the "greater good" is arguable. The traditional forms of punishment used in the school setting generally take on four forms: corporal punishment, exclusionary discipline (e.g., suspension, expulsion), isolation (i.e., time-out), or the loss of privileges. There is data showing (which is discussed below) that these forms of punishment are no longer effective and create negative outcomes such as increased absenteeism and eventually dropping out altogether.

Corporal Punishment

Corporal punishment, defined by the U.N. Committee on the Rights of the Child (United Nations, 2006), is any punishment in which physical force is used and intended to cause some degree of pain or discomfort, however light. In the U.S., corporal punishment continues to be a highly contested issue. Corporal Punishment was argued in the US Supreme Court case, Ingraham v. Wright, 430 US 651 (1977). The petitioners argued that corporal punishment violated their Eighth Amendment U.S. Constitutional right that "no person should be subject to cruel and unusual punishment." It was decided that paddling (or spanking) as corporal punishment is not cruel and unusual punishment; thus, it does not violate a child's eighth amendment right. As of 2016, 19 states (Alabama, Arizona, Arkansas, Colorado, Georgia, Florida, Idaho, Indiana, Kansas, Kentucky, Louisiana, Mississippi, Missouri, North Carolina, Oklahoma, South Carolina, Tennessee, Texas, Wyoming) allow corporal punishment in their classrooms (Gershoff and Font, 2016). As recently as May 2021, The State of Louisiana rejected a Louisiana State House Bill to ban the use of corporal punishment (Sentel, 2021). Some states (e.g., California, Massachusetts, and Hawaii) have expanded their respective statute's definition of corporal punishment to include "excessive exercising" (Russ et al., 2009).

In states where corporal punishment is practiced, parents sometimes feel there is no balance between their in-home discipline system and the school practitioner. These parents feel if there is a bruise or mark left on their child due to their use of corporal punishment, the teacher or administrator is a mandatory reporter and must call child protective services against the parent. However, if the parent sees a bruise or mark from a teacher's or administrator's use of corporal punishment, there is no natural consequence (Rico, 2002). Teachers and administrators are exempt from impunity due to their official capacity as government employees.

Qualified immunity is a doctrine that protects government workers or government agents from personal liability for their tortious acts so long as their actions were ministerial in nature and were not committed in gross negligence. Qualified immunity laws in most states set a gross negligence standard vs. an ordinary negligence standard for government workers operating in their official capacity. A gross negligence act is one committed recklessly and with wanton disregard for the harm it produces. Whereas an act committed in ordinary negligence is determined by the reasonable-prudent person's standard of care and a breach of the duty owed. Simply put, if a teacher or administrator uses corporal punishment to discipline a child, and it is within their power to do so under state law, it is unlikely they will be held culpable.

Exclusionary Discipline

According to the American Psychological Association Services (2019), exclusionary discipline is any school disciplinary action that removes or excludes a student from their usual educational setting. These actions include detention (or what is commonly referred to as in-school suspension), suspension, or expulsion. These actions are not without criticism. One such criticism is that exclusionary discipline is ineffective for correcting student misbehavior. According to Dr. Johnathan Zaff, executive director of the Center for Promise, the research institute of America's Promise Alliance, "exclusionary discipline practices do not make schools more conducive to learning, do not help improve student behavior, and do not make schools safer." Exclusionary methods of discipline frequently derail students' education. They miss valuable instructional time and are often pushed out or inevitably drop out (Luster, 2018). According to the National Education Association, teachers and administrators are finding it very challenging to balance an appropriate discipline with school safety, classroom effectiveness, and positive outcomes for the students (Luster, 2018). According to the United States Commission on Civil Rights (USCCR), exclusionary discipline is noted as harmful to the educational attainment of all students. The USCCR also had this to say regarding exclusionary discipline:

Exclusionary discipline practices place students at risk for experiencing a wide range of correlated educational, economic, and social problems, including school avoidance, increased likelihood of dropping out, and involvement with the juvenile justice system (USCCR, 2019).

Loss of Privileges and Isolation

Loss of privileges for infractions that violate schools' code of conduct is standard practice. Although the loss of privileges for a committed offense is pretty much without detractors, it's not void of criticism. However, several studies oppose using this method, mainly when it's about the withholding of recess (or gym) for K-8 students. The loss of recess is often used as a punishment in grades K-5. However, according to the Centers for Disease Control and Prevention (CDC) and the American Academy of Pediatrics, recess is necessary for a child's physical, social, and emotional development. For children with attention-deficit hyperactivity disorder (ADHD), it decreases outbursts and incidents related to the lack of recess. Contrary to this evidence, only 21% of school districts nationwide required daily recess for elementary school students (CDC, 2014).

Isolation is the act of placing a child in solitude as a result of unwarranted behavior. This is sometimes referred to as "time-out." Time-out has become a popular method among parents, teachers, and administrators since many have determined corporal punishment as detrimental to a child's development. However, there is also push back against the use of time-outs among parents, citing that overuse of time-outs in the classroom reduces their effectiveness. In a 2014 Time Magazine article by Daniel J. Siegel and Tina Payne Bryson, "Time-Outs Are Hurting Your Child," the authors stated, "the primary experience a time-out provides is isolation" (Siegel & Bryson, 2014). The lesson a practitioner hopes the child will learn from using time-out is that the child's actions are unacceptable. However, "the lesson often experienced, particularly by young children, is rejection" (Siegel & Bryson, 2014). There are thoughts that time-outs are not detrimental in concept but that the application by some is the reason for its ineffective results. According to an article written in Sage

Journals by Joseph B. Ryan, Sharon Sanders, Antonis Katsiyannis, and Mitchell Yell called "Using Time-Out Effectively in the Classroom" states, "Time-outs are subject to abuse when educators fail to understand and apply the behavioral principles that make the procedures effective in reducing problem behaviors." (Ryan et al., 2007). They also stated that some teachers continue to use the method even though it proves ineffective at curbing unwarranted behaviors (Ryan et al., 2007).

The Effects of Punishment on Minority and Students with Disabilities

According to the U.S. Government Accountability Office (GAO), black boys and students with disabilities are disproportionately suspended from school (GAO, 2018). Their research showed a persistent pattern even after controlling for disciplinary action taken by the district, socio-economic status, and the type of public school attended (GAO, 2018). The GAO found that although black students accounted for 15.5 percent of all public school students, they represented approximately 39 percent of students suspended from school. Regarding corporal punishment, in a 2019 article written by Brittany Barbee and Cheyenne Blackburn for the Southern Poverty Law Center, black girls were three times more likely to be struck than white girls, black boys were two times more likely to be struck than white boys, and students with disabilities were struck at higher rates than those without (Barbee & Blackburn, 2019). The USCCR findings regarding exclusionary discipline noted that minorities and students with disabilities are punished disproportionally. The correlation between the exclusionary discipline and the criminal justice system is well documented. Further, students who received harsher school punishments (e.g., suspension, expulsion) are four times more likely to report being arrested than those who didn't (Mowen & Brent, 2016).

The intersection of being a minority student combined with a disability designation results in a greater likelihood of exclusion. In the USCCR Briefing Report of July 2019, their research shows a "consistent pattern of schools suspending or expelling black students with disabilities at higher rates than their proportion of students with disabilities (USCCR, 2019)." These students are often punished with out-of-school suspensions for non-violent behavior. Students of color, except for Latinx and Asian American students with disabilities, are more likely than their white counterparts to be expelled without educational resources.

The effect of disproportional exclusionary punishment significantly increases the likelihood of disengagement by the student in the learning environment. Thus, increasing the possibility of these students being either retained in grade, dropping out of school, or funneling into the juvenile justice system.

Disparate Treatment, Disparate Impact

Implicit bias, according to the American Psychological Association Services, Inc. (APAS), "is the attitudes or stereotypes that influence our understanding, actions, and decisions in an unconscious manner" (APAS, 2019). These biases, if left unchecked, lead to irrational decisions that can have disastrous effects on segments of people who are the recipients of those irrational decisions. At least from a legal perspective, the outcome can either be disparate treatment or disparate impact. Disparate treatment is intentional discrimination against a protected group of people. In the United States, the protected group of people (or protected classes) are based on race, national origin, religion, alienage, disability, and gender. Disparate Impact relates to a policy that affects a group of individuals differently but was meant to be neutral in its application. In 2014, as a result of the United States Department of Education Office for Civil Rights Data Collection (CRDC), the U.S. Department of Justice Civil Rights Division and U.S. Department of Education Office for Civil Rights issued a joint letter titled, "Dear Colleague Letter on the Nondiscriminatory Administration of School Discipline." The letter lays out how districts may be subject to legal action by the federal government for the disparate treatment of protected classes (DoJ & DoE, 2014). Although suggestions set forth by the "Dear Colleague Letter" have largely been rescinded during the Trump Administration, the findings showed that black students were punished more harshly than white students (DoJ & DoE, 2014). The letter uses data from the CRDC indicating that teachers across the nation are still mainly in favor of "zero tolerance" policies. However, the CRDC data showed "zero tolerance" policies as the main culprit or exclusionary discipline disparities among minority and disabled students. In 2001, the American Bar Association also stated that zero-tolerance policies have:

become a one-size-fits-all solution to all the problems that schools confront. It has redefined students as criminals, with unfortunate consequences...most current policies eliminate the common sense that comes with discretion and, at great cost to society and children and families, do little to improve school safety (USCCR, 2019).

Also, a longitudinal study of almost one million middle school students observed the following:

researchers found that black students were more likely than white or Latinx students to be disciplined for "discretionary" offenses (e.g., tardiness, leaving class early, dress code violations); however, black, Latinx, and white students were removed from classes for mandatory offenses (e.g., possessing drugs or weapons) at similar rates. Moreover, the researchers found that white and Latinx students were more likely than black students to commit behavioral infractions that led to mandatory expulsions. These data indicate that discretion is closely correlated with higher discipline rates for students of color (Fabelo et al., 2011).

Due Process as a Concept

With increased talk about the disparities among minority students and school discipline more generally, the question becomes, have minority students been deprived of their rights to due process under the law? With regard to punishment in the United States, due process is a grindstone against which punishment must be shaped. Due process in the western world is born out of the Magna Carta Libertatum (i.e., The Great Charter of Freedoms), or for short, the Magna Carta.

The Magna Carta is an accord between King John of England and the feudal barons in the thirteenth century. King John of England was notorious for taking their property, money, levying taxes without reason, etc. (Breay & Harrison, 2014). Clause 39 of the document says, "No free-man shall be seized or imprisoned, or stripped of his rights or possession…except by the lawful judgment of his equals by the laws of the land" (Breay & Harrison, 2014). Translated 139 years later and written into the Liberty of Subject Act, statute 28 Edw. 3 states, "No man of what estate or condition that he be, shall be put out of land or tenement, nor taken, nor imprisoned, nor disinherited, nor put to death, without being in answer by due process of the law" (Breay & Harrison, 2014). Some five hundred years later, the very same story would play out in a land called America, ultimately resulting in a new nation.

During the colonial years of the 13 Colonies, colonists desperately wanted to assert economic independence from the British Kingdom (Declaration of Independence). They also had a sentiment similar to the one the feudal barons had that their king, George III, was guilty of levying taxes without good reason and taking their property for the benefit of the Kingdom, all to delay the economic independence of the 13 Colonies (Declaration of Independence). These colonists all came together and listed in a document the various arbitrary and capricious transgressions committed by King George III, which would be called the Declaration of Independence (Declaration of Independence). The Second Continental Congress signed and adopted the Declaration of Independence on July 4, 1776. The colonists believed they had an inalienable right to life, liberty, and the pursuit of happiness to be unrestricted from government intrusion without reason (Declaration of Independence). The 13 Colonies were no more with this document, and the United States of America was born.

The first governing document of the United States of America was the Articles of Confederation. Signed in 1777, It preserved the idea of individual states being separate sovereigns. It was later proved not to be a robust enough document to lead a nation but provided the framework for what would become the U.S. Constitution

(Constitution). The U.S. Constitution, signed September 17, 1787, is the succeeding governing document of the United States, consisting of seven articles (Constitution). Signed in 1791, the first ten amendments to the U.S. Constitution are considered the Bill of Rights (Bill of Rights). These rights are guaranteed to each recognized citizen of the United States and restrict specific government intrusion by United States Government and its citizens.

As previously stated, the concept of Due Process is extended to all U.S. citizens, including children. There is a clear empirical relationship between school discipline disparities and race/ethnicity. Minority K-12 students are disciplined at disproportionately higher rates than white contemporaries. Legal scholars and litigators alike are concerned that the lack of Due Process being observed in the discipline of these children may be the cause (Brady, 2002). It is worth exploring what Due Process is and how it relates to school discipline.

Due Process Clause

Due Process of Law is found in the Fifth Amendment of the United States Constitution and is commonly referred to as the Due Process Clause. It states, "no person shall be ... nor deprived of life, liberty or property without due process of law" (Fifth Amendment). Like the Magna Carta did for the feudal barons against King John, this guarantees that the U.S. government cannot take a person's life, freedom, or property without adhering to the legal process or "the laws of the land" (Breay & Harrison, 2014). As initially constructed, the Fifth Amendment was interpreted to only apply to the federal government. In Barron v. Baltimore, 32 U.S. 243 (1833), the Supreme Court decided that the Bill of Rights did not bind individual states, and the Fifth Amendment Taking Clause states, "nor shall private property be taken for public use, without just compensation" doesn't apply (Barron v. Baltimore, 1833). To close this loophole, the states ratified the Fourteenth Amendment on July 9, 1868. It states, "... nor shall any State deprive any person of life, liberty, or property, without due process of law..." (Fourteenth Amendment). After the civil war, this law required southern states to extend due process rights to newly freed slaves.

Procedural Due Process versus Substantive Due Process

There are two types of due process in the U.S. Constitution. The first focuses on the process, and the other focuses on the substance of the law and justification for the government intrusion. Procedural Due Process is the administration of the legal policy. If a U.S. citizen's life, liberty, or property is being taken or infringed upon by the government or extension thereof, then some resemblance of a legal process must occur. This process should include the following at a minimum:

1. facts by the state are presented;
2. the accused has an opportunity to tell their version of the facts;
3. this is usually in the presence of a neutral party or an arbiter;
4. the government must not act arbitrarily and capriciously towards a segment of the population (Procedural Due Process).

When the government is generally acting (or requiring compliance from everyone), there is no harm (e.g., requiring a license to drive). However, the government is said to be acting arbitrarily and capriciously when the government inequitably enforces laws or mandates against a particular segment of people or person.

Substantive Due Process focuses on the rights of the individual. As stated earlier, this country was founded on the premise that each U.S. citizen shall have the inalienable right to life, liberty, and the pursuit of happiness to be unrestricted from government intrusion without reason. These rights alluded to in the Declaration of Independence are now referred to as fundamental privacy rights. Through U.S. Supreme Court case law, fundamental privacy rights include the right to marriage, the right to contraception, the right to procreation, the right to intimacy, and the right to education. The right to education decided by Pierce v. Society of the Sisters of the Holy Names of Jesus and Mary, 268 U.S. 510 (1925), maintains parents' liberty interest in determining how their children are educated (private v. public).

Whether there is a violation of a Due Process right (whether procedural or substantive), the test the government must meet is referred to as "strict scrutiny." This is the highest judicial review test in determining a law's constitutionality. The government entity infringing on a fundamental liberty right of the individual must show it has a compelling overriding interest, and the law is narrowly tailored to that interest (Strict Scrutiny). What is considered a fundamental right determined by the U.S. Constitution is still evolving. Thus, through case holdings by the Supreme Court, it's determined what is regarded as a fundamental right. If the government cannot meet its burden, the infringement is considered unconstitutional.

However, if the infringement is not a fundamental right, the test used is called the "rational basis test." This is the lowest judicial review test in determining a law's constitutionality. In the rational basis test, the government's interest in the infringement need only be rationally related to a legitimate government interest (Rational Basis Test). It is the challenger's responsibility to prove there is no legitimate government interest in the infringement, and it is of an arbitrary and capricious nature. For example, a school district mandates that the only bookbag students may bring into its schools must be clear, or the student cannot enter. Many school districts used this policy in response to curbing contraband being brought into school buildings. So, if a student is disciplined due to the new mandate, the student (or parent) may believe this mandate infringes upon their privacy rights. The government (or school district) need only show a legitimate interest (however minimal) concerning the mandate, and it is the challenge's (or student) burden to disprove there is a relation. So, in this case, the school district need only show (however minimal) that clear bookbags will reduce the amount of contraband brought into its school buildings. It will then be the student's responsibility to show no relation to the school district's interest(s) and its new mandate.

Due Process in the K-12 School Setting

The establishment of procedural due process rights in the public K-12 school setting has been sluggish. Tinker v. Des Moines Independent Community School District, 393 U.S. 503 (1969) is the landmark case and precedent addressing children's fundamental Due Process rights. This case is distinctly a First Amendment Right to Free Speech case. Students attending a public school in Des Moines, Iowa, staged a protest wearing black armbands protesting the Vietnam War. The students were subsequently suspended for the duration of the protest (December 16 – December 31, 1965). The Supreme Court, in determining this was a violation of a student's First Amendment Right to Free Speech, stated, "It can hardly be argued that either students or teachers shed their constitutional rights to freedom of speech or expression at the schoolhouse gate" (Tinker v. Des Moines, 1969). This statement given by Justice Abe Fortas has formed the basis by which not only how freedom of expression school cases in the Supreme Court are analyzed and how most constitutional rights school cases are analyzed.

In Goss v. Lopez, 419 U.S. 565 (1975), the statement "shedding of constitutional rights at the schoolhouse door" was used in this landmark case dealing directly with due process. The Supreme Court held that the State of Ohio made education an individual property right, and therefore, the government must observe Due Process to infringe upon an individual's property right. Further, the Supreme Court stated,

...Although Ohio may not be constitutionally obligated to establish and maintain a public school system, it has nevertheless done so, and has required its children to attend. Those young people do not "shed their constitutional rights" at the schoolhouse door... (Goss v. Lopez, 1975)

Nine students were suspended for at least ten days or more by the Columbus Public School System (an Ohio school district) brought suit against the District because they hadn't been afforded minimal procedural Due Process (Goss v. Lopez, 1975). The Supreme Court determined that a 10-day suspension is not de minimis and cannot be exempt, barring an emergency, from the Due Process constitutional standard.

After the Goss case, the courts have largely contested what was considered a de minimis school punishment. In the Bethel School District No. 403 v. Fraser case, 478 U.S. 675 (1986), a student was suspended for two days following a lewd risqué speech given at a school-sanctioned student government rally. The student argued the suspension violated his First Amendment Right to Free Speech and his Fourteenth Amendment Due Process right. The Supreme Court found his arguments were without merit. Regarding his right to free speech, they determined that the school district sought only to regulate the appropriateness of his speech and not the content of his speech. Further, the Court also decided that his two-day suspension was not a violation of his due process right for the lack of notice. The student was warned that his speech was inappropriate and should not be given. The Court found this was adequate notice. The Court also stated two days are de minimis and "does not rise to the level of penal sanction call for the full panoply of procedural due process protections applicable to a criminal prosecution" (Bethel v. Fraser, 1986). Regarding punishment, mainly all types of school punishments mentioned in the previous section (i.e., corporal, exclusionary punishment ten days or less, loss of privileges, isolation) are considered de minimis and do not require full due process observations, and only concerning exclusionary punishment must there be minimum due process observations.

Zero Tolerance Policies and Due Process

It is often said that "today's solutions are tomorrow's problems." In the 1980s, the proliferation of crack cocaine in urban centers set off a series of events resulting in various unintended consequences. The influx of cash from drug sales and the low cost of guns during this period resulted in policies such as the Anti-Drug Abuse Act of 1986, which introduced "mandatory minimums" for various types of drug possession, and the Violent Crime Control and Law Enforcement Act of 1994, better known as the 1994 Crime Bill. Both bills have been linked to mass incarceration rates among minority men in urban centers. The increased violence and rampant drug addiction in these urban centers during this time started to spill over into the classroom. In 1994, The Gun-Free Schools Act was passed (Cerrone, 1999). States were forced to adopt mandatory expulsion laws for possessing a firearm on school grounds to receive federal funding. The mandatory length of the expulsion is one calendar year. This is widely considered the first form of a "zero-tolerance" policy school districts adopted. This policy made no mention of procedural due process, except as carved out to the Individuals with Disabilities Education Act (Cerrone, 1999). As the time passed, "zero-tolerance" policies morphed from being used solely for the discipline for gun possession on school grounds to punishing any unwarranted adolescent behavior. The justification lies in the school district's need to prevent an escalation of violence in the school setting. However, this has lumped violence-prone students and ordinary misbehaving students, or students who made an honest mistake, into one broad category without any regard for nuance within their respective circumstances (Cerrone, 1999). For instance, if one student purposefully brings a weapon onto school property with malicious intent, another student packs a knife in their lunch box to cut their apple for lunch, and yet another student eats a pastry shaped like a gun; all three students may suffer similar consequences under a "zero-tolerance" policy (Cerrone, 1999). School districts are not only given the latitude to enforce "zero-tolerance" policies according to their respective policy and procedures, but they can also determine what actions are worthy of "zero-tolerance." School districts may use exclusionary discipline under the guise of "zero-tolerance" as a swift punishment measure.

"Zero-tolerance" policies often subvert due process. Zero tolerance policies have an inherent aspect of absoluteness for punishment, but paradoxically they also have subjectivity in their definitions of punishable behaviors (Peden, 2001). According to a Faulkner Law Review article by John J. Garman and Ray Walker, "the latent fatal flaw in the basic concept of zero-tolerance discipline is the near presumption of guilt founded upon a mere statement of fact. The presumption of guilt imposes a heavy burden on the accused (Garman & Walker, 2010)." The presumption of guilt eviscerates the very notion of due process. Considering the Goss case, it was determined that a 10-day suspension from school is not de minimis and requires minimal due process procedures. However, the Supreme Court failed to provide criteria for establishing de minimis interpretations. Thusly, the Supreme Court left open the possibility that short-term suspensions, not exceeding ten days, are de minimis. The Supreme Court also stated that short-term suspensions need only have an informal give-and-take discussion between the student and the disciplinarian giving discretion to the administration of additional due process safeguards are required. The deference to school officials to determine, while in the administration of their own "zero-tolerance" policies, if they should observe additional due process rights for the student is problematic. Also, due to the social-economic status of many minorities, they are less likely to obtain the legal help necessary to fight for their child's due process rights.

The Equal Protection Clause

As previously stated, the passing of the fourteenth amendment closed a "loophole" individual states used to avoid giving U.S. Constitutional protections to their citizens, mainly affecting its black citizens. The Civil War formally brought an end to slavery in the U.S. However, many believe federal legislation was needed to prevent it from occurring again. Three constitutional amendments and several congressional acts later, the U.S. Government passed what is commonly referred to as the "reconstruction" or "civil rights" amendments. The ratification of the Thirteenth Amendment, which abolished slavery and involuntary servitude (except as a punishment for a crime), marked the beginning of the "Reconstruction Era."

The Fourteenth Amendment was ratified in 1868. As stated earlier in the chapter, the Fourteenth Amendment required the individual states to extend constitutional guarantees and protections to all citizens within their borders, especially the newly freed ones. The Fourteenth Amendment clarifies who qualifies as a citizen. There is the "Privileges and Immunities" clause which prevents individual states from restricting the rights of their citizens, the "Due Process" clause which was discussed at length earlier in the chapter, and the "Equal Protection" clause. The Fourteenth Amendment states the following:

All persons born or naturalized in the United States, and subject to the jurisdiction thereof, are citizens of the United States and of the State wherein they reside. No State shall make or enforce any law which shall abridge the privileges and immunities of citizens of the United States; nor shall any State deprive any person of life, liberty, or property, without due process of law; nor deny to any person within its jurisdiction the equal protection of the laws (Fourteenth Amendment).

The "Equal Protection" clause, as it is currently interpreted, prohibits any action taken by a state (or a state actor) resulting in the unequal treatment of citizens without a "qualified reason." However, the courts were unsure how this clause would be applied at the onset. Initially, the courts determined that "Equal Protection" meant enforcing political equality (to be explained later) (Plessy v. Ferguson, 1896). This resulted in court decisions divergent to the very purpose (or at least in part) of the amendment itself. One of the first cases where this lack of concurrence is evident is the case referred to as "separate, but equal," Plessy v. Ferguson, 163 US 537 (1896).

Equal Protection and Judicial Review

Strict scrutiny, a test used in Due Process cases, is also used in judicial review of Equal Protection cases. In Korematsu v. United States, 323 US 214 (1944), the following was determined "...all legal restrictions which curtail the civil rights of a single racial group is immediately suspect. That is not to say that all such restrictions are unconstitutional. It is to say that courts must subject them to the most rigid scrutiny. Pressing public necessity may sometimes justify the existence of such restrictions" (Korematsu v. United States, 1944). From this, the Supreme Court has determined that government regulations that infringe on the civil liberties of a particular race, national origin, or alienage must be narrowly tailored to a compelling government interest. Like in Due Process cases, the burden of proof rests with the government to prove. Two additional tests evolved to evaluate Equal Protection cases through other cases, and they are intermediate scrutiny and rational basis.

Intermediate scrutiny provides in cases dealing with gender and legitimacy (children born in wedlock), the government's regulation must be substantially related to a significant government interest (Intermediate Scrutiny). Like in strict scrutiny cases, this is the government's burden to prove. The petitioner must prove the government's regulation is not rationally related to a legitimate government interest. As mentioned before, the rational basis test is the lowest threshold. If the persons affected by government action are not of a suspect or a quasi-suspect class, they are subject to the rational basis standard of review.

Equal Protection in the K-12 Setting

Equal Protection is indirectly related to punishment. In analyzing Due Process cases, if a person is punished for their actions by the government or government agent, and the government doesn't follow the proper steps when intruding upon their civil liberties without a legal exception, it is unconstitutional. However, Equal Protection (as its name suggests) mandates if a person is punished for their actions by the government or a government agent and the punishment is not equal without a legal exception, it is unconstitutional.

Brown v. Board of Education of Topeka, 347 U.S. 483 (1954), is the landmark case that overturned Plessy v. Ferguson, the case sanctioning racial apartheid under the separate but equal doctrine. It was the lead case out of four others (Briggs v. Elliot, Davis v. Board of Education of Prince Edward County, Gebhart v. Ethel, Bolling v. Sharpe) that were combined into one case because they had a common issue of law due to segregation of public schools based on race is a violation of the Equal Protection Clause of the Fourteenth Amendment. Although the Court determined there was a negligible difference in the "tangible" amenities provided for both the black and white public schools (i.e., buildings, curricula, qualification of teachers, etc.), the psychological effects of segregation on young people must be considered (Brown v. Board of Education, 1954). In Plessy v. Ferguson, as stated earlier, it was decided that the notion of inferiority was a mere projection African-Americans placed on themselves, and separate but equal would not create a de facto caste system.

During the trial, an experiment proved vital in establishing the effects of a de facto caste system on young African-Americans. Using the "baby-doll test," it was determined that the majority of African-American children in this experiment preferred white dolls to black dolls. They thought of the black dolls as "bad" (Brown v. Board of Education, 1954). These cases demonstrated an undeniable negative psychological effect to this apartheid system that caused a feeling of inequity and inferiority among African-American children that the decision in Plessy, at best, negligently discounted, and at worst, purposefully and substantially disregarded. Using the decision in Bolling v. Sharpe, 347 US 497 (1954) (which provided the doctrine of reverse incorporation stating that "Though the Fifth Amendment doesn't contain an equal protection clause, as does the Fourteenth Amendment, which only applies to the States, the concepts of equal protection and due process are not mutually exclusive"), separate but equal public schools was determined as a violation of the Equal Protection Clause of the Fourteenth Amendment. As public schools were being desegregated in the 1970s, the issue of equality was being defined. Currently, there is inequality in the discipline of K-12 minority students, which raises Equal Protection implications as well. A good education is still the main conduit to realizing the American dream. Brown promised to provide a level playing field in education to achieve the American dream. Through the disproportionate enforcement of "zero-tolerance" policies, minority students' ability to achieve the American dream is diminished. "Zero-tolerance" policies are associated with students' contact with the criminal justice system (APAS, 2019). Research shows that students who experience a single suspension were two times more likely to encounter the criminal justice system than those who have not received a suspension. According to the John Hopkins University study "Sent Home and Put Off-Track," School expulsions and suspensions increase the chance of leaving school before graduation from 16 percent to 32 percent (Balfanz et al., 2012).

In the two federal lower court decisions in Pennsylvania Association for Retarded Children (PARC) v. Commonwealth of Pennsylvania, 334 F. Supp. 1257 (1971) and Mills v. Board of Education of the District of Columbia, 348 F. Supp. 866 (1972), the Equal Protection decision in Brown was used to stop the exclusion of students with disabilities from public schools. These two lower court decisions were used to form the basis for the U.S. Department of Education's Education of Handicapped Children Act of 1975. Currently, it is known as the Individuals with Disabilities Education Act (IDEA). In accordance with IDEA, a school receiving Department of Education funding is prohibited from discriminating against students with disabilities. Further, IDEA required public schools to provide all students with a Free and Appropriate Public Education (FAPE). It also prohibits schools from expelling or suspending (both of which are exclusionary punishments) disabled students for longer than ten days when the action the student is being disciplined for was due to their disability. With IDEA, the school district's disregard for disabled students was minimized but not completely eradicated. This was also true in the effects of IDEA on zero-tolerance policies. As stated above, disabled minority students are punished at higher rates. The CRDC data shows that black students with disabilities are almost four times more likely to receive out-of-school suspensions and nearly two times more likely to be expelled than white students with disabilities (USCCR, 2019). However, as persons with disabilities have some protection against zero-tolerance policies through IDEA, a better avenue for minority students to seek refuge is under Title VI of the Civil Rights Act of 1964, "CRA of 1964" (Siman, A., 2005). Under the CRA of 1964, race-based discrimination is prohibited in any activity that receives federal funding. With both the Equal Protection and Due Process Clauses of the U.S. Constitution, one must prove discriminatory intent behind the government policies. Establishing discriminatory intent in the actions perpetrated by school districts has proven very tough. It has proven ineffective in reducing the disparities of zero-tolerance policies and their effect on minority students (Siman, A., 2005). However, under the CRA 1964, there must be a preponderance of the evidence shown by the plaintiff in the matter. This follows a more traditional burden-shifting legal process, and the preponderance of the evidence is a shallow threshold to meet, unlike the discriminatory intent needed for the constitutional clauses. And, unlike the constitutional provisions, the CRA of 1964 must be enforced by the Department of Education as an administrative measure (Siman, A., 2005). The UCCCR data show that minorities, especially those with disabilities, are disproportionately affected more than their white counterparts while representing a significantly smaller student population ratio. Even with the "Dear Colleague" letter issued in 2014, and the USCCR Briefing of 2019, districts are still choosing antiquated zero-tolerance policies. However, as mentioned earlier, the Trump Administration essentially removed any enforcement power from the "Dear Colleague" letter. Currently, the recommendations given by the Trump Administration are under review by the Biden Administration. The enforcement of Title VI claims by the Department of Education may be restored.

CONCLUSION

"School discipline has traditionally been accomplished through corporal punishment, teacher-administrated discipline, and administrative proceedings (Hanson, 2005)." However, any progress that would materialize due to the style of punishment used is diminished when they are administered based on implicit or explicit bias. Report after report shows that minority students are disproportionately punished at exponentially higher rates than whites, even though they make up a significantly smaller percentage of the student population and engage in punishable behaviors at similar rates. The Due Process Clause, both Procedural and Substantive, and the Equal Protection Clause have provided much of the framework regarding punishment in grades K-12. They are frequently used to fight against egregious displays of punishment and abuses. From the Wright case and corporal punishment to the Goss case and procedural due process rights, Pierce v. Society of Sisters and substantial due process rights, and Brown v. Education and Equal Protection rights, these cases show which actions are in constitutional alignment as interpreted by the Supreme Court. However, inequity in punishment for minority children persists, and zero-tolerance policies are the main contributor. Zero-tolerance, at its inception, was an overreach of a response to the increase of violence in some school districts. Once the go-to procedure among school districts, these policies are now shown to have disproportionately adverse effects on minority students. And, at the intersection of minority students and disabilities, the outcomes are much worse. Zero tolerance policies allow school districts to punish a broad swath of behaviors with a disregard for Equal Protection and Due Process constitutional protections. The Office of Civil Rights (OCR) has provided guidance to school districts regarding zero-tolerance policies and their effect on minority and disabled children. And although there is some compliance, it is not enough. Many educators still favor zero-tolerance policies despite evidence showing they do little to reduce the behaviors they were implemented for (USCCR, 2019). Title VI of the Civil Rights Act of 1964 is also a valuable tool to fight against racial disparities in education. Many would-be plaintiffs are dissuaded from engaging in the process because of procedural requirements. The Magna Carta and the Declaration of Independence were spawned because citizens were unjustly treated and wanted the acts brought against them by the governing powers to be equitable. Zero-tolerance policies subvert the constitutional protections of Due Process and Equal Protection for minority students. The continued use creates disproportionate outcomes that lack fairness, equity, and equality. How Due Process and Equal Protection rights are interpreted did not occur overnight. The cases were used to provide context on how Due Process and Equal Protection cases are interpreted and illustrate what legal actions must be taken to fight against unfair disciplinary practices faced by minorities in the U.S. K-12 schools. These constitutional protections are the tools available to combat the disproportionate rates of punishment affecting minorities. Further, the constitutional Equal Protection and Due Process clauses, where applicable, and Title VI of the Civil Rights Act of 1964 are viable legal principles that can be invoked to fight institutionalized discrimination and mass exclusion. Although zero-tolerance school policies have yet to be argued at the U.S. Supreme Court level, an amicus brief was submitted in March 2021 against zero-tolerance school policies. Perhaps future cases will trigger the U.S. Supreme Court to rule on zero-tolerance policies in the school system under Equal Protection and Due Process, thus helping to reduce exclusion and increase educational opportunities for affected students.

REFERENCES

American Psychological Association Services, Inc. (2019). *The Pathway from Exclusionary Discipline to the School to Prison Pipeline.* Retrieved October 21, 2021, from https://www.apa.org/advocacy/health-disparities/discipline-facts.pdf

Balfanz, R., Byrnes, V., & Fox, J. (2012). *Sent Home and Put Off-Track: The Antecedents, Disproportionalities, and Consequences of Being Suspended in the Ninth Grade.* Johns Hopkins University School of Education Everyone Graduates Center.

Barbee, B., & Blackburn, C. (2019). *SPLC Report: Corporal punishment in school disproportionately affects black students, students with disabilities.* Southern Poverty Law Center. Retrieved October 21, 2021, from https://www.splcenter.org/news/20190611/splc-report-corporal-punishment-in-school

Barron v. Baltimore, 32 U.S. 243 (1833).

Bethel School District No 403 v. Fraser case, 478 U.S. 675 (1986).

Bolling v. Sharpe, 347 US 497 (1954).

Brady, K. (2002). Zero Tolerance or (In)Tolerance Policies? Weaponless School Violence, Due Process, and the Law of Student Suspensions and Expulsions: An Examination of Fuller v. Decatur Public School Board of Education School District. *BYU Educ. & L.J., 159.* Retrieved October 21, 2021, from https://digitalcommons.law.byu.edu/elj/vol2002/iss1/7

Breay, C., & Harrison, J. (2014). *Magna Carta: An Introduction.* British Library. Retrieved October 21, 2021, from https://www.bl.uk/magna-carta/articles/magna-carta-an-introduction

Brown v. Board of Education of Topeka, 347 U.S. 483 (1954).

Center for Disease Control and Prevention. (2014). *Policy Strategies for Supporting Recess in Schools 2012-2013 School Update* [Brief]. Retrieved October 21, 2021, from https://www.cdc.gov/healthyschools/npao/pdf/LWP_Recess _Brief_2012_13.pdf

Cerrone, K. (1999). The Gun-Free Schools Act of 1994: Zero Tolerance Takes Aim at Procedural Due Process. *Pace L. Rev., 20*(1), 131-188. Retrieved October 21, 2021, from https://digitalcommons.pace.edu/plr/vol20/iss1/7

Cornel University Legal Information Institute. (n.d.a). *Intermediate Scrutiny.* Retrieved October 21, 2021, from https://www.law.cornell.edu/wex/intermediate_scrutiny

Cornel University Legal Information Institute. (n.d.b). *Procedural Due Process*. Retrieved October 21, 2021, from https://www.law.cornell.edu/wex/procedural_due_process

Cornel University Legal Information Institute. (n.d.c). *Rational Basis Test*. Retrieved October 21, 2021, from https://www.law.cornell.edu/wex/rational_basis_test

Cornel University Legal Information Institute. (n.d.d). *Strict Scrutiny*. Retrieved October 21, 2021, from https://www.law.cornell.edu/wex/strict_scrutiny

Cornel University Legal Information Institute. (n.d.e). *U.S. Constitution Fifth Amendment*. Retrieved October 21, 2021, from https://www.law.cornell.edu/constitution/fifth_amendment

Cornel University Legal Information Institute. (n.d.f). *U.S. Constitution Fourteenth Amendment*. Retrieved October 21, 2021, from https://www.law.cornell.edu/constitution/amendmentxiv

Fabelo, T., Thompson, M., Plotkin, M., Carmichael, D., Marchbanks, M. III, & Booth, E. (2011). Breaking Schools' Rules: A Statewide Study of How School Discipline Relates to Students' Success and Juvenile Justice Involvement. *Justice Center The Council of State Governments & Public Policy Research Institute.*, (July), 41–43.

Garman, J., & Walker, R. (2010). The Zero-Tolerance Discipline Plan and Due Process: Elements of a Model Resolving Conflicts Between Discipline and Fairness. *Faulkner Law Review, 1*(3), 289–320.

Gershoff, E. T., & Font, S. A. (2016). Corporal Punishment in U.S. Public Schools: Prevalence, Disparities in Use, and Status in State and Federal Policy. *Social Policy Report, 30*(1), 1–26. doi:10.1002/j.2379-3988.2016.tb00086.x PMID:29333055

Goss v. Lopez, 419 U.S. 565 (1975).

Griswold v. Connecticut, 381 U.S. 479 (1965).

Hanson, A. (2005). Have Zero Tolerance School Discipline Policies Turned into a Nightmare? The American Dream's Promise of Equal Educational Opportunity Grounded in Brown v. Board of Education. *U.C. Davis Journal of Juvenile Law & Policy, 2*(9), 289-379.

History Channel Editors. (2019). *Dred Scott Case*. The History Channel. Retrieved October 21, 2021, from https://www.history.com/topics/black-history/dred-scott-case

Ingraham v. Wright, 430 US 651 (1977).

Korematsu v. United States, 323 US 214 (1944).

Luster, S. (2018). *How Exclusionary Discipline Creates Disconnected Students.* National Education Association NEA Today.

Mowen, T., & Brent, J. (2016). School Discipline as a Turning Point: The Cumulative Effect of Suspension on Arrest. *Sage Journals, 53*(5), 628–653. doi:10.1177/0022427816643135

Peden, J. (2001). Through A Glass Darkly: Educating with Zero Tolerance. *The Kansas Journal of Law & Public Policy, 10,* 369–389.

Pierce v. Society of the Sisters of the Holy Names of Jesus and Mary, 268 U.S. 510 (1925)

Plessy v. Ferguson, 163 US 537 (1896).

Rico, K. (2002). Excessive Exercise as Corporal Punishment in Moore v. Willis Independent School District - Has the Fifth Circuit Totally Isolated Itself in Its Position. *Jeffrey S. Moorad Sports L.J., 9*(2), 351-385. Retrieved October 21, 2021, from https://digitalcommons.law.villanova.edu/mslj/vol9/iss2/5

Russ, R., Donati, R., Rattigan, P., DiGrogorio, T., Abbadessa, E., & Richardson, K. (2009). *Physical activity used as punishment and/or behavior management* [Position statement]. National Association for Sport and Physical Education.

Ryan, J., Sanders, S., Katsiyannis, A., & Yell, M. (2007). Using Time-Out Effectively in the Classroom. *Sage Journals, 39*(4), 60–67. Retrieved October 21, 2021, from. doi:10.1177/004005990703900407

San Antonio ISD v. Rodriguez, 411 U.S. 1 (1973).

Sentell, W. (2021). Louisiana House rejects bid to ban spanking in public schools. *The Advocate.* https://www.theadvocate.com/baton_rouge/news/politics/legislature/article_7e8c322c-ad15-11eb-a844-d783f3245d1c.html

Siegel, D., & Bryson, T. (2014, September 23). 'Time-Outs' Are Hurting Your Child. *Time Magazine.* https://time.com/3404701/discipline-time-out-is-not-good/

Siman, A. (2005). Challenging Zero Tolerance: Federal and State Legal Remedies for Students of Color. *Cornell Journal of Law and Public Policy, 14*(2), 337–364. Retrieved October 21, 2021, from https://scholarship.law.cornell.edu/cgi/viewcontent.cgi?article=1082&context=cjlpp

The National Archives. (n.d.a). *Bill of Rights: What Does It Say?* Retrieved October 21, 2021, from https://www.archives.gov/founding-docs/bill-of-rights/what-does-it-say

The National Archives. (n.d.b). *Constitution of the United States - A History*. Retrieved October 21, 2021, from https://www.archives.gov/founding-docs/more-perfect-union

The National Archives. (n.d.c). *The Declaration of Independence: A History*. Retrieved October 21, 2021, from https://www.archives.gov/founding-docs/declaration-history

Tinker v. Des Moines Independent Community School District, 393 U.S. 503 (1969)

United Nations Committee on the Rights of the Child (CRC) CRC General Comment No. 8. (2006). *The Right of the Child to Protection from Corporal Punishment and Other Cruel or Degrading forms of Punishment* (U.N. CRC/C/GC/8) 2007 Mar 2. Retrieved October 21, 2021, from https://www.refworld.org/docid/460bc7772.html

United States Commission on Civil Rights. (2019). *Beyond Suspensions*. Retrieved October 21, 2021, from https://www.usccr.gov/files/pubs/2019/07-23-Beyond-Suspensions.pdf

United States Department of Justice & United States Department of Education. (2014). *Joint Dear Colleague Letter: Nondiscriminatory Administration of School Discipline*. Retrieved October 21, 2021, from https://www2.ed.gov/about/offices/list/ocr/letters/colleague-201401-title-vi.html

United States Government Accountability Office. (2018). *K-12 Education: Discipline Disparities for Black Students, Boys, and Students with Disabilities. GAO-18-258.* Author.

United States Department of Education. (n.d.). *A History of the Individuals With Disabilities Education Act*. Retrieved October 21, 2021, from https://sites.ed.gov/idea/IDEA-History#1950s-60s-70s

Young, D. B. (1983). Cesare Beccaria: Utilitarian or Retributivist? *Journal of Criminal Justice, 11*(4), 317–326. doi:10.1016/0047-2352(83)90071-5

KEY TERMS AND DEFINITIONS

Ad Valorem Taxes: "Ad Valorem" Latin for "according to value." Usually is used in reference to property taxes (either personal or real property).

Arbitrary and Capricious: A judgment or action not based on law or a previous precedent.

Free and Appropriate Public Education: An entitlement for students with disabilities guaranteeing they receive a free and appropriate public education reflective of their special individual needs.

Government Agent: A person granted the authority to act on behalf of a government entity.

Inalienable Right: A right that is inherent and cannot be given away.

Ministerial Acts: Acts carried out in connection with a particular function.

Qualified Immunity: Absolution for government workers or agents of personal liability for tortious acts when committed in connection with their job.

Retribution: To punish someone for an act based on revenge.

Utility: The use gained through a thing or an act.

Chapter 4
Corporal Punishment in Schools, "Still Legal?":
An Examination of the Phenomenon in the US and Guyana

Brenda Ingrid Gill
Alabama State University, USA

ABSTRACT

The chapter explores how two geographically distant countries are brought close by their cultural acceptance of corporal punishment (CP) in school. The chapter details that though both societies have formulated several bills engaged in numerous debates over a lengthy period, culture, religion, and politics sustain school CP. The Guyanese argument engages various stakeholders, significantly influenced by the US's "ban" on school CP and the perceived negative results from such "prohibitions." This study assesses the legality, prevalence, theories, and applicable corporal punishment laws in the US and Guyana. The findings suggest that corporal punishment remains legally sanctioned in 19 US states and Guyana. Annually, substantial numbers of children experience corporal punishment at school. Legal, political, educational, and familial institutions endorsed such use.

INTRODUCTION

Violence against children refutes human rights commitments and children's developmental needs (UNESCO, 2017). The UN Convention on the Child's Rights enshrines children's "Rights." Articles 19, 28(2), and 37 specifically require all State

DOI: 10.4018/978-1-6684-3359-1.ch004

Parties to forbid the use of corporal punishment. Corporal punishment is considered a severe violation of children's rights (UNICEF, 1990). This practice of punishing children corporally at school termed corporal punishment in educational settings, dates back to the days of the Roman Empire, the Middle Ages, and the 19th century and continues into the 21st century. It is a lingering relic of British colonial and penal practices that are systematically entrenched (Antoine, 2008). Despite years of trying to achieve global prohibition, the method remains pervasive. Though mainly controversial, corporal punishment is perceived by some as violent. This chapter focuses solely on corporal punishment at public schools in the United States (US) and Guyana, South America.

When asked about corporal punishment in US public schools, several persons are unsure about its legal standing. Prohibitionists argue that corporal punishment in public schools "is a thing of the past." Research suggests that though currently legal in 19 states and endured by several children annually, the practice of corporal punishment in the US remains unknown to some due to its application in principally southern states (Gershoff & Font, 2016).

These responses differ from members of the Guyanese community. It is common knowledge that corporal punishment is practiced widely in school settings in Guyana. The laws support the use of corporal punishment, and many persons condone it. Corporal punishment is despised and questioned by a few and persists from generation to generation. Debates that favor and oppose corporal punishment occur within the US and Guyana. So, despite differing in wealth, development, and legal structures, both countries continue to debate the use of the practice in public schools. The connection between Guyana and the US helps support the examination of corporal punishment in the two societies.

Guyana is a small (83,000 miles ^{2}) unique tropical country located on the northern coast of South America. It has an unusual racial mix of 6 races and is the only English-speaking country in South America due to its history as a British colony. Brazil bounds it to the South, Venezuela to the West, Suriname to its east, and the great Atlantic Ocean to its North. It is considered the seat of the Caribbean due to its language, proximity to several Caribbean islands, and its membership and housing of the CARICOM headquarters (Countryreports.org, 2022).

Though a slight majority in the US (as of 2013), 273,000 persons claimed Guyanese as their first ancestry. Of this number, 140,000 live in New York. This number makes Guyanese the fifth-largest foreign-born population in New York City (Nan, 2016). Annual estimates indicate that over 30,000 Guyanese immigrate to the US Nan (2016) outlines that the United States has the most Guyanese outside Guyana. There is no denying the US's influence on Guyanese culture, beliefs, and behaviors – including corporal punishment.

This chapter uses three relevant theories to help explain the present state of corporal punishment in societies: Durkheim's social capital, Messner and Rosenfeld"s theory of institutional anomie, and theory of culture. The three approaches offer brief snapshots into the role of laws, allowing for more straightforward discussions of the phenomenon as extant in the two societies. The chapter strives to inform and raise awareness about the obstinate use of corporal punishment in the two societies. It gauges the extent of corporal punishment's use as a disciplinary technique in both societies' public-school systems.

One aim of the chapter is to pinpoint the role of the legal and education systems as support mechanisms for continuing violence against children. Even though the comparison is not the goal, the author highlights areas of convergence and divergence between Guyana and the US's practices and beliefs about school corporal punishment. The chapter uses information from state laws to outline the regulations regarding corporal punishment in the US and Guyana. The author uses prevalence data (where available) to describe the present state of corporal punishment in the two societies.

The two public school systems serve the needs of about 49.4 million (US) (National Center for Education Statistics, 2020) and 171,000 (Ministry of Education, Guyana, 2022) children daily. These children spend most of their waking hours at school. Hence, it is essential to examine children's treatment at schools that administer corporal punishment. This chapter contributes to the literature on corporal punishment in education settings. This contribution is particularly relevant in three areas: First, it informs about the role of culture in supporting the practice of school corporal punishment even when considered violent, painful, and a violation of child rights. Second, it sheds light on the laws and legal guidelines of the phenomenon in two very different societies. Third, it presents the present prevalence statistics (where available).

BACKGROUND

Corporal Punishment

Research suggests that though used more frequently at the elementary school level, children experience corporal punishment at all school levels (Human Rights Watch & ACLU, 2008). Often, school corporal punishment entails using various objects (Gershoff, et. al., 2015). US teachers must use a paddle, an open hand, or a ruler (Public School Review, 2020). Guyana's teachers are legally allowed to use a cane or strap no longer than 24 inches (Ministry of Education, 1993).

There are several definitions proffered for corporal punishment. In some instances, it is culturally approved and often sanctioned and defined as legal by state and or country laws and statutes. Straus (1994) defines corporal punishment as "The use of physical force with the intention of causing a child to experience pain but not injury for the purposes of correction or control of the child's behavior" (p. 4). Corporal punishment is also defined as the willful and deliberate infliction of physical pain on another person to modify undesirable behavior (American Academy of Child & Adolescent Psychiatry, 2014).

Corporal punishment is "the most common form of violence against children worldwide… it includes…physical as well as non-physical forms of punishment that are cruel and degrading" (End Corporal Punishment.org, 2022, para. 1). Others consider it a form of established violence (Devries et al., 2015; Gershoff, 2017). Straus and Donnelly (2005) submit that corporal punishment involves physical force that causes no injury but imposes pain on the child. The goal is to stop the specific behavior permanently by soliciting the punishment to modify the specific behavior. Similarly, The American Academy of Child & Adolescent Psychiatry (2014) defines corporal punishment as "a discipline method in which a supervising adult deliberately inflicts pain upon a child in response to a child's unacceptable behavior and inappropriate language."

Commenting on this, Gershoff and Font (2016) maintain that corporal punishment usually entails a teacher or administrator hitting a student's buttocks with a wooden paddle for the US. This hitting occurs because corporal discipline requires intentional infliction of pain or discomfort via physical force upon students to punish them for a behavioral offense. Corporal punishment can be defined as a painful, intentionally inflicted (typically, by striking a child) physical penalty administered by a person in authority for disciplinary purposes. It can occur in various ways, anywhere from hitting, slapping, spanking, punching, shaking, shoving, and choking are specific forms of corporal punishment (Athirathan, 2018).

The present article adopts the definition of corporal punishment offered by Straus and Mouradian (1998), whereby corporal punishment is an act that sets out to cause a child pain, but not injury deliberately. The purpose is to correct or control the child's behavior (p. 354). The definition can also encompass varied methods such as hitting, slapping, shoving, choking, use of various objects (wooden paddles, belts, sticks, pins, switches, whips, or others), painful body postures (as placing in closed spaces), use of excessive exercise drills, or prevention of urine or stool elimination (Athirathan, 2018).

MAIN FOCUS OF THE CHAPTER

Issues, Controversies, and Problems
Related to Corporal Punishment

Several issues, controversies, and problems arise from the use and, in some instances, misuse of corporal punishment in schools. Some people argue against the use of corporal punishment. These persons believe that corporal chastisement violates children's rights and encourages violence. In some instances, though legally sanctioned and guidelines exist for its use, research suggests that some teachers deviate from the guidelines. These nonconformities often misuse the practice and cause physical, psychological, or emotional harm to children. Students are sometimes corporally disciplined in the classroom, in the presence of other classmates, by teachers who use disapproved instruments such as branches from trees, belts, pieces of wood, pieces of broken furniture, and their palms/fists.

When administered in the presence of other students, corporal punishment often tends to encourage teasing from classmates, low self-esteem, aggression, antisocial behavior, and eventual school dropout some students. Gershoff and Grogan-Kaylor (2016) suggest that corporal punishment is more effective at generating hostility than compliance. Bailey et al. (2014) drew a link between corporal punishment and increased levels of violence. Bearing the aforementioned in mind, let us examine the two countries of focus and why the two are under consideration in this chapter.

Issues, Controversies, and Problems: Focus on the US.

In 19 US states, school corporal punishment continues to be endorsed by some government officials, school administrators, teachers, parents, and even students. The following states use corporal punishment as part of their disciplinary methods: Alabama, Arkansas, Arizona, Colorado, Florida, Georgia, Idaho, Indiana, Kansas, Kentucky, Louisiana, Missouri, Mississippi, North Carolina, Oklahoma, South Carolina, Tennessee, Texas, and Wyoming (Caron, 2018; Walker, 2016). The annual introduction of several corporal punishment bills in the US does not mean prohibition exists at the federal level (ibid).

Although several persons in the US are aware of parental corporal punishment laws, some believe that school corporal punishment is a thing of the past or only occurs in "some other state" but theirs. Others who are informed demonstrate mixed feelings, with some in favor of stopping the practice and others preferring its continuation.

Attitudes in the US towards using corporal punishment in public schools have vacillated over the years, even though annually, over 160,000 children are corporally punished (Gershoff & Font, 2018). Despite this level of usage, recent initiatives by the

US government to improve school discipline primarily exclude corporal punishment (ibid, p. 1). The initial focus on public school corporal punishment received attention as early as 1867 when New Jersey banned its use. After one hundred years, the next state to ban school corporal punishment was Massachusetts (1971). Hawaii (1973) and Maine in 1975 followed suit. The Ingraham V. Wright case in 1977 was the first legal challenge brought against the practice in the US. At that time, corporal punishment in public schools became legal. States were permitted to make their own rules to guide its use. Since then, the questions against corporal punishment in schools on other constitutional grounds have continued.

Issues, Controversies, and Problems: The Guyana Scenario

In Guyana, corporal punishment use in public schools occurs nationwide. Whipping, beating, slapping, licks (use of any instrument on a body part for corporal punishment Mitchell, 2010), lashes, punching, kneeling, and shaking describe the practice some teachers use in Guyana. Like its Caribbean Community (CARICOM) sisters, Guyana has been debating how to handle the phenomenon of corporal punishment used in schools. Using physical punishment in schools arose following several allegations of teachers' use of violence toward children in 1999. The publicity led to a study of the phenomenon in 2000, presenting the findings at the well-advertised forum titled "New Research in the Social Sciences." The University of Guyana hosted the conference, and several prominent political and education officials attended. Following the presentation of the findings, the then President of Guyana, on November 27, 2000, renounced corporal punishment (Parliament of the Co-operative Republic of Guyana, 2012). In addition to raising local awareness of the problem, it also triggered several other research projects.

International Focus: Impact on Attitudes Towards Guyana's School Corporal Punishment

The United Nations, thru the Committee on the Rights of the Child at their 35th Session, held in Geneva on January 12-30, 2004, called on Guyana to prohibit the use of corporal punishment. Guyana was to develop policies to propose alternative methods of discipline, especially for educational settings (UN Committee on the Rights of the Child, 2004). The involvement of the international agency gave momentum to the corporal punishment issue. Since Guyana had both signed and ratified the Convention on the Child's Rights (in September 1990 and January 1991, respectively), this initiated the call to ban corporal punishment. The treaty ensures that children benefit from special protection measures and assistance, have access to services, grow up in environments conducive to development, and are informed about and participate in achieving these rights (United Nations Children's Fund (UNICEF, 1990). In addition to banning corporal punishment, Guyana raised public awareness about children's rights.

This heightened awareness of the misuse of corporal punishment, the potential harm to students, and UNICEF's admonition, saw some change. National debates, passage of new Bills, the creation of grass-root educational movements, and more research resulted (See Cabral & Speek-Warnery, 2004; Ministry of Labor, Human Services and Social Security, 2006, & Smith & Mbozi, 2008). An outcome of these activities caused one political party's activist to table a motion in Parliament seeking to abolish the practice of corporal punishment in schools (Kaieteur News, December 2006). The parliamentary hearing of the proposal for February 15, 2007, by the National Assembly of the First Session (2006-2007) was deferred to gather more information about alternate discipline techniques (Staff Reporter, 2015).

As the debates continued to simmer, several Guyanese advocates began looking to other societies for examples to support the continued use of school corporal punishment. The outcomes from disallowing school corporal punishment by other countries became a primary source for garnishing support in the corporal punishment debate in Guyana. One leading argument proposed by supporters of corporal punishment in Guyana is the perceived unacceptable behavior of children when corporal punishment is banned. Some strongly believe that more disruptions and student disorders at schools happen in societies where corporal punishment is forbidden. These disorders they attribute to teachers' inability to instill discipline corporally. With so many Guyanese having more readily access to western media, compounded with so many of them having relatives or friends living in the US, the US has become an essential reference point to most Guyanese. Like some Americans, several Guyanese believe that the US does not administer corporal punishment in schools.

These persons tend to use this misguided, unfounded, unresearched belief, often coupled with their narrow cultural definitions and opinions of "acceptable behaviors," to guide their conclusions. Some see a correlation between misconduct and other behaviors exhibited by some public-school students in the US and the removal of corporal punishment. These behaviors, they subjectively believe, stem from the removal of corporal punishment from US public schools. Several of the national debates in Guyana, therefore, reference what is occurring in US public schools (use of metal detectors, students disrespecting teachers, disrespectfully talking to teachers, rolling of eyes, arguing with teachers' instructions, refusing to follow instructions, etcetera) as a direct result of the removal of corporal punishment from public schools.

This chapter explores corporal punishment in the US and Guyana's public school systems to raise awareness of the current state of the phenomenon. It examines the laws, policies, statutes, politics, the role of religion, initiatives, and interventions, that influence the use of corporal punishment. The intent is to highlight what is happening versus what some "think" about corporal punishment in the US. It describes the Guyanese and US laws on school corporal punishment to enrich and inform future discussions and debates in the two societies.

THEORY AND REASONS FOR USING CORPORAL PUNISHMENT

Linking Theory and Reasons for Corporal Punishment's Continuation

Three sociological theories guide this discussion: Durkheim's social capital, Messner and Rosenfeld" s theory of institutional anomie, and culture as explanations for the continued use of corporal punishment.

Social Capital

Previous research has established a relationship between the amount of social or cultural capital and the legality and use of corporal punishment (Coleman, 1988; McClure & May, 2007; Owen, 2005). Owen (2005) and McClure and May (2007) applied this concept in their research. Durkheim (1961) postulated this idea of social networks being essential for the welfare of society with his reference to secular morality. He emphasized the need for citizens to be dedicated to societal activities and to shaping and improving character when he stated, "If a man is to be a moral being, he must be devoted to something other than himself; he must feel at one with a society…" (P.79).

Social capital further refers to the degree of involvement in community matters. It is the networks between and among individuals and the societies in which they live. It involves a multiplicity of friendships and political and social ties with institutions (Owens, 2005). Social capital may also include reciprocal relationships among individuals, information networks, and the enforcement of norms through informal social capital (Coleman,1988). Coleman argues that children from communities characterized by outstanding interpersonal and generations of closure may exhibit more confirmatory behaviors.

The cultural capital by Xu, Tung, and Dunaway (2000) applied primarily to parental discipline but could also apply to education settings. The cultural norms, values, and symbolic meanings to which educators invest and are exposed allow them to use such criteria to impose specific disciplinary measures to control children's classroom behavior. Like parents, teachers also selectively consume the dominant cultural values and norms that approve physical force, thereby legitimating and culturally justifying corporal punishment (Xu et al., 2000). Cultural capital may include church adherence rate, total voter registration rate, total voter turnout rate (McClure & May, 2008), religious theme, and doctrine (Xu et al., 2000).

Institutional Anomie

Merton (1938) examined the concept of anomie or strain and its resultant effects on deviant societal behavior. He tried to explain how some social structures can pressure individuals to engage in nonconformist conduct. Merton identified two social and cultural systems elements: societal goals and the regulations and controls to achieve these goals. Often these two elements conflict because, while individuals seek to maximize their goals, institutional regulatory norms and moral imperatives often hinder such aspirations. Institutional standards hamper choice and make it difficult to achieve goals (Ibid p. 673).

Merton's (1938) and Agnew's (2005) arguments explain high incidents of corporal punishment and its relationship to lower socioeconomic status. They draw connections between social deviance, societal goals, and an individual's means of achieving them. Therefore, corporal punishment may be a function of not having the means (Ex. time, class sizes, and highly trained teachers) to use other discipline techniques such as in-school suspension and individualized education programs.

Using Merton's strain theory, Messner and Rosenfeld (2001) extended its application from an individual focus on strain to institutional strain. They suggest that, like individuals, institutions may also experience tension when other institutions control the means to achieve specific goals. Thus, while one of the goals of schools is to provide a safe environment in which learning may take place, not all schools have the means to accomplish this. Some schools may be in disadvantaged areas where drugs and crime are rife. Some of these schools may have several poorly-trained teachers. Often, substitutes may be the ones teaching the students. Thus, while the school may wish to keep the students safe, the environment around the school is itself unsafe, and the budget may be too small to hire security personnel and security devices such as body scanners. Other institutions exert constraints on schools that often result in strain. The political, religious, and economic institutions are mainly instrumental in putting pressure on schools to fulfill their goals.

Messner and Rosenfeld (2001) point out that the family, polity, and economic systems may control education policies such as corporal punishment. Parents, politicians, religious members, and others may insist on retaining corporal punishment at school and exert pressure to maintain it as part of its disciplinary policies. In their political positions, school boards, teachers' unions, and the state legislature may endorse corporal punishment use, and when teachers refuse to use it, the economic institutions may withdraw funding. The financial institution is considered by Messner and Rosenfeld (2001) as very influential owing to American capitalism, its materialist culture, and the financial contributions made to schools. In Guyana's Culture, parents play an essential role in supporting, opposing, and adding pressure on the education system to conform to "expected" cultural behavior, including using corporal punishment as a norm.

Previous research shows an association between rates of corporal punishment and poverty at the state level that supports Messner et al.'s (2000) premise. Schools will endeavor to achieve their goals in poor areas regardless of the measures involved. Even though corporal punishment may not be the best way to ensure a safe learning environment, this may be the most financially efficient way to achieve that goal (Arcus, 2002; McClure et al., 2008).

Culture

Culture is a determinant of the use of corporal punishment. Assessing the link between corporal discipline and culture has been the focus of several research endeavors (Baptiste, et al., 1997; Horn, Cheng, & Joseph, 22004; RipollNúñez & Rohner, 2006; Lansford & Dodge, 2008; Straus & Donnelly, 2017;). Durkheim (1933) stated that as societies become heterogeneous and more economically interdependent, their punishment methods change. Heterogeneous communities tend to determine punishment based on individual rights and practices rather than those based primarily on religious values and emotions.

Durkheim's theory implies that societies characterized by several religious and political varieties may more likely support corporal punishment in schools. Increased corporal punishment might occur more in Guyana, where religious conservatism and less religious and political heterogeneity prevail. Likewise, research findings for the US reveal a link between the use of corporal punishment and states with similar characteristics (Flynn 1994), such as religious conservativism (Ellison & Sherkat,1993). Research from Guyana support this relationship (Cabral & Speek-Warnery, 2004; Ministry of Labour, Human Services, and Social Security, 2006; Smith & Mbozi, 2008).

The prevalence of school corporal punishment in the conservative US south and Guyana supports Durkheim's theory. The Southern states focus more on decisions based on religious values and emotions rather than individual "rights," evidenced more in Northern states. This shift is noted in the recent developments internationally for corporal punishment, where children know that they have "rights" and are encouraged to pursue them (Paintal, 2007). The United States tends to use children's rights as one explanation for banning corporal punishment.

As the social capital, institutional anomie, and culture theories show, several explanations and factors can explain the retention of school corporal punishment in the US and Guyana. In Guyana's case, one of the main reasons is that it is part of the Guyanese culture and enshrined in the law. Other reasons include cultural and religious support. Some persons refer to their having experienced corporal punishment in school as kids and how well they have "turned out" as adults. Guyanese continue to question what will happen to Guyana's schools if teachers cannot punish students corporally. One question posed consistently is: What discipline style can effectively replace corporal punishment in schools? The fear is that maintaining school discipline will be difficult, albeit impossible, with the removal of corporal punishment. This question has become the backbone of parliamentary arguments in favor of retaining corporal punishment in Guyana's public schools (Parliament of the Co-operative Republic of Guyana, 2012).

PREVALENCE OF SCHOOL CORPORAL PUNISHMENT

The US.

While consensus exists that the incidents of corporal punishment in schools in the US seem to have declined, it remains a common practice in 19 states: Alabama, Arizona, Arkansas, Colorado, Florida, Georgia, Idaho, Indiana, Kansas, Kentucky, Louisiana, Mississippi, Missouri, North Carolina, Oklahoma, South Carolina, Tennessee, Texas, and Wyoming (End Corporal Punishment, 2021). Data from the US Department of Education, Office for Civil Rights for school years 2011-2012, 2013-14, 2015-16, and 2017-18 show that corporal punishment figures may be declining. The data reveal reduced usage for the 19 states that legally allow corporal punishment. The data indicate that from a high of 152,659 cases in 2011-2012, the number fell to 105,896 for 2013-14. It tumbled to 92,370 for 2015-2016, and the 2017-18 school year usage decreased to a low of 69,199. Despite the noted decline, while some states' totals are dropping yearly, the high incidents reported in states such as Mississippi, Texas, Alabama, and Arkansas, continue to be a source of unease for some. These data further indicate that while some children enjoy protection from corporal punishment at school, this is not true for all American children.

Table 1 shows the frequency and percent of students experiencing corporal punishment from the 19 states with legal corporal punishment during the 2017-18 school year. The first ten states listed in the table are those with the highest frequency of corporal punishment. These states (in order of usage) are Mississippi (20,309, 29.3%), Texas (13,892, 20.1%), Alabama (9,168, 13.2%), Arkansas (8,932, 12.9%), Oklahoma (3,968, 5.7%), Tennessee (3,765, 5.4%), Georgia (3,697, 5.3%), Missouri

Table 1. Number and percentage of US students that received corporal punishment in the 19 states where corporal punishment is legal: 2017-18 school year

States	Number of Children	%	States	Number of Children	%
Mississippi	20,309	29.3	Kentucky	207	0.3
Texas	13,892	20.1	Indiana	16	0.0
Alabama	9,168	13.2	Arizona	71	0.1
Arkansas	8,932	12.9	North Carolina	57	0.1
Georgia	3,697	5.3	Colorado	0	0.0
Oklahoma	3,968	5.7	South Carolina	23	0.0
Tennessee	3,765	5.4	Idaho	0	0.0
Missouri	2,461	3.6	Kansas	0	0.0

Source: US Department of Education, Office for Civil Rights, 2017-18.

(2,461, 3.6%), Florida (1,332, 1.9%), and Louisiana (1,301, 1.9%). Mississippi, Texas, Alabama, and Arkansas retain the top four slots. The data also show that the five states reporting the highest numbers account for more than three-quarters of all the school paddling done in the 19 schools with legal corporal punishment for the 2017-18 school year.

Previous studies found widespread racial differences in school corporal punishment in states such as Alabama and Mississippi (Gershoff & Font, 2016; Smith & Harper, 2015). Citing several authorities (APA Zero Tolerance Task Force, 2008; Kinsler, 2011; Smith & Harper, 2015), Gershoff and Font (2016) refer to the dilemma in which Black children are disproportionately disciplined compared to their non-black peers and, at times, for the same behavior. Regardless of the school's racial composition, Black students were more likely to experience more corporal punishment than white peers. Also, some researchers report a trend of boys experiencing corporal punishment more than girls (American Civil Liberties Union and Human Rights Watch, 2010; Gershoff & Font, 2016).

Guyana

Unlike in the US, prevalence statistics for corporal punishment in Guyana's schools are not readily available. Some research findings provide glimpses into the usage of corporal punishment in Guyana. Prevalence statistics from the mixed-methods study conducted by Gill-Marshall (2000) revealed that while teachers were aware of the Ministry's guidelines on discipline, classroom teachers were nonetheless administering corporal punishment in their classrooms without the knowledge or consent of Head Teachers. Often, teachers applied lashes to parts of the body disapproved by law or the Ministry of Education's guidelines. This behavior is still prevalent (See Carmichael, 2017; Stabroek News, 2014). In some instances, the instruments ranged from wood, wild canes, broken pieces of furniture, metal strips, belts, and other objects.

An examination of the response data collected by Gill-Marshall (2000) reveals teachers' use of five corporal punishment methods. Children reported they were whipped, slapped by teachers, made to kneel, stand on benches, and shaken by teachers. Nearly two-thirds (65 percent) of the respondents reported that they were whipped. Thirty-eight percent stated that corporal punishment occurred often or sometimes, respectively, and 28.2 percent were rarely physically punished. Kneeling (36 percent) was the next frequently reported method of corporal punishment. Other forms of corporal punishment revealed; slapped by teachers (16 percent), shaken by teachers (14 percent), and made to stand on the bench (13 percent). More boys than girls experienced these varied forms of discipline. Research findings suggest that boys experience harsher corporal punishment (UNICEF, 2019).

Other Guyanese studies bear this out. In 2005 a survey of 4000 children (ages 3-17 years) gathered students' opinions about experiences with all kinds of violence. Regarding violence at school, some students said that their teachers walked around the classroom with small whips (branches cut from trees), which they used to threaten, give tap warnings, or beat them. The children recounted teachers administering quick lashes to their backs and arms. They also described that some teachers slapped them on their heads as they walked around the class (Cabral & Speek-Warnery, 2004, p. 43). In a similar study, teachers customarily administered corporal punishment in the classroom instead of following the Ministry's disciplinary guidelines (Smith & Mbozi, 2008).

There is a trend of more acceptance of corporal punishment use at the primary level than secondary school students' acceptance of such discipline. Cebral and Speek-Warnery (2004) found that (73%-77%) of primary school students compared to (50%-64%) either agreed or strongly agreed that if they did something wrong, teachers should beat them (Cabral & Speek-Warnery, 2004, cited in Smith & Mbozi, 2008, p.10). The report further suggests that 53% of Guyana's schools use corporal punishment to maintain discipline. The researchers also confirmed that the frequent use of corporal punishment often involved methods that infringed on the Ministry of Education's guidelines and the laws of Guyana. They mention corporal punishment by unauthorized teachers, disapproved instruments, and inappropriate administration of the wrong parts of children's bodies. Such findings lead to a discussion of what is legally allowed.

LINKING THEORIES TO CORPORAL PUNISHMENT'S PERSISTENCE

The previously discussed theories explained the prevalence of school corporal punishment in both societies. Durkheim's culture theory facilitated an understanding of corporal punishment's continued use and predominance when the US and Guyana. Nonetheless, the findings from this chapter suggest that both countries tend to justify the continued use of corporal punishment on the foundation of individual, emotional, and religious arguments. Some religious leaders, along with other activists, politicians, government officials, and educators, in the US and Guyana use religion often to support their decisions. The warning from Proverbs 13:34, "He who spares his rod hates his son, But he who loves him disciplines him promptly" (The New King James Version, n.d), permeates even political debates related to the abolition of the practice.

Merton's strain theory is also applicable to the continued use of school corporal punishment. Some teachers and parents argue for its use as a practical discipline that helps preserve culturally acceptable behavior and hence, social order. Others, even some children who attend public schools in both countries, opine that corporal punishment helps keep order at school and is an effective measure for maintaining order at school. Similarly, some politicians and school officials debate its usage and perceive their involvement in stopping the practice as potentially affecting their popularity and appointments to political offices.

Messner and Rosenfeld's (2001) institutional theory also aptly aids comprehension of the continued practice in Guyana. The interplay of politics, economics, education, and the family is crucial when explaining corporal punishment's prolonged acceptance and use in Guyanese society. Survival of the practice is easier for Guyana since the method remains enshrined in the laws. The institutional strain between and within various institutions also explains its continuation. The institutions of politics, economics, family, education, and religion uphold and support its usefulness or exert pressure. However, the theory is less effective for the US in explaining support in the 19 states that still allow such practice. The fact that 31 states do not condone the use of corporal punishment makes this theory somewhat weak for accounting for such disparity in the US.

LEGISLATIVE APPROACHES TO CORPORAL PUNISHMENT

The US.

Before 1977, few state statutes addressed corporal punishment's use in schools. This situation changed in 1977 after the ruling by the US Supreme Court in the Ingram V. Wright case. Schools learned that they might use corporal punishment despite protestation from parents. While noting that the districts in some states have banned corporal punishment, the focus here is on state laws and the State laws and School Codes that guide teachers in the US on the use and application of corporal punishment. The concern here is that school districts that have banned corporal punishment can revert to state laws and reintroduce corporal punishment's help in their schools.

Generally, though some districts have chosen not to enforce the use of corporal punishment or impose regulations "banning" its use in public schools in those districts, such restrictions do not make the act illegal. Corporal punishment use remains legal in those states. Therefore, while the 19 states mentioned before in this chapter legally allow the practice of corporal punishment in public schools, some cities within the state have abolished any type of corporal punishment. Such abolition means that a county, city, or school district in a state where corporal punishment is allowed in public schools may decide to change its regulation/abolition and revert to using corporal punishment in schools. Such a change in regulation will be legal. Bearing this in mind then, the author's interest is in the content of State laws and not specific county/city regulations.

Table 2 contains the state law granting authority and statutes for each of the 19 states that permit corporal punishment. As shown in the table, states often give Boards and educators the legal right to use corporal punishment in schools. Further examination of the statutes for some states reveals that each state approaches the practice differently. Statutory definitions sometimes provide details about the acceptable use of corporal punishment and outline ways to administer the method. Alabama, Kansas, Kentucky, Wyoming, Mississippi, and Texas statutes give school boards control over decisions about how to govern corporal punishment. Furthermore, educators are immune from suit for using corporal punishment in each state. While the regulations are silent, the active use is often not without controversy.

Though corporal punishment persists and affects several US children annually, this does not mean that efforts to either ban or retain its use in the US are nonexistent. On the contrary, at the National and state levels, some antagonists of school corporal punishment consistently propose bills to ban school corporal punishment, while protagonists introduce bills to bolster usage. The information in Table 3 below, though not exhaustive, outlines some of the more recent national and state levels bills

Table 2. States allowing corporal punishment by state law granting authority and statutes

State	Statutes	State Law Granting Authority
Indiana Arkansas Texas North Carolina Idaho Wyoming	IND. CODE Sec. 20-8.1-5.1-3 (Authority- Family Law) ARK. CODE ANN. Sec. 6-18-505 TEX. PENAL CODE Sec. Texas Education Code Chapter 37: Law and Order NC. GEN. STAT. Sec. 115C-391-4 ID. Sec. 33-1224 WY. Sec. 21-4-308.	Grant of Board Authority to Educators for the use of corporal punishment.
Arizona Florida Kentucky Louisiana Missouri South Carolina Tennessee	ARIZ. REV STATE. Sec 15-843 FLA. STAT. Sec 1003.32 KRS. Sec. 161.180, 503.110 LA. REV STAT. Sec. 17.233 and Sec. 17:416.1 MO. REV STAT. Sec. 160-261.1 SC Sec. 59-63-260 TCA. Sec. 49-6-4103; 4104	Grant of Authority to School Boards to Permit corporal punishment within statutory guidelines.
Georgia Oklahoma Alabama Mississippi	GA. CODE ANN. Sec 20-2-730, Sec 20-2-731 OKLA. STAT. Sec. 24-100.4 (Includes spanking, switching, or paddling) AL. Sec. 16-1-24.1 MS. Sec. 37-11-57	Justification for the use of force by certain persons. Use of ordinary (not excessive) force as a means of discipline is not prohibited.
Colorado Kansas	CO. Sec. 27-10.5-115, 2509-8, 7.702.66, 7.712.55, 7.713.22, and 7.715.46 KS. No statutory provisions	corporal punishment not directly addressed. It may be addressed indirectly through powers given to school boards for control of discipline or through immunity from suit for educators using corporal punishment.

Source: Table information compiled from FindLaw, 2022.

and their outcomes. The presented information shows that disparity and consensus at the national and state levels exist. While most national proposals seek to ban school corporal punishment entirely, several proposed or passed state legislation favor fixing or altering the practice, including stopping its use for children with disabilities. Overall, some states seem interested in retaining the approach.

Guyana

The Ministry of Education's "Manual of Guidelines for the Maintenance of Order and Discipline in Schools" (2002) (referred to as the "Manual") is the current regulation followed by schools. In 2008 the Education Task Force circulated a draft Education Bill, section 52 of which deals with corporal punishment. The plan

Table 3. National and state level bills for some select US states

Bills	Origin	Outcome
The Ending Corporal punishment in Schools Bill 2015 (HR 2268). [a]	National	Failed
Ending Corporal punishment in Schools Bill 2017 (HR 160). [b]	National	Failed
The Ending Corporal Punishment Corporal in Schools Bill 2019 (HR 727).[c]	National	Referred to the House Committee on Education and Labor.
Protecting Our Students in Schools Act of 2020 (HR 8460). [d]	National	Introduced in the House of Representatives. Not Adopted. Resubmitted.
A Companion Bill of the Protecting Our Students in Schools Act, 2020.[e]	National	Not Adopted.
The Ending PUSHOUT Bill 2019 (HR 5325). [f]	National	Pending
Protecting Our Students in Schools Act (HR 8460), 2021[g]	National	Reintroduced to new US Congress; pending.
Corporal punishment in Public Schools - "Sofia Taddeo-Goldstein Act" (SB 858), 2021.[h]	State Florida	Died
Stephanie Hilferty's House Bill (324). 2021.[i]	State Louisiana	Failed
Corporal punishment. Prohibit the use of corporal punishment in public schools to discipline a student with a disability (MS HB 1182). [j]	State Mississippi	Passed 3/21/2019
House B*ill* 760. An act to amend section 37-11-57, *Mississippi* code of 1972. [k]	State Mississippi	Enacted July 1, 2021.
House Bill 1623, or the "Bryan Young Act," protects students with disabilities from corporal punishment...[l]	State Oklahoma	Passed March 7, 2017.
Relating to the use of Corporal punishment in public schools, Texas SB 1595, 2021.[m]	State Texas	In Committee
A BILL to be entitled an Act to amend Part 2 of Article 16 of Chapter 2 of Title 20 of thee OCGA, relating to student discipline	State	In the House, being read.

Source: Items [a, b, c, d, e, f], and [g] cited from End Corporal Punishment, 2021

[h] The Florida Senate, 2021.https://www.flsenate.gov/Session/Bill/2021/858

[i] Louisiana State Legislature, 2021,https://www.legis.la.gov/legis/BillInfo.aspx?i=240209

[j] Mississippi Legislature, 2019.http://billstatus.ls.state.ms.us/2019/pdf/history/HB/HB1182.xml

[k] Mississippi Legislature, 2021.http://billstatus.ls.state.ms.us/documents/2021/html/HB/0700-0799/ HB0760IN.htm

[l] Oklahoma State Legislature, 2017.https://www.okhouse.gov/Media/News_Story.aspx?NewsID=5218

[m]. Texas Legislature online, n.d.https://capitol.texas.gov/BillLookup/History. aspx?LegSess=87R&Bill=SB1595

[n]. Openstates, February 2021

was to reform school discipline. It seems plausible that this section was to replace

Education Code Regulations 93 and 94, which govern corporal punishment. This Bill was eventually tabled in the National Assembly in June 2014 (Parliament of the Co-operative Republic of Guyana, 2014-2022). The tabled June Bill would likely replace an outdated Education Act, first passed in 1876 and later amended in 1976.

Interestingly, this tabled Bill does not unequivocally outlaw corporal punishment in schools. Instead, it outlines the benefits of maintaining school order and discipline (End Corporal Punishment, 2021). Additionally, it summarizes the role of the Headteacher, other teachers, students or "Learners," and parents/guardians in maintaining order and discipline at schools.

An earlier document: the Ministry of Education (MOE) circular No. 3 (1993), had previously provided a more in-depth outline and discussion of corporal punishment laws applicable to schools in Guyana. While admonishing that "Physical intervention must be appropriate and reasonable," the definitions of what constitutes these two terms are not provided (MOE 2002:20). The Ministry of Education's Manual (2002) outlines six uses for physical intervention by school staff: To restrain a learner from an act of wrongdoing, quell a disturbance threatening bodily injury to others, obtain possession of a weapon or dangerous object from a learner, protection of personal property, and preservation of order (Ibid: p.20). Other education policies concerning corporal punishment question: Where and by whom should it be administered?

1) Corporal punishment must only be administered by the Head Teacher, Deputy Head Teacher, or designated Senior Master/Mistress (ibid, p. 20).
2) Males should be punished by striking only their hands or on their buttocks, while females must be struck only on their hands (ibid, p. 20).
3) Learners are not to be punished in the presence of other learners (ibid, p.20). Infringement of this rule falls under Chapter 8:01 section 43, for simple assault. A charge of Simple assault could result in the person being found guilty of a misdemeanour and imprisonment for one year.

Applicable Offences

4) It must be restricted for use in circumstances such as fighting, use of indecent language, and gross insubordination (ibid, p.20).
5) It must only be used in cases of continued display of unacceptable behaviours or in grave circumstances (ibid, p.20).

Instruments to be used

6) In administering corporal punishment, the Headteacher must use either a cane or strap no longer than 24 inches (ibid, p.20).

Other Legal Requirements

7) Cases of corporal punishment must be carefully documented in the misdemeanours book on the same day the punishment is administered (Ibid: 20).

Elaborating on this, Circular No. 3 (1993) states that the statement of the nature and extent of the punishment and the reason for inflicting it should be stated.

Any infringement of these previously mentioned regulations constitutes some form of illegal practice and hence a violation of the law. In cases where corporal punishment results in the injury of a child, a teacher can be charged with a criminal offense that falls under chapter 8:01 section 50, which states:

Everyone who unlawfully and maliciously wounds or inflicts any grievous bodily harm upon any person whether with or without any weapon or instrument shall be guilty of a misdemeanour and liable to imprisonment for five years (Laws of Guyana, p. 37).

Guyana has held several debates to reach a consensus and develop a workable plan to ban corporal punishment in schools legally. Despite these debates, the problem persists.

SOLUTIONS AND RECOMMENDATIONS

The problem of violence against children is deep-rooted and complex. To change what is an accustomed feature of school life is to uproot a sensitive and persistent tradition. Violence towards children at schools brings into focus other problems. Legislative and institutional reform can be positive paths to addressing social issues. Noteworthy is that a society's acceptance of change does not come easily. Society can resist change, especially if the policies do not mirror views from the dominant social groups' cultural ideals, practices, and beliefs. The difficulty of change requires the urgent use of persuasive change mechanisms such as counseling, education, and training.

Teacher training must include alternate methods of discipline for students. This way, teachers can more confidently maintain order and successfully impart course content to students. Additionally, as learned from research involving teachers, parents, and students, more support to realize positive school culture is required. Everyone, especially education officials, must champion teachers' abilities and appreciate their selfless job. Administrators must allow teachers to voice precisely how they feel and the challenges they face in their daily tasks so that parents, students themselves, and administrators can help.

Parents must become partners with the schools their children attend. Schools must seek out workable ways to do so. Engage children, parents, and the community in its plans and decisions to get better support and ideas that may be more suitable to the service population. Find creative ways to motivate parents to do their part by assisting with their children's behaviors, helping with homework assignments, and generally establishing a partnership with the school.

Be proactive instead of reactive to problems, as is the present norm. Education officials, school administrators, teachers, parents, and children must meet before conduct problems arise to plan appropriate responses earnestly and collaboratively. Children do have workable ideas. Allow students to share their thoughts. After all, it is the school that serves students. Discipline should not be a teacher-only problem but a team effort. Hold regular debriefing sessions with students and teachers to gauge the mood, determine how things are, and plan new approaches.

In both societies, teacher training should involve studying courses such as sociology, psychology, social work, and communication. Such studies must address the cultural acceptance of corporal punishment, the adverse effects of such violence, and some steppingstones for attaining cultural change. The fundamental techniques in these subject areas will allow teachers to know more about actions, age-appropriate child development tasks and expectations, discipline methods, and the adverse effects of violence against students. As this chapter shows via the theories earlier, societies' recognition of the role of culture, individual beliefs, goals, socialization, institutional norms, regulations, and standards on corporal punishment in schools as a social problem can help provide workable remedies to reduce its use. Though happening to some extent in both the US and Guyana, discussions at the individual and institutional levels must be more deliberate, well-organized, and goal-oriented.

The encouragement of different and more diverse corrective actions via workshops, public opinion polls, plays, school curriculum, and so on can help transmit various discipline techniques. Addressing the familial institution via the holding of family forums to educate parents about different ways to communicate, correct, and control children's in-school behaviors may have a trickle-down effect on educational institutions. Such education can contribute to cultural shifts in institutional standards, regulatory norms, moral imperatives, laws, and aspirations of both Americans and Guyanese. These shifts may allow greater acceptance for banning corporal punishment's use in schools and, eventually, even a ban on its use in other settings, including the home.

FUTURE RESEARCH DIRECTIONS

As expected, prevalence statistics and studies are more available in the US than Guyana. To this end, Guyana must mandate, collect, and document corporal punishment data from each school. These data must be publicly available and easily accessible. There is no denying the power of information and qualitative data for helping to establish prevalence, show trends, and pinpoint where changes are needed. Having access to up-to-date data cannot be overstated. There is a considerable lag time between data collection of national statistics and the availability of these data to the public in the US. Having readily available access to recent data will allow researchers, other entities, and organizations to conduct much-needed analyses. Both non-professionals and professionals will be in better stead to offer workable suggestions to the ongoing debates about ending school corporal punishment. More studies should also be performed with the active constituents to gather their opinions and recommendations about school corporal punishment.

CONCLUSION

Despite state and education statutes governing the use of school corporal punishment, research establishes that it persists amidst strong undercurrents of opinions in both societies. In some cases, culture often based on religious beliefs preponderates and influences the inappropriate use of corporal punishment in public schools in both US and Guyana. In some US states, residents are more accepting of a "culture of violence." Wherever it may be allowed in US states, some parents opt out of corporal punishment for their children. Various children may choose to receive corporal in place of suspension, parent conferences, and other methods of punishment. Interestingly, even though some parents never corporally discipline their children, they may allow their children's teachers who stand in or assume parental status (standing in loco parentis) to administer corporal punishment to their children.

Fischer (1969) posits that "punishment must be reasonable, but the question of reasonableness is always related to the facts of a particular situation. It must be related to a legitimate educational purpose and not merely express teacher frustration, anger, or malice" (p. 329). Drye (n.d.) outlined situations where teachers may become legally liable in a school-related lawsuit (termed *Tort Liability*). In a section on corporal punishment, Drye (n.d.) states that teachers may become exposed in the courts based on the reasonableness of the punishment provided and how administered. He outlines in part, ".to be reasonable, punishment must relate to an educational purpose and not to the expression of a teacher's anger or frustration..." (Corporal Punishment, paragraph 2). This study found that in both the US and Guyana, the issue of reasonableness needs to be defined clearly. On some occasions, teachers misuse their positions of authority in apparent contravention of the law and statutes governing such use.

In the US, school officials and local school boards have wide-ranging power to make and enforce rules and regulations related to the operation of schools. These powers may be granted expressly by state law or implied as necessary to carry out other educational responsibilities. Research also revealed that excessive punishment by teachers or administrators remains unprotected by policies and laws in both societies. Violation can result in lawsuits against teachers for their students' injuries incurred. Teachers may lose their jobs for violating accepted statutes or regulations related to corporal punishment.

It, therefore, follows that the severity of punishment should be appropriate to the gravity of the offenses and should consider the child's ability to sustain the discipline. Courts are reluctant to interfere with the daily operation of the schools if disciplinary rules and procedures are reasonable and non-discriminatory. For both societies to fully meet the requirements as member states of the World Health Organization, they should,

Advocate for the adoption or reform of laws and policies, ensure their alignment with international human rights standards (37), and enforce existing laws and policies to prevent violence against children and adolescents, including corporal punishment, in all settings and, in particular, in the home, schools, communities, and residential care and detention facilities (World Health Organization, 2016 p. 23).

A legal ban on school corporal punishment is one sure way to start. In response to the question asked in the title, the answer is, yes, corporal punishment is still legal in the US and Guyana.

REFERENCES

Agnew, R. (2005). *Why do criminals offend? A general theory of crime and delinquency.* Roxbury.

American Academy of Child & Adolescent Psychiatry. (2014). *Corporal punishment in schools.* https://www.aacap.org/aacap/Policy_Statements/1988/Corporal_ Punishment_in_Schools.aspx

American Civil Liberties Union and Human Rights Watch. (2010). *Corporal punishment in schools and its effect on academic success: Joint HRW/ACLU statement.* Retrieved from: https:// www.hrw.org/news/2010/04/15/corporal-punishment-schools-and-its-effect-academic-success-jointhrw/aclu-statement

American Psychological Association Zero Tolerance Task Force. (2008). Are zero tolerance policies effective in the schools? An eviden-tiary review and recommendations. *The American Psychologist, 63*(9), 852–862. doi:10.1037/0003-066X.63.9.852 PMID:19086747

American School Counselor Association. (2007). *Position statement: Corporal punishment the professional school counselor.* https://www.schoolcounselor.org/content.asp?contentid=199

Antoine, R. (2008). *Commonwealth Caribbean: law and legal systems* (2nd ed.). Routledge-Cavendish. doi:10.4324/9780203930397

Arcus, D. (2002). School shooting fatalities and school corporal punishment: A look at the states. *Aggressive Behavior, 28*(3), 173–183. https://psycnet.apa.org/doi/10.1002/ab.90020. doi:10.1002/ab.90020

Athirathan, S. (2018). Corporal punishment and its effects on learning in Sri Lanka. *International Journal of Agriculture, 3*, 413–420. https://ijaeb.org/uploads2018/AEB_03_287.pdf

Bailey, C., Robinson, T., & Coore-Desai, C. (2014). Corporal punishment in the Caribbean: Attitudes and Practices. *Social and Economic Studies, 63*(3&4), 207–233.

Baptiste, D. A., Hardy, K. V., & Lewis, L. (1997). Clinical practice and Caribbean immigrant families in the United States: The intersection of emigration, immigration, culture, and race. In J. L. Roopnarine & J. Brown (Eds.), *Caribbean families: diversity among ethnic groups.* Ablex.

Biblestudytools. (2022). *The New King James Version 1982.* https://www.biblestudytools.com/nkjv/proverbs/13.html

Cabral, C., & Speek-Warnery, V. (Eds.). (2004). *Voices of children: Experiences with violence.* Report produced for Ministry of Labor, Human Services and Social Security, Red Thread Women's Development Programme, and UNICEF-Guyana. https://www.devnet.org.gy/sdnp/csoc/childviolreport.pdf

Carmichael, A. (2017, October 3). Student bleeds after 'wild cane' beating by teacher. *Guyana Times.* https://guyanatimesgy.com/student-bleeds-after-wild-cane-beating-by-teacher/

Caron, C. (2018, December 13). In 19 States, It's still legal to spank children in public schools. *The New York Times.* https://www.nytimes.com/2018/12/13/us/corporal-punishment-school-tennessee.html

Chen, G. (2020, February 14). *Teachers in 19 states allowed to physically punish students.* Public School Review. https://www.publicschoolreview.com/blog/teachers-in-19-states-allowed-to-physically-punish-students

Coleman, J. (1988). Social capital in the creation of human capital. *American Journal of Sociology, 94,* 195–120. doi:10.1086/228943

Countryreports.org. (2022). *Guyana facts and culture.* https://www.countryreports.org/country/Guyana.htm

Devries, K. M., Knight, L., Child, J. C., Mirembe, A., Nakuti, J., Jones, R., Sturgess, J., Allen, E., Kyegombe, N., Parkes, J., Walakira, E., Elbourne, D., Watts, C., & Naker, D. (2015). The good school toolkit for reducing physical violence from school staff to primary school students: A cluster-randomised controlled trial in Uganda. *The Lancet. Global Health, 3*(7), E378–E386. doi:10.1016/S2214-109X(15)00060-1 PMID:26087985

Drye, J. M. (n.d.). *Tort liability 101: When are teachers liable?* Education Resources. https://educator-resources.com/tort-liability101-when-are-teachers-liable/

Durkheim, E. (1961). *Moral education: A study in the theory and application of the sociology of education.* Free Press of Glencoe.

Ellison, C. G., & Sherkat, D. (1993). Conservative Protestantism and support for corporal punishment. *American Sociological Review, 58*(1), 131–144. doi:10.2307/2096222

End Corporal Punishment. (2020). *Country report for Guyana, June 2020.* https://endcorporalpunishment.org/reports-on-every-state-and-territory/guyana/

End Corporal Punishment. (2021). *Country report for the USA.* https://endcorporalpunishment.org/reports-on-every-state-and-territory/usa/

End Corporal Punishment. (2022). https://endcorporalpunishment.org/

FindLaw. (2021). *Find laws, legal information, and attorneys.* https://www.findlaw.com/

Flynn, C. P. (1994). Regional differences in attitudes toward corporal punishment. *Journal of Marriage and Family, 56*(2), 314–324. doi:10.2307/353102

Froelich, J. (2016, December 2) *Arkansas spanks: The natural state still practices public school corporal punishment.* Arkansas Public Media. https://www.arkansaspublicmedia.org/education/2016-12-02/arkansas-spanks-the-natural-state-still-practices-public-school-corporal-punishment

Gershoff, E. T. (2017). School corporal punishment in global perspective: Prevalence, outcomes, and efforts at intervention. *Psychology, Health & Medicine, 22*(sup1), 224–239. doi:10.1080/13548506.2016.1271955

Gershoff, E. T., & Font, S. A. (2016). Corporal punishment in US public schools: Prevalence, disparities in use, and status in state and federal policy. *Social Policy Report, 30*(1), 1–26. doi:10.1002/j.2379-3988.2016.tb00086.x PMID:29333055

Gershoff, E. T., & Grogan-Kaylor, A. (2016). Spanking and child outcomes: Old controversies and new meta-analyses. *Journal of Family Psychology, 30*(4), 453–469. doi:10.1037/fam0000191 PMID:27055181

Gershoff, E. T., Purtell, K. M., & Holas, I. (2015). *Corporal punishment in US public schools: Legal precedents, current practices, and future policy. 2015th Edition.* Springer Briefs in Psychology.

Gill-Marshall, B. I. (2000). *Child abuse in Guyana: A study of teacher abuse of children in secondary schools in Guyana* [Unpublished Master's thesis]. University of Guyana.

Horn, I. B., Cheng, T., & Joseph, J. (2004). Discipline in the African American community: The impact of socioeconomic status on attitudes, beliefs, and practices. *Pediatrics, 113*(5), 1236–1241. doi:10.1542/peds.113.5.1236 PMID:15121935

House Media News Story. (2017, March 3). *Bill scaling back corporal punishment for students with disabilities.* Oklahoma State Legislature. https://www.okhouse.gov/Media/News_Story.aspx?NewsID=5218

Human Rights Watch and the ACLU. (2008). *A Violent Education: Corporal punishment in US Public Schools.* https://www.hrw.org/sites/default/files/reports/us0808_1.pdf

Kaieteur News. (2006, December 8). House defers debate on corporal punishment: AFC member optimistic government will change position. *Kaieteur News.* http://www.landofsixpeoples.com/news604/nk612082.html

Kinsler, J. (2011). Understanding the black-white school discipline gap. *Economics of Education Review, 30*(6), 1370–1383. doi:10.1016/j.econedurev.2011.07.004

Lansford, J. E., & Dodge, K. A. (2008). Cultural norms for adult corporal punishment of children and societal rates of endorsement and use of violence. *Parenting, Science and Practice, 8*(3), 257–270. doi:10.1080/15295190802204843 PMID:19898651

Laws of Guyana. (n.d.). *Chapter 8.01. Criminal Law (Offences) Act.* https://www.oas.org/juridico/spanish/mesicic2_guy_criminal_law_act.pdf

Louisiana State Legislature. (2021). *HB324.* https://www.legis.la.gov/legis/BillInfo.aspx?i=240209

McClure, T. E., & May, D. C. (2008). Dealing with misbehavior at schools in Kentucky: Theoretical and contextual predictors of use of corporal punishment. *Youth & Society, 39*(3), 406–429. doi:10.1177/0044118X06296698

Merton, R. K. (1938). Social structure and anomie. *American Sociological Review, 3*(5), 672–682. doi:10.2307/2084686

Messner, S. E., & Rosenfeld, R. (2001). *Crime and the American dream.* Wadsworth-Thompson.

Ministry of Education. (2002). *Ministry of Education Manual of Guidelines for the Maintenance of Order and Discipline in schools.* https://www.education.gov.gy/web2/index.php/or/other-files/policy-documents/709-manual-of-guidelines-for-the-maintenance-of-order-and-discipline-in-schools/file

Ministry of Education, Guyana. (2022). *Digest of Education Statistics 2016-2017.* https://education.gov.gy/web2/index.php/or/digest-of-education-statistics

Ministry of Education and Cultural Development. (1993). *Corporal punishment in Schools.* Circular No. 3/1993.

Ministry of Labor, Human Services and Social Security. (2006). *Assessment of procedural and physical standards in children's residential care institutions in Guyana. Summary and Recommendations.* https://bettercarenetwork.org/sites/default/files/attachments/Assessment%20of%20procedural%20and%20physical%20standards.pdf

Mississippi Legislature. (2019, July 1). *House bill 1182.* http://billstatus.ls.state.ms.us/2019/pdf/history/HB/HB1182.xml

Mississippi Legislature. (2021). *House bill 760.* http://billstatus.ls.state.ms.us/documents/2021/html/HB/0700-0799/HB0760IN.htm

Mitchell, C. (2010). Corporal punishment in the public schools: An analysis of federal constitutional claims. *Law and Contemporary Problems, 73,* 321–341.

Nan. (2016). 10 Fast facts about Guyanese Immigrants in the US you should know. *News Americas.* https://guyaneseonline.net/2016/05/12/facts-about-guyanese-immigrants-in-the-us-you-should-know-newsamericas/

National Association of State Boards of Education. (n.d.). *Corporal Punishment, Mississippi.* Retrieved from https://statepolicies.nasbe.org/health/categories/physical-environment/corporal-punishment/mississippi

National Center for Education Statistics. (2020). *Digest of education statistics 2020.* https://nces.ed.gov/fastfacts/display.asp?id=372

Orentlicher, D. (1992). Corporal punishment in schools. *Journal of the American Medical Association, 267*(23), 3205. doi:10.1001/jama.1992.03480230105036 PMID:1593744

Owen, S. S. (2005). The relationship between social capital and corporal punishment in schools a theoretical inquiry. *Youth & Society, 37*(1), 85–112. doi:10.1177/0044118X04271027

Paintal, S. (2007). *Banning corporal punishment of children. A position paper.* Association for Childhood Education International. International Focus Issue 2007. Accessed 3/27/2008. http://www.stophitting.com/disathome/sureshrani.php

Parliament of the Co-operative Republic of Guyana. (2012). *Corporal punishment.* Speeches in the National Assembly. Speech delivered at: 28th Sitting - Tenth Parliament - August 9, 2012. Accessed January 13, 2022. https://parliament.gov.gy/media-centre/speeches/corporal-punishment1

Ripoll-Núñez, K. J., & Rohner, R. P. (2006). Corporal punishment in cross-cultural perspective: Directions for a research agenda. *The Journal of Cross-Cultural Research, 40*(3), 220–249. doi:10.1177/1069397105284395

Smith, C., & Mbozi, J. (2008). *Removing corporal punishment corporal from schools: Integrating partner efforts.* Business Unlimited Consulting Services. https://www.hands.org.gy/files/Corporal%20Punishment%20Report%20-%202008.pdf

Smith, E. J., & Harper, S. R. (2015). *Disproportionate impact of K-12 school suspension and expulsion on Black students in southern states.* University of Pennsylvania, Center for the Study of Race and Equity in Education.

Stabroek News. (2014). West Ruimveldt pupil severely whipped - Ministry probing headmistress. *Stabroek News* https://www.stabroeknews.com/2014/02/01/news/guyana/west-ruimveldt-pupil-severely-whipped/

Staff Reporter. (2015, October 20). Corporal punishment to be totally banned soon – Dr. Roopnaraine …says alternative disciplinary measures being sought. *Guyana Chronicle.*

Staff Reporter. (2015). Rupununi teachers charged for flogging female students – Ministry to intervene once action taken. *Guyana Chronicle.* https://guyanachronicle. com/2015/07/10/rupununi-teachers-charged-for-flogging-female-students-ministry-to-intervene-once-action-taken/

Straus, M. A. (1994). *Beating the devil out of them: Corporal punishment in American families.* Jossey-Bass/Lexington Books.

Straus, M. A., & Donnelly, D. A. (2017). *Beating the devil out of them: Corporal punishment in American families and its effects on children* (1st ed.). Taylor & Francis Group. doi:10.4324/9781351314688

Straus, M. A., & Mouradian, V. E. (1998). Impulsive corporal punishment by mothers and antisocial behavior and impulsiveness of children. *Behavioral Sciences & the Law, 16*(3), 353–374. doi:10.1002/(SICI)1099-0798(199822)16:3<353::AID-BSL313>3.0.CO;2-O PMID:9768466

Texas Legislature Online. (2021, March 24). *Bill: SB 1595.* https://capitol.texas. gov/BillLookup/History.aspx?LegSess=87R&Bill=SB1595

The Florida Senate. (2021, July 7). *SB 858: Corporal punishment in public schools.* https://www.flsenate.gov/Session/Bill/2021/858

The United Nations Educational, Scientific and Cultural Organization (UNESCO). (2017, January 19). Knocking out school violence and bullying. *Building peace in the minds of men and women.* https://en.unesco.org/

UNICEF. (2019). *Study of social norms in Guyana as it pertains to sexual, physical and emotional violence against children.* Final Report. https://www.unicef.org/ guyanasuriname/media/1166/file/Study%20of%20Social%20Norms%20on%20 Violence%20against%20Children.pdf

United Nations Children's Fund (UNICEF). (1990). First *call for children.* World Declaration and Plan of Action from the World Summit for Children: Convention on the Rights of the Child. https://www.unicef.org/media/85571/file/WSC-declaration-first-call-for-children.pdf

United Nations (UN). (2004). *Committee on the Rights of the Child.* Thirty-fifth sessions consideration of reports submitted. UN.

US Department of Education. (n.d.a). *Office for Civil Rights Data Collection, 2011-2012.* Available at http://ocrdata.ed.gov

US Department of Education. (n.d.b). *Office for Civil Rights Data Collection, 2013-14.* Available at http://ocrdata.ed.gov

US Department of Education. (n.d.c). *Office for Civil Rights Data Collection, 2015-16.* available at http://ocrdata.ed.gov

US Department of Education. (n.d.d). *Office for Civil Rights Data Collection, 2017-18.* available at http://ocrdata.ed.gov

Walker, T. (2016). *Why are 19 states still allowing corporal punishment corporal in schools?* National Education Association (NEA). https://www.nea.org/advocating-for-change/new-from-nea/why-are-19-states-still-allowing-corporal-punishment-schools

World Health Organization (WHO). (2016). *Global plan of action to strengthen the role of the health system within a national multisectoral response to address interpersonal violence, in particular against women and girls, and against children.* https://www.who.int/reproductivehealth/publications/violence/global-plan-of-action/en/

Xu, X., Tung, Y., & Dunaway, R. G. (2000). Cultural, human, and social capital as determinants of corporal punishment: Toward an integrated theoretical model. *Journal of Interpersonal Violence, 15*(6), 603–630. doi:10.1177/088626000015006004

Section 2
Research

Chapters 5-6 provide current research on school discipline.

Chapter 5

Relative Rate Index, Racial Disparity, and School Suspensions

Jennifer Wyatt Bourgeois
Texas Southern University, USA

Melissa Kwende
Texas Southern University, USA

Howard Henderson
Texas Southern University, USA

ABSTRACT

This chapter will analyze school disciplinary actions across large metropolitan school districts. In recent decades, K-12 school disciplinary practices have garnered national attention from researchers, policymakers, and educators. Racial disparity among school discipline raises serious questions about continued violations of the 1954 Brown vs. Board of Education decision. The purpose of the chapter is to provide a series of evidence-supported recommendations for the dismantling of the school-to-prison pipeline. The current chapter will examine the discipline records for the 2016-2017 academic school year in 19 independent school districts to identify the equitable assignment of suspensions and expulsions. Disparity ratio analysis will help us understand the relationship between race, ethnicity, and school suspension. The findings will be utilized to guide policy recommendations. The results will provide an evidence-based understanding of racial disparity in school suspensions.

DOI: 10.4018/978-1-6684-3359-1.ch005

INTRODUCTION

The school-to-prison pipeline debate has garnered great debate nationally. In fact, racial disparity among school discipline practices raises serious questions about continued violations of the 1954 Brown vs. Board of Education decision. Stemming from the conversation about the school-to-prison pipeline is national and state-level data showing that minorities who receive school disciplinary actions are impacted at a disproportionate rate (Losen & Whitaker, 2018; Fabelo et al., 2011). The need to address patterns of racial inequities in public schools has surfaced as a key focus for education system reform efforts. However, much of the research up to now has been descriptive in nature and at the national and state level. The following chapter represents a localized movement toward education reform. Harris County has a population of 4.6 million residents and contains 19 independent school districts (ISDs). Based on the 2016-2017 academic school year, the ISD's racial and ethnic composition was approximately 6% Asian, 19% Black or African American, 55% Hispanic/Latino, 18% White, less than 2% two or more races, and American Indian or Alaska Native and Native/Hawaiian each account for less than 1%. The purpose of this chapter is to examine school disciplinary actions by race and ethnicity in the county's public school districts.

African American students are suspended and expelled at a higher frequency than their peers who represent other racial groups. This is a consequence of zero tolerance policies which were introduced into the school administrative system as a means to expand school safety among all students (Skiba et al., 2006). Yet, in recent years, these policies have become excessively rigid, and they have directly contributed to racial inequities in school discipline. Additionally, these policies have directly impacted students of color in a negative manner. Zero-tolerance policies are frequently authorized through unyielding practices and predestined penalties that significantly hamper any type of discretion in specific cases. The application of zero-tolerance policies has augmented the commonness of suspension and expulsion to deal with behaviors that run the gamut from improper dress code violations and talking back to teachers to the worst-case situations involving weapons possession and selling narcotics. These policies damage and disproportionately hurt students of color, students with disabilities, and low-income students (Curran, 2019; Hackett, 2018). Simply stated, zero-tolerance policies resulting in school removals do not work because Students suspended or expelled are associated with the stigma of being labeled as a "problem child." Consequently, as research shows, these students who are removed from school for disciplinary actions are more apt to end up at-risk, ultimately placed into an alternative disciplinary school, or worse. This is signified as the school-to-prison pipeline, and while it's a worst-case scenario, for many students, it becomes their reality (Wheeler, 2017).

Under President Barack Obama's administration in 2014, the U.S. Departments of Education and Justice released recommendations for educational leaders as guidance to assist schools in creating progressive practices and strategies to ensure equality in school discipline. If applied correctly, the purpose is to use alternative penalties for suspensions and expulsions, which do not remove students from classroom time, while simultaneously avoiding discriminating against specific racial and ethnic groups at a disproportionate rate.

The influence of school disciplinary actions has strong implications for students' entrance into the juvenile justice system (Fabelo et al., 2011). Previous literature that documents discriminatory practices in school disciplinary actions solely describes the levels of disparity. What is less clear is the context in which inequities in school discipline practices happen. Therefore, this chapter aims to examine racial disparity among the total population for each school district in Harris County in order to work towards school discipline equity.

OVERVIEW OF SCHOOL DISCIPLINE

The school discipline system is a permanent fixture of the educational system. School districts have different policies that modulate the discipline of their learning environments. However, there are five types of disciplinary actions that can be observed in most schools, if not all, of the schools in the United States. The first and most commonly used form of disciplinary action is *In-School Suspension* (Chen et al., 2021; Green et al., 2021). In-school suspension (ISS) is a form of disciplining students without removing them from the educational environment. Students undergoing in-school suspensions have limited privileges in the classroom and are often designated a study area away from their peers, so they may have a timeout and refocus on classwork. Some educational administrators posit that in-school suspension is infinitely better than the other forms of discipline because the student is able to rejoin the class without missing any education. According to the Kids Count Data Center, approximately 5% or more of the K-12 student population of the United States have received in-school suspensions since 2013. Our data shows that in at least one county in Texas, in-school suspensions account for the highest percentage of disciplinary actions.

The second most commonly used form of disciplinary action is *out-of-school suspension*. Out-of-school suspension (OSS) is defined as a temporary, complete exclusion from school and activities wherein a student is banned from being on school property. A typical out-of-school suspension lasts a few days, though it can range from a few hours to weeks long. This penalty is one of the most severe a school district can enforce and stops short only of expulsion or being completely kicked out. According to the National Center for Education Statistics, approximately five percent of the K-12 student population for the academic year 2013-2014 received out-of-school suspensions and Black students represented the highest percentage of this population. The data collected for this research also reflects what the existing literature (Pearman, 2021) states which is that Black students receive out-of-school suspensions at a significantly disproportionate rate to their peers.

The Juvenile Justice Alternative Education Program (JJAEP) and Disciplinary Alternative Education Program (DAEP) are alternative education programs designed to serve students that have committed specific grievances pursuant to Chapter 37 of the Texas Education Code. The *Juvenile Justice Alternative Education Program* (JJAEP) is a placement for some students who have been expelled from school for certain offenses such as bringing a firearm to school while the *Disciplinary Alternative Education Program* (DAEP) is an alternative education program for students who violate a district's Student Code of Conduct or certain other offenses such as a felony offense. These disciplinary actions are similar in scope and are utilized only in the event of severe infractions; therefore, as the data shows, the percentage of students that receive this disciplinary action is significantly lower than the sum percentage of in-school and out-of-school suspensions.

Expulsions is the last disciplinary action and it is the most severe. Expulsion, in this context, is defined as forcing someone to leave a school, university or organization. Due to the severity of this action, it is often used as a last resort. According to the National Center for Education Statistics, the number and percentage of school expulsions in the country and the state is below one percent of the K-12 student body population. Black students also represent the highest percentage of expulsions in the country.

Overview of Disparity in the Educational System

The demographic population of schools in the United States over the past few decades has evolved and become more diverse. Even so, according to the 2019 census, White students still represent the highest student population at fifty-two percent, Hispanics at twenty-four percent, Blacks at sixteen percent, Asians at six percent and the other minorities at three percent (U.S. Census Bureau, 2019). Given these student population demographics, it is logical and statistically sound to assume that the White students will represent the highest students suspended population but research shows that Black and Hispanic students often represent the highest percentage of students suspended or expelled (Owens & McLanahan, 2019). This supports the argument that students from minority communities are disciplined at a disproportionate rate to their White counterparts.

The purpose of schools as social institutions is to provide an environment that supports acquiring knowledge and socialization. Essential to the learning process is a space in which everyone feels a sense of safety; however, zero-tolerance policies neither maintain a level of security nor protection both teachers and students. These zero-tolerance policies only serve to exacerbate an already volatile social problem by taking away the only chance some students have of escaping a criminal lifestyle. Preserving order and school safety is integral to the educational system, juvenile justice system, and the mental well-being of children (Cornell & Mayer, 2010; Chen et al., 2021) but the removal of students from the educational environment is more apt to increase disruptive behavior rather than lessen it as evidenced by the percentage of students that receive multiple suspensions in an academic year. Past research shows that minority students are removed from the classroom at a disparate rate (Crenshaw et al., 2015; Rios & Vigil, 2017; Skiba et al., 2011; Skiba et al., 2014; Loveless, 2017) and they often represent the highest percentage of students with multiple suspensions. According to a report by the U.S. Department of Education Office for Civil Rights in 2014, in comparison to White students, Black students were three times more likely to receive an out-of-school suspension disciplinary action during the 2011-2012 academic school year. Those that are under the assumption that harsh school discipline policies are effective argue that minority students are removed from the classroom at a disproportionate rate simply due to misbehaving at a higher rate in comparison to their fellow classmates. However, this statement is inaccurate and not supported by empirical studies (Green et al., 2021; Skiba, 2013; Peguero & Shekarkhar, 2011).

The Impact of School Disciplinary Policies

Removal from the classroom setting is a disadvantage for students (Edwards, 2016). Students that are removed from the classroom are labeled as "at-risk" and as "problem" students who are disrupting the learning process of their fellow classmates. When a student is removed from the classroom due to a school disciplinary action, they experience short and long-term effects. Research has shown that students that are suspended or expelled have lower grades and test scores, a higher likelihood of being placed into special education classes, delayed academic progress, higher dropout rates, and an increase in the odds of arrest (Gregory et al., 2010; Mattison & Aber, 2007; Kupchik, 2016; Peguero et al., 2017; Mowen & Brent, 2016). The short-term impacts of school discipline resulting in the removal from the classroom can lead to a series of events that can follow students into their adulthood. Research shows that students who receive school discipline sanctions are more likely to drop out, which results in economic losses due to fewer opportunities for gainful employment (Marchbanks III et al., 2015). The outcomes of students that are removed from the classroom parallel those of the criminal justice system. The reentry process for students back into the classroom after their removal is met with several obstacles (Skiba et al., 2014; Kirk & Sampson, 2013). Even a few days away from the classroom might cause a student to fall behind in their studies. Students' relationships with their instructors and peers are also affected by suspensions and expulsions. Therefore, a reengagement plan should be put into place to ensure that the student is comfortable with their return back to the classroom.

Context of School Discipline Disparity (School-to-Prison Pipeline)

The majority of court-involved youth have experienced academic failure, school exclusion, and dropouts. Many school-based policies and practices worsen the risks for court involvement among Black male youth. School-level leadership, a dedicated staff, a school-wide behavior management system, and evidence-based academic instruction can help lessen the risks for youth delinquency and stymie the level of students of color being disciplined at harsher rates (Christle et al., 2005). Prior studies have determined that schools' unrestricted decisions to suspend, expel, and criminalize student misconduct contribute to student push-out and dropout rates (Fowler, 2011).

METHODOLOGY

Consistent with the suggestions in Nishioka (2017), we used data known to be accessible, accurate, and reliable. The data analyzed for this study came from two sources, The Texas Education Agency (TEA) and individual school districts within Harris County. The management of funding and oversight for the state's public education system is the responsibility of TEA. This study focused on the 2016-2017 academic school year. The dependent variable in this study is the type of school disciplinary sanction measured by the number of actions per category. There are five school disciplinary sanctions that school districts report to TEA: in-school suspensions, out-school suspensions, disciplinary alternative programs – Disciplinary Alternative Education Programs (DAEPs) and Juvenile Justice Alternative Education Programs (JJAEPs) (DAEP & JJAEP), and expulsions were analyzed. For the purposes of this study, DAEP, JJAEP, and expulsions were grouped together in one category. To get the percentage of all students that were suspended or removed from class in any capacity, the five disciplinary sanctions – ISS, OSS, DAEP, JJAEP and Expulsions were grouped together under the category 'total classroom removals'. DAEP, JJAEP, and expulsion actions marked as N/A in TEA's data indicated counts or percentages that were not available or masked. For the purpose of this study, N/A was counted as 0 actions. The independent variable in the study was race and ethnicity. Race and ethnicity was separated into seven different categories: American Indian or Alaskan, Asian, Black or African American, Hispanic/Latino, Native Hawaiian, Two or more races, and White. School district sizes were operationalized as the following: small up to 10,000 students, medium districts had an enrollment of 10,000-50,000 students, and large districts hand an enrollment of 50,000 or more students.

ANALYSIS METHODS

This chapter focused on the descriptions of relationships between two variables, for example, race and ethnicity and the type of school disciplinary action. For the purposes of this study, Black and Hispanics were the only two race and ethnicities compared to Whites due to the other ethnicities' frequencies being too small for analysis purposes. Descriptive statistics were calculated for all students by race and ethnicity from Kindergarten through 12th grade and by type of discipline administered. Refer to the Texas Compilation of School Discipline Law and Regulations (2021) regarding specific criteria regarding out-of-school suspensions for students that are in the grade level three or below.

Three different types of analysis methods were used in the study: absolute numbers and percentages, rates, and relative rate ratios. Due to rates failing to show whether or not disparity exists in each disciplinary action category across different groups, relative rate ratios were calculated. By calculating relative rate ratios, this study was able to answer questions regarding how the classroom removal rate among Black students compare with the classroom removal rate among White students, as well as provide additional context such as whether the rate is higher or lower (Nishioka, 2017; Boneshefski & Runge, 2014; Bollmer et al., 2007). Below explains the calculations for rates and relative rate ratios.

Rate (risk index) = Number of students in a specified disciplinary sanction category divided by Total number of students in the group and then multiplied by 100. For example, the number of Black students removed from the classroom due to ISS divided by total number of Black students and then multiplied by 100.

Relative Rate Ratio = Rate of students in a specified disciplinary sanctions category divided by Rate of students in the comparison group in the same disciplinary sanction. For example, rate of Black students removed from the classroom due to ISS divided by rate of White students removed from the classroom due to ISS.

In this study, rates were calculated for in-school suspensions and out-of-school suspensions. Disciplinary Alternative Education Programs (DAEPs), Juvenile Justice Alternative Education Programs (JJAEPs), and expulsion categories were first combined together, and then the relative rate was calculated. In this chapter, the formula used to calculate the relative rate ratio shows the between-group disparity with Black and Hispanic students being compared to White students. For the remainder of the chapter, the relative rate ratio is referred to as the disparity ratio. Due to using aggregate data, the disparity ratios reflect the number of students disciplined but do not distinguish between the number of occurrences per student. Simply stated, the data does not distinguish between students that may have had more than one disciplinary occurrence. It should also be noted that in some instances, the data indicated N/A for certain disciplinary sanctions, and in those instances, the information was coded as 0. Due to some districts having N/A or 0 occurrences, disparity ratios were not able to be calculated.

Harris County Independent School Districts

The study's sample contained 19 independent Harris County school districts, which consisted of Houston ISD, Cypress-Fairbanks (CyFair) ISD, Katy ISD, Aldine ISD, Pasadena ISD, Klein ISD, Alief ISD, Humble ISD, Spring ISD, Spring Branch ISD, Goose Creek ISD, Galena Park ISD, Tomball ISD, Deer Park ISD, Channel View ISD, Sheldon ISD, LaPorte, ISD Crosby ISD, and Huffman ISD. Katy ISD is a large school district that sits in three different counties; however, the majority of the school district is located in Harris County and therefore is included in this chapter for analysis. For the academic year 2016-2017, the 19 school districts enrolled approximately 818,251 students, representing approximately 16% of K–12 students in the state of Texas.

FINDINGS

Figure 1 illustrates the race and ethnicity of students in Texas and the 19 school districts in the county studied for the 2016-2017 academic school year. In the state of Texas, during the 2016-2017 academic school year, Hispanic students were the majority of the total student population at 52%. White students accounted for 28%, Black students 13%, and other students (Native Hawaiian/Other Pacific, American Indian or Alaska Native, Asian, and Two or More Races) accounted for approximately less than 7%.

Figures 2 and 3 ethnicities' frequencies were provided in order to provide context; however for additional figures, the other ethnicities' frequencies are too small for analysis purposes and were subsequently removed. Figure 2 shows for the 2016-2017 academic school year the percentage of the total population of all 19 Harris County Independent School Districts in comparison to the percentage of total classroom removal of students in the county by race and ethnicity. In Harris County, Black students represent 19% of the total student population; however, they account for 36% of total classroom removals.

Figure 1. Texas and Harris County's independent school districts' student demographics for the 2016-2017 academic school year

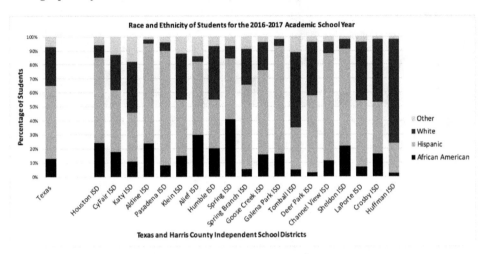

Figure 2. Percentage of total classroom removals for the Harris County independent school districts for the 2016-2017 academic school year

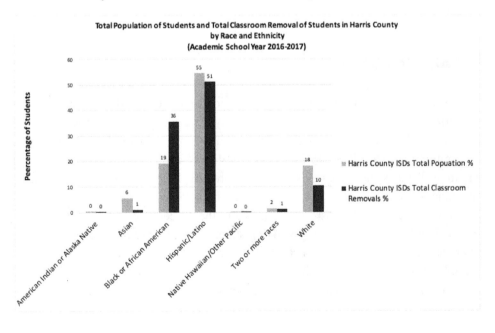

Figure 3. Disparity ratios comparing rates of each race and ethnic group with the rate of total removals rate of white students in Texas overall compared to Harris County independent school districts

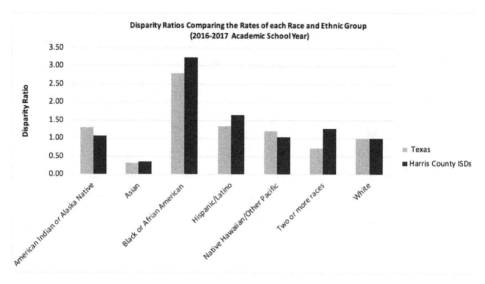

In order to examine in more detail classroom removals within the county, Figure 3 illustrates the disparity ratio for classroom removals for the 2016-2017 academic school year. Black students were almost three times more likely than White students to be removed from the classroom, which is more than the Texas ratio. The Texas disparity ratio is 2.74, and Harris County's ratio is 3.23.

TOTAL REMOVALS

This section of the chapter displays disparity ratios for the 2016-2017 academic school year for total classroom removals in the county. As mentioned in the methodology section, for the purpose of this chapter, total classroom removals were determined by grouping together ISS, OSS, DAEP, JJAEP, and expulsions into one category. Figure 4 displays the disparity ratio of total removals by race and ethnicity from the county's six largest school districts. The bars represent the disparity ratio of the percentage of total classroom removals to the percentage of the student body. For each of the 19 school districts, Black students were more likely to be removed from the classroom at a disproportionate rate. As shown in Figure 4, out of the large school districts, Black students in Houston, Katy, and Klein ISDs surpassed the Texas disparity ratio of 2.74. In Houston ISD, Black students were almost five times more

Figure 4. Disparity Ratios comparing the rates of Black and Hispanic students with the rate of total classroom removals among white students for large Harris County independent school districts

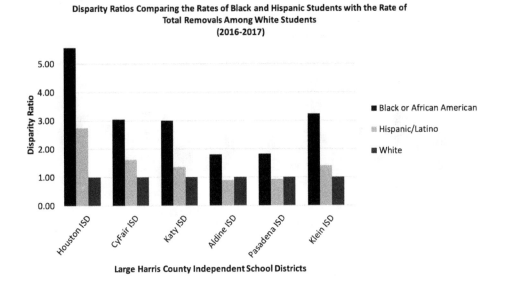

likely to be removed from the classroom in comparison to White students, with a disparity ratio of 5.56.

Figure 5 represents eight medium-sized school districts. Within the five medium districts, Black students in Humble, Spring, Spring Branch, and Deer Park ISDs surpassed the Texas disparity ratio. Humble and Spring Branch had the highest levels of disparity ratios for Black students at 4.20 and 4.51; the disparity ratio for the state of Texas is 2.74.

Figure 6 shows the five smallest school districts in the county. Black students' disparity ratios in all five small school districts were below the Texas 2016-2017 disparity ratio; however, Black students were still removed from the classroom at higher rates in comparison to White students.

IN-SCHOOL SUSPENSIONS

This section of the chapter displays disparity ratios for the 2016-2017 academic school year for in-school suspensions (ISS) in the county. Similar to the prior section, schools were categorized into three categories based on the school student body population size. Figure 7 shows a breakdown of large county School districts. Black

Figure 5. Disparity ratios comparing the rates of Black and Hispanic students with the rate of total classroom removals among white students for medium Harris County independent school districts

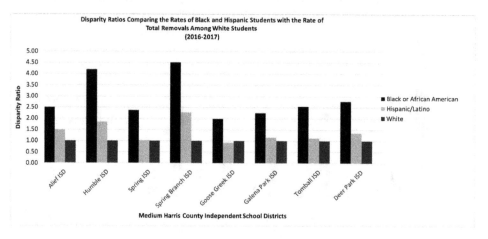

Figure 6. Disparity ratios comparing the rates of Black and Hispanic students with the rate of total classroom removals among white students for small Harris County independent school districts

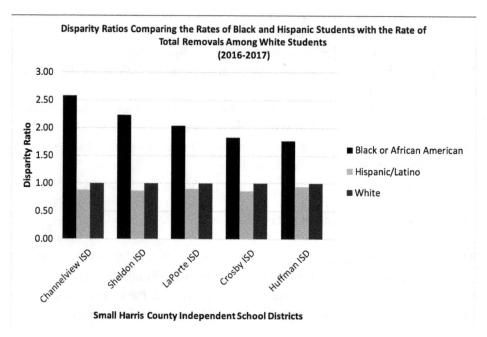

Figure 7. Disparity ratios comparing the rates of Black and Hispanic students with the rate of in-school suspensions among white students for large Harris County independent school districts

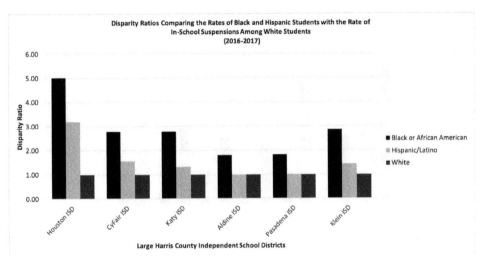

students were impacted at a disproportionate rate in comparison to White students in each large school district. Additionally, Black students in three of the six large districts' disparity ratios were above the Texas disparity ratio for Black students at 2.22; Houston ISD had the highest disparity ratio at 5.00.

Figure 8 illustrates in-school suspensions of medium-sized schools in the county. Consistent with large school districts, Black students were impacted at a disparate rate for ISS sanctions also. The disparity ratios for Black students in Humble, Spring Branch, Tomball, and Deer Park ISDs were all above the Texas ratio of 2.22. In Humble ISD, Black students had the highest disparity ratio and were over four times more likely, in comparison to White students, to receive ISS disciplinary action.

There are five school districts in the county that have a student body population of less than 10,000. Channelview ISD was the only small district whose disparity ratio for Black students was above the Texas ratio. Figure 9 shows the ratio of In-School Suspensions of students by race and ethnicity. Black students' ISS disparity ratio was lower than the Texas ratio of 2.22 in each of the small districts; however, Black students were still more likely to receive in-school suspension in comparison to White and Hispanic students.

Figure 8. Disparity ratios comparing the rates of Black and Hispanic students with the rate of in-school suspensions among white students for medium Harris County independent school districts

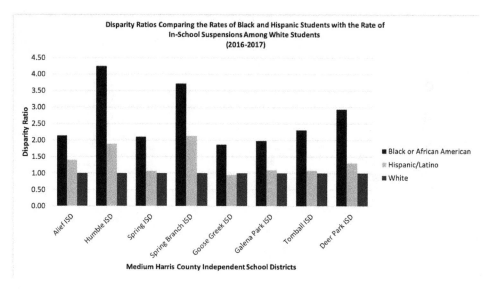

Figure 9. Disparity ratios comparing the rates of Black and Hispanic students with the rate of in-school suspensions among white students for small Harris County independent school districts

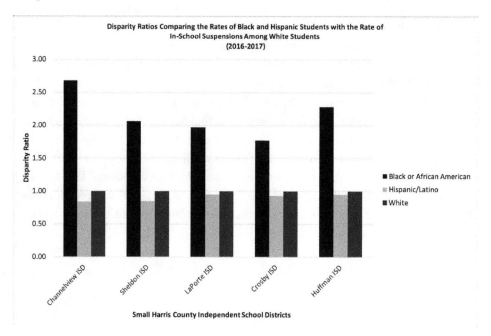

Figure 10. Disparity ratios comparing the rates of Black and Hispanic students with the rate of out-of-school suspensions among white students for large Harris County independent school districts

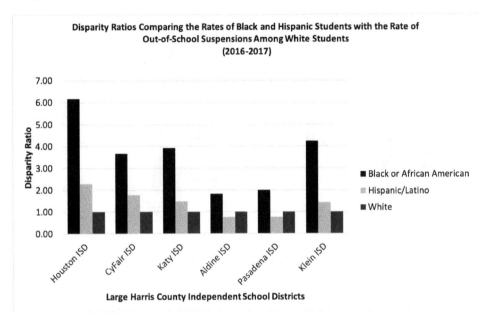

OUT-OF-SCHOOL SUSPENSIONS

Although out-of-school suspensions cannot exceed three days, this is a significant amount of time for a student to be removed from the classroom, which can hinder their learning experience. The following section of this chapter shows the disparity ratio for the 2016-2017 academic school year for out-of-school suspensions (OSS) in the county. Figure 10 illustrates the disparity ratio of OSS for large school districts, and Black students in all six districts received OSS sanctions at a disparate rate. Out of the six large school districts, Houston ISD was the only one above the Texas disparity ratio of 4.49. Black students in Houston ISD were more than six times more likely to receive out-of-school suspension. The Katy ISD disparity ratio was 3.92, and Klein ISD was 4.24.

Figure 11 shows the disparity ratios for eight of the medium-sized school districts in the county. For each medium school district, Black students were more likely to receive out-of-school suspensions in comparison to White students. Humble and Spring Branch ISDs had an alarming OSS disparity ratio for Black students at rates of 5.38 and 6.28, respectively.

Figure 11. Disparity ratios comparing the rates of Black and Hispanic students with the rate of out-of-school suspensions among white students for medium Harris County independent school districts

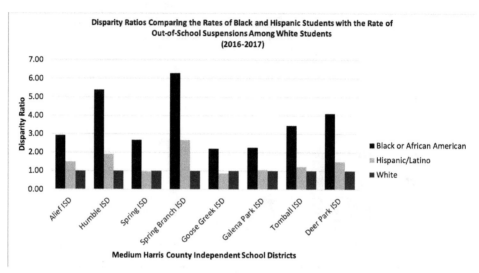

Figure 12 illustrates OSS disciplinary sanctions for school districts in the county with a population of less than 10,000 students. For small school districts, the disparity ratio for Black students for each of the schools was under the Texas ratio of 4.49; however, in four of the five districts, Black students were still more likely than their White counterparts to receive out-of-school suspensions. Huffman ISD has a very small population of Black students and did not indicate any disparity in OSS sanctions.

DISCIPLINARY ALTERNATIVE EDUCATION PROGRAMS (DAEPS), JUVENILE JUSTICE ALTERNATIVE EDUCATION PROGRAMS (JJAEPS), AND EXPULSIONS

After observing ISS and OSS removals, a pattern was also observed for Disciplinary Alternative Education Programs (DAEPs), Juvenile Justice Alternative Education Programs (JJAEPs), and expulsions. The Juvenile Justice Alternative Education Program (JJAEP) and Disciplinary Alternative Education Program (DAEP) are alternative education programs designed to serve students that have committed specific grievances pursuant to Chapter 37 of the Texas Education Code. The *Juvenile Justice Alternative Education Program* (JJAEP) is a placement for some students who have been expelled from school for certain offenses such as bringing

Figure 12. Disparity ratios comparing the rates of Black and Hispanic students with the rate of out-of-school suspensions among white students for small Harris County independent school districts

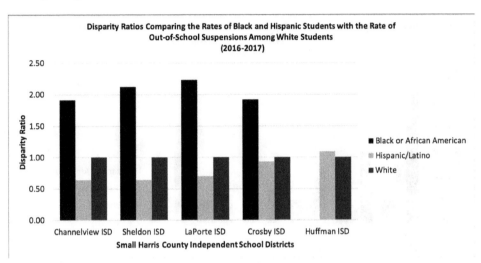

a firearm to school while the *Disciplinary Alternative Education Program* (DAEP) is an alternative education program for students who violate a district's Student Code of Conduct or certain other offenses such as a felony offense. Expulsion is the nuclear disciplinary sanction and the most severe because it results in the removal of a student from the school and its premises. These disciplinary actions are similar in scope and are utilized only in the event of severe infractions.

This section of the chapter displays the disparity ratio for the 2016-2017 academic school year for DAEPs, JJAEPs, and expulsions in the county. Due to the small representation of students under the disciplinary sanctions – Disciplinary Alternative Education Programs (DAEPs), Juvenile Justice Alternative Education Programs (JJAEPs), and expulsions – we grouped all three sanctions together. Similar to the prior sections, schools were categorized into three categories based on the school student body population size. Black students were disproportionately impacted by expulsions and placement into DAEP and JJAEP programs. Figure 13 depicts the disparity ratio for large school districts, and Houston and Klein ISDs had the highest disparity ratios; in the largest school district, Houston ISD, Black students were over five and half times more likely to receive DAEP, JJAEP, or expulsion sanction. CyFair and Klein ISDs disparity ratios for Black students were both above the Texas ratio of 2.54 at 3.08 and 3.01, respectively.

Figure 14 shows the disparity ratios for the 2016-2017 academic school year of DAEP/JJAEP/Expulsions to the student body by race and ethnicity. For the medium

Figure 13. Disparity ratios comparing the rates of Black and Hispanic students with the rate of DAEP/JJAEP/Expulsions among white students for large Harris County independent school districts

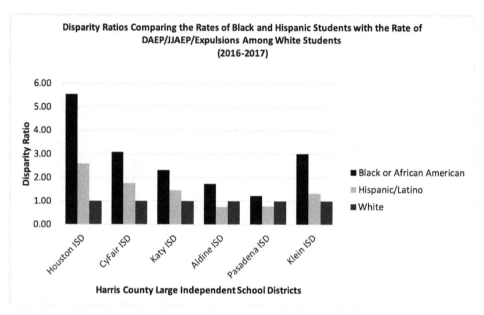

school districts group, Galena Park and Spring Branch ISDs had the highest disparity ratio for Black students at 4.03 and 5.89, respectively, in comparison to White students. Four of the eight medium school districts' disparity ratios for Black students receiving Disciplinary Alternative Education Programs (DAEPs), Juvenile Justice Alternative Education Programs (JJAEPs), or expulsions as disciplinary sanctions were above the Texas disparity ratio of 2.54 for Black students.

As shown in Figure 15, one out of the five small districts indicated Black students were placed into alternative programs or expelled at a disparate rate in comparison to White students. Channelview and Huffman ISDs did not reveal disparity for Black students.

Research has shown teacher demographics impacts school discipline; therefore figure 16 illustrates the race and ethnicity of teachers in Texas and the 19 school districts in Harris Couny. Throughout the state of Texas and Harris County, the majority of K-12 students are minorities.

Figure 14. disparity ratios comparing the rates of Black and Hispanic students with the rate of DAEP/JJAEP/Expulsions among white students for medium Harris County independent school districts

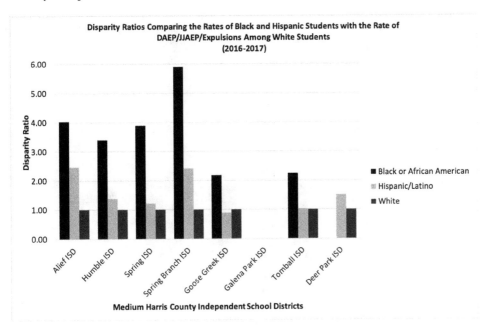

DISCUSSION

This research yielded findings consistent with the statement that Black students are disciplined at a disparate rate. During the 2016-2017 academic school year, Black students were over three times more likely to be removed from the classroom in comparison to White students. Out of 918, 449 students in public schools during the 2016-2017 academic school year, 145,175 (16%) students were removed from the classroom. Although Black students accounted for 19% of the total student population, they represented 36% of classroom removals. Based on disparity ratios for the 2016-2017 academic school year, Black students were disproportionately more likely to be removed from the classroom for disciplinary reasons. For each school size (small, medium, and large), Black students were more likely to be removed from the classroom in comparison to their White classmates. Black students were more likely to receive in-school suspension in each school district. Eleven out of 19 school districts' 2016-2017 disparity ratio for Black students receiving in-school suspension was above the Texas ratio.

For the strictest categories of school disciplinary sanctions, Disciplinary Alternative Education Programs (DAEP), Juvenile Justice Alternative Education

Figure 15. Disparity ratios comparing the rates of Black and Hispanic students with the rate of DAEP/JJAEP/expulsions among white students for small Harris County independent school districts

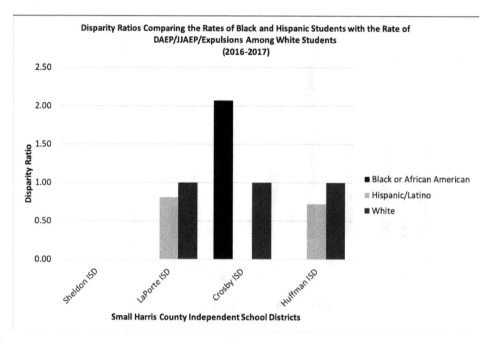

Figure 16. Texas and Harris County independent school district race and ethnicity of teachers (2017)

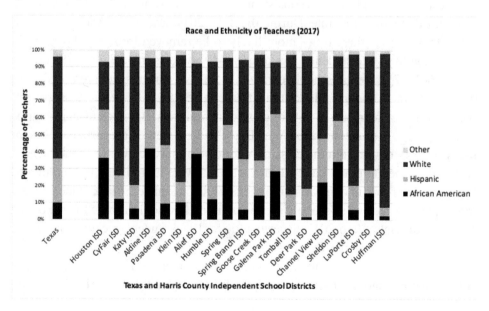

Programs (JJAEP), and expulsions, Black students were impacted at a disparate rate. The largest school district reflected the highest 2016-2017 disparity ratio at 5.52. There is a lack of diversity in educators in school districts. The majority of K-12 students are from minority communities; however, the majority of teachers are White. Black students were impacted by school discipline sanctions at a disproportionate rate; however, further analysis of individual campus level characteristics is needed in order to fully answer the question of why. Aggregate school, district-level information, is available on Texas Education Agency's website; however, there is minimal accessible individual campus-level data.

RECOMMENDATIONS

Recommendation 1

Disaggregate Data Analysis

In order to acquire a better understanding of which variables have a relationship with inequitable disciplinary trends and provide effective recommendations countywide, disaggregate data analysis is necessary. Consistent with the model created by Osher et al. (2015), this chapter is an example of the first step in the model, which is examining available data in order to determine if the administration of school discipline disparities exists in the county. Our findings showed that racial disparity is persistent throughout each district in the county, with Black students being impacted at a disproportionate rate. While using data that was accessible for our key findings, we realized additional information was needed for future studies.

Data provided on TEA's website reports the number of disciplinary actions per student group. For the purposes of this study, this chapter used the number of students in each school discipline category per student group. However, the data does not distinguish between which students may have been suspended multiple times. Since TEA is responsible for compiling school disciplinary information from each school, our recommendation is that TEA requires each school within each district to provide disaggregated discipline information based on race and ethnicity, gender, and grade level.

Example: North Carolina

The State of North Carolina school discipline data includes information regarding multiple suspensions per student.

https://www.dpi.nc.gov/media/14171/open

Recommendation 2

Focus on Implementing, Adapting, and Evaluating Evidence-Based Interventions to Decrease Classroom Removals

Within the state of Texas, there have been some schools that have taken a proactive approach to address racial disparity. In order to determine what works and what does not work, it is essential to review current policies and evaluate programs. The evaluation of programs will provide insight into what measures have been taken to ensure equitable school discipline practices and whether or not the implementation of certain programs has been effective. In situations in which evidence-based interventions do not exist, an interdisciplinary and collaborative approach involving educators, community partners, and researchers should work together to develop and implement new interventions with clearly defined measurable outcomes (Rathvon, 2008).

Recommendation 3

Cultural Awareness Training

In addition to evidence-based interventions, the management of classrooms should take into consideration that each student learns differently. The acquiring of knowledge needs to consist of classrooms that encourage a safe place to learn while recognizing the diversity of students and their learning capabilities (Rathvon, 2008). For example, organize short training sessions on topics about diversity and cultural competence. The training sessions should be in-depth and require a hands-on approach. The purpose of the training sessions is for individuals to obtain knowledge about their own biases, discuss them, and provide tools and methods to reduce racial and ethnic disparities.

Recommendation 4

Positive Behavioral Interventions and Supports

As an alternative to suspension or school removal, one plan that has gained traction is the use of Positive Behavioral Interventions and Supports (PBIS). Positive Behavioral Interventions and Supports is the application of using evidence-based prevention strategies along with a layered scale of measures and outcomes that supports the academic, emotional, social, and behavioral needs of a student in order for said students to succeed (Garbacz et al., 2016). The effects tend to work among children who are exposed to PBIS in Kindergarten. There is evidence-based support that there is a reduction in behavior problems and improvements in positive behavior and successful emotion regulation after training in PBIS. The PBIS framework is a hopeful approach for reducing problems and promoting correction among elementary school children (Bradshaw & Waasdorp, 2012).

Recommendation 5

Professional Development and Support for Teachers

Teachers are the gatekeepers for students and have broad discretion as to which students they recommend need removal from the classroom. Therefore, school districts need to ask themselves if they are supporting their teachers as much as possible? Are they giving them essential tools to ensure they are able to manage their classrooms without the last result of removing a student from the classroom? Providing professional development for teachers can assist in improving their academic instruction model and lessen the suspension rate through positive behavioral interventions. There is growing acknowledgment that young children's social ability is important since it is positively connected with their school readiness and educational success. However, professional development opportunities for teachers to augment their role in promoting these students are limited (Han, 2014). Programs such as REACH, an intervention-designed program used to grow the capacity of early childhood teachers to support children's social and emotional development, have shown great promise (Conners-Burrow et al., 2017). Research shows that effective classroom management and building trust between teachers and adolescents resulted in improved outcomes (Skiba, 2008). This suggests that providing better funding and training for teachers could help lessen suspension rates. Negative behaviors that violate school policies are based on juvenile development; therefore, teachers may need specialized training in this particular area. Programs such as The My Teaching Partner-Secondary (MTP-S), which focus on teacher-student interactions in a sustained manner using a rigorous approach, can reduce the disparate use of exclusionary discipline with African American students. Findings per districts that used MTP-S show policymakers a direction to identify different types of professional development programs that have promise for decreasing the racial discipline gap (Gregory et al., 2014).

Recommendation 6

Community-School Partnerships

Community-School partnerships allow schools to provide a wide-ranging support structure to help students succeed instead of interrupting their learning process with suspensions. Working in tandem to combine resources to support children in an all-inclusive learning environment can help guarantee positive academic and non-academic success. Schools are the foundation of many communities, linking students with much-needed means and encouragement. Schools that follow these enterprises, such as the YMCA, have been fruitful in increasing family engagement and cultivating student learning, increasing better attendance, better behavior and development as well (Owen et al., 2015). These partnerships create a sort of "connected science" in which real-world problems are used as contextual scaffolds for bridging students' community-based knowledge and school evidence-based knowledge as a way to provide opportunities for meaningful and intellectual challenges for students (Bouillion & Gomez, 2001). Partnerships between school staff, faculty, families, and communities are vital for establishing success for all students (Haines et al., 2015).

Recommendation 7

Restorative Justice

About forty years ago, criminal justice academics and activists in North America and Europe began studying justice across different cultures and studying the viewpoints of perpetrators. "Eye for an eye" justice may be an established part of Western society, yet it's not true to be that way in all cultures. Many communities put compromise above revenge. Inspired by this awareness, restorative justice was born. Behavioral science alludes to the many advantages of this methodology. Suspension rates for students of color are far higher than for White students, even in schools that apply alternatives to suspension, such as restorative justice practices. Even with people's hearts being in the right place, there is still a disconnect (Lustick, 2017). Yes, punishment is necessary at times, and reckless or negative actions should have consequences; however, the disciplinary action should fit the act. In criminal justice, experts generally recognize that people convicted of crimes have a probability of going back to jail or prison, which is referred to as recidivism and the revolving criminal justice door. Restorative justice, on the other hand, emphasizes working within the community, giving empathy, and perspective-talking. This, in turn, can account for some of the deficiencies of outdated punitive actions (Yuhas, 2018). Restorative justice practices may produce benefits for students, but they may result in only minimal lessening of the inequalities in suspension rates between Black and White students. What this shows is that greater attention is needed to address the unbalanced school contexts in which disparities come from (Gregory et al., 2018).

CONCLUSION

This chapter puts forth empirically justified solutions for rethinking school discipline in the Twenty-First Century and conceptualizes the ideal components of a fair system of punishments and rewards, most notably by disaggregating data, focusing on implementing, adapting, and evaluating evidence-based interventions, putting forth cultural awareness trainings, along with police behavioral interventions and supports, professional development for teachers, community-school partnerships, and restorative justice. To maximize the effect of our recommendations, they must not be viewed as mutually exclusive. However, a more nuanced strategic plan outlining precisely what is necessary to persuade policymakers and key stakeholders to adopt a twenty-first-century discipline plan, as it should be, including an understanding of our proposed plan's implications. Doing so has been shown to significantly decrease disparities in school suspensions and intentionally divorce the school's pipeline to prison.

Although we discussed the demographics of teachers in Texas and in the 19 school districts in comparison to students, future research needs to look at individual districts in order to determine the impact of teacher demographics on school discipline throughout Harris County. Despite our contributions, we were limited by our access to data. Therefore, we had no ability to examine any of the environmental factors that may have increased the likelihood of a student being disciplined. Though doing so would create a nightmarish interaction with a university's institutional review board, the benefits of doing so far outweigh the researcher's frustration with the process.

The Center for Justice Research will continue research in order to ask several unanswered questions about school discipline sanctions in Houston area schools to work towards fairness in the public school districts. Determining the causes for excessive use of harsh school discipline sanctions can assist with decreasing the funneling of students into the school-to-prison pipeline. Black students across Harris County are removed from the classroom at higher rates than their fellow classmates, which is the trend statewide and nationally. Several national policymakers have expressed the need for education reform; however, each school district at the local level has a responsibility to examine what is happening inside their districts, campus by campus. Although our analysis is ongoing, we feel comfortable saying that the Harris County schools need an action plan to address racial disparity.

REFERENCES

Bollmer, J., Bethel, J., Garrison-Mogren, R., & Brauen, M. (2007). Using the risk ratio to assess racial/ethnic disproportionality in special education at the school-district level. *The Journal of Special Education, 41*(3), 186–198. doi:10.1177/002 24669070410030401

Boneshefski, M. J., & Runge, T. J. (2014). Addressing disproportionate discipline practices within a school-wide positive behavioral interventions and supports framework: A practical guide for calculating and using disproportionality rates. *Journal of Positive Behavior Interventions, 16*(3), 149–158. doi:10.1177/1098300713484064

Bouillion, L. M., & Gomez, L. M. (2001). Connecting school and community with science learning: Real world problems and school–community partnerships as contextual scaffolds. *Journal of Research in Science Teaching: The Official Journal of the National Association for Research in Science Teaching, 38*(8), 878–898. doi:10.1002/tea.1037

Bradshaw, C. P., Waasdorp, T. E., & Leaf, P. J. (2012). Effects of school-wide positive behavioral interventions and supports on child behavior problems. *Pediatrics, 130*(5), e1136–e1145. doi:10.1542/peds.2012-0243 PMID:23071207

Chen, E., Brody, G. H., Yu, T., Hoffer, L. C., Russak-Pribble, A., & Miller, G. E. (2021). Disproportionate School Punishment and Significant Life Outcomes: A Prospective Analysis of Black Youths. *Psychological Science, 32*(9), 1375–1390. doi:10.1177/0956797621998308 PMID:34387518

Conners-Burrow, N. A., Patrick, T., Kyzer, A., & McKelvey, L. (2017). A preliminary evaluation of REACH: Training early childhood teachers to support children's social and emotional development. *Early Childhood Education Journal, 45*(2), 187–199. doi:10.100710643-016-0781-2

Cornell, D. G., & Mayer, M. J. (2010). Why do school order and safety matter? *Educational Researcher, 39*(1), 7–15. doi:10.3102/0013189X09357616

Crenshaw, K., Ocen, P., & Nanda, J. (2015). *Black girls matter: Pushed out, overpoliced, and underprotected.* Center for Intersectionality and Social Policy Studies, Columbia University.

Christle, C. A., Jolivette, K., & Nelson, C. M. (2005, January 01). Breaking the School to Prison Pipeline: Identifying School Risk and Protective Factors for Youth Delinquency. *Exceptionality, 13*(2), 69–88. doi:10.120715327035ex1302_2

Curran, F. C. (2019). The law, policy, and portrayal of zero tolerance school discipline: Examining prevalence and characteristics across levels of governance and school districts. *Educational Policy, 33*(2), 319–349. doi:10.1177/0895904817691840

Duffy, H. J. (2018). School Racial Composition and Discipline. Rice University's Kinder Institute for Urban Research. *Research Brief for the Houston Independent School District, 6*(4).

Edwards, L. (2016). Homogeneity and inequality: School discipline inequality and the role of racial composition. *Social Forces, 95*(1), 55–76. doi:10.1093fow038

Fabelo, T., Thompson, M. D., Plotkin, M., Carmichael, D., Marchbanks, M. P., & Booth, E. A. (2011). *Breaking schools' rules: A statewide study of how school discipline relates to students' success and juvenile justice involvement.* Council of State Governments Justice Center.

Fenning, P., & Jenkins, K. (2018). Racial and Ethnic Disparities in Exclusionary School Discipline: Implications for Administrators Leading Discipline Reform Efforts. *NASSP Bulletin, 102*(4), 291–302. doi:10.1177/0192636518812699

Fowler, D. (2011, October 1). School Discipline Feeds the "Pipeline to Prison". *Phi Delta Kappan, 93*(2), 14–19. doi:10.1177/003172171109300204

Garbacz, S. A., McIntosh, K., Eagle, J. W., Dowd-Eagle, S. E., Hirano, K. A., & Ruppert, T. (2016). Family engagement within school wide positive behavioral interventions and supports. *Preventing School Failure, 60*(1), 60–69. doi:10.1080/1045988X.2014.976809

González, T. (2015). *Socializing schools: Addressing racial disparities in discipline through restorative justice.* Academic Press.

Green, A. L., Hatton, H., Stegenga, S. M., Eliason, B., & Nese, R. N. T. (2021). Examining Commitment to Prevention, Equity, and Meaningful Engagement: A Review of School District Discipline Policies. *Journal of Positive Behavior Interventions, 23*(3), 137–148. doi:10.1177/1098300720951940

Gregory, A., Allen, J. P., Mikami, A. Y., Hafen, C. A., & Pianta, R. C. (2014). The promise of a teacher professional development program in reducing racial disparity in classroom exclusionary discipline. *Closing the school discipline gap: Equitable remedies for excessive exclusion*, 166-179.

Gregory, A., Huang, F. L., Anyon, Y., Greer, E., & Downing, B. (2018). An examination of restorative interventions and racial equity in out-of-school suspensions. *School Psychology Review, 47*(2), 167–182. doi:10.17105/SPR-2017-0073.V47-2

Gregory, A., Skiba, R. J., & Noguera, P. A. (2010). The achievement gap and the discipline gap: Two sides of the same coin? *Educational Researcher, 39*(1), 59–68. doi:10.3102/0013189X09357621

Hackett, A. (2018). *Black Students Are Disproportionately Disciplined in Public Schools*. Retrieved from https://psmag.com/education/Black-students-are-disproportionately-disciplined-in-public-schools

Haines, S. J., Gross, J. M., Blue-Banning, M., Francis, G. L., & Turnbull, A. P. (2015). Fostering family– school and community–school partnerships in inclusive schools: Using practice as a guide. *Research and Practice for Persons with Severe Disabilities, 40*(3), 227–239. doi:10.1177/1540796915594141

Han, H. S. (2014). Supporting early childhood teachers to promote children's social competence: Components for best professional development practices. *Early Childhood Education Journal, 42*(3), 171–179. doi:10.100710643-013-0584-7

Kirk, D. S., & Sampson, R. J. (2013). Juvenile arrest and collateral educational damage in the transition to adulthood. *Sociology of Education, 86*(1), 36–62. doi:10.1177/0038040712448862 PMID:25309003

Kupchik, A. (2016). *The real school safety problem: The long-term consequences of harsh school punishment.* Univ of California Press. doi:10.1525/california/9780520284197.001.0001

Losen, D., & Whitaker, A. (2018). *Eleven million days lost: Race, discipline, and safety at U. S Public Schools.* ACLU.

Loveless, T. (2017). How well are American students learning? With sections on the latest international test scores, foreign exchange students, and school suspensions. *The 2017 Brown Center Report on Education, 3*(6).

Lustick, H. (2017). "Restorative Justice" or Restoring Order? Restorative School Discipline Practices in Urban Public Schools. *Urban Education.*

Marchbanks III, M. P., Blake, J. J., Booth, E. A., Carmichael, D., Seibert, A. L., & Fabelo, T. (2015). The economic effects of exclusionary discipline on grade retention and high school dropout. *Closing the school discipline gap: Equitable remedies for excessive exclusion,* 59-74.

Mattison, E., & Aber, M. S. (2007). Closing the achievement gap: The association of racial climate with achievement and behavioral outcomes. *American Journal of Community Psychology, 40*(1-2), 1–12. doi:10.100710464-007-9128-x PMID:17587175

Mowen, T., & Brent, J. (2016). School discipline as a turning point: The cumulative effect of suspension on arrest. *Journal of Research in Crime and Delinquency, 53*(5), 628–653. doi:10.1177/0022427816643135

Na, C., & Gottfredson, D. C. (2013). Police officers in schools: Effects on school crime and the processing of offending behaviors. *Justice Quarterly, 30*(4), 619–650. doi:10.1080/07418825.2011.615754

Nance, J. P. (2015). Students, police, and the school-to-prison pipeline. *Wash. UL Rev., 93*, 919.

Nishioka, V. (2017). *School Discipline Data Indicators: A Guide for Districts and Schools. REL 2017-240*. Regional Educational Laboratory Northwest.

Sugai, G., Horner, R. H., Dunlap, G., Hieneman, M., Lewis, T. J., Nelson, C. M., Scott, T., Liaupsin, C., Sailor, W., Turnbull, A. P., Turnbull, H. R. III, Wickham, D., Wilcox, B., & Ruef, M. OSEP Center on Positive Behavioral Interventions. (2000). Applying positive behavior support and functional behavioral assessment in schools. *Journal of Positive Behavior Interventions, 2*(3), 131–143. doi:10.1177/109830070000200302

Osher, D., Fisher, D., Amos, L., Katz, J., Dwyer, K., Duffey, T., & Colombi, G. D. (2015). Addressing the root causes of disparities in school discipline: An educator's action planning guide. Washington, DC: National Center on Safe Supportive Learning Environments (Support and Collaboration with U.S. Department of Education).

Owen, J., Wettach, J., & Hoffman, K. C. (2015). *Instead of suspension: Alternative strategies for effective school discipline*. Duke Center for Child and Family Policy and Duke Law School.

Owens, J., & McLanahan, S. (2019). Unpacking the Drivers of Racial Disparities in School Suspension and Expulsion. *Social Forces, 98*(4), 1548–1577. doi:10.1093foz095 PMID:34017149

Pearman, F. II. (2021). Gentrified Discipline: The Impact of Gentrification on Exclusionary Punishment in Public Schools. *Social Problems*, spab028. Advance online publication. doi:10.1093ocpropab028

Peguero, A. A., Bondy, J. M., & Shekarkhar, Z. (2017). Punishing latina/o youth: School justice, fairness, order, dropping out, and gender disparities. *Hispanic Journal of Behavioral Sciences, 39*(1), 98–125. doi:10.1177/0739986316679633

Peguero, A. A., & Shekarkhar, Z. (2011). Latino/a student misbehavior and school punishment. *Hispanic Journal of Behavioral Sciences, 33*(1), 54–70. doi:10.1177/0739986310388021

Rathvon, N. (2008). *Effective school interventions: Evidence-based strategies for improving student outcomes.* Guilford Press.

Rios, V. M., & Vigil, J. D. (2017). *Human targets: Schools, police, and the criminalization of Latino youth.* University of Chicago Press. doi:10.7208/chicago/9780226091044.001.0001

Sheldon, S. B. (2007). Improving student attendance with school, family, and community partnerships. *The Journal of Educational Research, 100*(5), 267–275. doi:10.3200/JOER.100.5.267-275

Skiba, R. J., & Knesting, K. (2001). Zero tolerance, zero evidence: An analysis of school disciplinary practice. *New Directions for Youth Development, 2001*(92), 17–43. doi:10.1002/yd.23320019204 PMID:12170829

Skiba, R. J., Reynolds, C. R., Graham, S., Sheras, P., Conoley, J. C., & Garcia Vazquez, E. (2006). *Are zero tolerance policies effective in the schools? An evidentiary review and recommendations.* A Report by the American Psychological Associate Zero Tolerance Task Force.

Skiba, R., & Sprague, J. (2008). Without suspensions. *Educational Leadership, 66*(1), 38–43.

Skiba, R. J., Horner, R. H., Chung, C. G., Rausch, M. K., May, S. L., & Tobin, T. (2011). Race is not neutral: A national investigation of African American and Latino disproportionality in school discipline. *School Psychology Review, 40*(1), 85–108.

Skiba, R. J. (2013). Reaching a critical juncture for our kids: The need to reassess school-justice practices. *Family Court Review, 51*(3), 380–387. doi:10.1111/fcre.12034

Skiba, R. J., Arredondo, M. I., & Williams, N. T. (2014). More than a metaphor: The contribution of exclusionary discipline to a school-to-prison pipeline. *Equity & Excellence in Education, 47*(4), 546–564. doi:10.1080/10665684.2014.958965

Texas Compilation of School Discipline Law and Regulations. (2021). Retrieved from: https://safesupportivelearning.ed.gov/sites/default/files/discipline-compendium/Texas%20School%20Discipline%20Laws%20and%20Regulations.pdf

Texas Education Agency. (2018). *District Type Glossary of Terms.* Retrieved from: https://tea.texas.gov/reports-and-data/school-data/district-type-data-search/district-type-glossary-of-terms-2018-19

Tomar, D. A. (2018). *Cops in Schools: Have we built a school-to-prison pipeline.* The Best Schools.

Yuhas, D. (2018). *Restorative justice is about more than just reducing suspensions. The Hechinger Report.*

Varela, K. S., Peguero, A. A., Eason, J. M., Marchbanks, M. P. T. III, & Blake, J. (2018). School strictness and education: Investigating racial and ethnic educational inequalities associated with being pushed out. *Sociology of Race and Ethnicity (Thousand Oaks, Calif.)*, 4(2), 261–280. doi:10.1177/2332649217730086

U.S. Department of Education Office for Civil Rights. (2014). *Civil Rights Data Collection. Data Snap Shot: School Discipline. Brief No. 1.* Author.

U.S. Census Bureau. (2019). *Census Bureau Reports Nearly 77 Million Students Enrolled in U.S. Schools.* Retrieved from https://www.census.gov/newsroom/press-releases/2019/school-enrollment.html

Wheeler, R. (2017). *Suspensions Don't Teach.* Retrieved from https://www.edutopia.org/article/suspensions-dont-teach

Whitaker, A., Torres-Guillen, S., Morton, M., Jordan, H., Coyle, S., Mann, A., & Wei-Ling, S. (2019). *Cops and no counselors: How the lack of school mental health is harming students.* American Civil Liberties Union.

Chapter 6
Separate and Still Unequal:
An Analysis of School Discipline

Melissa F. Kwende
Texas Southern University, USA

Jennifer Wyatt Bourgeois
Texas Southern University, USA

Howard Henderson
Texas Southern University, USA

Julian Scott
Texas Southern University, USA

ABSTRACT

This chapter will examine the disproportionate rate of minority school suspensions relative to race/ethnicity, gender, socioeconomic status, grade level, and school population size. Although Black students account for 20% of the school population for this chapter's study, the rate of in-school discipline for Black students far exceeded the rates for White and Hispanic students. Notably, the authors find that race, gender, socioeconomic status, and grade level are correlated with the disproportionate disciplinary practices imposed upon minority students regardless of grade level. In this chapter, the authors review the previous research on race, gender, poverty, grade level, and school discipline before laying out their methodological approach for understanding suspension disparities. After analysis, they conclude with recommendations for improvement.

DOI: 10.4018/978-1-6684-3359-1.ch006

ZERO TOLERANCE POLICIES AND SCHOOL SUSPENSIONS

Prior research highlights the ineffectiveness of zero-tolerance school disciplinary policies (Cramer et al., 2014; Noguera, 2010). These policies - established to create safer learning environments for all students - have negatively and disproportionately impacted students of color, the economically disadvantaged, and those classified for special education. This is evidenced by the over-representation of Black, poor, and developmentally challenged students disciplined within schools. School-based zero-tolerance policies were originally derived from federal drug policies designed to deter drug trafficking through immediate, harsh, and legally mandated punishments and initially focused on weapons and substance use. However, many schools nationwide later expanded these policies to include infractions which have relatively negligible impact on school safety (Smith & Harper, 2015; Wallace Jr et al., 2008). The continued implementation of zero-tolerance policies for all infractions, including discretionary ones, has marginalized students of color, the economically disadvantaged, and those classified for special education, and led to these groups overrepresentation in the school discipline system. The high rate at which racial minority students receive multiple suspensions is the clearest evidence against these zero-tolerance policies. An analysis of Texas student suspension data demonstrated African American students were four-times more likely to receive suspensions than White or Hispanic students for similar behavioral infractions (Fabelo et al., 2011). While the suspension rates are disproportionately high for Black, poor, and developmentally challenged or special education students, it is important to note that some students may fall into more than one of these categories (Texans Care for Children, 2019).

The current research examines reasons for school discipline and the influence of student's racial classification. To do so, a convenience sampling of 262 students from a small, rural Texas school district were analyzed. Convenience sampling was used due to time constraints and was retrieved from the Texas Education Agency (TEA). In the school district we examined, Black students accounted for almost 20% of the students in Grades 3 - 12 during the 2016 – 2017 academic year; however, the rates at which they were suspended were disproportionately higher than White and Hispanic students. Though, of the three racial groups, Hispanic students had the lowest suspension rates.

Our study also shows that high school students - in grades nine through twelve - represent the highest percentage of all students suspended, at 47 percent. Additionally, middle school students - in grades six through eight - represent the lowest percentage of the student suspension population at 21 percent. Moreover, 33 percent of students in grades 3 - 12 were suspended, and 17 percent of all students were disciplined, 47 percent of which were Black. We argue that this school district's zero-tolerance policies contribute to these suspension frequencies and the racial disparity observed in the school discipline system.

RACE AND SUSPENSIONS

Across the United States, Black and Hispanic students are more likely than their White classmates to be suspended (Lindsay & Hart, 2017). According to the United States Department of Education Office for Civil Rights, Black students are suspended and expelled at a rate three-times greater than White or Hispanic students. On average, 5 percent of White students are suspended, compared to 16 percent of Black students (OCR, 2014). Research shows that White and Asian students are more likely to be given in-school suspension (ISS), whereas Black and Hispanic students have higher rates of out-of-school suspension (OSS) (Besse & Canastota, 2018; Kamenetz, 2018; Losen et al., 2015). Further, Black high school students are twice as likely (12.8%) to be suspended as White (6.1%) or Hispanic (6.3%) high school students (Riddle & Sinclair, 2019; Kamenetz, 2018).

Approximately 2.6-million public school students (5.3%) received one or more OSS in an academic year. A higher percentage of Black students (13.7%) than any other race of students received an OSS. Hispanic students represented 4.5% of OSSs, while White students accounted for 3.4%. Asian and American Indian or Alaska Native students represented 1.1% and 6.7% of OSSs population, respectively (National Center for Education Statistics, 2019). The percentage of all Black students (4%) who were expelled was higher than the percentages for students of all other racial groups. Among other racial groups, 2% of White students and 1% of Hispanic students were expelled (National Center for Education Statistics, 2019).

Black students are more likely to be referred for discipline or suspended as well as experience more severe forms of discipline, like corporal punishment (Lundberg, 2020; Riddle & Sinclair, 2019). Research shows Black and Hispanic youth are often sent to the office for distinctive and subjective reasons, such as disrespect and perceived threat. Conversely, White students were more likely to be referred for more objective reasons, including smoking, vandalism, and leaving school without permission (Wallace Jr et al., 2008). Black students are also more likely to receive multiple suspensions than their White counterparts.

As the data shows, school suspensions and expulsions disproportionately affect students of color. Examining a small rural Texas city's school district, our study found Black students are suspended at similar rates to Black students around the state and the country, which prompted examining underlying patterns of behavior or official responses to that behavior. What we find interesting is that Hispanic students in this school district had the lowest rate of suspension compared to the Black and White racial/ethnic groups.

GENDER AND SUSPENSIONS

Male students are more likely to receive suspensions than female students, irrespective of race or age. An examination of 2.6-million public schools showed male students received twice as many (7.3%) OSS when compared to female students (3.2%) (National Center for Education Statistics, 2019). Male students when compared to female students received more out-of-school suspensions in all the racial groups. Approximately 18 percent of Black male students received one or more OSS compared to 9.6 percent of Black female students. The percentage of Black male students (17.6%) who received OSS was the highest of male students from any racial group. A similar pattern was observed among female students, with Black female students (9.6%) receiving the highest percentage of OSS (National Center for Education Statistics, 2019). As such, Black female students are two times more likely to receive office discipline referrals, and five times more likely to experience expulsion than their White and Hispanic counterparts (Lundberg, 2020; Wallace Jr et al., 2008). While males receive more than two-thirds of suspensions, Black females are suspended at higher rates (12%) than female students of any other race or ethnicity and most Hispanic/White boys (OCR, 2014).

ECONOMICALLY DISADVANTAGED AND SUSPENSIONS

Students coming from economically disadvantaged backgrounds are disciplined at disproportionate rates compared to their more economically stable counterparts (Balfanz et al., 2014). Economically disadvantaged students come from households with incomes that are below average for either the State or the United States of America. Non-White youth are often less economically advantaged than White youth (Wallace Jr. et al., 2009). Black economically disadvantaged students have higher rates of suspension than their White and Hispanic counterparts. Male students from disadvantaged families have higher rates of disciplinary problems, lower achievement scores, and fewer high school completions than female students from comparable backgrounds (Autor et al., 2019). Moreover, lower social class children are more likely to experience traumatic and frightening experiences which influence their behavior - likely contributing to their overrepresentation in the school discipline system (Morsy & Rothstein, 2019). In our study of the small rural Texas cities' discipline reports, we found 95 percent of the suspended Black students were economically disadvantaged. Conversely, 58 percent of the White students suspended were economically disadvantaged, and 79 percent of the suspended Hispanic student population were economically disadvantaged.

GRADE LEVEL AND SUSPENSIONS

Studies have shown middle school students are disciplined more than elementary and high school students. Skiba et al. (1997) reported 41 percent of students from 19-midwestern middle schools were involved in disciplinary actions, and 33 percent of those disciplinary actions were OSS. Additionally, 32 percent of suspensions were high school students. Moreover, research suggests these suspensions peak in 9th grade (Raffaele Mendez et al., 2002). Within the current research, the highest frequency of school suspensions was recorded for Grades nine through twelve, with 52-Black students representing the largest population. The lowest number of school suspensions was recorded for Grades six through eight, with Hispanic students representing the smallest population.

CURRENT STUDY

The current research examines reasons for school discipline and the influence of student's racial classification. To do so, a convenience sampling of 262 students from a small, rural Texas school district were analyzed. Convenience sampling was used due to time constraints and was retrieved from the Texas Education Agency (TEA). In the school district we examined, Black students accounted for almost 20% of the students in Grades 3 - 12 during the 2016 – 2017 academic year; however, the rates at which they were suspended were disproportionately higher than White and Hispanic students. Though, of the three racial groups, Hispanic students had the lowest suspension rates.

The student behavior used to justify disciplinary action during the 2016 and 2017 academic year was controlled for. This was done by analyzing the reasons for suspensions and coding the data. By doing so, our study was able to better understand which behaviors motivated school disciplinary actions. We evaluated the *Race/ Ethnicity, Grade Level, Gender, Economic Disadvantage, and Reasons for Suspension* of each student disciplined. To better understand the nature of multiple suspensions and the ability of suspensions to deter subsequent suspensions, we examined how often multiple suspensions occur. As such, our study aimed to address the following research questions: 1) do student suspensions vary based on student race? and 2) does racial grouping predict the number of student suspensions?

Table 1. Suspension Types

ISS	OSS	DAEP
In School Suspension	Out of School Suspension (3 Day Limit)	Continue Other Districts DAEP
Partial Day ISS	Partial Day OSS	Continue Prior Year DAEP
Partial Day Time Out		DAEP Placement (Student Not Expelled)
School Detention		
Time Out		

METHODOLOGY

Participant and Setting

Secondary data was collected and analyzed to determine if there are racial disparities in school discipline of a Texas school district. School discipline was measured by tracking the number of school suspensions and classifying them into distinct types. From the various suspension types, related suspension types were grouped into three major categories: In-School Suspension (ISS), Out-of-School Suspension (OSS), and Disciplinary Alternative Education Program (DAEP). Table 1 displays the three major suspension categories (ISS, OSS and DAEP) and their respective subcategories to directly compare the suspension categories.

The current sample comprised of students from a small rural Texas school district, between Grade 3 through 12. In Table 2, the total student population for Grades 3 to 12 was 1,588. White students represented the highest subsample (n) within the sample (N), n = 715, and Hispanic students (n = 550) were the next highest population. Black students represented the lowest population with 323 students, which accounts for 20.3% of the student population; however, Black students also represented 48 percent of the student suspension population. During this academic year, 722 suspensions were documented, and 262 students were reportedly suspended. Therein suggesting some students were suspended multiple times. Despite being the smallest racial minority, Black students were overly represented in the student suspension population.

Throughout the research article, ISS, OSS, and DAEP grouped together are referred to as suspensions. We ran a cross tabular analysis to determine if *Race/Ethnicity, Gender, Economic Disadvantage, Number of Times Suspended* were correlated. We

Table 2. Student Population Demographics

	Student Population
Race	n (%)
White	715 (45)
Hispanic	550 (35)
Black	323 (20)
Total	1588

Source: Texas Education Agency

also examined the degree to which students were suspended multiple times. Then, we calculated the percent differences of the students to determine the comparative percentages of Black, White, and Hispanic student suspension. Aggregate data were used for this study, and the focus of the study was on students suspended, not the suspension occurrences. As such, the percent difference is critical in determining the comparative percentage of suspensions for each student in each racial/ethnic group.

Two separate datasets comprised the current sample of student suspension information. The first contained information regarding 262 students which had been suspended. The second dataset contained categorical suspension information for each of the 722 instances wherein these 262 students were suspended. The first dataset contained the following variables: 1) student ID; 2) gender; 3) race; 4) grade level; 5) economically disadvantaged status; 6) number of suspensions; and 7) multiple suspension occurrences. Dataset two contained the subgroup discipline types, and three-major group discipline types amongst the variables mentioned in dataset one.

Measures

Several variables in the study were coded with subcategories to provide the structure for subsequent statistical analysis. The race variable was coded as follows: Black = 1, White = 2, and Hispanic = 3. Gender was coded as Male = 0 and Female = 1. For grade levels, Grades 3 through 5 = 0, Grades 6 through 8 = 1, and Grades 9 through 12 = 2. Economically disadvantaged students, those who qualify for free and or reduced priced lunches, were classified with a code of "1", and non-economically disadvantaged students with "0". The major discipline categories of ISS, OSS, and DAEP were coded "0", "1", and "2" respectively. The response variable for both analyses is the number of suspensions that occurred.

Statistical Analysis

The statistical analyses conducted in this study include calculating percent difference, Relative Rate Index (RRI), a standard multiple regression, and ANOVA.

The percentage difference is usually calculated to find the difference in percentage between two numbers/values. Percentage difference equals the absolute value of the change in value, divided by the average of the 2 numbers, all multiplied by 100. The percent difference is calculated using equation one below.

$$\% \text{ Difference} = \frac{New\,Value - Initial\,Value}{\left(\dfrac{New\,Value + Initial\,Value}{2}\right)} \times 100 \tag{1}$$

The percent difference was used to determine the difference in suspension between Black, White, and Hispanic students.

The RRI provides a single index number indicating the likelihood with which school suspensions differ for minority (Black and Hispanic students) and White students. To determine the difference between the rates of suspension for the different races and ethnicity in this school district, we calculated the RRI of the student suspended population. There are two steps to take when calculating the RRI. First, the rate of the index group (each race) needs to be determined, followed by the rate of the minority group(s) that need to be divided by the rate of the White group. Equation two below represents the formula for the Relative Rate Index.

$$RRI = \frac{Rate\,of\,Index\,Group}{Rate\,of\,Reference\,Group} \tag{2}$$

The Relative Rate Index provides a picture of the disparity in school discipline across races.

A standard multiple regression was conducted for the variables contained in the dataset to determine their impact on the number of suspensions. The predictors involved in the multiple regression included race, gender, grade level, economic disadvantage, and discipline type. All the predictors-were dummy variables coded to provide a reference variable for the analysis. The reference variables for the predictors used were White, males, Grades 3 through 5, not economically disadvantaged, and ISS for discipline type. A total of eight-variables were entered into the regression analysis. The standard multiple regression was conducted to determine which predictors had a significant impact on the number of suspensions that occur.

After conducting the regression analysis, a two-way ANOVA was conducted to determine if there were significant differences among race and discipline types. These two variables were used as outputs from the regression analysis. The two independent variables, race and discipline type, could be used in the analysis using the original codes for the race variable and discipline type. The response variable remained as suspensions for the analysis.

Results

In Table 3, student suspensions are displayed by grade level and race. In the three levels consisting of Grades 3 through 5, 6 through 8, and 9 through 12, Black students account for the most suspensions as compared to White students and Hispanic students (47%). Across the racial groups, grade levels 9 through 12 have the highest percentage of suspensions when compared to the lower grade levels.

Table 3. Student Suspensions by Grade Level and Race

Grades	Black n (%)
3 - 5	39 (31)
6 – 8	33 (27)
9 - 12	52 (42)
Total	124 (100)

Note. *indicates percentages that exceed 100% due to rounding of percentages, but represent 100%

Table 4 shows how student suspensions differ by gender and race. Black, Hispanic and White male students tend to have more suspensions than all female students (63%). The largest gap between males and females in each group occurs among Hispanic students (46%), with the lowest gap between Black males and females (12%).

Table 4. Student Suspensions by Gender and Race

Suspension Occurrence	Black n (%)
Male	69 (56)
Female	55 (44)
Total	124 (100)

Source: Texas Education Agency

In Table 5, students that were economically disadvantaged were compared with those that were not. For each race, it is evident that economically disadvantaged students have a higher percentage of overall suspension as opposed to those not economically disadvantaged (80%). Black students have the highest percentage of suspensions among the races (95%) for economically disadvantaged students. The next highest within their race is Hispanic students (79%), followed by White students (58%).

Table 5. Student Suspensions by Economically Disadvantaged Students and Race

Status	Blacks n (%)
Not Economically Disadvantaged	5 (5)
Economically Disadvantaged	115 (95)
Total	120 (100)

Source: Texas Education Agency

Single and multiple suspension occurrences are compared in Table 6. The percentage of multiple suspension occurrences is greater than 1.5-times the number of single suspension occurrences (63%). As such, the same students tend to have multiple offenses, with 262 students accumulating 722 suspensions. Of these, Black students had the highest percentage of multiple suspensions at (68%).

Table 6. Single and Multiple Suspension Occurrences

Suspension Occurrence	Black n (%)
Single	40 (32)
Multiple	84 (68)
Total	124 (100)

Source: Texas Education Agency

In Table 7, suspensions by discipline type are displayed relative to race. Among the discipline types, ISS is the most common type (72%) administered to students, followed by OSS and then DAEP. When comparing the racial gap by discipline type, Black students experience more suspensions than White and Hispanic students. For ISS, Black students exceed White students at about three-times the occurrences and Hispanic students by about five-times. With OSS, Black students exceed their White classmates by five-times and Hispanic classmates by more than 10-times.

DAEP for Black students exceeds White students and Hispanic students by three-times for both races.

Table 7. Suspension by Discipline Types and Race

Race	ISS n (%)
Black	177 (49)
White	124 (34)
Hispanic	61 (17)
TOTAL	362 (100)

Note: *indicates percentages which exceed 100% due to rounding of percentages, but represent 100%
Source: Texas Education Agency

The percentage difference of students suspended by race was calculated using the three races included in the study. The percent difference of Black to White students suspended is 31.80%, while the percent difference of Black to Hispanic Students Suspended is 88.37%. The percent difference between Black students suspended and Hispanic students suspended (88.37%) is higher than the percent difference between Black students and White students (31.77%). This suggests Black students are 88 percent more likely to be suspended than Hispanic students and 31 percent more likely to be suspended than White students.

The relative rate index was calculated for Black and Hispanic students to compare suspension rates relative to White students. The rates of the White, Black, and Hispanic students were 12.6%, 38.4%, and 8.7%, respectively, leading to a RRI of 3.05 for Black to White students and 0.69 for Hispanic to White students. The RRI's show Black students are three-times more likely to be suspended than their White counterparts. Hispanic students are about half as likely to be suspended as White students. Black students make up only 20% of the student population, but they are three-times more likely than White students (45% of the student population) to receive school suspensions.

The standard multiple regression procedure was used to test whether a relationship exists between race, gender, grade level, economic disadvantage, discipline type, and

Table 8. Standard Multiple Regression for Factors Impacting Number of Suspensions

Predictor	B	SE	Beta	t	p
(Constant)	2.019	.399		5.062	.000
Black	.889	.399	.187	2.169	.009*
Hispanic	-.261	.409	-.042	-.637	.524
Female	-.413	.302	-.084	-1.369	.172
Grade 6-8	.026	.416	.004	.062	.950
Grade 9-12	.413	.330	.087	1.252	.212
EconDisAdv	.290	.383	.049	.756	.451
OSS	-.733	.438	-.101	-1.674	.095
DAEP	2.387	.565	.267	4.224	.000**

Note: R = .402; R Square = .161; Adjusted R Square = .135; F = 6.058; DF = 8,252; p = .000
*Significant at the .01 level
*Significant at the .001 level

the number of suspensions. As shown in Table 8, the regression model produced a multiple correlation coefficient of .402. Predictors in the model accounted for 16.1 percent (Adjusted = 13.5%) of the variance in the number of suspensions. A linear relationship was found to exist between all predictors and the number of suspensions (F (8, 252) = 6.058; p = .000). Black race is .889 points higher than White race in the number of suspensions. DAEP is 2.387 points higher than ISS in the number of suspensions for the discipline type. Black (t(252) = 2.169, p<.009) and DAEP (t(252) = 4.224, p<.000) were independent predictors of the number of suspensions among students in Grades 3 to 12.

A two-way ANOVA was used to test whether there were differences between race and discipline type on the number of suspensions. As shown in Table 9, the ANOVA analysis produced a significant difference based on the main effect of

Table 9. Differences in Suspension Occurrence Based on Race and Suspension Type

Source	Sum of Squares	df	Mean Square	F	p
(Intercept)					
Race	26.020	2	13.010	2.639	.073
Discipline Type	65.231	2	32.615	6.615	.002**
Race*Discipline Type	13.997	4	3.499	.710	.586
Error	1242.421	252	4.930		

R Squared = .159 (Adjusted R Squared = .132)
***Significant at the .001 level

Discipline Type (F(2, 252) = 6.615; p = .002). Race did not produce a significant difference (F(2, 252) = 2.639; p = .073), although the results were slightly above the significance criterion. The interaction between Race and Discipline Type did not register a significant result (F (4, 252) = .710; p = .586).

As a result of the Two-Way ANOVA, a Scheffe test was conducted to determine where the significance lies regarding Discipline Type. The post-hoc comparison test indicated a significant difference between DAEP and OSS, p=.001, and DAEP and ISS, p=.001. There was a greater difference between DAEP and OSS which means more students were likely to receive OSS than DAEP.

Table 10. Multiple Comparisons of Suspension Type

(I) Discipline Type	(J) Discipline Type	Mean Difference (I – J)	Std. Error	Sig.
ISS	OSS	.59	.421	.376
	DAEP	-2.78*	.520	.000
OSS	ISS	-.59	.421	.376
	DAEP	-3.37*	.633	.000
DAEP	ISS	2.78*	.520	.000
	OSS	3.37*	.633	.000

*Significant at the .05 level
** Significant at the .001 level

Utilizing data relevant to n = 262 suspended students, two Multiple Linear Regression (MLR) analyses were conducted to estimate the proportion of variance in the number of suspensions accounted for by economic disadvantage, gender, Hispanic/Latino, Grade, and race.

Prior to conducting the MLR, assumptions testing was performed to examine the dataset for normality, outliers, and multicollinearity, as well as normality, linearity, and homoscedasticity of residuals. Histograms indicated all variables were normally distributed and free from outliers. A bivariate Pearson Product-Moment Correlation (PPC) matrix was created to inspect for the absence of multicollinearity, and this assumption was violated for the race variables of White and Black/African American. Because these variables could not be merged and still calculate interpretable findings, multiple MLRs were conducted. Inspection of a histogram for standardized residuals and a scatterplot for standardized residuals against standardized predicted values indicated assumptions of normality, linearity, and homoscedasticity of residuals were violated. One identified outlier was removed (.38%), and afterward, the sample met these assumptions. Table 11 summarizes the results of the MLR wherein White

Table 11. Standard Multiple Regression for Factors Impacting Number of Suspensions, including Black/African American Race

Predictor	B	SE	Beta	t	p
(Constant)	1.49	.09	0	17.31	.00*
Economic Disadvantage	.09	.08	.07	1.05	.29
Sex	-.12	.06	-.12	-1.85	.07
Hispanic/ Latino	-.02	.09	-.02	-.27	.79
Grade	.07	.03	.13	1.98	.05*
Black/African American	.07	.07	.08	.99	.33

Note: R = .18; R Square = .03; Adjusted R Square = .02; F = 1.8; DF = 5, 255; p = .144

race as a dummy-coded variable was removed, but Black/African American race was included.

Table 12 summarizes the results of the MLR wherein Black/African American race as a dichotomous variable was removed, and White race was included.

Table 12. Standard Multiple Regression for Predictors of Number of suspensions, including White Race

Predictor	B	SE	Beta	t	p
(Constant)	1.57	.11	0	14.86	.00
Economic Disadvantage	.09	.08	.07	1.05	.29
Sex	-.12	.06	-.12	-1.85	.07
Hispanic/ Latino	-.10	.09	-.08	-1.16	.25
Grade	.07	.03	.13	1.98	.05*
White	-.07	.07	-.07	-.99	.33

Note: R = .18; R Square = .03; Adjusted R Square = .02; F = 1.8; DF = 5, 255; p = .144

DISCUSSION

The primary purpose of this study was to establish whether the practices in levying suspensions were disproportionate regarding race, gender, economic disadvantage, and discipline type in a small rural Texas school district. While previous research covers such topics, our study is unique in that reported reasonings for student suspensions within a single Texas school district were consistent with more robust findings. As such, our study constitutes somewhat of a case-study for school suspensions within this small, rural Texas school district. When first looking at the number of suspensions by race and grade level, we found that suspension levels were consistently higher for students in grades 9-12. Also, Black students incurred a greater number of suspensions than other races (Lacoe & Steinberg, 2019; Riddle & Sinclair, 2019) while their Hispanic counterparts had the lowest rate of suspension compared to the Black and White racial/ethnic groups. This was an interesting discovery because while Hispanic students represented the second highest student population in the school district, they are still a minority population. Therefore, how do the Hispanic students differ from the Black students and why do they have the lowest student suspended population while Black students with the lowest student population represent the highest number of students suspended? This is a question that can be evaluated in future research.

For gender and race, males tend to have higher rates of suspension than females. Black males and females are relatively balanced in the number of suspensions experienced, while Hispanic males and females have a much greater difference in the number of males suspended versus Hispanic females (Angton, 2020; Kamenetz, 2018; Losen & Skiba, 2011).

Economically disadvantaged students have more suspensions than those students not economically disadvantaged. Students from low socioeconomic backgrounds often do not have the pre-academic skills and advantages that their peers do; therefore, they are set up for low academic performance, which in turn lowers their teachers' expectations of them. This negative bias of teachers towards their economically disadvantaged students increases the chances of economically disadvantaged students being suspended (Jennings, 2020). Also, our research shows that Black students make up a higher percentage of suspensions among students who were economically disadvantaged. There appears to be a relatively strong correlation between Black students and economic disadvantage (Loveless, 2017; Welsh & Little, 2018).

Multiple suspension occurrences are significantly higher than the occurrences with single suspensions. This parallels the fact that Black students, in comparison to their White and Hispanic counterparts, have more multiple suspensions than single suspensions (Riddle & Sinclair, 2019; Losen & Skiba, 2011). Overall, some students tend to consistently have multiple suspensions, which contributes to the high ratio of suspension occurrences to students suspended (722:262).

Comparing the three-major category discipline types of ISS, OSS, and DAEP, Black students appear to have more suspensions as compared to other races. In fact, Black students are suspended in the range of 1.5 to 3-times more than Hispanic and White students, respectively. As predicted by the statistical analysis, race and discipline types are relatively strong predictors of the number of suspensions. The discipline type of DAEP goes along with the occurrences for Black students among the other races. This suggests, on average, Black students not only are suspended more, but they are levied greater penalties in terms of suspensions with more DAEP for discipline.

In the first two MLR models, economic disadvantage, gender, Hispanic/Latino, Grade, and race accounted for 18% of the variability in suspensions among white and Black/African American students; however, both models were non-significant. This means it is uncertain if the variance explained by either model is due to chance. Moreover, none of the predictors in either model was significant using alpha .01. While the variance explained may be due to chance, the strongest predictor in both models was Grade. In both models, students having more-than-one suspension could be predicted by a .13 increase in grade level.

Despite the value of this research, there are limitations to the study that we must consider. The data used in this research was derived from the Texas Education Agency (TEA), and was only relevant to a small, rural Texas school district. As such, the findings herein are not representative of a larger population but do offer an insight into the specific Texas school district. Moreover, from our study, future research can begin to infer and examine whether the relationships found within our study exist more broadly. Additionally, while the secondary data collected from this agency is concise, it does not allow researchers to follow individual students' history. As such, the data is without detailed information about either the pathway to an exclusionary discipline event or students' background. There is no information about the mental and behavioral status of the students. Existing literature posits students who have experienced trauma or *adverse childhood experiences (ACE)*, and students with mental impairments like *attention deficit hyperactivity disorder (ADHD)* tend to act-out at school. Suspensions seem like quick fixes to these student outbursts and serve as an incentive for continued unruly behavior (Patrick Skahill et al., 2019; Ford et al., 2017; Iselin, 2011). That is, knowing the behavioral and mental make-up of suspended students is vital to the study of disproportionate school discipline. The behavioral data of the students suspended can help policymakers assess and understand how exclusionary discipline is used at individual schools and what areas of policy and practice need changing (Weinstein, 2019; Acevedo, 2016). Behavioral data of students disciplined also provides insight into the mindset of the students and alternative perspectives of why some students are more likely to receive multiple suspensions. The analysis of discipline data in conjunction with behavioral data provides a more in-depth overview of the specific challenges students and teachers face. Moreover, this presents school administrations and policymakers with reliable data they can use to implement more effective policies (Weinstein, 2019).

The sample used within this study comprised of high populations of White students and a low population of Black and Hispanic students. As such, when analyzing the school discipline data, the overrepresentation of the Black students in the school discipline population highlights racial disparities; however, no discipline data from predominantly Black schools were analyzed. Such schools may have differing disparities, and White students as racial minorities may be overrepresented in the school discipline population (Acevedo, 2016). That is, observations made from the current sample are not generalizable beyond the current case study.

This study is not able to directly measure and account for school or administrators' propensity to offer students Restorative Interventions instead of Exclusionary Discipline in response to a discipline incident (Anyon et al., 2020; Gordon, 2018). The high number of multiple suspensions may be a consequence of not enough Restorative Interventions. More data on this factor of school discipline may help us determine if Restorative Interventions influence the rates of suspension (Kline, 2016).

The dataset used in this project was three-years old. Many changes in school discipline and school policies may have occurred in the past three-years. For example, the school district for this dataset placed a moratorium on discretionary suspension and has seen a reduction in the total number of suspensions and the racial and ethnic disparities in school suspensions. As such, whatever observations are made from this data may no longer be applicable to the school district currently (Anyon et al., 2020; Gordon, 2018; Marchbanks III & Blake, 2018). In 2019, the 86th Texas Legislature passed several bills that made changes in the education code dealing with issues of school safety and student discipline. Some of these changes may alter how schools in Texas are disciplined moving forward. One such change bans schools from issuing exclusionary discipline to students at the elementary level and below. Recent school discipline statistics show that exclusionary discipline has decreased overall, however school suspensions are still high in K – 12 grades (Anderson & McKenzie, 2022: Rafa, 2022). Colorado's largest school district has implemented and evaluated restorative practices at several school sites since 2003 and over the period of implementation, suspension rates have decreased, racial disparities have reduced, and test scores have improved for all student groups in nearly every subject, every year (Rafa, 2022).

Another important limitation of this study is the narrow assessment of disproportionality in school discipline. This study compares the discipline rates across races and assesses the differences in economic disadvantage among the students disciplined population, but the study does not assess the disproportion of school discipline among those with disabilities and those of the Lesbian, Gay, Bisexual, Transgender, and Queer (LGBTQ) community (Anyon et al., 2020; Marchbanks III & Blake, 2018). Other disproportionalities in the school discipline of this small

Texas school district may account for the uneven frequency of disciplinary actions against certain students.

Existing literature on school discipline focuses on suspension categories, and not the reasons given for individual student suspensions (Acevedo, 2016; Losen & Skiba, 2011). The lack of access to disaggregate data forced previous researchers to focus on group suspensions and suspension categories as opposed to individual student suspensions and reasons for suspensions. However, with access to disaggregate data, our study was not only able to observe the disparities in school discipline, but also able to ascertain the reason each student was suspended (Losen, 2011). Also, in this study, we observed that 69.25% of all suspensions were for discretionary reasons like failure to comply, dress code violations, cell phone usage, missed assignments, tardiness, parking issues, false reports, and cheating. Black students accounted for 57.8% of the suspensions resulting from discretionary reasons above, and they were over 20-times more likely to receive In-School Suspensions (ISS) for Verbal Altercations and Stealing compared to their White and Hispanic classmates (Gordon, 2018).

RECOMMENDATIONS

Despite the well-documented history and current status of racially and ethnically disparate school discipline, there remains a lack of research on the behavioral justifications for the use of school discipline. Just as there are many school districts who have yet to identify and properly implement tested approaches, only a few states, such as California and Texas, are implementing reliable approaches such as a moratorium on discretionary suspensions (Agrawal, 2019; Texans Care for Children, 2019; Washburn, 2018; Michels, 2016). Our results indicate that despite motivation to address school discipline, the manner in which it is expressed is 17-times more likely to be utilized on Black students. We also found that 63% of the students suspended had multiple suspensions within an academic year. As a result, we conclude this report with a few recommendations that will assist school districts seeking to reduce disparities, increasing student compliance, and improving the overall school-community relationship.

Our first recommendation is a moratorium placed on discretionary suspensions. Our results indicated that 69.25% of all suspensions were for discretionary reasons. Black students account for 57.8% of the suspensions resulting from discretionary reasons beyond those experienced by their White (25.4%) and Hispanic (16.8%) counterparts. Black students were over 20-times more likely to receive ISS for Verbal Altercations and Stealing compared to their White and Hispanic classmates. As a result, classroom removals for these behaviors must be weighed against the immediate and long-term impact of suspension. Exclusionary discipline should never be administered for discretionary infractions/behaviors.

A review of the previous research has demonstrated that by placing moratoriums on discretionary suspensions, school districts have been able to significantly reduce suspensions. California, Florida, New York, and Texas have recently banned suspensions of kindergarten through second-grade students for discretionary reasons such as willful defiance. With time, the effectiveness of the program will be determined (Berwick, 2016; Michels, 2016). California passed a new bill in September 2019 that placed moratoriums on suspensions from kindergarten through 8th Grade. This new bill went into effect in July 2020.

In 2015, the Seattle School Board placed a moratorium on out-of-school suspensions (OSS) for elementary grade students. A district-wide plan was also developed to further reduce OSS for all Grades. Between 2015 and 2017, there was only a 0.69% reduction in suspensions in the district. Texas has had more luck with the suspension ban on kindergarten through 2nd Grade with a 30% reduction in suspensions (Texans Care for Children, 2019; Zelinski & Bureau, 2019).

Second, we recommend the implementation and use of focus groups to grapple with the school disciplinary concerns. Focus Groups are a viable option for examining disparate discipline and safety problems. There are two-studies which applied the use of focus groups to implement school discipline reform (Griffith & Tyner, 2019; Davis, 2016; Flannery et al., 2013). The first study, Suspended Students Experiences with In-School Suspension: A Phenomenological Investigation" by Katherine Rene Evans of the University of Tennessee, Knoxville, highlighted the use of focus groups to determine the effectiveness and consequences of exclusionary discipline. The study found participants - middle and high school public school teachers - expressed frustration with administrators' inconsistent application of suspension and expulsion. The study also found most reported threats to school safety reported by teachers was a lack of cohesive culture and relationships between staff and students. The second study, "Translating Research into Effective Practice: The Effects of a Universal Staff and Student Intervention on Key Indicators of School Safety and Discipline," by the University of Oregon faculty highlighted the use of focus groups to describe the effects of a universal intervention package. The package aimed at improving the safety and social behavior of students in elementary and middle schools. Nine-treatment and six-comparison, or no-intervention elementary and middle schools in three-communities participated. In a focus group interview across some treatment and comparison schools, treatment school personnel generally reported improved operation of their schools and motivation to continue with the intervention. Comparison schools cited the need for school-wide intervention and technical assistance as a top need.

By creating focus groups, schools are better able to collect qualitative information that can be used to improve upon the school's disciplinary approaches. These focus groups may also be used to improve communication and help move the conversation from observation to solution in real-time. Such an approach could lead to greater official responses for change and essentially close the racial gap in school disciplinary practices.

Utilizing findings from the focus groups in conjunction with external evaluators, our third recommendation, is for school districts to formulate a strategic task force that reports directly to the school board and superintendent. This task force should be charged with examining the school district's disciplinary policies, practices, and procedures. The overall goal would be to determine the impact of these practices and provide recommendations for reducing unnecessary disciplinary actions and racial/ethnic disparities. In addition to examining district-level data, the task force would be charged with recommending proven disciplinary models for consideration. Each year the task force would submit a report to the school board and superintendent before releasing the report for public consumption.

Schools that have implemented community-level task forces have been able to increase family engagement and cultivate student learning while at the same time improving attendance, behavior, and development (Duke Children's Law Clinic, 2015). These types of partnerships create a "connected science" in which real-world problems are used as contextual scaffolds for bridging students' community and evidence-based knowledge as a way to provide opportunities for meaningful and intellectual challenges for students (Gross et al., 2015; Bouillion & Gomez, 2001).

Similar to approaches in Maryland, Washington, Michigan, and New Jersey, the task force serves as a unique opportunity for community involvement in a pressing educational issue (Salmon, 2019; Colombi & Osher, 2015; APA, 2008). At a minimum, the task force would serve as a real-time oversight evaluator and recommender of disciplinary policies and practices.

Cultural norms across race, ethnicity, and social class, contrasting with the behavioral norms of teachers and students, may provide fertile ground for misunderstandings that contribute to the race-discipline relationship (Monroe, 2005). As a result, our fourth recommendation is the adoption of regular diversity and cultural competence training for all district teachers, staff, and administrators.

Research has shown the benefits of cultural awareness training as it relates to suspension reductions. In fact, a North Carolina middle school was able to successfully reduce racially disproportionate suspensions after requiring cultural awareness training for its teachers (Moore & Ratchford, 2007). The Boys to Men Program and Cultural Diversity training in North Carolina led to a 59.7% reduction in the discipline referrals for African American male students used in the experiment. Students who participated in the experiment were chosen because they had the highest repeated offenses. Moreover, their academic achievements reflected the negative effect of the repeated suspensions (Moore & Ratchford, 2007).

As an alternative to suspension or school removal, one plan that has gained traction is the use of Positive Behavioral Interventions and Supports (PBIS). The PBIS framework is a promising approach for reducing insubordinate student behavior and promoting cohesive and exemplary behavior among children Kindergarten through- 12. PBIS is the application of evidence-based prevention strategies with the use of layered scales of measures and outcomes which support student academic, emotional, social, and behavioral needs (Garbacz et al., 2015).

There is evidence-based support that there is a reduction in behavior problems and improvements in positive behavior and successful emotion regulation after training in PBIS (Bradshaw et al., 2012). Their results indicated positive effects on student behavior problems, student ability to focus, social-emotional functioning, and prosocial behavior. Students in PBIS schools were 33% less likely to receive a disciplinary referral than those in non-participating schools. The effects tended to be greater among children who were first exposed to PBIS in their earlier years. Nearly 46% of North Carolina's schools were PBIS trained or had enacted the program's model. They saw a 72% decrease in the number of in-school suspensions within two years of PBIS implementation. Therefore, we not only recommend using positive behavioral interventions and supports, but the research also supports our fifth recommendation.

Lastly, we recommend the creation of a data collection and analysis portal that would ease the ability to share identified student disciplinary-specific data. Such a system would help school leaders craft a sound blueprint with measurable results for continuously improving schools so that there could be more evidence-informed decisions (American Association of School Administrators - AASA, 2004).

Similar to the Texas Education Agency's Discipline Action Group Summary Reports, most state educational databases lack individual-level disciplinary. For instance, the number of suspensions each child received in a given year. In order to better determine the necessary steps to address disciplinary challenges, researchers need to be able to determine the degree to which individual students are disciplined. In the San Francisco Unified School District, data was at the core of the district's efforts to reduce suspension. They were able to see which schools, classrooms, and teachers were suspending students the most; what interventions specific students received; and how restorative practices have been used to help students (AASA & Children's Defense Fund, 2014).

In order to identify bright spots and challenges, allocate resources effectively and ensure success for all students, educators need to be able to make data-driven decisions. Data do not necessarily evidence students are being discriminated against, but without data, it is difficult to know if all students are being treated fairly. Best practices may be employed without school or district-specific data, but without data, it will be difficult to know what is working and what needs to be adjusted (AASA & Children's Defense Fund, 2014).

CONCLUSION

Approaches to school discipline are similar to the 'three strikes policies utilized by the criminal justice system. Both have grave consequences, the least of which is that they precipitate the school to prison pipeline. Zero tolerance policies are archaic and thus we suggest re-imagining alternative strategies to discipling children within the school setting. Zero tolerance adversely affects Black and Hispanic students more disproportionately than other students (Cramer et al., 2014, Sealey-Ruiz, 2011). Progressive action is needed to reform discipline policies to negate the racial, gender, socioeconomic, grade level, and school size determinants that sustain systemic disproportionate disciplinary sanctions meted against vulnerable populations. One such example is that of a California-based program that saw a 57%-65% reduction in school disciplinary infractions (Goyer, Parker, Cohen, Master, Apfel, Lew, & Watson, 2019). Exclusionary discipline must be reserved for the most severe disciplinary infractions to protect the student from harm.

Research suggests that students exposed to educators of the same race and similar backgrounds perform better in the classroom and do not experience as disproportionate an experience with school discipline (Lindsay & Hart, 2017). Recognizing the value in culturally- sensitive pedagogy has its benefits: 1). It forces school administrators, educators, and staff to confront implicit biases and recognize that culture, learning styles, and behavior go hand-in-hand and 2). understanding cultural differences assists in the development of comprehensive approaches to student disciplinary problems. Therefore, comprehensive knowledge of vulnerable student populations can counter negative perceptions of student culture, behavior, and academic ability.

In closing, this chapter's examination of disproportionate suspensions seeks to build upon the research with the intention of finding solutions to an ever-present problem. It is apparent that current disciplinary practices have negatively affected African American student success and progressive disciplinary practices are needed to ensure a reasonable and fair educational experience.

REFERENCES

AASA, & Children's Defense Fund. (2014). *School Discipline Data*. Retrieved 15 April 2020, from https://www.childrensdefense.org/wp-content/uploads/2018/06/school-discipline-data.pdf

Acevedo, F. (2016). *Beyond Race: A Quantitative Study Of The Discipline Gap Among Predominantly Black High Schools In Chicago*. Retrieved 25 November 2020, from https://via.library.depaul.edu/cgi/viewcontent.cgi?article=1090&context=soe_etd

Agrawal, N. (2019). *California expands ban on 'willful defiance' suspensions in schools*. Retrieved 25 June 2021, from https://www.latimes.com/california/story/2019-09-10/school-suspension-willful-defiance-california

Allen, Q., & White-Smith, K. A. (2014). *Just as Bad as Prisons": The Challenge of Dismantling the School-to-Prison Pipeline Through Teacher and Community Education*. Retrieved from Taylor & Francis https://www.tandfonline.com/doi/full/10.1080/10665684.2014.958961?src=recsys

American Association of School Administrators - AASA. (2004). *Using Data to Improve Schools: What's Working*. https://aasa.org/uploadedFiles/Policy_and_Advocacy/files/UsingDataToImproveSchools.pdf

Anderson, K. P., & McKenzie, S. (2022). *Local Implementation of State-Level Discipline Policy: Administrator Perspectives and Contextual Factors Associated With Compliance*. AERA. https://journals.sagepub.com/doi/full/10.1177/23328584221075341

Angton, A. (2020). *Black girls and the discipline gap: Exploring the early stages of the school-to-prison pipeline*. Retrieved from https://lib.dr.iastate.edu/cgi/viewcontent.cgi?article=9280&context=etd

Anyon, Y., Gregory, A., & Stone, S. (2016). *Restorative Interventions and School Discipline Sanctions in a Large Urban School District*. Retrieved 25 November 2020, from https://journals.sagepub.com/doi/full/10.3102/0002831216675719?casa_token=u2l0rK0EMegAAAAA%3AfU5CSDfSvnAp0qEd84SdNFkYOS6JZp6OVMurfn--x5yxy63I5ACEbgOmKggLsqL1Pjy8YnYgB23w

APA (American Psychological Association). (2008). Are Zero Tolerance Policies Effective in the Schools? *The American Psychologist*, *63*(9), 852–862. doi:10.1037/0003-066X.63.9.852 PMID:19086747

Autor, D., Figlio, D., Karbownik, K., Roth, J., & Wasserman, M. (2019). Family Disadvantage and the Gender Gap in Behavioral and Educational Outcomes. *American Economic Journal. Applied Economics, 11*(3), 338–381. doi:10.1257/app.20170571

Balfanz, R., Byrnes, V., & Fox, J. (2014) *Sent Home and Put Off-Track: The Antecedents, Disproportionalities, and Consequences of Being Suspended in the Ninth Grad.* Retrieved 5 July 2020, from https://digitalcommons.library.tmc.edu/cgi/viewcontent.cgi?referer=https://scholar.google.com/&httpsredir=1&article=1217&context=childrenatrisk

Berwick, C. (2016). *Ban school suspensions!* Retrieved 31 March 2020, from https://theweek.com/articles/640318/ban-school-suspensions

Besse, R., & Capatosto, K. (2018). *Ending Racial Inequity in Out of School Suspensions: Mapping the Policy Landscape and Equity Impact.* Retrieved October 27, 2020, from https://kirwaninstitute.osu.edu/implicit-bias-training/resources/OSS-racial-inequity-02.pdf

Bouillion, L., & Gomez, L. (2001). Connecting school and community with science learning: Real world problems and school-community partnerships as contextual scaffolds. *Journal of Research in Science Teaching, 38*(8), 878–898. doi:10.1002/tea.1037

Bradshaw, C., Waasdorp, T., & Leaf, P. (2012). Effects of School-Wide Positive Behavioral Interventions and Supports on Child Behavior Problems. *Pediatrics, 130*(5), e1136–e1145. Advance online publication. doi:10.1542/peds.2012-0243 PMID:23071207

Colombi, G., & Osher, D. (2015). *Advancing School Discipline Reform.* Retrieved 15 April 2020, from https://www.air.org/sites/default/files/downloads/report/Advancing-School-Discipline-Reform-Sept-2015.pdf

Cramer, E. D., Gonzalez, L., & Pellegrini-Lafont, C. (2014, November 14). *From Classmates to Inmates: An Integrated Approach to Break the School-to-Prison Pipeline.* Retrieved from Taylor & Francis Online: https://www.tandfonline.com/doi/full/10.1080/10665684.2014.958962?src=recsys

Davis, C. J. (2016). *Teacher Beliefs Regarding Positive Behavior Support Programs in Mississippi Middle Schools.* Retrieved 15 July 2020, from https://aquila.usm.edu/cgi/viewcontent.cgi?article=1416&context=dissertations

Duke Children's Law Clinic. (2015). *A Parents' Guide to Special Education in North Carolina.* Available at: https://law.duke.edu/childedlaw/docs/Parents%27_guide.pdf

Fabelo, T., Thompson, M. D., Plotkin, M., Carmichael, D., Marchbanks, M. P. III, & Booth, E. A. (2011). *Breaking Schools' Rules: A Statewide Study of How School Discipline Relates to Students' Success and Juvenile Justice Involvement*. Council of State Governments Justice Center.

Flannery, K. B., Frank, J. L., Kato, M. M., Doren, B., & Fenning, P. (2013). Implementing school-wide positive behavior support in high school settings: Analysis of eight high schools. *High School Journal*, *96*(4), 267–282. doi:10.1353/hsj.2013.0015

Ford, T., Parker, C., Salim, J., Goodman, R., Logan, S., & Henley, W. (2017). The relationship between exclusion from school and mental health: A secondary analysis of the British Child and Adolescent Mental Health Surveys 2004 and 2007. *Psychological Medicine*, *48*(4), 629–641. doi:10.1017/S003329171700215X PMID:28838327

Garbacz, S., McIntosh, K., Eagle, J. W., Dowd-Eagle, S. E., Hirano, K. A., & Ruppert, T. (2015). Family Engagement Within School-wide Positive Behavioral Interventions and Supports. *Preventing School Failure*, *60*(1), 1–10. doi:10.1080/1045988X.2014.976809

Gordon, N. (2018). *Disproportionality in student discipline: Connecting policy to research*. Retrieved 25 November 2020, from https://www.brookings.edu/research/disproportionality-in-student-discipline-connecting-policy-to-research/

Goyer, J. P., Cohen, G. L., Cook, J. E., Master, A., Apfel, N., Lee, W., Henderson, A. G., Reeves, S. L., Okonofua, J. A., & Walton, G. M. (2019). Targeted identity-safety interventions cause lasting reductions in discipline citations among negatively stereotyped boys. *Journal of Personality and Social Psychology*, *117*(2), 229–259. doi:10.1037/pspa0000152 PMID:30920278

Griffith, D., & Tyner, A. (2019). *Discipline Reform through the Eyes of Teachers*. Thomas B. Fordham Institute. Retrieved from https://eric.ed.gov/?id=ED597759

Gross, J., Haines, S., Hill, C., Francis, G., Blue-Banning, M., & Turnbull, A. (2015). Strong School–Community Partnerships in Inclusive Schools Are "Part of the Fabric of the School….We Count on Them". *School Community Journal*, *25*, 9.

Hannon, L., DeFina, R., & Bruch, S. (2013). The Relationship Between Skin Tone and School Suspension for African Americans. *Race and Social Problems*, *5*(4), 281–295. doi:10.100712552-013-9104-z

Iselin, A.-M. (2011). *Research on School Suspension*. Retrieved 25 June 2021, from https://www.purdue.edu/hhs/hdfs/fii/wp-content/uploads/2015/07/s_ncfis06report.pdf

Jennings, M. (2020). *Excluded from Education: The Impact of Socioeconomic Status on Suspension Rates*. https://socialequity.duke.edu/wp-content/uploads/2021/07/Michael-Jennings.pdf

Kamenetz, A. (2018). *Suspensions Are Down In U.S. Schools But Large Racial Gaps Remain*. Retrieved October 28, 2020, from https://www.npr.org/2018/12/17/677508707/suspensions-are-down-in-u-s-schools-but-large-racial-gaps-remain

Kline, D. (2016). *Can Restorative Practices Help to Reduce Disparities in School Discipline Data? A Review of the Literature*. Retrieved 25 November 2020, from https://www.tandfonline.com/doi/abs/10.1080/15210960.2016.1159099

Lacoe, J., & Steinberg, M. P. (2019) *Do Suspensions Affect Student Outcomes?* Educational Evaluation And Policy Analysis. Retrieved from https://journals.sagepub.com/doi/full/10.3102/0162373718794897

Lindsay, C., & Hart, C. (2017). Teacher race and school discipline: Are students suspended less often when they have a teacher of the same race? *Education Next*, *17*(1), 72–79. https://go.gale.com/ps/anonymous?id=GALE%7CA474717812&sid=googleScholar&v=2.1&it=r&linkaccess=abs&issn=15399664&p=AONE&sw=w

Losen, D. (2011). *Discipline policies, successful schools, and racial justice*. Retrieved 25 June 2021, from https://nepc.colorado.edu/publication/discipline-policies

Losen, D., Hodson, C., Keith, I. I. M., Morrison, K., & Belway, S. (2015). *Are we closing the school discipline gap?* Retrieved October 28, 2020, from https://www.civilrightsproject.ucla.edu/resources/projects/center-for-civil-rights-remedies/school-to-prison-folder/federal-reports/are-we-closing-the-school-discipline-gap/AreWeClosingTheSchoolDisciplineGap_FINAL221.pdf

Losen, D., & Skiba, R. (2011). *Suspended Education Urban Middle Schools in Crisis*. Retrieved 25 November 2020, from https://civilrightsproject.ucla.edu/research/k-12-education/school-discipline/suspended-education-urban-middle-schools-in-crisis/Suspended-Education_FINAL-2.pdf

Loveless, T. (2017). *2017 Brown Center Report on American Education: Race and school suspensions*. Retrieved October 28, 2020, from https://www.brookings.edu/research/2017-brown-center-report-part-iii-race-and-school-suspensions/

Lundberg, I. (2020). *Exclusionary Discipline Disparities: A Case Study*. Retrieved 4 July 2020, from https://red.mnstate.edu/cgi/viewcontent.cgi?article=1366&context=thesis

Lurie, J., & Rios, E. (2016). *Black Kids Are 4 Times More Likely to Be Suspended Than White Kids*. Mother Jones. Available at: https://www.motherjones.com/politics/2016/06/department-education-rights-data-inequality-suspension-preschool/

Luster, S. (2018, July 19). *How Exclusionary Discipline Creates Disconnected Students*. Retrieved October 28, 2020, from https://www.nea.org/advocating-for-change/new-from-nea/how-exclusionary-discipline-creates-disconnected-students

Marchbanks, M., III, & Blake, J. (2018). *Assessing the Role of School Discipline in Disproportionate Minority Contact with the Juvenile Justice System: Final Technical Report*. Retrieved 25 November 2020, from https://www.ncjrs.gov/pdffiles1/ojjdp/grants/252059.pdf

McFadden, A. C., Marsh, G. E., Price, B. J., & Hwang, Y. (1992). A study of race and gender bias in the punishment of school children. *Education & Treatment of Children*, 140–146.

Michels, P. (2016). *Houston Schools Ban Suspensions in Early Grades*. Retrieved 25 June 2021, from https://www.texasobserver.org/houston-schools-ban-suspensions/

Michels, P., Beckner, A., Coronado, A., & Bova, G. (2016). *Houston Schools Ban Suspensions in Early Grades*. Retrieved 31 March 2020, from https://www.texasobserver.org/houston-schools-ban-suspensions/

Monroe, C. R. (2005). *Understanding the discipline gap through a cultural lens: implications for the education of African American students*. Intercultural Education. Retrieved from https://www.tandfonline.com/doi/abs/10.1080/14675980500303795?src=recsys&journalCode=ceji20

Moore, E., Jr., & Ratchford, V. (2007). *Decreasing Discipline Referrals for African American Males in Middle School*. Retrieved 30 March 2020, from https://eric.ed.gov/?id=EJ831292

Morsy, L., & Rothstein, R. (2019) *Toxic stress and children's outcomes: African American children growing up poor are at greater risk of disrupted physiological functioning and depressed academic achievement*. Retrieved 9 July 2020, from https://www.epi.org/publication/toxic-stress-and-childrens-outcomes-african-american-children-growing-up-poor-are-at-greater-risk-of-disrupted-physiological-functioning-and-depressed-academic-achievement/

National Center for Education Statistics. (2019). *Indicator 15: Retention, Suspension, and Expulsion*. Retrieved 9 July 2020, from https://nces.ed.gov/programs/raceindicators/indicator_RDA.asp#:~:text=A%20higher%20percentage%20of%20Black%20students%20(13.7%20percent)%20than%20of,and%20Pacific%20Islander%20students%2C%203.4

Noguera, P. A. (2010, June 24). *Schools, Prisons, and Social Implications of Punishment: Rethinking Disciplinary Practices*. Retrieved from Taylor & Francis Online: https://www.tandfonline.com/doi/abs/10.1207/s15430421tip4204_12?src=recsys

OCR. (2014). *U.S. Department of Education Office for Civil Rights*. Retrieved 9 July 2020, from https://ocrdata.ed.gov/Downloads/CRDC-School-Discipline-Snapshot.pdf

Owens, J., & McLanahan, S. (2019, June 20). *Unpacking the Drivers of Racial Disparities in School Suspension and Expulsion*. Retrieved October 28, 2020, from https://academic.oup.com/sf/article-abstract/98/4/1548/5521044?redirectedFrom=fulltext

Patrick Skahill, D., Watson, A., Thomas, J., Watson, A., Watson, A., & Thomas, J. (2019). *Students With "Emotional Disturbances" Face High Rate of Suspensions*. Retrieved 25 June 2021, from https://ctmirror.org/2019/05/20/students-with-emotional-disturbances-face-high-rate-of-suspensions/

Pierre, M. (2019). *The Push Out: A Disproportionality Study on Discipline in the State of Florida*. Retrieved from https://stars.library.ucf.edu/cgi/viewcontent.cgi?article=7725&context=etd

Rafa, A. (2022). *The Status of School Discipline in State Policy*. Education Commission of the States. https://www.ecs.org/wp-content/uploads/The-Status-of-School-Discipline-in-State-Policy.pdf

Raffaele Mendez, L. M., Knoff, H. M., & Ferron, J. M. (2002). *School Demographic Variables and Out-of-School Suspension Rates: A Quantitative and Qualitative Analysis of a Large Ethnically Diverse School District*. Retrieved 7 July 2020, from https://www.researchgate.net/profile/Linda_Mendez/publication/229731457_School_demographic_variables_and_out-of-school_suspension_rates_A_quantitative_and_qualitative_analysis_of_a_large_ethnically_diverse_school_district/links/5a7cc3200f7e9b9da8d6fee2/School-demographic-variables-and-out-of-school-suspension-rates-A-quantitative-and-qualitative-analysis-of-a-large-ethnically-diverse-school-district.pdf

Riddle, T., & Sinclair, S. (2019). Racial disparities in school-based disciplinary actions are associated with county-level rates of racial bias. *Proceedings of the National Academy of Sciences of the United States of America, 116*(17), 8255–8260. doi:10.1073/pnas.1808307116 PMID:30940747

Rios, E. (2018, April 25). *New data shows that America's schools are still disproportionately punishing students of color.* Retrieved October 28, 2020, from https://www.motherjones.com/politics/2018/04/new-data-america-schools-suspend-punish-arrest-black-students/

Salmon, K. (2019). *Task Force on Student Discipline Regulations.* Retrieved 15 April 2020, from https://marylandpublicschools.org/stateboard/Documents/08272019/TaskForceStudentDisciplineRegulations082019.pdf

Sealey-Ruiz, Y. (2011, December 19). *Dismantling the School-to-Prison Pipeline Through Racial Literacy Development in Teacher Education.* Retrieved from Taylor & Francis Online: https://www.tandfonline.com/doi/full/10.1080/15505170.2011.624892?src=recsys

Shollenberger, T. L. (2015). Racial disparities in school suspension and subsequent outcomes: Evidence from the National Longitudinal Study of Youth. In D. J. Losen (Ed.), *Closing the school discipline gap: Equitable remedies for excessive exclusion* (pp. 31–43). Teachers College Press.

Skiba, R., Michael, R., Nardo, A., & Peterson, R. (2002). *The Color of Discipline: Sources of Racial and Gender Disproportionality in School Punishment.* Available at: https://www.indiana.edu/~equity/docs/ColorofDiscipline2002.pdf

Skiba, R. J., Peterson, R. L., & Williams, T. (1997). Office referrals and suspension: Disciplinary intervention in middle schools. *Education & Treatment of Children*, 295–315.

Smith, E. J., & Harper, S. R. (2015). *Disproportionate Impact Of K-12 School Suspension and Expulsion On Black Students In Southern States.* Retrieved from Penn GSE: https://web-app.usc.edu/web/rossier/publications/231/Smith%20and%20Harper%20(2015)-573.pdf

Texans Care for Children. (2019). *Report: TX Schools Still Suspending Many Pre-k – 2nd Graders, But Out-of-School Suspensions Dropped Sharply — Texans Care for Children.* Retrieved 15 July 2020, from https://txchildren.org/posts/2019/8/27/report-tx-schools-still-suspending-many-pre-k-2nd-graders-but-out-of-school-suspensions-dropped-sharply

Texans Care for Children. (2021). *Keeping Kids in Class: Pre-K Through 2nd Grade Suspension in Texas and a Better Way Forward.* Retrieved 25 June 2021, from https://static1.squarespace.com/static/5728d34462cd94b84dc567ed/t/5b1ea6c270 a6ad846fb7cbc9/1528735440357/keeping-kids-in-schools.pdf

Wallace, J. Jr, Goodkind, S., Wallace, C. M., & Bachman, J. G. (2008). Racial, Ethnic, and Gender Differences in School Discipline among U.S. High School Students: 1991-2005. *Negro Educational Review*, *59*(1-2), 47. https://www.ncbi. nlm.nih.gov/pmc/articles/PMC2678799/ PMID:19430541

Washburn, D. (2018). *Countdown to expand ban on 'willful defiance' suspensions in California schools.* Retrieved 25 June 2021, from https://edsource.org/2018/ youth-advocates-pushing-to-expand-californias-ban-on-willful-defiance-suspensions/593754

Weinstein, B. (2019). *Behavioral Data is as Important as Academic Data (maybe more).* Retrieved 25 November 2020, from https://blog.behaviorflip.com/ behavioraldata/

Welsh, R. O., & Little, S. (2018). The School Discipline Dilemma: A Comprehensive Review of Disparities and Alternative Approaches. *Review of Educational Research*, *88*(5), 752–794. doi:10.3102/0034654318791582

Zelinski, A., & Bureau, A. (2019). *Texas banned out-of-school suspensions for most young children. 4,500 kids were suspended anyway.* Retrieved 25 June 2021, from https://www.houstonchronicle.com/politics/texas/article/Texas-banned-out-of-school-suspensions-for-most-14398476.php

Section 3
Practice

Chapters 7-8 offer creative alternative approaches to exclusionary discipline.

Chapter 7

Digital Storytelling:
A Student–Centered Approach for Shifting the School Discipline Narrative Using Story, Technology, and Data as Interventions

Kisha Solomon
Independent Researcher, USA

ABSTRACT

Storytelling is an effective technique for resolving disputes and conflict while preserving relationships, self-image, and cultural standards. With increased access to the internet and social media, digital storytelling has become instrumental in spurring awareness and change in areas of social injustice and inequality. This chapter briefly examines the science and culture of storytelling and explores the use of digital storytelling in multiple contexts. The author establishes evidence-based support for the use of storytelling and/or digital storytelling 1) to mitigate educator bias in school discipline policy and practices; 2) to counteract and/or reduce negative psychological, emotional, and cultural impacts of excessive or disparate disciplinary practices; 3) to increase cross-sector awareness, advocacy, and engagement on exclusionary discipline issues. The author also proposes a counter-storytelling method for enhanced qualitative and quantitative data-gathering in school discipline cases.

DOI: 10.4018/978-1-6684-3359-1.ch007

INTRODUCTION

Storytelling is an activity found in every culture. It has been used for knowledge-sharing, cultural preservation and dispute resolution for generations (Reese, 2012; McCullum et al., 2014; Utley, 2008). When properly utilized, storytelling can also have a profound effect on human psychology, neurology and behavioral responses (Pak, 2013). Storytelling can change how we think and feel about ourselves and others, and how we act on those thoughts and feelings.

Storytelling and structured story have been used in a wide variety of behavior modification approaches – from child-rearing and disciplinary practices in Inuit culture, to psychotherapy techniques for people recovering from trauma (Doucleff and Greenhalgh, 2019; Vanden Poel and Hermans, 2019). When combined with digital technology and media, storytelling becomes an even more reliable and effective tool for shaping behaviors, sharing contextualized data, and transforming cultures and communities. By combining visuals, text and sound, digital storytelling allows for the transmission of rich information, meaning and context.

Context is critically important with regards to school discipline outcomes. The more context there is, the more accurate conclusions can be drawn from both individual cases of school discipline and the systemic trends and patterns in school disciplinary actions and policies. Two contextual themes seem to regularly appear at the epicenter of the decades-long discussion about school discipline disparities: interpersonal conflict and internal bias. With both of these themes, story and narrative play a significant role. Behind every interpersonal conflict there is a story of differing perspectives. Behind all internal bias there is a story that lacks perspective. The stories being told by educators about students involved in disciplinary actions are often one-sided. When classroom conflict stories are told solely from the perspective of the educator or disciplinarian, the storyteller is considered to be infallible – their version of the truth is often the only version of the truth that is allowed to be heard or documented (Bell, 2020). More stories from varied perspectives are desperately needed to shift the balance of power in schools and the dominant narrative surrounding school discipline disparities from school-centered to student-centered.

Much of the effort toward reducing school discipline disparities has focused specifically on identifying the causes of, and implementing deterrents to students' bad behavior in the classroom. Yet, research has shown that differences in rates of disciplinary referrals, suspensions and expulsions cannot be attributed solely to students' behavior (Carter et al., 2014, p. 1). Evidence suggests that personal and interpersonal differences between educators and students – and the incomplete or incorrect stories that often accompany them – are primary contributing factors to schools' disciplinary disparities (Gregory et al., 2014; Fallon et al., 2021). Where educators are unfamiliar with or have internal bias against students of a different race, sexual orientation or gender identity, students within those demographic subgroups experience higher and more excessive incidences of disciplinary action. When student infractions are more subjective in nature, that is, when a disciplinary decision relies more heavily on the personal judgment of the teacher or administrator, there is evidence of greater unfairness in the punishment dispensed (Carter et al., 2014, p. 2). One study even revealed that one of the most powerful determining factors for discipline disparities within a school was the school administrator's personal perspective on expulsion and suspension (Skiba et al., 2014, p. 3).

The impact of one-sided school discipline stories extends far beyond the classroom. In attempting to tell their side of the story to school administrators, students and parents report feeling silenced, labeled, stereotyped, like they don't belong, violated, and without faith or hope (Fallon et al., 2021). These experiences leave a lasting impression, and often lead to students developing a negative self-image and low self-esteem. This can ultimately impede student success. Students who have experienced exclusionary discipline at school are more likely drop out of school and more likely to become entangled in the criminal justice system (McIntosh et al., 2014; Miller et al., 2020). Thus, discriminatory and exclusionary discipline practices can have the long-tail effect of reducing students' future prospects or completely removing them as productive members of their families and communities.

Relatively few interventions have been specifically designed to target educator bias, and recommendations for improving school culture and increasing educators' cultural responsiveness are often generalized. Because of the difficulty with identifying bias and the equally challenging lack of school resources, there are few – if any – investments in educator training or new classroom methods that actually produce lasting change in educator perspectives and behaviors (Boudreau 2020, para. 2, 6). Instead, popular and heavily-promoted models like Multi-Tiered Systems of Support for Behavior (MTSS-B) continue to target student behavior. While schools are required to gather data on school disciplinary actions by race, gender or sexual orientation, too often, the data is neither rigorously examined or acted upon. One study found that of all schools that collected student ethnicity data, fewer than 50% of them actually reviewed disciplinary data by ethnic group at least once a year (Fallon et al., 2021). By taking this 'color-blind' approach, school leadership may – intentionally or not – be telling one story about their school's progress as a whole, while obscuring a less positive story about how demographic subgroups may still be disproportionately disciplined (Gregory et al., 2014, p. 6). Additionally, MTSS-B frameworks like Schoolwide Positive Behavioral Interventions and Supports (SW-PBIS) do little to shift cultural norms within schools where discipline disparities exist. Instead, these interventions maintain an imbalance of power, prevent students from participating in reshaping school culture, and fail to specifically address racial disparities in school discipline (Beyl, 2020; Fallon et al., 2021).

One of the most promising interventions to date in reducing educator bias is the My Teaching Partner-Secondary program (MTP-S). The key components of the intervention include: regular teacher coaching, reframing conflict through storytelling and the use of digital media. Teachers that participated in the one-year coaching program had no significant racial disparities in discipline cases coming from their classrooms, while racial disparities remained for teachers in the control group who did not participate in MTP-S. The research of Miller et al., (2020) suggests the use of counter-narratives as a means of promoting more equitable school cultures. Counter-narratives give members of marginalized groups the power to protect their psyches and center their own self-concepts, while affording dominant groups the opportunity to shift their perspectives by seeing reality through someone else's point of view (Miller et al., 2020). Counter-narratives can also help reveal the hidden realities of racial and gender discrimination in schools and educational systems and even expose them to others outside of educational and academic circles. Gregory et al., (2014) divide proposed solutions for school discipline disparities and educator bias into two categories: conflict prevention – strategies that target school culture and educator bias; and conflict intervention – strategies that focus on learning and relationship-building via conflict resolution versus punitive discipline. Other research suggests that in order to mitigate the possibility of bias-influenced disciplinary decisions, schools should use a multi-step decision-making process to determine disciplinary action for more subjective offenses like student insubordination (Gregory et al., 2014, p. 6).

This chapter proposes the use of storytelling and digital storytelling as a relatively low-cost, high-impact tactic for conflict prevention, conflict intervention and cultural change in schools with evidence of discipline disparities. It also offers an illustrative example of a multi-step digital storytelling process that could be used as a formative, classroom-level intervention in school discipline cases. This process would have the added benefits of: facilitating more thorough data collection on school discipline cases, better enabling the identification of educator bias and including student and parent voices as counter-narratives in the documentation of disciplinary incidents. As disparities in school discipline in the United States appear to be a systemic cultural problem whose effects have lasting impact on marginalized communities and American society as a whole, the author also recommends increased leverage of digital storytelling to engage audiences, journalists and activists outside of academia to help influence individual, local and national-level cultural change in perceptions, practices and policy related to school discipline disparities.

BACKGROUND

We are living the stories planted in us early or along the way... we are also living the stories we planted—knowingly or unknowingly—in ourselves.... If we change the stories we live by, quite possibly we change our lives. (Okri, 1997, p. 46)

STORYTELLING AS A TOOL TO REFRAME CONFLICT, AND INFLUENCE BEHAVIOR, SELF-CONCEPT AND CULTURAL NORMS

Throughout history and across continents and cultures, narrative and story have been used to both define individual identity and to influence and preserve collective identity and culture (Reese, 2012; McCullum et al., 2014; Utley, 2008). While there is no single definition of storytelling, there are common characteristics within the myriad definitions that do exist. Most concur that storytelling is interactive, that it evokes emotion and promotes insight. Storytelling is multi-sensory, and it is intimate – it either requires or results in an implied bond, or, at a minimum, a mutual investment of time and attention between the storyteller and the story receiver (McCullum et al., 2014, p. 9). Mello's definition of storytelling (2001, para. 2), highlights three notable characteristics that make it highly suitable for use in both conflict prevention and conflict resolution.

1. **Storytelling is linguistic**: it is accessible to anyone who has language skills whether they be verbal, written or visual.
2. **Storytelling is educative:** it can be used to transmit and share personal understanding, thereby allowing the storyteller to assume the role of teacher or guide.
3. **Storytelling facilitates negotiated transactions:** a process that creates a certain default equity among its participants.

The Narrative Mediation Approach to Conflict Resolution

Unlike a story or novel, where there is usually a single protagonist with a clearly defined conflict, interpersonal conflicts – like those between teachers and students in classrooms – can become distorted by the judgment and emotion of the parties involved. Each party in an interpersonal conflict sees themselves as the protagonist, and each holds their own story of the events. In narrative mediation, storytelling is used to bring the conflicting stories of the parties involved to light, and reconstruct them in a way that allows for enhanced understanding of both perspectives. As in other forms of mediation, narrative mediation requires a go-between, a non-biased third party who guides those in conflict through the process of storytelling, reflection, reframing and resolution. The mediator's role is multi-fold. Using structured methods, the mediator helps parties in conflict first share how they view the other in the dispute and then dis-identify with those emotions and reconstruct a story that focuses on the impact of each individual's actions, instead of on the individuals themselves (Winslade and Monk, 2000).

The narrative mediation process has three stages (Winslade, 2020, para. 8):

Stage 1: Individual meetings between the mediator and each party to the conflict,
Stage 2: A joint meeting with all parties,
Stage 3: Follow-up meetings with the parties involved to ensure expanded understanding, shared ownership of the conflict resolution and adherence to agreements reached.

It is the mediator's job to bridge the gap, leveraging each of the three definitive characteristics of storytelling. The linguistic aspect of storytelling allows the parties to bring the often-unheard story in their mind to life with words. These words are then used by the mediator to facilitate the education of both parties on their respective stories – revealing that both are protagonists. Finally, with the mediator's guidance, each party, both now fully aware of the facts and tangible impacts – not just the personal emotions – surrounding the conflict, can negotiate an outcome from equitable positions.

Within school settings, there is usually no mediator to serve as unbiased third party – no gathering of differing perspectives as mutual education, and an inherent lack of equity between student and teacher. Teachers and administrators act as judges or interpreters of classroom conflict, not as facilitators and fact-gatherers. Narrative mediation works well when parties are on equal footing, but what happens when interpersonal conflict occurs between parties who are not in equitable positions? How can interpersonal conflict be resolved when one party has more authority or situational power, as is the case between teacher and student? What role can storytelling play in this context?

The Inuit Way of Disciplining Children through Dramatic Storytelling

Among Inuit tribes, a form of dramatic storytelling is used as a disciplinary method for children. When a child misbehaves, parents and elders who observe the incident wait until the situation has blown over and the child is calm. The child is not punished. Instead, the parents or elders perform a kind of morality play designed to help the child think more rationally about the situation – both their actions and the consequences of those actions. The elders act out how the child has misbehaved and even playfully question and provoke the child during the interactive story. With the child no longer in a state of high emotion, she is able to see the impact of her actions, not only on others but on her own identity. By comparing the actions in the dramatized story to the ideas she has about herself, the child is able to choose a different behavioral norm, one that is more closely aligned with her own self-concept and influenced by her elder role models cajoling examples (Doucleff and Greenhalgh, 2019). It is a participative act for both. The elder acts as mirror and guide, engaging the child's reason and judgment to re-work the conflict story within the framework of the culture's values and standards of behavior. The child learns what is 'right' by working through the conflict and becoming aware of her own behavioral blind spots with the help of an engaged teacher.

Unlike the administration of rule and punishment, the Inuit's form of presenting behavioral norms as entertaining narrative engages the would-be-punished in visualizing the impact of their actions. Perhaps the most important feature of this story-based disciplinary method is that it prioritizes the preservation of a positive relationship between the child and the adult disciplinarian. Jean Briggs – a Harvard researcher who spent eighteen months living among an Inuit tribe in the 1960s, remarked how Inuit adults were exceptionally good at controlling their anger, even in particularly upsetting moments (Doucleff and Greenhalgh, 2019). This propensity for emotional self-control in Inuit adults appears to be a direct result of the dramatic storytelling disciplinary approach used by the Inuits in early childhood. Through repeated practice and role-play of how to respond appropriately in emotionally charged situations, Inuit children become adults who are slow to anger and able to respond appropriately in moments of frustration or interpersonal conflict (Doucleff and Greenhalgh, 2019).

The idea of addressing or responding to a child's negative behavior after the moment of conflict has passed, i.e., 'letting cooler heads prevail', allows for the separation of emotion from the dispensing of corrective action or guidance – neither the child nor the disciplining adult are in a heightened state of emotion when the conflict story is dramatized and reflected upon. The cool-headedness of Inuit adults hints at the long-lasting, emotion-stabilizing impact of such a disciplinary tactic.

How Storytelling Influences our Minds and Emotions

There is neurological evidence to support the Inuit concept of disciplinary behavioral modification. In moments of stress or conflict, an individual's ability to make rational decisions is diminished. The so-called fight-or-flight response is engaged, and effectively overrides higher brain function that would allow one to engage in critical thinking and respond appropriately to stress or perceived threat. Research on collaborative problem solving (CPS) in schools shows that a specific sequence of engagement can reliably and effectively disrupt the fight-or-flight response and directly address the neurological basis of inappropriate student behavior (Pollastri et al., 2019, p. 26). The 3-step process known as 'Plan B' stresses the following sequence: regulate, relate and reason. To regulate, the educator listens to and empathizes with the student's concerns; to relate, the educator clarifies their concerns and asks the student to empathize, and to reason, the educator invites the student to brainstorm possible solutions and outcomes. Note that the act of telling the conflict story from their own perspective is the first step in helping students move out of the fight-or-flight mode and into a state of problem-solving and conflict resolution. The 3-step 'Plan B' approach is also effective for adults and educators. In the heat of a classroom conflict, educators' nervous systems may also become dysregulated. Taking time to view a disciplinary incident with empathy and compassion rather than as an act of willful defiance or transgression allows educators to access their higher reasoning skills when determining appropriate disciplinary action or response (Pollatsri, et al., 2019, p. 29).

The stories that are most likely to cause someone to take action or to change their behavior have a well-defined structure that initially grabs, then holds the attention and causes the receiver to emotionally relate to or empathize with the characters in the story (Zak, 2013). Table 1 highlights both the essential elements of conflict narratives (Laursen and Hafen, 2010, para. 2) and the elements of an effective digital story (Bouchrika, 2021). Table 1 reveals how the elements of an effective digital story can be mapped onto the core elements of a conflict narrative.

These elements of story structure are also mirrored in various storytelling disciplines and methods used in literature, television and film. From the hero's journey to Dan Harmon's story circle, the narrative arc of a conflict that builds, reaches a max point, then ends with a clear resolution is a familiar one. Why is this important to highlight? Not all stories have the same ability to impact emotions and spur behavioral change. Structured stories have proven to be most effective in this capacity. In one study, participants were instructed to engage in either an emotionally-expressive or a narrative writing exercise about a painful life event. Those who engaged in the narrative writing exercise – one that had to follow a defined, coherent structure – showed lower markers of 'fight-or-flight' stress after completing the exercise. Researchers theorized that when people can distance themselves from the heightened emotion of stress or conflict through the construction of a cohesive story, they are able to overcome egocentric impulses and respond more rationally to those events (Bergland, 2017).

When there is information lacking to fill in the full details of a story, the brain tends to fill in the details for us (Whitenton, 2017, para. 7). For instance, when there is no

Table 1. Comparison of elements of conflict narratives to elements of an effective digital story

Elements of Conflict Narratives	Elements of an Effective Digital Story
The main characters	Point of view; Soundtrack; Recording one's voice
The theme: i.e., what the story or conflict is about.	
A complication: an initial moment of difficulty of opposition between the protagonist and antagonist.	Dramatic question
Rising action: the conflict behaviors or responses that occur as a result of the initial complication.	Emotional content, Economy, Pacing
Climax or Crisis: the actions taken to end or resolve the conflict.	
Denouement: the effect or outcome of the conflict resolution actions.	

Source: (Laursen and Hafen, 2010; Bouchrika, 2021)

clear antagonist or when there is little knowledge of the antagonist's backstory, the brain, feeling dissatisfied with an incomplete narrative, will use whatever available information it has to fill in the blanks. Media influences, personal experiences, the opinions of others – all are sources that the brain may draw on to complete an incomplete story. This is precisely how internal bias can replace objective thinking. Bias – or the pre-conceived notions that we already have about a person or situation – provides the missing material needed to make an incomplete story make sense. This is not necessarily always a bad thing. When an incomplete story is filled in with details that are self-affirming or optimistic, the result is generally positive. The brain seems to encourage the story protagonist to either act out the positive effect in real-life or to view any subsequent real-life effect or outcome as positive. By contrast, when an incomplete story is filled in with details that are self-negating or pessimistic, negative outcomes and perceptions are more likely. In a particularly salient example, participants in a research study were asked to fabricate a story in which they placed the blame for a negative outcome on a particular person. Even after the participants had forgotten the details of the story they had completely made up themselves, they continued to blame that person (Dingfelder, 2011, p. 42). This demonstrates the lasting affect that even a wholly imagined story can have on one's memory and decision-making.

The phenomenon known as the Pygmalion Effect explains how both positive and negative teacher expectations can act as a self-fulfilling prophecy and actually influence the direction of student performance (Rosenthal and Jacobsen, 1968). In schools where marginalized students report lack of understanding, lack of cultural sensitivity or a lack of supportive relationships from teachers, there is likely to be a higher degree of mistrust and greater conflict between students and teachers. Conversely, when teachers get to know students better, it can lead to greater empathy and trust and enable teachers to view student behaviors as part of the student's larger story, versus automatically assigning the role of antagonist to a misbehaving student (Gregory et al., 2014, p. 3).

Digital Storytelling and the Importance of Recording One's Own Voice

As illustrated in Table 1, one of the uniquely distinguishing elements of digital storytelling is the recording of one's own voice. Self-constructed stories can also have a lasting influence on individual psychology and emotions. In a study where participants were asked to write stories about a difficult, life-changing moment, those who wrote stories with happy endings reported feeling happier when surveyed two years later. A separate study of adults in an outpatient psychotherapy program revealed that patients who centered themselves – not their therapists – as the main actors in their recovery stories were the most likely to show improvement (Dingfelder, 2011, p. 42). Nigerian cultural storyteller Chinua Achebe (1994) is quoted as saying, "If you don't like my story, write your own" ("The Danger of"). In this simple statement, the author reveals the powerful, empowering, and often necessary imperative of creating and recording one's own narrative.

Recent research strongly supports the use of student-constructed counter-narratives as a method for increasing equity and decreasing bias in school culture and disciplinary policies (Miller et al., 2020). Storytelling in classroom settings can help children develop their own sense of identity and examine and clarify their values (Mello, 2001). Counter-narratives allow marginalized students to reframe stories of interpersonal conflict and discriminatory discipline through a self-affirming perspective, one that centers the student – not the teacher – as the story's protagonist. Counter-narrative also provides a foundation for the student to explore alternate endings to discipline stories, enabling the student to subvert being defined by a single moment of discriminatory or exclusionary discipline.

An examination of Smyth's learner-centered constellation illustrates that voice and identity – students' ability to be heard, to use their voices against imbalanced power relationships in school and to be involved in real decision-making – are foundational to developing a sense of equity and "relational power" in school and classroom settings (Smyth, 2006, p. 292). When students are given the space to tell their own stories and given tools and knowledge to bring their stories to life, they are able to counteract the stories being told about them, re-imagine their own futures, and in some cases actually spur transformative change within their school's culture and policies. Miller et al. (2020) make reference to a study that required students' participatory action in addressing school discipline. One student composed a poem as his response to a disciplinary incident in which a symbol of his cultural identity – a Mexican flag – was confiscated and labeled a gang symbol by a school security guard. The student's recitation of the poem in front of school administrators and district officials, led to the school changing its policy on the display of cultural symbols. In another cited example, counter-narratives of Black students and parents in Baltimore were used to effectively advocate against neighborhood school closures.

Digital stories that use more than just text to convey a message are more likely to hold the receiver's attention and more likely to provoke an empathetic response (Zak, 2013). The research of neurobiologist Paul Zak suggests that certain stories can influence levels of oxytocin in the recipients' brains, leading them to behave more compassionately and charitably toward others (Zak, 2013). By making use of technology to combine narrative with images, sound, and audio (Wake, 2012, p. 26), digital storytelling can be even more useful than traditional storytelling for inspiring transformative action to reduce school discipline disparities. With digital storytelling technologies – video, the internet, mobile devices, social media – being widely available and relatively low-cost, the ability to tell rich, engaging stories is now accessible to almost anyone who has a smartphone and a compelling story to tell.

For well-established systems, the greatest transformation often comes from the outside. The need for transformative action – not just scholarly discussion or inert data reports – in reducing school discipline disparities is often underemphasized within school systems. Outside pressure from activists, journalists and communities surrounding the school is often just the catalyzing force needed to spur change in discriminatory and exclusionary discipline practices inside of schools. Digital storytelling has repeatedly proven effective in bringing issues of disproportionate discipline to mass audiences that may not even be directly associated with the school system. By broadening the audience and amplifying the voices of the students, parents and teachers, digital storytelling has the potential to spark a widespread social movement that can lead to more dramatic and long-lasting improvements in school discipline policy and practices.

The documentary film, *Pushout* – originally produced as a book – exposes the emotion-tinged narratives of Black girls who experienced exclusionary discipline at school. The film garnered the attention and support of Congresswoman Ayanna Pressley, who premiered the film at an annual conference of the Congressional Black Caucus. The documentary also inspired the name of the bill that Rep. Pressley co-sponsored and subsequently introduced in Congress – the Ending PUSHOUT (Punitive, Unfair, School-Based Harm that is Overt and Unresponsive to Trauma) Act. Months after the film premiered, it was featured on 48 PBS affiliate stations across the country, potentially reaching hundreds of thousands of viewers ("About", 2021, https://pushoutfilm.com/about). *Pushout* is but one example of how digital storytelling can be used to maximize the emotional impact of a story and to increase awareness, support and policy change for students affected by discipline disproportionality.

In 2021, the independent investigative journalism outlet *Propublica*, published a multi-part digital story of exclusionary discipline to their social media profile. The story centered around four Black girls at a Tennessee elementary school who were arrested and jailed for having watched a fight. The investigative report revealed a systemic and pervasive pattern of racial discrimination, illegal jailing of juveniles and lax governmental oversight within the county. The story highlighted how students, parents, teachers and even police officers involved in the incident were rendered powerless to contradict or combat the deeply entrenched policies and procedures that local courts and politicians routinely established and enforced (Propublica, 2021). The compelling digital story went viral – receiving widespread attention and gaining support from state lawmakers and local clergy. The impact of the story was resounding. A local university publicly severed ties with the juvenile court judge implicated in Propublica's story. The president of the NAACP Legal Defense and Education Fund initiated the call for a Justice Department investigation into the people and events surrounding the story; eleven members of Congress soon followed suit. Months after the digital story was published, the juvenile court judge at the center of it announced that she would retire and not seek re-election (Propublica, 2021).

These examples reveal the critical role that both storytelling and digital storytelling can play in identifying, deconstructing and recreating the stories of bias and interpersonal conflict that form the foundation for school discipline disparities. It is also evident that digital storytelling has significant potential for creating widespread awareness that can ultimately lead to transformational change in school policies and behavior that contribute to discipline disparities.

ON THE WRONG SIDE OF STORY: HOW EDUCATOR BIAS AND SCHOOL-CENTERED NARRATIVES PERPETUATE INEQUITIES IN SCHOOL DISCIPLINE

Educator Bias Contributes to School Discipline Disparities – Yet There Are Few Effective Interventions to Address It

Teachers who come from different racial, ethnic or class backgrounds than their students, often have little understanding of students' personal stories – as a result, they may fill in the missing details about misbehaving students with imagined or fabricated details that allow them to more readily characterize a student as hero or villain. Teachers' stories about and expectations of students can have a reinforcing impact on student outcomes. The data tells a consistently compelling story about the impact that educator bias has on which students are more likely to be disciplined and the severity of discipline those students receive. Several studies have shown that Black males, students in special education programs, and LGBTQ students disproportionately receive exclusionary discipline – disparities that cannot be completely attributed to differences in these students' behaviors (Carter et al., 2014). In counties where educators are shown to have average or higher levels of pro-white bias, Black students are more likely to receive both in-school and out-of-school suspensions than their White counterparts in (Dhaliwal et al., 2020).

Yet the most popular intervention for improving school disciplinary issues - known as Positive Behavioral Interventions and Supports (PBIS), seems to address the impact of educator bias on disciplinary inequity as an afterthought. Figure 1 illustrates the three-tiered PBIS framework. The framework focuses almost exclusively on student behaviors. Ironically, PBIS could actually contribute to educator bias as teachers may inadvertently begin to identify students as 'Tier 1' or 'Tier 2' students, a risk that even PBIS promotional and training material cautions educators against (PBIS Implementation Blueprint, 2021, https://www.pbis.org/resource/pbis-implementation-blueprint). Despite being aware of the impact of educator bias on the implementation and administration of PBIS, the current PBIS published guidance gives broad-based instruction on how to address or mitigate their implicit bias, with little insight on detailed implementation steps or which methods have proven most effective. Unsurprisingly, the PBIS framework has not proven effective at reducing bias. If schools are unable to discover and implement proven, reliable methods for mitigating educator bias, they will remain unable to solve the issue of exclusionary and inequitable school discipline practices.

One of the most common interventions for addressing and reducing educator bias is implicit bias training. Despite the popularity of the intervention, its effectiveness has not been proven. Evidence suggests that even when external interventions like training do reduce bias, they do so only minimally, and there is often no associated change in behavior after training (Boudreau, 2020).

One intervention known as the My Teaching Partner – Secondary (MTP-S) program, appears to be more effective than classroom training in significantly reducing educator bias – the disparity in discipline referrals for Black and White students was effectively eliminated for those teachers who participated in the program (Gregory et al., 2014, p. 4). In MTP-S, teachers videotape their classroom instruction and student interactions and send the footage to a coach, who reviews the footage and records feedback prompts. The coach and teacher then review and discuss the video and feedback together. Through questioning and self-reflection, the teacher develops a different plan of action with the support and feedback of the coach ("Coaching Cycles", 2021, https://www.secondarycoaching.org/mtps-model). The MTP-S approach also contains all of the story elements that are most likely

Figure 1. Three-tiered Positive Behavioral Interventions and Supports (PBIS) model - original, and as modified in 2007
Source: OSEP Technical Assistance Center on Positive Behavioral Interventions and Supports, 2015

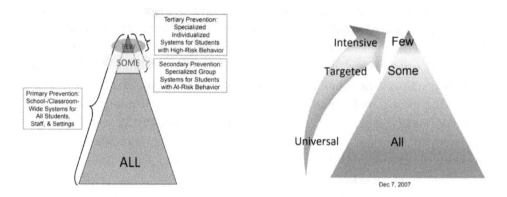

to cause a change in behavior – it places the teacher in the role of protagonist, it has an obstacle to overcome (the teacher's own perceptions or behaviors), and it follows a reliable series of actions leading to a resolution (Laursen and Hafen, 2010, para. 2; Zak, 2013). While seemingly effective, the year-long commitment and the hands-on coaching required in MTP-S makes it somewhat impractical for mass adoption, as the associated cost and time investment may be out of reach for many schools. Where effective interventions for exposing and reducing educator bias are found, they must also be easily replicable and relatively low-cost to be viable for widespread implementation in schools where financial, technological and personnel resources may be limited.

The Voices of Marginalized Students and Parents Are Ignored or Dismissed Throughout the Disciplinary Process

In addition to the one-sided perspective that educator bias introduces into school discipline practices, educators and administrators may also deliberately or inadvertently exclude students and parents from the conversation on resolving school discipline issues. When schools fail to involve the affected students and their parents in decision-making and problem-solving for individual conflicts or for schoolwide interventions, it contributes to families' feelings of powerlessness and objectification (Gregory et al., 2014, p. 8). The theme of both voicelessness and powerlessness is one that resounds within marginalized student populations. Students and parents who have been involved in cases of excessive or discriminatory disciplinary action report feeling invisible, unable to have their stories heard and powerless to change the outcome of the situation (Bell, 2020; Gregory et al., 2014, p. 8).

They aint let us tell the story or nothing. Maybe if they let us tell the story I wouldn't have gotten suspended (Bell, 2020, p. 5).

This quote from a student reveals the lingering frustration of not having one's voice heard. Students who have felt silenced during school disciplinary cases aAre often left with more than just a mark on their school record. They are marked mentally and emotionally as well. Students have reported feeling violated, losing their faith in justice and fairness, and like they'd been defined as a 'bad kid' based on a single incident (Fallon et al., 2021, p. 6). Students who feel unfairly mischaracterized or unfairly punished can begin to develop negative self-concepts and accompanying behavioral patterns. In the short-term, this can show up as decreased student engagement, increased alienation from their peers, and more hostile attitudes or behaviors (Smyth, 2006). The long-term impact of this negative self-image could result in eventual dropout or later involvement in the criminal justice system, a well-documented phenomenon known as the school-to-prison pipeline.

To achieve equitable outcomes in school discipline, there must be equity in the creation of school discipline policies and the resolution of school discipline issues – especially when there is evidence of unfairness. And who better to judge the fairness of a system or set of practices than those on the receiving end of those practices? Historically, the interventions aimed at increasing equity in school disciplinary practice and policy have relied on the administrators and educators within school systems to report on, judge and then act upon the fairness or unfairness that exists within their school discipline cases. Without the voices of students and parents to tell a complete and contextualized story, the most valuable perspective of the school discipline narrative remains glaringly absent.

Demographic-Only School Discipline Data is Insufficient for Developing Equity-Driven Solutions

Without story, data is lifeless. When school systems and policymakers rely solely on data to determine the practices and policies that will shape countless young American lives, they are doing those lives a disservice. In the business and marketing world, demographic data was once the only way to predict consumer behavior. Age, gender, zip code, income, past buying behavior – these were all inert data points that marketers used to make complicated (and often inaccurate) guesses about how a new product or service might perform in the market. With the rise of social media and the advancement of digital technology, user-generated content – a form of digital storytelling – has revolutionized the way companies develop new products and services and improvements to existing offerings. The ability to get instant, real-life, richly nuanced feedback and insight into how a customer uses or consumes a product or service and how that product or service makes them feel – about the product or service itself, about the company and about themselves – is as close to clairvoyance as a corporation could hope to come. Corporations who ignore or discount customer feedback experience inevitable declines in their customer base and their bottom lines. The American school system is not a corporation, however. It has a captive audience: students and parents that have little choice in who provides their compulsory education. And as such, school systems have yet to recognize the need for timely, real-life feedback from these customers.

Yet, if schools and policymakers are truly invested in improving their school discipline practices and in reducing inequities in school discipline, then they must grow beyond the demographic-only approach to data collection and engage students and parents to add context to the growing mass of disciplinary data that has yet to tell the full story. Student-generated stories have helped educators broaden their own perspectives on the 'whys' behind behavioral problems, thus leading to disciplinary solutions that consider, rather than neglect the students' point of view (Miller, et al., 2020).

The lack of rich, contextualized data can conceal the fact that disparities still exist for students in different subgroups and make it more difficult to spot patterns of bias and discrimination. Key gaps in data affecting school discipline disparities include a lack of data on: conditions in schools, reasons for discipline, outcomes associated with discipline, and LGBTQ students and issues (Gregory et al., 2014, p. 7). Often, the data that is made available to teachers and administrators about school discipline cases is not readily available to students and parents. This can perpetuate the perceived power imbalance between educators and students and leaves students and their families without information that could enable them to take their own actions to address disciplinary disparities (Gregory et al., 2014, p. 6).

But the collection and analysis of student-generated discipline stories remains inconsistent. School discipline policies, approaches and decisions continue to be made based on lifeless demographic data, without the additional context or empathetic understanding that student-centered stories could reliably provide. If schools fail to capture student-generated stories from school disciplinary incidents, the ability to develop truly equitable solutions and effective interventions will continue to be limited.

Limiting The Discussion on School Discipline Disparities to Academic Circles Limits the Potential for Cross-Sector Advocacy and Innovation

Inequities in school discipline are often framed as a school issue or an issue for a particular student or family to be concerned with. Persistent disparities in school discipline often lead to a long-tail series of issues for affected students, including increased dropout rates and higher rates of mental health issues (Carter et al., 2014, p. 3). Disparities in school discipline have been shown to be a contributing element in the school-to-prison pipeline (Gregory et al., 2014, p. 7), a phenomenon that impacts not only the affected student but the community to which he or she belongs. Wider community involvement could place additional pressure on schools to resolve disciplinary disparities. Varying perspectives and possible solutions from non-academic sectors could provide innovative approaches and interventions for consideration. However, much of the discussion surrounding the issue, and, consequently, many of the recommended solutions and interventions come from scholars, researchers and academicians who may not even intend for their ideas to be readily accessible to or consumed by mass audiences. Without the infusion of perspectives and approaches from other professional sectors and without more widespread awareness of and advocacy for systemic changes in discriminatory school disciplinary policies and practices, the ongoing palaver about disparities in school discipline runs the risk of becoming an echo chamber of ideas without accompanying actions.

SOLUTIONS AND RECOMMENDATIONS

Educators, like students, need continual, well-structured and timely support in the form of clear guidance and expectations in order to influence changes in their own mindsets and behaviors. It cannot be left up to individual teachers to determine for themselves what anti-racist or unbiased data gathering and decision-making looks like. School districts and administrators are obligated to guide teachers and aid in their professional development by providing not just policy, but practical classroom-level practices.

Since stories can be so widely and reliably used to create shifts in emotions, behaviors and outcomes, it is reasonable to consider storytelling as a tool in shifting not only the perspectives but also the outcomes of current approaches to disparities in school discipline. The following recommendations are proposed for using the tenets of traditional storytelling combined with the multimedia technology of digital storytelling to create equitable alternatives to the educator-centered narratives that perpetuate continued school discipline disparities for marginalized students.

Recommendation #1: *Initiate the use of a multi-step, digitally-enabled structured storytelling method for decision-making and data collection in subjective or exclusionary discipline cases.* This recommendation is supported by research that proposes the use of a multi-step screening process before discipline is issued for more subjective behavioral offences like insubordination or willful defiance. (Gregory et al., 2014, p. 6). Since cases of subjective discipline present the greatest potential for educator bias to affect equitable decision-making, this recommendation focuses specifically on those cases (Carter et al., 2014, p. 2). Using elements of story structure as a guide, educators would deconstruct the key elements of the conflict story surrounding the student's misbehavior. These details could be captured in existing classroom management software or in a short online form made available to teachers, and could be completed along with the day's classroom notes or administrative tasks. Teacher-recorded details could include the following conflict story elements: the main characters; type of conflict; background situation / environment; student's action that led to the decision to discipline; classroom impact; disciplinary action taken. Once the teacher has entered details about the behavioral incident, subsequent steps in the process could allow for: the student to enter their own version of the conflict story details using a similar digitally-enabled tool or form; automatic notification of the student's parent or guardian with a link to view the conflict story details entered by the teacher and / or student; scheduling of a mediated session where both the teacher and the student are allowed to present their own story and hear the other's version of the story with the guidance of a coach or counselor. Specific steps in the process could be tailored to fit individual school resources and capabilities. However, it is recommended that all of the following stages or key actions be present in the implemented process:

- Conflict story data collection from both teacher and student.
- Student and teacher reflection time.
- Joint review of collected conflict story data.
- Recording of conflict story resolution and final disciplinary action.

Implementation of this multi-step process would also enable the consistent capture of additional relevant data such as type of student infraction, type of discipline issued, and number of disciplinary referrals per student (Gregory et al., 2014, p. 6; Carter et al., 2014, p. 4). In keeping with research findings, allowing time for teacher self-reflection, giving teachers more insight on student perspectives of conflict stories and providing teachers with a structured decision-making process to use when disciplining students all contribute to a decrease in educator bias and promotes more equitable outcomes in school disciplinary actions (Gregory et al., 2014, p. 6).

Recommendation #2: *Enable the recording and collection of short, student-generated digital narratives in subjective or exclusionary disciplinary incidents.* As part of the multi-step process for recording and resolving subjective disciplinary cases, students should be given the option to submit a digital story – a video, audio recording or digital presentation – that captures their perspective of the conflict story surrounding the discipline referral. This recording could be done either individually as a solo student activity or in pairs or groups, allowing students to assist each other in recording, reflecting and reframing their version of the conflict story. The confessional-style video recording made popular by reality tv shows provides a model for the type of student-centered content that could be produced from this optional exercise. Students could be given access to school equipment like PCs with webcams and / or audio recorders, podcasting or video equipment, mobile phones, or handheld digital voice recorders. The digital artifact could then be uploaded to the student's record in existing school or classroom management software or otherwise saved in a way that could be readily shared with educators and / or parents.

Recommendation #3: *Expand current required school discipline data reporting to include student and parent assessments of school discipline practices.* School districts are currently required to provide regular reports of data related to the percentage of students receiving in-school and out-of-school suspensions. But this data alone is not enough to provide information on the contributing factors to discipline disparities (Nishioka, 2017, p. 5). Through the use of the previously recommended multi-step data collection process or a separate periodic data collection exercise, schools could expand their current data collection and reporting to include a student's and / or parent's assessment of the fairness or equity of a disciplinary decision. Through the administration of a single-question customer-satisfaction-style survey, schools would be able to more clearly assess student and parent perceptions of disciplinary inequities. This data could also be further explored to help develop more effective and equitable interventions.

Recommendation #4: *Educators, parents, students and researchers should rely more heavily on digital storytelling to raise awareness, attract supporters and increase advocacy related to school discipline disparities.* Students and parents can add balance to one-sided discipline narratives by using the democratic tools of digital media to document and share their own perspectives. Educators and researchers studying school discipline disparities – especially those engaged in research using first-person narratives or interviews as means of data collection – should leverage digital storytelling methods and complementary disciplines like data visualization to create more widely-accessible formats and presentations of key research findings and recommendations that could have an impact on public policy or interventions. Academics and researchers should also seek to collaborate with skilled and experienced digital storytellers in other sectors and disciplines to create digital stories based their research insights and findings.Students, parents and supporters should leverage digital storytelling platforms to create and distribute their first-hand accounts of excessive or unfair discipline. Openly available platforms like YouTube, Instagram, Tik Tok and Twitter are ideal for sharing student-centered narratives with the community at-large. Creating and using common hashtags can help others find similar content and content creators, and, over time, can help develop a digital awareness and advocacy movement that is diverse and self-sustaining. Existing digital stories and collections – like *Pushout* and *Suspension Stories* – that provide more nuanced accounts of those affected by and the effects of discriminatory discipline practices should be made available to teachers and school administrators, and incorporated into training programs and curricula on implicit bias and cultural sensitivity for educators.

FUTURE RESEARCH DIRECTIONS

Since the use of digital storytelling as an equity-based disciplinary intervention has not yet been fully explored, future research might include studies on the feasibility and cost of implementing the above recommendations in an average school or school system. Next steps might logically include piloting this chapter's recommendations within a selected group of schools and reporting initial and continued outcomes. The establishment of baseline measures for the time to successfully implement and adopt the recommended digital storytelling process would make a worthwhile contribution to future research efforts on this topic. Baseline measures for student and parent 'disciplinary fairness assessments' would also add significant value to ongoing research and policy discussions related to inequities in school discipline. Additionally, more research is needed on identifying evidence-based interventions that are effective at reducing or mitigating educator bias.

CONCLUSION

There are many ways that stories can be used to influence changes in perceptions and behaviors. Moments where there is a lack of clarity or perspective, or where there is unresolved interpersonal conflict present uniquely ripe opportunities for using conflict stories to dissect and reframe the narrative. By using what is known of standard story structure and applying the sensory-stimulating and emotionally engaging elements of digital storytelling, it is possible to create several smaller, integrated interventions that address multiple issues stemming from disparities in school discipline. Through the collection, review, sharing of and reflection on conflict story information, the ability to make more rational and equitable decisions can be increased. By empowering students and communities with the tools and data to create and change their own narratives of discriminatory disciplinary practices, schools can begin to shift the story of school discipline disparities from educator-centered to community-centered. This can lead to increased awareness and advocacy by supporters, policy makers and activists from different sectors which would likely spur more diverse insights on and innovative approaches to reducing disparities in school discipline.

REFERENCES

@ProPublica [@ProPublica]. (2021, October 10). *Three police officers went to an *elementary* school in Tennessee & arrested four Black girls* [Instagram photograph]. Retrieved from https://www.instagram.com/p/CUz7ZUILDcj/

Achebe, C. (1958). *Things Fall Apart*. William Heinemann Ltd.

Bell, C. (2020). "Maybe if they let us tell the story I wouldn't have gotten suspended": Understanding Black students' and parents' perceptions of school discipline. *Children and Youth Services Review, 110*. doi:10.1016/j.childyouth.2020.104757

Bergland, C. (2017, May). Narrative Expressive Journaling Could Help Your Vagus Nerve. *Psychology Today*. https://www.psychologytoday.com/us/blog/the-athletes-way/201705/narrative-expressive-journaling-could-help-your-vagus-nerve

Beyl, S. (2020). *Questioning the Rule: The Civic Implications of Positive Behavioral Interventions and Supports (PBIS) as a Pedagogy of Power* (Unpublished Education Studies capstone). Yale University, New Haven, CT.

Bouchrika, I. (2021, February). *Digital Storytelling: Benefits, Examples, Tools & Tips*. https://research.com/education/digital-storytelling#elements

Boudreau, E. (2020, August). Measuring implicit bias in schools: A Harvard study shows implicit bias affects discipline disparities. *Usable Knowledge*. https://www.gse.harvard.edu/news/uk/20/08/measuring-implicit-bias-schools

Carter, P., Fine, M., & Russell, S. (2014). Discipline disparities series: Overview. *Discipline Disparities Series*. https://indrc.indiana.edu/tools-resources/pdf-disciplineseries/disparity_overview_040414.pdf

Corcoran, B., & Ahrens, M. (2018). *Every kid has a story to tell.* https://www.edutopia.org/article/project-every-kid-has-story-tell

Dhaliwal, T. K., Chin, M. J., Lovison, V. S., & Quinn, D. M. (2020, July 20). *Educator bias is associated with racial disparities in student achievement and discipline.* Brown Center Chalkboard. https://www.brookings.edu/blog/brown-center-chalkboard/2020/07/20/educator-bias-is-associated-with-racial-disparities-in-student-achievement-and-discipline/

Dingfelder, S. F. (2011). Our stories, ourselves. *Monitor on Psychology, 42*(1), 42.

Doucleff, M., & Greenhalgh, J. (2019, March). *How Inuit parents teach kids to control their anger.* NPR. https://www.npr.org/sections/goatsandsoda/2019/03/13/685533353/a-playful-way-to-teach-kids-to-control-their-anger

Fallon, L. M., Veiga, M., & Sugai, G. (2021). Strengthening MTSS for Behavior (MTSS-B) to Promote Racial Equity. *School Psychology Review.* doi:10.1080/2372966X.2021.1972333

Forscher, P. S., Lai, C. K., Axt, J. R., Ebersole, C. R., Herman, M., Devine, P. G., & Nosek, B. A. (2019). A meta-analysis of procedures to change implicit measures. *Journal of Personality and Social Psychology, 117*(3), 522–559. https://doi.org/10.1037/pspa0000160

Gregory, A., Bell, J., & Pollock, M. (2014). How educators can eradicate disparities in school discipline: A briefing paper on school-based interventions. *Discipline Disparities Series.* https://indrc.indiana.edu/tools-resources/pdf-disciplineseries/disparity_intervention_full_040414.pdf

Laursen, B., & Hafen, C. (2010). Future directions in the study of close relationships: Conflict is bad (except when it's not). *Social Development, 19*(4), 858–872. https://doi.org/10.1111/j.1467-9507.2009.00546.x

McCullum, M. M., Maldonado, N., & Baltes, B. (2014). Storytelling to teach cultural awareness: The right story at the right time. *LEARNing Landscapes, 7*(2), 219–223. https://files.eric.ed.gov/fulltext/ED546872.pdf

McIntosh, K., Girvan, E. J., Horner, R. H., & Smolkowski, K. (2014). Education not Incarceration: A Conceptual Model for Reducing Racial and Ethnic Disproportionality in School Discipline. *The Journal of Applied Research on Children, 5*(2). https://digitalcommons.library.tmc.edu/childrenatrisk/vol5/iss2/4

Mello, R. (2001). The power of storytelling: How oral narrative influences children's relationships in classrooms. *International Journal of Education & the Arts, 2*(1). http://www.ijea.org/v2n1/

Miller, R., Katrina Liu, K., & Ball, A. F. (2020, April). Critical Counter-Narrative as Transformative Methodology for Educational Equity. *Review of Research in Education, 44*(1), 269–300. https://doi.org/10.3102/0091732X20908501

My Teaching Partner Secondary Project. (2021). *Coaching Cycles.* https://www.secondarycoaching.org/mtps-model

Nishioka, V. (2017). *School discipline data indicators: A guide for districts and schools (REL 2017–240).* Washington, DC: U.S. Department of Education, Institute of Education Sciences, National Center for Education Evaluation and Regional Assistance, Regional Educational Laboratory Northwest. Retrieved from https://ies.ed.gov/ncee/edlabs

Okri, B. (1997). *A way of being free.* W&N.

OSEP Technical Assistance Center on Positive Behavioral Interventions and Supports. (2015). *PBIS Implementation Blueprint.* https://www.pbis.org/resource/pbis-implementation-blueprint

Perry, B. D., & Ablon, J. S. (2019). CPS as Neurodevelopmentally Sensitive and Trauma-Informed Approach. In A. R. Pollastri, J. S. Ablon, & M. J. G. Hone (Eds.), *Collaborative Problem Solving. An Evidence-Based Approach to Implementation and Practice* (pp. 122–138). Springer International Publishing.

Pushout Film. (2021). *About.* https://pushoutfilm.com/about

Reese, L. (2012). Storytelling in Mexican homes: Connections between oral and literacy practices. *Bilingual Research Journal, 35*(3). https:// doi:10.1080/15235882.2012.734006

Skiba, R. J., Arredondo, M. I., & Rausch, M. K. (2014). New and developing research on disparities in discipline. *Discipline Disparities Series.* https://indrc.indiana.edu/tools-resources/pdf-disciplineseries/disparity_newresearch_full_040414.pdf

Smyth, J. (2006). 'When students have power': Student engagement, student voice, and the possibilities for school reform around 'dropping out' of school. *International Journal of Leadership in Education, 9*(4), 285–298. https:// doi:10.1080/13603120600894232

Staley, B., & Freeman, L. A. (2017). Digital storytelling as student-centred pedagogy: Empowering high school students to frame their futures. Research and Practice in Technology Enhanced *Learning, 12*(21). doi:10.1186/s41039-017-0061-9

Suspension Stories. (2021). *About the Author.* https://www.suspensionstories.com/

Utley, O. (2008). Keeping the tradition of African storytelling alive. *Yale National Initiative.* https://teachers.yale.edu/curriculum/viewer/initiative_09.01.08_u

Vanden Poel, L., & Hermans, D. (2019). Narrative coherence and identity: Associations with psychological well-being and internalizing symptoms. *Frontiers in Psychology.* doi:10.3389/fpsyg.2019.01171

Wake, D. G. (2012). Exploring Rural Contexts with Digital Storytelling. *Rural Educator, 33*(3), 23–37.

Whitenton, K. (2017). *Narrative biases: When storytelling hurts user experience.* https://www.nngroup.com/articles/narrative-biases/

Winslade, J., & Monk, G. (2000). *Narrative mediation: A new approach to conflict resolution.* https://www.researchgate.net/publication/240132907

Zak, P. J. (2013, October). How stories change the brain. *Greater Good Magazine.* https://greatergood.berkeley.edu/profile/paul_zak

ADDITIONAL READING

Fracassini, E. (2018). Checking Yourself for Bias in the Classroom. *Learning for Justice.* https://www.learningforjustice.org/magazine/checking-yourself-for-bias-in-the-classroom

Gonser, S. (2019, December 13). Key Strategies for Reducing Friction Over Student Discipline. *Edutopia.* https://www.edutopia.org/article/key-strategies-reducing-friction-over-student-discipline

Hooper, L. (2019, January 21). Using data storytelling to disrupt white supremacy culture. Lydia Hooper. http://lydiahooper.com/blog/white-supremacy

Hurst, K. W. (2016, December 7). Biased Discipline at My School. *Edutopia.* https://www.edutopia.org/article/biased-discipline-at-my-school-kelly-wickham-hurst

Knight, M. (2021, October 13). Outrage Grows Over Jailing of Children as Tennessee University Cuts Ties With Judge Involved. ProPublica. https://www.propublica.org/article/outrage-grows-over-jailing-of-children-as-tennessee-university-cuts-ties-with-judge-involved

Stevenson, N. (2018). Developing cultural understanding through storytelling. *Journal of Teaching in Travel & Tourism*, *19*(2), 1–14. doi:10.1080/15313220.2018.1560528

Stratton-Berkessel, R. (Host). (2020, September 8). How Narrative Mediation Promotes Respectful Relationships (Episode 136) [Audio podcast episode]. *Positivity Strategist*. https://positivitystrategist.com/narrative-mediation/

Weismann, M. (2017). *Prelude to Prison: Student Perspectives on School Suspension*. Syracuse Studies on Peace and Conflict Resolution.

Wright, S. E. (2020). *Redefining Trauma: Understanding and Coping with a Cortisoaked Brain*. Taylor & Francis. doi:10.4324/9780429269110

KEY TERMS AND DEFINITIONS

Bias: A misaligned personal assumption about an external situation, group, or person that conflicts with the truth or reality about that situation, group or person.

Conflict Story: A narrative summary of an instance of interpersonal conflict.

Counter-Narrative: A self-constructed story developed in contrast to a story that often paints a less than favorable or unfair picture of the events or individuals involved.

Digital Storytelling: The creation and delivery of a story or narrative using common digital platforms and technologies, such as social media and mobile devices.

Equity-Driven Data: Data and data collection practices that incorporate non-dominant cultural perspectives, social structures, identities, and value systems.

Interpersonal Conflict: A disagreement or unresolved issue between two or more persons.

Morality Play: A dramatized performance of a story or narrative that is designed to teach a moral or ethical lesson.

Narrative Mediation: An interpersonal conflict resolution method that involves a neutral, 3rd party mediator who guides parties through the process of first telling, then reframing a conflict story.

Pygmalion Effect: Aka, self-fulfilling prophecy. The phenomenon describing the effect of teacher perceptions of students on student performance.

Subjective Discipline: Instances of school discipline or behavioral infractions that are more subjective in nature – such as defiance or insubordination – as opposed to more objective infractions like violence or theft.

Chapter 8
Rethinking Exclusionary Discipline Consequences for Discretionary Reasons for Economically Disadvantaged Youth

Thelma Laredo Clark
https://orcid.org/0000-0002-2047-2123
Baylor University, USA

Brandi R. Ray
Baylor University, USA

Elizabeth Anne Murray
Baylor University, USA

ABSTRACT

Exclusionary discipline practices are continuously pushing economically disadvantaged students out of their traditional home campuses instead of rehabilitating them with the ability to become productive members of their communities. This chapter explores the development of exclusionary discipline consequences and the known outcomes of these consequences on economically disadvantaged students. The chapter provides background information regarding the initial appeal of exclusionary discipline practices followed by the subsequent harm it created for certain groups of students. The chapter identifies the possibilities for decreasing the use of exclusionary discipline by adopting strategies like PBIS and restorative justice practices. The chapter closes with a discussion of the importance of schools moving away from exclusionary discipline practices. The authors argue transparency from school leaders with school community members is essential for the initial and continued success of restorative practices and the curbing of the damage of exclusionary consequences for students.

DOI: 10.4018/978-1-6684-3359-1.ch008

INTRODUCTION

The Gun-Free Schools Act of 1994 (GFSA) pushed school districts to use more punitive discipline measures to maintain safety on school grounds. School districts quickly adapted codes of conduct to reflect the new act. Swift action was required to subdue the concerns of the recent spike in violence and drug-related incidents. However, the GFSA became the gateway for school administrators to assign exclusionary discipline for offenses that are not safety concerns; suddenly, not all students were good enough to receive an education on their home campus. Economically disadvantaged students are the most affected by exclusionary discipline consequences since they often have difficulty connecting to their school community. Yet, they are most often assigned exclusionary discipline for discretionary reasons. For example, Texas school administrators assigned more than 58,000 economically disadvantaged students to a Discipline Alternative Education Program (DAEP) (Texas Education Agency, 2020). While school districts are currently adopting discipline strategies like Positive Behavioral Intervention and Supports (PBIS), restorative justice, and rehabilitative practices, school districts must rethink discipline consequences for discretionary reasons to ensure students needing the most support are kept in their home campus. The proposed chapter explores the need for decreasing exclusionary discipline for discretionary reasons, the lack of restorative discipline options and rehabilitative transition plans for school administrators to use, and the need to focus on connecting students to their schools.

BACKGROUND: THE DEVELOPMENT, INCREASE, AND DAMAGE OF EXCLUSIONARY DISCIPLINE PRACTICES

After an uptick in school shootings during the first half of the 1990s, legislatures passed the Gun-Free Schools Act of 1994 (GFSA) to curtail the increase in school violence. With the passing of GFSA, schools also began to adapt their student codes of conduct to reflect the new act and increase their use of exclusionary discipline practices, those which exclude students from their typical classroom. Schools needed to take swift action to quell concerns of the recent spike in violence and drug-related incidents (Skiba, 2014; Skiba & Losen, 2015; Skiba & Peterson, 1999; Tajalli & Garba, 2014). Shortly after the GFSA was signed, school leaders in many districts adopted zero-tolerance policies. Though created out of concern for the well-being and safety of students, the GFSA became a gateway for school administrators to assign exclusionary discipline for offenses that were not safety concerns. Fear has been a primary driving force behind the adoption of zero-tolerance and exclusionary discipline policies, making communities feel that if minor disruptions are not punished, they will lose control (Skiba, 2014).

Exclusionary discipline practices assigned to students who commit infractions under zero-tolerance policies include out-of-school suspension (OSS), in-school suspension (ISS), and expulsion (Cruz et al., 2021). The most commonly used form of exclusionary discipline is out-of-school suspension. When an administrator assigns a student OSS, the student is removed from the campus and asked to stay home for a few days based on the offense and what guidelines or policy each district follows. School districts also use ISS to keep students in school but separated from their peers after a discipline incident. Schools that use ISS have students remain on school grounds, but the student is isolated to the assigned ISS classroom. In some schools, the students are assigned to cubicle-like seating arrangements to not engage with other students in the room. Students who have committed an offense that falls under the category of drugs or violence are assigned to a Disciplinary Alternative Education Program (DAEP). These programs are used to house students for an extended period outlined by the school districts' board policy and student code of conduct. Some DAEPs are housed within the traditional school in a separate classroom. Still, most school districts also have an off-campus DAEP option in which the student is removed from their traditional home school to attend DAEP for the recommended days after a discipline hearing.

Some researchers consider exclusionary discipline consequences to be negative discipline consequences because of the student's removal and how the removal impacts some of the most vulnerable student populations (Anyon et al., 2018; Carver et al., 2010; Cramer et al., 2014; Skiba & Losen, 2015; Skiba & Peterson, 1999). Although DAEP classrooms vary from state to state, a DAEP is much different from a traditional school; teachers only concentrate on delivering instruction for core subjects, students adhere to a uniform policy, and there are no after-school activities or clubs. According to Texas Education Code (TEC) Chapter 37, the DAEP setting for schools must include the following: students assigned to DAEP are to be in a different classroom from their peers, teachers are to focus their instruction on the four core subjects and self-discipline, and the staff, which is made up of fully certified teachers, is trained to provide counseling and supervision.

DAEPS were created to serve students that have committed mandatory DAEP offenses specifically. These include-assault, possession of alcohol, or possession of marijuana. However, school administrators may send students to DAEP for discretionary reasons if they feel other discipline strategies have been exhausted. Every state has a list of reasons considered mandatory DAEP recommendation reasons and other discipline offenses that are not mandated to have a DAEP recommendation. The reasons are known as discretionary reasons and include such offenses as being rude and disrespectful and creating a class disruption (Texas Education Data Standards,

2019). Administrators often use exclusionary discipline practices like OSS and DAEP to set an example so that other students will not engage in the same behavior (Gregory et al., 2010; Skiba, 2014). The use of exclusionary discipline consequences has not helped school leaders decrease discipline incidents, increase-academic success in students, or improve-school climate (Cramer et al., 2014; Kang-Brown, 2013; Lehr et al., 2009; Skiba, 2014; Wilkerson et al., 2016; Wilkerson & Afacan, 2009). Furthermore, substantiating evidence that those exclusionary disciplinary consequences are helping school administrators improve behavior is scarce (Skiba et al., 2011; Skiba, 2014; Wilkerson et al., 2016).

Evidence shows that students removed to DAEP struggle to reconnect with their home campuses due to feeling excluded and isolated (Kennedy, 2019; Owens & Konkol, 2004; Selman, 2017). Not only do these discipline consequences affect students socially and emotionally, but they also generate feelings of disconnectedness and adverse outcomes in academics (Kang-Brown et al., 2013; Kennedy et al., 2019; Skiba, 2014). Administrators recommending a DAEP deprive students of equal educational opportunities. Furthermore, research indicates that students from economically disadvantaged backgrounds suffer more from the negative impact of exclusionary discipline policies than their peers (Anderson & Ritter, 2020; Selman, 2017).

District administrators often overlook that exclusionary discipline consequences add to the achievement gaps of minority and economically disadvantaged students, despite them being the group that needs the most support (Gregory et al., 2010, Selman, 2017). Economically disadvantaged students often have difficulty connecting to their school community, to begin with, but exclusionary consequences like DAEP further exacerbate this (Anderson & Ritter, 2017; Lehr et al., 2009; Selman, 2017; Skiba, 2014; Tajalli & Garba, 2014). Economically disadvantaged students will be kept from developing a sense of community in their schools as long as exclusionary discipline strategies like DAEP continue to push them out. Assigning exclusionary discipline consequences leads to more repeat recommendations to DAEP, more encounters with law enforcement, and dropping out of school (Booker & Mitchell, 2011; Cramer et al., 2014; Skiba & Losen, 2015; Spence, 2020).

Some school district codes of conduct allow the use of DAEP for students who engage in repetitive disciplinary issues that are not mandatory reasons related to violence or drugs. Administrators face deciding whether or not to use an exclusionary discipline consequence. This process makes the use of exclusionary discipline consequences subjective, and the decision is left entirely up to the perception of the administrator (Fenning & Jenkins, 2019). School districts have done little to correct the possibility of bias when the use of DAEP is increasing, and the recommendations for placement are so subjective (Booker & Mitchell, 2011).

School districts implementing DAEPs make it easier to push students out of schools, further contributing to inequality and the exclusion of minority students (Selman, 2017). Although advocates of zero-tolerance policies believe that benefits exist with removing the problem student, through the use of exclusionary discipline, research has not proven that student removal is a solution to the problem or has improved academic success or school climate (Cramer et al., 2014; Kang-Brown, 2013; Lehr et al., 2009; Skiba, 2014; Wilkerson et al., 2016, Wilkerson & Afacan, 2009).

The use of exclusionary discipline is a way for school administrators to show that they have restored safety on campus by removing the problem, abiding by zero-tolerance policies, and satisfying parents. When administrators remove students, they are also released from rehabilitating them; they send the message that a specific type of student does not belong on school grounds (Cramer et al., 2014; Fenning & Jenkins, 2019; Geronimo, 2011). DAEP schools are not desirable places. School administrators have lined DAEP schools' entrances with metal detectors and have strict dress codes, making the campuses comparable to jails. The students do not speak to one another except for designated times. ISS classrooms are similar; students sit away from each other, are not allowed to talk to each other, or remain on school grounds when the school day ends. DAEP schools often mimic a site for criminals, which only helps to create a society that is no longer prosperous in the future (Phillips, 2013; Selman, 2017; Spence, 2020). The student sent to DAEP will often return to the home campus and often engage in another behavior that will send them back to DAEP, building a cycle of recidivism. Zero-tolerance policies do not necessarily make schools safer; instead, they push students out.

On the contrary, students feel less secure, leading stakeholders to question if these policies genuinely aim to help students (Dutil, 2020; Kang-Brown et al., 2013; Skiba & Losen, 2015). To find a positive outcome from the use of exclusionary discipline on economically disadvantaged students is challenging. The use of DAEPs assists in marginalizing students and pushing them out of school because the school staff has already labeled them as "undesirable and low-achieving" (Geronimo, p. 430). Exclusionary discipline focuses on fixing behaviors, not providing support to students (Cruz et al., 2021).

The same year the GFSA legislation passed, President Clinton signed Improving America's School Act of 1994 (IASA) to help disadvantaged students by increasing technology in education, keeping schools and communities safe and drug-free, and helping students at risk of dropping out. However, these two policies seemed to cancel each other out when it came to economically disadvantaged students by giving schools the tools to remove these students for discipline offenses that were not always mandatory. School administrators continued to send economically disadvantaged students to DAEP more often than others, proving that the use of the GFSA kept students from receiving the help the IASA was supposed to provide (Anderson & Ritter, 2020; Selman, 2017). Exclusionary discipline strategies like those that came into practice after the GFSA was signed are linked to causing anti-social behaviors in students, low academic growth, low attendance rates, and low graduation rates (Cramer et al., 2014; Skiba & Losen, 2015). The consequences of exclusionary discipline policies seem to lead to more harm than good for these students. Reacting to discipline concerns with zero-tolerance policies that came from the GFSA has not shown to be effective; instead, negative feelings toward schools have emerged along with lowered academic success for students because it has allowed the use of exclusionary discipline consequences (Cramer et al., 2014; Skiba & Losen, 2015).

The lack of rehabilitative transition programs and interventions may increase the continued use of DAEP assignments for economically disadvantaged students. The data regarding why students are assigned DAEP is abundant. Administrators place students in DAEP when they no longer fit the mold of expectations at their traditional home campus; it is of concern that few states report the outcomes of students placed in DAEP (Lehr et al., 2009; Novak, 2019). Students are continuously moved from DAEP to regular classes without documenting the effects.

Exclusionary discipline does not curtail poor behaviors; instead, it has adverse effects on students' learning by creating discouraging learning environments and depriving students of educational opportunities (Fenning et al., 2010; Gregory et al., 2016; Kang-Brown et al., 2013; Spence, 2020; Skiba, 2014). Schools reacting with high exclusionary discipline use prove that schools are becoming more reliant on responding to disciplinary concerns instead of finding strategies to correct behaviors by rebuilding, reinforcing, and redirecting (Simonsen & Sugai, 2013). Schools that serve more economically disadvantaged students have fewer resources and tools for discipline; therefore, they utilize exclusionary discipline more often (Kang-Brown et al., 2013). Administrators are forced to choose between removing students after repetitive incidents like class disruption, one of the most common offenses in schools, instead of finding solutions for their behaviors through restorative or rehabilitative practices.

ALTERNATIVES TO EXCLUSIONARY DISCIPLINE: RESTORATIVE DISCIPLINE APPROACHES AND POSITIVE BEHAVIOR INTERVENTION SUPPORTS (PBIS)

Schools are responsible for providing an equitable education for all students regardless of their economic status, ability, race, ethnicity, religion, gender, and sexual orientation. Educators' beliefs regarding economically disadvantaged students shape the type of instruction they receive, the type of relationships faculty will develop with them, and whether or not faculty will advocate for their equitable education (Gorski, 2018). However, ensuring that all students receive an equitable education necessitates differentiation among discipline strategies and consequences. School administrators will have difficulty connecting education and socio-economic status unless they can understand the biases and barriers students experience that affect how they interact with school personnel and peers (Gorksi, 2018). Schools with high records of DAEP assignments substantiates that administrators are becoming more reliant on reactive disciplinary measures. Especially, students assigned to a DAEP for discretionary reasons would benefit more from a rehabilitation-type program or restorative program that attempts to redirect and correct the behavior rather than removal to a different setting, like a DAEP. Rather than focusing their efforts on proactive approaches to discipline and finding strategies that offer students the opportunities to rebuild, reinforce, and redirect their actions toward positive behavior, they continually place students in DAEP programs (Simonsen & Sugai, 2013).

When administrators remove students from their schools, they are released from rehabilitating them, thereby sending the message that a specific type of student does not belong on traditional school grounds (Cramer et al., 2014; Fenning & Jenkins, 2019; Geronimo, 2011). Students who do not follow the rules are often assigned exclusionary discipline because it is a prompt response to their disruption of the learning environment; however, administrators fail to see that this will alleviate the issue temporarily (Gerlinger et al., 2021). When student behaviors are not corrected by campus administrators using strategies other than exclusion, the rates of recidivism increase and the revolving door of DAEPs is repeatedly used (Booker & Mitchell, 2011). Because students from specific demographics are overrepresented in exclusionary discipline programs, students often attribute the constant use of exclusionary discipline as a reaction from school administrators to the differences between students and school staff based on race or socioeconomic status (Cramer et al., 2014).

Applying restorative practices to discipline helps remove the beliefs that discipline in schools is simply about authority, zero-tolerance strategies, and exclusion (Velez et al., 2020). Teachers recognize their own need for the development of new skills in classroom management and fear that without the ability to connect or relate to students, classroom behaviors may continue to be seen by school staff as worthy of an exclusionary discipline consequence (Spence, 2020). Lessening the chances of negative school experiences begins with lowering repeated discipline offenses by implementing strategies to help students early in their schooling (Albrecht & Braten, 2008). While the numbers surrounding exclusionary discipline practices are distressing, alternative approaches exist. Specifically, research supports the use of restorative discipline approaches. Restorative practices focus on helping students focus on mending relationships and repairing harm.

Most importantly, helping them learn to recognize how harm and damage are consequences of their actions (Payne & Welch, 2015). Restorative justice practices provide students with time to reflect on their actions so that recognition of harm occurs, and they explore ways to repair damaged relationships (Calhoun & Pelech, 2010; Childs et al., 2016; Gregory et al., 2016; Simson, 2014; Skiba & Losen, 2015). Strategies used in the restorative justice model include addressing discipline concerns through conferences with students, peer mediation sessions, community service assignments, and other activities that help students restore relationships their behavior may have damaged (Payne & Welch, 2015). Restorative practices are flexible and applicable in the school and community setting. They encompass community meetings, discussion circles, and other engaging activities that focus on approaching harm with the intent to understand how it happened and how to repair the damage done (Velez et al., 2020).

Benefits of Restorative Approaches

Restorative practices benefit students in several ways. These include increasing student engagement, building a stronger school community, and helping students recognize and reflect on their actions and thoughts. Of particular importance to the positive student behavior is developing a strong school community. Connections between school faculty and staff and students are crucial to student success. Students that feel content and have become involved in their school community will develop a sense of loyalty to their community; through these feelings of connectedness, they will create a sense of purpose and empowerment (McMillan & Chavis, 1986; Thurman et al., 2018). Students who bond with their school community also are less likely to be involved in lawbreaking behaviors (Gregory et al., 2010). Restorative practices are more likely to help administrators increase inclusivity in their schools and create a more welcoming environment to promote equality (Simson, 2014). Researchers believe that when student engagement increases, negative behaviors will decrease because better engagement usually means better student/teacher relationships (Fredericks et al., 2019; Skiba & Losen, 2015). When students are not involved in school activities, it often means they will not have the academic and emotional support needed for school success (Cramer et al., 2014). Teachers who can interact with their students through more positive conversations have students who are more successful both socially and academically (Reinke et al., 2013).

Making students feel like they are a part of the school community becomes more challenging if an administrator has issued a consequence to a student that forces them to withdraw from their home campus. When students are removed from their typical school communities, they are not allowed to reflect on their actions and how they have affected others. Removing a student from their traditional home campus as a consequence does not necessarily mean that the student understands their actions were wrong and that they should not repeat the behavior. Furthermore, when exclusionary discipline occurs, students do not have the opportunity to rebuild or repair relationships, leading to repeated behavior (Calhoun & Pelech, 2010). The ideal time to step in and make sure students remain connected to their home campus would be when they initially exhibit behavioral issues, instead of allowing the behavior to lead them to disengage further through exclusionary discipline (Andrews et al., 1998; Kang-Brown, 2013). In addition to building stronger school communities, restorative approaches to discipline allow for rehabilitation by providing students the help they need to understand what they did wrong and how to correct it and prevent it in the future (Brown, 2007). Owens and Konkol (2004) found in their examination of school settings that students, although wanting to return to their home campus, felt confused and wondered if the DAEP school was a better fit for them because they started to build relationships and found support.

Implementing restorative practices teaches students that some of their actions harm others, and hurting others impacts their ability to trust one another. They learn that when trust is violated, there are ways to heal the relationship, and this will encourage students to follow the rules so that the relationships they have built are not harmed (Payne & Welch, 2015). Offering restorative approaches to behavior involves more than simply avoiding exclusionary discipline practices; it requires education for all concerned parties. Educating students on what contributes to negative behavior should be supported by educating teachers and parents about discipline. Using restorative justice strategies encourages an environment of reflection and repairing relationships as a whole community simultaneously reduces the number of discipline incidents in school (Payne & Welch, 2015). Trauma-informed teaching is a strategy that has helped schools understand more minority and economically disadvantaged students.

Like trauma-informed teaching, social-emotional learning should be significant in education because it helps build trust, patience, and respect, thereby bettering the climate for learning (Brown, 2007; Phillips, 2013). Parent involvement is another beneficial practice in preventing exclusionary discipline, specifically for economically disadvantaged students. (Skiba, 2014; Stacy et al., 2019). By using more inclusive restorative strategies, schools and communities will be working together to ensure more awareness of the equity of discipline consequences (Kennedy, 2019).

Recognizing Obstructions to and Opportunities for Successful Restorative Practices

Exclusionary consequences like DAEP and OSS have not helped improve behavior; in fact, several authors reiterate that removing students negatively affects them and does not improve school climate (Cramer et al., 2014; Skiba, 2014; Skiba & Peterson, 1999). Utilizing "proactive support" instead of "reactive punishment" would be more effective and would reduce exclusionary discipline (Skiba & Losen, 2015 p. 11). Strategies like PBIS are available to school districts, yet exclusionary discipline practices usually take precedence for various reasons. Training administrators and teachers on what effects trauma has on students are essential to understand better the need for less exclusionary consequences (Dutil, 2020).

Change requires time, work, and resources. Exclusionary discipline practices offer an easy solution to a complex problem. They are easy to assign and do not require much follow-up. The student is removed from the classroom or campus, and business goes on as usual. The reluctance to use rehabilitative transition programs and interventions allows for the continued use of exclusionary discipline for economically disadvantaged students. In creating and implementing more restorative plans for student discipline, an administrator may experience "push-back" as developing such practices is time-consuming, unlike the "quick fix" exclusionary discipline provides (Skiba & Peterson, 1999, p. 382). Progress in school districts focused on restorative practices for discipline is becoming more apparent and has grown from a few initial schools to entire communities and states (Freeman et al., 2016). Finding restorative programs to use in schools is not the difficult part of this journey; implementing and fidelity to those programs are the challenges.

Successfully implementing restorative justice programs requires buy-in from the involved parties. Administrators and teachers must recognize their overreliance on exclusionary discipline practices and identify the damage they create for students, especially students from economically disadvantaged homes. Administrators need support in using techniques that will help them increase equity in disciplinary actions and decrease exclusionary discipline (Kennedy, 2019; Skiba & Losen, 2015). The success of programs like PBIS is not possible without help from the school community and parents. Administrators have continually assigned exclusionary consequences due to pressure from parents and community members that expect them to keep students under control (Fenning & Jenkins, 2019). Zero-tolerance policies have pushed school administrators to use a one-size-fits-all style when assigning consequences rather than looking at the context of each situation (Cramer et al., 2014). District administrators should recognize the importance of keeping students a part of their school communities and stress the significance of positive interactions between teachers and students. Administrators need to endorse preventative strategies and do more to encourage the building of positive relationships between school personnel and students (Fenning et al., 2012; Gregory et al., 2016, Skiba & Losen, 2015; Skiba & Peterson, 1999; Spence, 2020).

In addition to buy-in and support from administrators, parents, teachers, and school communities, successful intervention programs require education. These programs necessitate teachers and administrators to look at the disciplinary data in their local settings to pinpoint specific trends and patterns. Learning to do this requires training and professional development, and time to draft new disciplinary policies and then educate all involved parties about those new policies. When creating these new policies, one way of decreasing the use of exclusionary discipline assignments is to set limits on the assignment of DAEP for discretionary reasons for specific populations of students such as those in elementary school, special education, and those with 504 plans.

Seeing the adverse outcomes exclusionary discipline has on students should encourage school districts and administrators to reexamine how they handle conflict and fundamental rule deviation and what they are doing to engage students (Gregory et al., 2016; Phillips, 2013). As Booker & Mitchell (2011) note, school administrators need to reevaluate the kinds of behaviors severe enough to merit a DAEP recommendation and learn that the majority of student infractions do not justify exclusionary consequences. Professional development for administrators and teachers that focus on strategies to diffuse conflict has proven beneficial to schools in reducing exclusionary discipline (Gregory et al., 2010). Trauma-informed teaching and social-emotional learning also show success in helping faculty, staff, and students build trust, patience, and respect, maximizing the climate for learning (Brown, 2007; Phillips, 2013).

Successful intervention programs require more from administrators than assigning a consequence; they include teaching and involving the students. Giving students voices by making the discipline process less one-sided helps build better relationships and decrease reoccurrences as students learn to take responsibility for their actions (Anyon et al., 2018). These programs also teach students how to self-regulate and encourage them to remain connected to their home campuses to begin restoring and building positive relationships (Gregory et al., 2010; Novak, 2019). Central, to the involvement of students is the role of the school counselor or counseling team. Unlike teachers and administrators, counselors have specialized training on implementing strategies like solution-focused brief therapy and restorative models, which change the focus from the problem to the solution. Counselors also assist students in developing goals focused on solutions, taking responsibility for their actions, and repairing relationships (Calhoun & Pelech, 2010; Moore et al., 2020). With the knowledge and support of counselors, techniques like "Time Away" and deescalating/calming rooms make their way into schools and provide students with a safe place to reflect on and discuss the behavior with a facilitator and begin a redirection plan (Albrecht & Braten, 2008).

Alternatives to exclusionary discipline practices are available to schools. Programs like PBIS allow greater student success and a stronger school community, but these programs do not appear overnight; they take time and effort. Until these programs are fully implemented, schools should work on helping students have more successful transitions out of DAEP and back into their home schools. DAEPs should include transition steps that serve as interventions so that students can return to their home campus and be successful; however, they are lacking (Moore et al., 2020). As with any transition to a new approach, restorative discipline programs need to be given time to prove successful. When schools begin to implement programs like PBIS, administrators have to be willing to offer support to teachers, and teachers have to be ready to try these new strategies with fidelity.

Positive Behavioral Interventions and Supports (PBIS)

Since the early 2000s, school districts nationwide have been looking for discipline strategies that are less punitive and more student-centered. Factors needed in techniques to decrease exclusionary discipline are: building relationships through restorative practices, helping students understand and regulate their emotions, increasing the use of PBIS, and restricting codes of conduct to reflect the changes made (Skiba & Losen, 2015). Developed in 1998, Positive Behavioral Interventions and Supports (PBIS) is a program that teaches school administrators to use student data to learn how different discipline strategies are affecting students in their school, helping them set goals to support further the success of all students (Center on PBIS, 2021). Administrators decipher the data to find specific places and reasons or times where negative student behavior occurs. Using this data, school faculty and staff can collaborate to create more equitable plans to help students remain on task, grow socially, and reach higher levels of success (Center on PBIS, 2021). Although exclusionary discipline targets students after negative behavior occurs, PBIS supports all students. Research has shown that PBIS decreases disruptive behaviors, improves school climate, helps foster positive relationships school-wide, reduces exclusionary discipline consequences, and contributes to higher academic achievement over time (James et al., 2019; Pas et al., 2019; Reinke et al., 2013). When PBIS is implemented appropriately, school staff and students see more engagement and less exclusionary discipline consequences (Center on PBIS, 2021). Administrators need the support of their districts to adequately staff their schools to have programs like PBIS become fully functional.

SOLUTIONS AND RECOMMENDATIONS

Finding a solution or alternative to exclusionary discipline is no longer the problem. Now that programs focused on rebuilding relationships, building a sense of community, and restorative practices are effective, the problem is ensuring their successful implementation in the schools (Payne & Welch, 2015; Velez et al., 2020). One recommendation central to ensuring a smooth transition and implementation process is recognizing the importance of open and continuous communication with all involved stakeholders. The communication between school administrators and their faculty and staff and between school officials and the parents and communities is particularly significant.

The Broad School Community

Schools belong to the community they serve. Communities need to be involved in the changes to discipline practices to support their schools and community members. Removing students with behavior problems has become an expectation with little success. Community members need to be made aware of the issues that exclusionary discipline practices may bring for a community in the long run, including lower academic success, lower attendance rates, and lower graduation rates.

Schools also have to be accountable to the communities and families they serve. The well-being of students is and should remain a top concern for schools. Student well-being, however, should not be limited to just the students who have not committed disciplinary infractions. Schools and communities must consider what practices accomplish the most for all students, not just those from economically privileged homes. Zero-tolerance policies were created to keep schools safe but stretched beyond their original intent. Unfortunately, students are assigned exclusionary discipline consequences for discretionary reasons like insubordination and excessive tardiness—the kinds of infractions that do not necessarily affect the safety of the school. Students deserve to be safe in schools that encourage learning; relying on zero-tolerance strategies that exclude and punish students negatively affects their outcomes (Skiba & Losen, 2015). While student safety and success are essential for the individual student, they are also crucial for healthy communities. Stakeholders need to be made aware that if the student sent to DAEP is isolated and not rehabilitated with skills to reintegrate into their home school, they will return to DAEP and have a greater likelihood of dropping out of school and becoming involved in criminal activity (Anderson & Ritter, 2017; Gregory et al., 2010; Skiba, 2014). Excluding students for exhibiting unwanted behaviors will not improve their chances of success or the school's ratings (Fenning et al., 2010; Skiba, 2014). Stakeholders need to be aware of the negative shift in a school culture that the continuous use of exclusionary discipline practices can bring.

Changes to disciplinary policies should be handled carefully, taking the time to do research and outreach so that all involved parties can become invested in the success of new policies. Communities need to understand the benefits of programs like PBIS and how these programs proactively support all students. School leaders have to communicate that even though school discipline policies are changing, the safety and wellbeing of students are still the school's top priority. School community members need to understand that safety concerns would still be addressed accordingly. Resolving and redirecting negative behavior is better for students' social and academic success than assigning exclusionary discipline consequences. The goals of restorative justice programs need to be transparent, and the community needs to be involved in implementing and transitioning to these new approaches to achieve success. When students succeed, communities benefit, but when students fail, communities suffer the consequences.

School Faculty and Staff

Convincing faculty and staff can be a daunting task that district-level administrators face when recommending a change in discipline procedures. Implementing a new approach to discipline requires a great deal of learning and unlearning, especially when moving from a reactive to a proactive style. Since their development, school districts have felt the need to use punitive discipline practices like DAEP to ensure that school staff will not tolerate certain behaviors that prevent them from teaching their students (Skiba, 2014). Educators have been led to believe that removing a disruptive student is the best practice. As a result, school administrators have allowed the exclusion of students that do not fit the norm established in schools and further the divide between students and their traditional home campus.

School leaders were concerned about maintaining school safety and student success and felt these acts and policies supplied the needed support to remove obstacles from their paths. Academic achievement is a significant concern during the transition to a new discipline plan. Teachers want to do their jobs effectively and help their students learn and succeed. However, suppose the goal is to implement policies that support the most significant number of students. In that case, teachers must recognize the academic damage connected with programs like DAEP, ISS, and OSS. Students often have a noticeable gap in learning due to their DAEP placements, making them more likely to return to DAEP due to repeated disruptive behavior due to an academic gap (Wilkinson et al., 2020). Academic gaps often contribute to disruptive behavior in the first place. Researchers have found that failures in learning are culprits for the disruptive behaviors that students are issued DAEP for; removing students further allows schools to disconnect students from the learning process (Phillips, 2013; Spence, 2020). DAEPs are not seen as schools where academics are the top priority (Brown, 2007; Novak, 2019; Spence, 2020). The movement between DAEP and the traditional home campus creates an even more significant gap in their learning due to lost instructional time that often makes grade level gaps or retention (Brown, 2007; Fenning et al., 2012; Novak, 2019).

The students miss out on learning, fall further behind, and do not receive positive support from programs like PBIS. Teachers need to learn that these programs offer a way of handling disciplinary issues without sacrificing the learning opportunities for their students.

Parents and Students

When implementing disciplinary policies, the third stakeholder to consider is parents and their students. Students are the most affected when campuses rely on reactive measures instead of preventative measures. Communication between schools and families is essential for the success of restorative disciplinary programs. Unfortunately, in many situations, a disconnect exists between parents and school administrators, and sometimes the possibility for a relationship is tarnished before it begins. Schools need proactive support from parents, but in many cases, the initial time parents and schools work together to help a student is after a significant infraction has already occurred. Reaching out to a parent at the first sign of behavior issues may help them develop a better solution together. Transparency with parents is essential. Not all parents favor restorative practices but informing families of the school's goals and reasons for implementing these approaches is critical for gaining their support (Skiba & Losen, 2015). Parents have been told for the last 30 years that exclusionary discipline practices are what works best, so now they need to be told the truth about the harm these practices may bring.

When students are sent to DAEP, their state is often unknown and unaccounted for; some return to their home campus and graduate, others never re-enroll (Kennedy et al., 2019). If parents could see that removing a student does not help school administrators curtail behaviors but somewhat further impedes students' success, they would be more willing to consider alternate discipline strategies. If parents feel that students are being pushed out due to exclusionary discipline, parent engagement will be lacking (Skiba, 2014). Additionally, some administrators often use exclusionary discipline practices like DAEP to set an example so that other students will not engage in the same behavior (Gregory et al., 2010). DAEP schools appear to prepare students for jail (Kennedy, 2019; Spence, 2020). Parents need to be more aware of the consequences if the schools are set on making examples of students by sending them to schools that mimic the prison system.

Finally, the students themselves need to be brought into the implementation process. Students feel less safe and more disconnected as the rates of DAEP usage rise. McMillan and Chavis (1986), who developed the sense of community theory, define the four major components needed to create a sense of community: membership, influence, integration, fulfillment of needs, and shared emotional connections. Although students will not always express it, one of the things they long for the most is feeling connected; having that sense of belonging while in school is crucial. Furthermore, the seclusion that comes with exclusionary discipline practices is being forced on students during a critical time for adolescents as they learn to build a community within their school (Selman, 2017; Thurman et al., 2018).

Students' voices are vital in understanding the reasons for their behavior to be provided with strategies to cope with and overcome their negative behavior triggers. School leaders need to listen to their students when creating new disciplinary policies and show that they value their opinions. Parents and school staff need to be aware of student reactions regarding relationship building and how they feel better about learning from teachers who build relationships. Students feel more connected to teachers that encourage them rather than yell at them (Fredricks et al., 2019). Schools have a responsibility for educating students—the whole student—and that education must include teaching them strategies and methods for strengthening their prosocial behavior.

FUTURE RESEARCH DIRECTIONS

Due to the negative impact of exclusionary discipline, school communities, including educational researchers, must continue to advocate for access to more rehabilitative transition programs and interventions for economically disadvantaged students. For these programs to be implemented in schools, complete transparency is needed within the community. The voices of students and administrators need to be utilized to deliver the message to school district leaders and community members about the need to rehabilitate students and decrease exclusionary discipline consequences. These practices have adverse effects on students, schools, and communities. Further research is needed examining the implementation and transition processes and the community involvement and support of these programs. Year after year, data surrounding exclusionary discipline practices continually proves these consequences negatively impact economically disadvantaged students. This data should be reason enough for school district leaders and community members to devote time to find transition programs that will shut the revolving door opened through the use of DAEP. Of particular need are studies focused on exploring the voices of administrators and students regarding the outcomes of exclusionary discipline and their experiences in restorative justice.

CONCLUSION

School administrators trusting that exclusionary discipline practices will help reduce common office referrals is a misconception. Using exclusionary discipline practices to curtail behaviors by exemplifying students has not proved successful (Gregory et al., 2010; Skiba, 2014). Economically disadvantaged students are often in need of the most support while in school, yet exclusionary discipline practices remove these students from their home campuses, subjecting them to a lower quality of instruction and furthering academic gaps (Geronimo, 2011; Gregory et al., 2010; Wilkerson et al., 2016). Furthermore, the lack of alternate discipline consequences affects students in states where the percentage of economically disadvantaged students is high (Texas Education Agency, 2020). Economically disadvantaged students assigned exclusionary discipline consequences will lack the ability to make connections to their school communities and contribute to a cyclical pattern of negative behavior (Anderson & Ritter, 2017; Anyon et al., 2018; Carver et al., 2007; Cramer et al., 2014; Lehr et al., 2009; Selman, 2017; Skiba, 2014; Skiba & Losen, 2015; Skiba & Peterson, 1999; Tajalli & Garba, 2014).

Without implementing alternate disciplinary practices, rehabilitative transition programs, and interventions, DAEP assignments for economically disadvantaged students will continue to rise. Administrators and school leaders must advocate for transition programs to address the gaps that exclusionary discipline consequences have created. Communicating with community members and other stakeholders about the advantages of using more restorative or rehabilitative practices would benefit the entire school community and economically disadvantaged students. Instead of immediately turning to exclusionary discipline practices, using restorative practices or PBIS with fidelity could help shut the revolving door of exclusionary discipline practices and promote more successful educational experiences for all students.

ACKNOWLEDGMENT

The authors wish to express their gratitude to Nicholas R. Werse for his recommendations during the chapter's development.

REFERENCES

Anderson, K. P., & Ritter, G. W. (2020). Do school discipline policies treat students fairly? Evidence from Arkansas. *Educational Policy*, *34*(5), 707–734. doi:10.1177/0895904818802085

Anyon, Y., Atteberry-Ash, B., Yang, J., Pauline, M., Wiley, K., Cash, D., Downing, B., Greer, E., & Pisciotta, L. (2018). It's all about the relationships: Educators' rationales and strategies for building connections with students to prevent exclusionary school discipline outcomes. *Children & Schools*, *40*(4), 221–230. doi:10.1093/cs/cdy017

Carver, P. R., Lewis, L., & Tice, P. (2010). *Alternative schools and programs for public school students at risk of educational failure: 2007–08*. National Center for Education Statistics, Institute of Education Sciences, U.S. Dept. of Education.

Center on PBIS. (2021). *Positive Behavioral Interventions and Supports*. www.pbis.org

Cramer, E. D., Gonzalez, L., & Pellegrini-Lafont, C. (2014). From classmates to inmates: An integrated approach to break the school-to-prison pipeline. *Equity & Excellence in Education*, *47*(4), 461–475. doi:10.1080/10665684.2014.958962

Cruz, R. A., Firestorne, A. R., & Rodl, J. E. (2021). Disproportionality reduction in exclusionary school discipline: A best-evidence synthesis. *Review of Educational Research*, *91*(3), 397–431. doi:10.3102/0034654321995255

Fenning, P. A., Pulaski, S., Gomez, M., Morello, M., Maciel, L., Maroney, E., Schmidt, A., Dahlvig, K., McArdle, L., Morello, T., Wilson, R., Horwitz, A., & Maltese, R. (2012). Call to action: A critical need for designing alternatives to suspension and expulsion. *Journal of School Violence*, *11*(2), 105–117. doi:10.10 80/15388220.2011.646643

Freeman, J., Simonsen, B., McCoach, D. B., Sugai, G., Lombardi, A., & Homer, R. (2016). Relationship between school-wide positive behavior interventions and supports and academic, attendance and behavior outcomes in high schools. *Journal of Positive Behavior Interventions*, *18*(1), 41–51. doi:10.1177/1098300715580992

Gerlinger, J., Viano, S., Gardella, J. H., Fisher, B. W., Chris Curran, F., & Higgins, E. M. (2021). Exclusionary School Discipline and Delinquent Outcomes: A Meta-Analysis. *Journal of Youth and Adolescence*, *50*(8), 1493–1509. doi:10.100710964-021-01459-3 PMID:34117607

Geronimo, I. (2011). Deconstructing the marginalization of "underclass" students: Disciplinary alternative education. *University of Toledo Law Review. University of Toledo. College of Law*, *42*(2), 429–465.

Gorski, P. (2018). *Reaching and teaching students in poverty: strategies for erasing the opportunity gap* (2nd ed.). Teachers College Press.

Gregory, A., Clawson, K., Davis, A., & Gerewitz, J. (2016). The promise of restorative practices to transform teacher-student relationships and achieve equity in school discipline. *Journal of Educational & Psychological Consultation, 26*(4), 325–353. doi:10.1080/10474412.2014.929950

Gregory, A., Skiba, R. J., & Noguera, P. A. (2010). The achievement gap and the discipline gap: Two sides of the same coin? *Educational Researcher, 39*(1), 59–68. doi:10.3102/0013189X09357621

James, A. G., Noltemeyer, A., Ritchie, R., Palmer, K., & University, M. (2019). Longitudinal disciplinary and achievement outcomes associated with school-wide PBIS implementation level. *Psychology in the Schools, 56*(9), 1512–1521. doi:10.1002/pits.22282

Kang-Brown, J., Trone, J., Fratello, J., & Daftary-Kapur, T. (2013). *A generation later: What we've learned about zero tolerance in schools.* Vera Institute of Justice.

Kennedy, B. L., Acosta, M. M., & Soutullo, O. (2019). Counternarratives of students' experiences returning to comprehensive schools from an involuntary disciplinary alternative school. *Race, Ethnicity and Education, 22*(1), 130–149. doi:10.1080/1 3613324.2017.1376634

Lehr, C. A., Tan, C. S., & Ysseldyke, J. (2009). Alternative schools: A synthesis of state-level policy and research. *Remedial and Special Education, 30*(1), 19–32. doi:10.1177/0741932508315645

National Center for Education Statistics. (2019). *Table 102.40. Poverty rates for all persons and poverty status of related children under age 18.* https://nces.ed.gov/ programs/digest/d20/tables/dt20_102.40.asp

Owens, L., & Konkol, L. (2004). Transitioning from alternative to traditional school settings: A student perspective. *Reclaiming Children and Youth, 13*(3), 173–176.

Pas, E. T., Ryoo, J. H., Musci, R. J., & Bradshaw, C. P. (2019). A state-wide quasi-experimental effectiveness study of the scale-up of school-wide Positive Behavioral Interventions and Supports. *Journal of School Psychology, 73*, 41–55. doi:10.1016/j. jsp.2019.03.001 PMID:30961880

Payne, A. A., & Welch, K. (2015). Restorative justice in schools: The influence of race on restorative discipline. *Youth & Society, 47*(4), 539–564. doi:10.1177/0044118X12473125

Reinke, W. M., Herman, K. C., & Stormont, M. (2013). Classroom-level positive behavior supports in schools implementing SW-PBIS: Identifying areas for enhancement. *Journal of Positive Behavior Interventions, 15*(1), 39–50. doi:10.1177/109800712459079

Selman, K. J. (2017). Imprisoning 'those' kids: Neoliberal logics and the disciplinary alternative school. *Youth Justice, 17*(3), 213–231. doi:10.1177/1473225417712607

Simonsen, B., & Sugai, G. (2013). PBIS in alternative education settings: Positive support for youth with high-risk behavior. *Education & Treatment of Children, 36*(3), 3–14. doi:10.1353/etc.2013.0030

Skiba, R. J. (2008). Are zero tolerance policies effective in the schools? An evidentiary review and recommendations. *The American Psychologist, 63*(9), 852–862. doi:10.1037/0003-066X.63.9.852 PMID:19086747

Skiba, R. J. (2014). The failure of zero tolerance. *Reclaiming Children and Youth, 22*(4), 27–33.

Skiba, R. J., & Losen, D. J. (2015). From reaction to prevention. *American Educator, 39*(4), 4–46.

Skiba, R. J., & Peterson, R. (1999). The dark side of zero tolerance. *Phi Delta Kappan, 80*(5), 372–376.

Spence, R. N. (2020). Saved by the bell: Reclaiming home court advantage for at-risk youth funneled into the school-to-prison pipeline. *Family Court Review, 58*(1), 227–242. doi:10.1111/fcre.12464

Tajalli, H., & Garba, H. (2014). Discipline or prejudice? Overrepresentation of minority students in disciplinary alternative education programs. *The Urban Review, 46*(4), 620–631. doi:10.100711256-014-0274-9

Texas Education Agency. (2020). *Comprehensive biennial report on Texas public schools.* https://tea.texas.gov/sites/default/files/comp_annual_biennial_2020.pdf

Velez, G., Hahn, M., Recchia, H., & Wainryb, C. (2020). Rethinking response to youth rebellion: Recent growth and development of restorative practices in schools. *Current Opinion in Psychology, 35,* 36–40. doi:10.1016/j.copsyc.2020.02.011 PMID:32283520

Welsh, R. O., & Little, S. (2018). The school discipline dilemma: A comprehensive review of disparities and alternative approaches. *Review of Educational Research, 88*(5), 752–794. doi:10.3102/0034654318791582

Wilkerson, K. L., Afacan, K., Yan, M.-C., Justin, W., & Datar, S. D. (2016). Academic remediation–focused alternative schools: Impact on student outcomes. *Remedial and Special Education*, *37*(2), 67–77. doi:10.1177/0741932515620842

KEY TERMS AND DEFINITIONS

Disciplinary Alternative Education Program (DAEP): The Disciplinary Alternative Education Program is implemented in schools for students recommended serving a specified number of days after a discipline hearing for behavior offenses. DAEPs are housed away from the general population in schools, including separate school buildings.

Discretionary Reasons: Students are recommended to DAEP for reasons that are considered non-mandatory, meaning they do not have ties to a criminal report. Some reasons include class disruption, insubordination, and dress-code offenses.

Exclusionary Discipline Practices: Consequences including Out-of-School-Suspension (OSS) and DAEP are considered exclusionary discipline practices since they remove students from traditional home campuses.

GFSA: The Gun-Free Schools Act of 1994 deriving from the IASA intended to decrease the uptick in violence and drugs in school.

IASA: Improving America's Schools Act of 1994 is intended to help disadvantaged students increase technology in education, keep schools and communities safe and drug-free, and prevent students from dropping out.

PBIS: Positive Behavioral Interventions and Supports is a program that teaches school administrators to use student data to learn how different discipline strategies affect students in their school, helping them set goals to support further the success of all students (Center on PBIS, 2021).

Restorative Practices: Discipline practices guide students to accept responsibility for their actions and repair damaged relationships through counseling and other reflective practices.

Zero-Tolerance Policies: Policies that were put into place by school districts after the launch of the GFSA, in which school districts declared their schools zero-tolerance sites for offenses pertaining to drugs, alcohol, and violence.

Section 4
Social Change

Chapters 9-12 approach school disciplinary disparities from a social change perspective. These chapters offer innovative approaches and strategies for combatting school discipline disparities. The chapters sought guidance from teachers and practitioners regarding their lived experiences and ideas for approaching school discipline disparities.

Chapter 9
Administrators Leveraging School Counseling Supports to Address Disparities in School Discipline

Caroline Lopez-Perry
(iD) https://orcid.org/0000-0003-2333-556X
California State University, Long Beach, USA

Edwin Hernandez
California State University, San Bernardino, USA

Enrique Espinoza
University of California, Riverside, USA

ABSTRACT

Across the nation, various movements have persistently called for the removal of punitive practices in school; this includes removing law enforcement officers (LEOs) and school resource officers (SROs) and prioritizing funding toward student support services. This chapter brings attention to the role of school administrators and how they can leverage and support school counselors to address disparities in school discipline that impact racially minoritized youth. The authors draw on the theory of racialized organizations to demonstrate how schools are a racialized space, as individual agency is constrained or enabled by their social position within the organization, and how schools further reproduce inequity through their unequal distribution of resources. This chapter offers some practical approaches to reveal how school administrators can leverage school counselors to dismantle disparities in school discipline and prioritize practices of care.

DOI: 10.4018/978-1-6684-3359-1.ch009

INTRODUCTION

Well technically actually we have more campus security. We have more of them than we have counselors because we have campus security, we have a probation officer, and we have a school police. I don't see school police. He's not on campus all the time I don't think, but the probation officer is here all the time and the campus security is here all the time and that outnumbers the number of counselors that we have. - Monica, School Counselor

Monica (*pseudonym*) is one of the thousands of school counselors in the state of California who are tasked with the critical role of supporting the academic, career, and socio-emotional development of students (California Association for School Counselors [CASC], 2019). In her own words, presented in the epigraph of this chapter, she shares a commonly disturbing practice that many administrators and school districts use by over-relying on law enforcement officers (LEOs) and school resource officers (SROs) to address issues of school discipline in schools that serve predominantly racially minoritized youth (Annamma, 2018; Hernandez & Espinoza, 2021; Shedd, 2015; Whitaker et al., 2019). Like Monica, she makes note of how a combination of school police, school resource officers, and probation officers outnumber the number of school counselors at her institution. Not surprisingly, this has direct implications on racially minoritized youth as they are surrounded by a more punitive approach to addressing student needs and fewer services directed toward academic and mental wellness supports that are often provided by school counselors (Serrano, 2020; Whitaker et al., 2019), who in many cases are the first and only mental health providers in schools (CASC, 2019). Given this case, how school counselors respond to the overpolicing of racially minoritized youth and how administrators support by funding these punitive approaches requires further investigation.

The significant presence of law enforcement officers and school resource officers on campuses has persistently shown how their excessive force contributes to the physical and psychological harm for many Black and Latinx youth (Annamma, 2018; Shedd, 2015; Whitaker et al., 2019). Recent events have continued to fuel the movement to abolish all forms of policing that harm Black, Indigenous, and People of Color (BIPOC) communities. Such events include the racial reckoning that occurred in 2020 across the country against police brutality over the murders of George Floyd, Breonna Taylor, Ahmaud Arbery, and many others. More recently, in September 2021, Manuela (Mona) Rodriguez, an 18-year-old, Latina was shot and murdered by a Long Beach Unified School District (LBUSD) School Safety Officer (SSO) near the campus of Milikan High School (Black Lives Matter Long Beach [BLMLB], 2021). According to LBUSD policies, SSOs can carry and use weapons, such as guns, batons, or other weapons on combative students. As a result, this clearly shows how school district policies support and contribute to the physical and psychological harm of Black and Latinx youth (BLMLB, 2021).

In community spaces, various partners have and continue to persistently advocate towards police-free schools, as Omar Cardenas, Organizing Director for Californians for Justice in Long Beach, brings attention to the systems that perpetuate injustice, as he shared, "Mona Rodriguez should be here, holding her 5-month-old baby. For too long we've seen a system of 'safety' that harms Black and Brown youth and our communities. Only we can keep us safe. True safety starts with relationship-building, trust, and healing" (Californians for Justice, 2021). He pointed to the ongoing criminalization of communities of color and the pressing need to combat inequities by abolishing all forms of policing. Therefore, this serves as a reminder of the various moments across the nation that are calling for abolishing all forms of policing and redirecting more services towards school-based mental health professionals who can attend to the care of youth of Color (Serrano, 2020; Whitaker et al., 2019).

This chapter is guided by the following question posed by Black Lives Matter Long Beach, "What would school safety look like if we reinvested some of these funds into school counselors and other forms of care that actually keep our students and school safe?" (BLMLB, 2021, para. 4). Many school districts, like LBUSD, utilize excessive funds and resources on school safety officers. Recent research from BLMLB Community Briefing indicated that the school district salaries for their campus officers were a combined total of $1,429,110 - $1,678, 251. Yet, those funds could be used in ways that center on the mental wellness of the nearly 68,000 students that LBUSD serves (BLMLB, 2021). They are not alone; school leaders continue to spend millions of dollars on law enforcement and security while only a fraction of that is spent on mental wellness and social-emotional supports. For example, in 2019-20, Inglewood Unified spent $1.3 million on school police, but only $66,400 in Positive Behavior Intervention Supports (PBIS) training (Gon Ochi et al., 2020). In cases such as these, school districts and administrators play an important role in how resources are utilized and allocated, including support personnel, programs, funding, and professional development training to support the wellness of Black and Brown youth. Recognizing this, in this chapter the authors bring attention to the role of school counselors, who, as previously noted, might be the first and only mental health providers in a school setting (CASC, 2019). Specifically, this chapter focuses on how school administrators can support and leverage school counselors' unique training to address issues of school discipline that impact racially minoritized youth, rather than relying on the presence and excessive reliance of school safety officers.

While recognizing the important role of school administrators and counselors in this work, Annamma (2018) calls to attention that many educators enter the helping profession to serve and support marginalized students, yet they are infused with carceral logics as they utilize a pedagogy of pathologization that psychologically and physically harms youth of Color. Specifically, Annamma (2018) states that many school personnel employ carceral logics as they are guided by a prison nation that "encourages a mindset of observing for problems (surveillance), identifying issues (labeling), and fixing (punishing) those considered abnormal" (p.6). Consequently, many school administrators and counselors engage in these carceral logics that further reproduce harm to racially minoritized youth through hyper-surveillance, hyper-labeling, and hyper-punishment (Annamma, 2018). Similarly, Williams (2021) notes how "police, counselors, and social workers alike often work to normalize behavior that adheres to a set of standards determined and enforced by predominantly white and wealthy people" (p. 321). Therefore, Williams (2021) argues that policing is not only a profession, but in the exchanges between any relationship, as in the case of counselors and their students, counselors can also further perpetuate harm in their role of power (Williams, 2021).

As school districts across the nation grapple with defunding and abolishing school police and redirecting funds towards mental health programs and services (Turner III, 2021; Williams, 2021), it is important these new programs and supports are not weaponized through carceral logics. Camangian and Cariaga (2021) bring attention to the rise in social and emotional learning (SEL) and how a majority of these efforts focus on modifying and controlling student behaviors, without a critique and analysis of oppression that exist in schools and communities. To this point, school counselors can further contribute to the marginalization of students through their various forms of policing (Williams, 2021), this can include hegemonic SEL pedagogies and practices that are rooted in controlling student behavior (Camangian & Cariaga, 2021). As Camangian and Cariaga (2021) state, "any framework that focuses on changing people's maladaptive social and emotional orientation to oppression – rather than aiming towards transforming oppressive social conditions itself – is hegemonic because it anesthetizes the political will of a people" (p. 3).

Therefore, critically conscious educators must recognize the need to abolish all forms of policing (Williams, 2021), as research has consistently shown that many educators or social service providers still hold racial biases towards racially minoritized youth, which directly informs their deficit-centered approaches towards youth of Color (Annamma, 2018; Camangian & Cariaga, 2021; Howard, 2003; Kohli & Solorzano, 2012). The purpose of this chapter is to outline opportunities for collaboration among school administrators and counselors to remove policing and center an approach of care rather than punitive measures that contribute to the school-to-prison nexus.

By the end of this chapter, readers will:

- Enhance their knowledge of the structures, policies, and practices that contribute to the school-to-prison pipeline
- Understand the concepts of racialized organizations and carceral logic
- Identify specific ways administrators can collaborate with school counselors on interventions to address disparities in discipline

THE SCHOOL-TO-PRISON PIPELINE

The School-to-prison pipeline (STPP) is a metaphor that has been challenged due to its narrow focus on school disciplinary policies practices, nevertheless, it has been used to describe the increasing pattern of contact students in the U.S. public school system have with law enforcement and the criminal justice system through discriminatory policies and practices at the federal, state, and local level (Welfare et al., 2021). Examples include inadequate resources in public schools, zero-tolerance policies, lack of due process for students, schools' increased reliance on police, school resource officers, and school-based arrests, and youth contact with courts (Welfare et al., 2021). The process of students being pushed out of school and into continuation schools and then prisons often begins with a "push out" from educators. *Pushout* refers to punitive discipline practices schools use that exclude students from class, instruction, and peers. Examples include office discipline referrals, in-house suspension, out-of-school suspension, and expulsion. Furthermore, several studies have indicated that racially minoritized youth, students receiving special education services, and youth with unmet mental health needs disproportionately comprise those being pushed out into the school-to-prison pipeline (Maschi et al., 2008; Skiba et al., 2011).

The Effects of Police Presence on the Mental Wellness of BIYOC

Within the STPP concept, increased attention has been given to the effects of police presence in schools. Research has indicated that the presence of LEOs and SROs can have detrimental effects on youth, particularly Black, Indigenous, Youth of Color (BIYOC). Urban youth whom police had stopped at school (relative to other locations) reported significantly higher levels of emotional distress during the stop and posttraumatic stress after the stop (Jackson et al., 2019). A growing body of literature indicates that police contact among adolescents is associated with mental health impairments including, depressive symptoms (Baćak & Nowotny, 2020), anxiety (Geller, 2017; Geller et al., 2014), post-traumatic stress (Geller, 2017; Geller et al., 2014) and emotional distress (Jackson et al., 2019). Further, the overpolicing of BIYOC coupled with the everyday racism they encounter can lead to the development of racism-induced traumatic stress - or racial trauma (Saleem et al., 2020). Racism-induced traumatic stress is the development of traumatic stress symptoms like hypervigilance, loss of sleep, impaired emotional regulation, and tensed muscles (Carter, 2007; Saleem et al., 2020). School policing can exacerbate these symptoms by continuously targeting Black and Brown youth. Stressors can also be caused by direct or indirect (witnessing) contact with racist acts like school discipline. Ample research has documented how racism can negatively impact BIYOC both mentally and academically (Kohli & Solorzano, 2012; Saleem et al., 2020). Thus, the need to remove harsh punitive disciplinary practices is imperative to the mental well-being of students.

The presence of LEOs and SROs on campus can also shape the culture of a school and its response to student misbehavior. Historically, teachers and administrators were the principal agents of socialization, and classrooms, hallways, and playgrounds are the primary sites where socialization occurs (Brint, 2017). One result of increased policing in schools is that educators have increasingly withdrawn from teaching of school norms in favor of security personnel (Simon, 2009). LEOs and SROs are increasingly called to deal with disruptive behavior in the classroom, and the hallways of secondary schools have become spaces for security personnel. Simon (2009) contends that "through the introduction of police, probation officers, prosecutors and a host of private security professionals into the schools, new forms of expertise now openly compete with pedagogic knowledge and authority for shaping routines and rituals of schools (p. 209)." Rather than responding to students' mental well-being and social-emotional development through social emotional learning and mental wellness supports, funding that could be utilized to develop systems of care is diverted to systems of punishment and policing.

Limitations of the STPP

The STPP metaphor is not without limitations. Scholars have argued that the STPP lacks historical context and theoretical grounding (Crawley & Hirschfield, 2018; McGrew, 2016). Research also shows that this model contributes to deficit assumptions that position many students as "at-risk." It also fails to recognize that Black and Brown youth are predominantly targeted (McGrew, 2016). Another critique is that the STPP metaphor does not address the complex relationship between the school process of criminalization and poverty, unemployment, and the weaknesses of child welfare and mental health systems (Crawley & Hirschfield, 2018). The model also fails to elaborate on other intermediary steps between school exclusion and justice system involvement. Therefore, while the model has been helpful to identify the various social practices that contribute to the removal of children from schools,

Black and Brown youth are punished in other spaces outside of school. Recognizing that schools are not the only space that contributes to the punishment of Black and Brown youth is vital for educators to understand (Annamma, 2018). For instance, Annamma's (2018) work revealed how girls of color were criminalized and pushed out from various institutions, which included: foster care, social services, public schools, police custody, and alternative education.

Erica Meiners (2007) demonstrated the connection between schools and prisons, which was conceptualized as the "school-to-prison nexus" that shows the common "web of punitive threads...which capture the historic, systemic, and multifaceted nature of the intersections of education and incarceration" (p.32). Schools as microcosms of a prison nation-state are influenced by and employ carceral logic, the idea that the goal of society is to maintain safety and order through unquestioned social control (Foucault, 1977). Rooted in white supremacy, the goal is not to surveillance all bodies but to socially and spatially monitor Black and Brown bodies (Annamma, 2018). This process weaponizes racial and gender stereotypes (e.g. loud, aggressive, disruptive, defiant, ghetto) to criminalize Black and Brown youth and reinforce beliefs about behavioral deficiencies in need of correction. Thus, within carceral logics is the notion that Black and Brown bodies must be under constant observation, scrutiny, and correction. To address disproportionate discipline, a mindset and behavior shift must occur to move schools from a carceral culture to one of care. While a summary of punitive policies and practices within STPP has been provided in this section, it is important to note that the STPP is a complex topic that cannot be fully explained within one chapter.

BEYOND CARCERAL CULTURE AND PUNITIVE PEDAGOGY

As noted, multiple factors influence disparities in school discipline and the practices of school exclusion which ultimately require multi-prong approaches at various levels (e.g., school, district, local, state, national). This chapter focuses on the school level and how school counselors can be critical agents to addressing disproportionate discipline and move schools' beyond carceral culture to a culture of care. Carceral logic commits to punishment, imprisonment, exclusion, and disposability. In schools, carceral logic suggests that 1) like laws, rules and the enforcement of such rules are required to keep students safe, 2) punishment prevents people from repeating wrongdoings, and 3) it is ok to throw away people who do not follow the rules (Shalaby, 2021). As a result, administrators continue to prioritize funding LEOs and SRO's over student support personnel such as school counselors (Gon Ochi et al., 2020). The American Civil Liberties Union (ACLU) found that 1.7 million students are in schools with police but no school counselors (Whitaker et al., 2019).

In California, 5.9 million of the state's 6.2 million students (96 percent) were in schools where counselor caseloads exceeded the ratio (250-1) recommended by the American School Counselor Association ([ASCA] Whitaker et al., 2019).

Rather than investing in punitive measures such as LEOs and SROs, districts and administrators should prioritize a culture of care. Recent advocacy efforts by the Black Organizing Project (BOP) resulted in a momentous achievement when Oakland Unified School District became the first district in California to eliminate its school police department (Turner III, 2021; Whitaker et al., 2021). Consequently, a coalition of community organizations and student advocates pushed and convinced board members from the Los Angeles Unified School District (LAUSD) to reduce the school district's police department budget by nearly $25 million and reallocate those funds in a Black Student Achievement Plan (Turner III, 2021; Whitaker et al., 2021). The Black Student Achievement Plan directs $36.5 million annually to provide supplemental services and supports to 53 schools that have high numbers of Black students and high need indicators (Math and English Language Arts proficiency rates below the district average, higher than average referral and suspension rates, below-average school experience survey responses, and/or higher than average chronic absenteeism).

One of the main goals of this plan is to reduce over-identification of Black students in suspensions, discipline and other measures through targeted intervention to address students' academic and social-emotional needs (Whitaker et al., 2021). Collectively this requires diverting funds from LEOs and SROs to support staff such as school counselors and leveraging the training, expertise, and time of school counselors to programming and resources that support, educate, and guide students in their social-emotional development and mental wellness. Such actions shift from a prioritization of law and order to empathy and care. It is one important step toward implementing a whole child approach to teaching and learning to address students' fundamental psychological and safety needs. It recognizes the humanity of Black and Brown students. It affords them the same grace provided to White students, the opportunity to be seen within their full spectrum of growth and cognitive development, to think, explore, make mistakes, and figure things out without retribution.

UNDERSTANDING THE CRITICAL ROLE OF SCHOOL COUNSELORS AS CHANGE AGENTS

While there is a common misconception that school counselors function as disciplinarians or clerks whose main focus is to schedule student classes, the role of school counselors has changed dramatically over the last twenty years (Gysbers, 2010). School counselors work with all students to remove individual and systemic barriers to learning by addressing students' academic concerns, career awareness in post-secondary options, and social-emotional skills (ASCA, 2019b). School counselors provide support via direct and indirect services. Through classroom lessons, small group interventions, and individual counseling, school counselors help students develop the knowledge, attitudes, and skills to enhance academic achievement and healthy behaviors. School counselors also work on behalf of students by supporting those closest to them, including teachers, parents, and administrators through collaboration, consultation, and referrals (ASCA, 2019a).

School counselors often collaborate with school administrators, who are stakeholders on what roles and duties counselors have (Karatas & Kaya, 2015). As a result, school administrators must be aware of the role of a school counselor so that counselors can provide the much-needed support for students in the domains of social-emotional, academics, and college and career. Unfortunately, many administrators have inaccurate understandings of the role of a school counselor. Too often, school counselors are understood as "guidance counselors" working predominantly as academic and college advisors for students (Karatas & Kaya, 2015). Others see school counselors as pseudo administrators and are expected to participate in school discipline, campus supervision, and other non-counseling related duties that consume time that should be dedicated to supporting and connecting with students (Cisler & Bruce, 2013; Karatas & Kaya, 2015). School counselors are in a unique position to be agents of change that intentionally address issues of social justice that impart the students they work with (ASCA, 2019a). They are the liaison between students and many other educators (teachers, administrators), their parents/caregivers (home), and community agencies (mental agencies, social services; ASCA, 2018).

School counselors indeed wear many hats, none of which should be that of a disciplinarian (ASCA 2019b). However, this does not mean they are not involved or connected with discipline. ASCA (2019a) clearly states in their professional standards, standard B-PA 2., that school counselors should "identify gaps in achievement, attendance, discipline, opportunity and resources" (p.2). School counselors should be paying attention to their schools' discipline data and policies to identify what, if any, patterns of injustice and equity are occurring. Then, using their positions as social justice agents bring light to these issues and collaborate in this process to dismantle these disciplinary practices and procedures that are further reproducing inequities.

To help develop a comprehensive school counseling program, Lane and colleagues (2020) argue that it is essential that school administrators attend professional development to familiarize themselves with the role and duties of counselors. This can help influence how school counselors are viewed, and ultimately as a means to remove non-counselor-related duties assigned to them. Scholars also argue that school counselors can and should advocate for their roles and profession (ASCA, 2019a; Dollarhide et al., 2007). Engaging in a critical conversation about what support and services they can offer and their training with school-based mental health interventions can inform school administrators on utilizing school counselors better. In turn, this may lead to the use of school counselors in preventive work towards discipline.

RACIALIZED ORGANIZATION FRAMEWORK

The theory of racialized organization by Ray (2019) is used in this chapter to show how schools as an organization is a racialized space and brings attention to how administrators and school counselors can collaborate to address issues of school discipline and remove all forms of policing that disproportionately impact racially minoritized youth. Specifically, Ray (2019) describes that an individual's personal agency "is constrained (or enabled) by racialized organizations" (p. 11). Consequently, an individual's social position or role within a racialized organization also influences their personal agency. For example, in schools, the agency of school counselors is mediated by their social status, which is influenced by administrators' perception and knowledge of the role of school counselors. Therefore, the location of administrators and school counselors within racialized schools is critical in how they collaborate and support each other's collective efforts to dismantle punitive policies and practices that hinder the educational and mental wellness of racially minoritized youth.

Ray (2019) also notes that racialized organizations further reproduce inequity as they legitimize the unequal distribution of resources. Research has shown how schools that enroll a high proportion of racially minoritized youth are persistently under-resourced in comparison to schools that serve a high number of White students (Ray, 2019). Schools that enroll Black and Brown youth frequently overinvest their resources in school police and school resource officers (SROs) to punish and criminalize racially minoritized youth (Annamma, 2018; Hernandez & Espinoza, 2021; Rios, 2011; Whitaker et al., 2019). In sum, the theory of racialized organization is a helpful lens to better understand institutions, specifically the role of administrators in how they allocate resources, but also how they support or hinder the agency of school counselors in addressing issues of school discipline that significantly harm racially minoritized youth.

DISMANTLING RACIALIZED SPACES: ADMINISTRATORS AND COUNSELORS AS COLLABORATORS

In this section, the authors offer a method for administrators and school counselors to collaborate to dismantle racialized spaces in schools to address disparities in school discipline. Because institutional decision-making factors racialize the process of punishment, administrators and educators must become equity-minded. Equity-minded practitioners are mindful of and call attention to structures, policies, and practices that produce patterns of inequity (Bensimon & Malcom, 2012). They take personal and institutional responsibility for the success and setbacks of their students by examining their policies and practices.

Too often, school administrators focus on punitive practices, like out-of-school suspension or detention, towards youth who are in one way or another challenging school rules like not following dress code policies. Research has shown how school dress codes are another form for disciplining and punishing youth of Color for how they wear their hair and clothes, specifically Black girls (Morris, 2016). In response, Morris (2016) notes that "when Black girls respond to this treatment with cries of discrimination, it's important to see them as disruptors of oppression, not as defiant, willfully or otherwise" (p. 94). Therefore, administrators and school counselors need to collaborate closely and recognize that students have agency and often resist the punitive policies that harm and dehumanize them. Thus, the need to dismantle racialized spaces that punish Black girls and other minoritized groups is critical, as Morris (2016) reminds us that "adults and the policies they create should model for girls that it is the development of their brains, not their bodies, that is most salient in the school environment" (p. 216).

Another common punitive practice is when students do not adhere to school policies, such as constantly being late to class. While, not all school administrators are previous school counselors or lack the skills to truly dig out the real cause of a student's misconduct. Administrators run the risk of only briefly talking to kids without truly going in-depth to learn what life factors may be acting as barriers for them and therefore getting them in trouble. For instance, a student who is frequently late to first period may be misunderstood as lazy, not punctual, and lacking time management skills. In reality, if more time was given to explore what is causing the student to arrive late to school, one might learn that they have younger siblings to care for, to take to school, or other duties they need to complete prior to arriving at school. This is a consequence of zero-tolerance policies and infamous "tardy sweeps" where students are not given an opportunity to share and reflect on what is happening. A review of school disciplinary practices shows that students who are suspended and kept out of their general education courses are often frequent flyers with discipline because the actions do not address the issue at hand (Allman & Slate,

2011). To remedy this situation, school administrators should leverage school support staff like school counselors, who possess the training and skills to counsel students and bring to light structural barriers that are the root cause of a student's problems. The following sections offer recommendations for how school administrators can leverage the training, expertise, and time of school counselors to create a culture of care, one that engages educators in love filled action by valuing the whole child, prioritizing relationships, and recognizing that no child is disposable.

Integrate School Counseling Services within the MTSS framework

School administrators can, and should, build partnerships with school support staff like school counselors to move away from carceral logics and instead employ more equity-driven and restorative-focused interventions. School counselors are in a unique position to coordinate school-wide positive behavior interventions and supports (PBIS) and have the skill set to apply targeted interventions through multi-tiered systems of support ([MTSS] Ziomek-Daigle, et al., 2016). Multi-tiered systems of support (MTSS) is a comprehensive framework that focuses on aligning the entire system of initiatives, supports, and resources (Goodman-Scott et al., 2020). Unfortunately, the support and resources in a school's typical MTSS framework often focus solely on academics and instruction, social-emotional, and mental health supports are often left out of this framework. In a culture of care, schools recognize the whole child and tend to students' psychological and emotional safety needs.

School administrators should consider expanding their school's framework to align with the Multi-tiered, multi-domain system of supports (MTMDSS). Heavily influenced by MTSS, the MTMDSS recognizes the various developmental needs of all students and outlines the school counselor's role and duties across three specific domains: college and career, social/emotional, and academics (Hatch et al., 2018). Moreover, MTMDSS explains what the three counseling domains look like across the three tiers: tier 1, 2, and 3 of the traditional MTSS framework (Hatch et al., 2018; Sink 2016). Generally, *Tier 1 interventions* are implemented school-wide, servicing 100% of the student population. *Tier 2 interventions* are developed for students who may need added support; roughly 20%. Support here may look like group counseling and restorative circles. *Tier 3 interventions* are targeted at students in great need of help - 5-10% of the student population (Hatch et al., 2018; Sink, 2016).

School counselors are encouraged to align their school counseling activities with their schools MTSS activities. Within Tier 1, school counselors engage in data collection, interpretation, and decision-making that focus on the needs of the entire student population. Needs assessment surveys can be distributed to stakeholders (e.g. students, parents, families, community members, etc.) to identify academic and behavioral supports (Zyromski & Mariani, 2016). This type of data collection allows students, families, and the community to drive the decision-making. Utilizing MTMDSS, school counselors could implement tier 1, universal support, to all students with counseling lessons on self-awareness, self-management, relationships skills, responsible decision-making, conflict resolution, coping strategies, and emotional regulation. Doing so is proactive and can inform students about ways to manage their emotions or whom they can connect with on campus in times of need (Geiger & Oehrtman, 2020).

School counselors can also collaborate with administrators to examine disciplinary data and identify students in need of tier 2 support. School counselors can then facilitate targeted interventions like restorative circles or group counseling. These care-focused interventions allow for student voices to be heard and critical reflection and dialogue to occur. Restorative practices, or circles, empower the individuals affected and the responsible student by making them a part of restoring an injustice (Smith et al., 2017). Restorative practices are commonly used in the field of education as a means to combat harsh disciplinary practices like zero-tolerance rules (Smith et al., 2017). Restorative practices prioritize relationships and provide a more equity-centered way to help improve student academics and behavior. Instead of removing students from the classroom and having them unsupervised at home through out-of-school suspension or clumped into a classroom for in-house suspension where they are working independently, these interventions purposely seek to keep them in school and understand what causes these behaviors and what can be done to minimize or eliminate them. As a result, students can connect with school personnel, develop interventions and strategies, and ultimately improve both behaviorally and academically.

School counselors also play a critical role in identifying students with chronic and severe needs. At tier 3 school counselors provide intensified interventions for a few students who need a higher level of support. This can include individual counseling, community referrals, and progress monitoring. School counselors can support the development of behavior intervention plans by conducting a functional behavior assessment and collecting and analyzing data to identify the root function of students' behaviors through a holistic approach. Finally, they can consult and collaborate with other school support providers (e.g. nurses, school psychologists, social workers) and community agency partners (clinicians, mentors, social service agencies) via wrap-around teams to provide individualized, coordinated, and family-driven care.

While various ways have been outlined to discuss how school counseling supports can be integrated within MTSS to address issues of school discipline, it is important to note the constraints with this framework as it mainly focuses on supporting individual students without an analysis that interrogates and addresses racist systems that contribute to the reproduction of inequities. Annamma (2018) refers to this as "pedagogy of pathologization because it is situated in teaching the girls--positioning their problems as internal, while simultaneously ignoring structural inequities" (p. 13). In response, this chapter draws on the framework of racialized organizations (Ray, 2019) to show how schools as racialized spaces further reproduce inequity through their programs and services, as school counselors and administrators can employ carceral logics and produce new ways of harming students. As school counselors and administrators integrate MTTS or any other frameworks in their practice, it is imperative that they recognize and shift away from employing carceral logics that positions the student as the problem, instead collective efforts should prioritize identifying and transforming the oppressive social conditions (Camangian & Cariaga, 2021). The following section focuses on how school counselors can collaborate with students, communities, and other school personnel to enhance care in school settings.

Enhancing Care Through School Counselor Collaboration and Consultation

Administrators can also utilize school counselors' training and expertise to support teachers and students experiencing social-emotional issues by providing consultation. School counselors are trained in child and adolescent development, mental health, solution-focused strategies, group facilitation, relationship-building, and trauma-informed practices. Rather than policing the bodies of BIYOC, administrators can utilize school counselors to facilitate workshops with teachers and other leaders on campus regarding discussion on child and adolescent development, identities, and racial and gender stereotypes. These professional development opportunities can help educators recognize how racial biases influence their interactions with BIYOC and the classroom and school policies and potentially shift educators from socially and spatially monitoring Black and Brown bodies to co-constructing communities of care with students.

Utilizing their training in group facilitation and group development, school counselors can train educators in restorative circles (Smith et al., 2017) and on building classroom communities (Keenan, 2021). Drawing on their training in mental health, brain development, and trauma, school counselors can provide professional development and one-to-one consultation with administrators and teachers on trauma-informed practices (Howell et al., 2019). This can include training teachers on how to engage in educator-student interactions rooted in trauma-responsive practices and tools for engaging with children and youth in distress in ways that prevent retraumatization. For example, school counselors can consult with teachers and yard supervisors on how to co-regulate, the process of helping a student who has made a poor choice of behavior to regain their composure. It involves building a warm, responsive relationship, modifying and adjusting the environment, and coaching the student through self-regulation skills (Keels, 2020). Training in coregulation shifts the focus from student behavior to how educators can behave in ways that demonstrate attunement and provide supportive, consistent responses.

Finally, and most importantly, school counselors and administrators should collaborate and consult with their students who are directly impacted by the present hostile conditions embedded in school settings. Turner III (2021) in his work reveals the need for adult educators to take a step back and leverage resources and opportunities for Black boys and young men to enact their agency to transform their relationships with peers and conditions within the social institutions they navigate. Therefore, administrators and school counselors can benefit and learn from youth that are directly involved in youth organizing (Turner III, 2021), specifically in social movements that are centered around removing school police and abolishing all forms of policing. In return, this allows for individual and collective organizing to take place to dismantle systems that are harming BIYOC in schools. In revisiting the statement of Omar Cardenas presented earlier, there is an urgency to abolish the current system in place that harms and dehumanizes Black and Brown youth, and truly invest in relationship-building, trust, and healing (Californians for Justice, 2021), this includes BIYOC leading the way with support from community-centered spaces along with the critical conscious administrators and school counselors that are committed to co-creating conditions that humanize students.

CONCLUSION

This chapter has demonstrated how institutions through their structures, policies, and practices contribute to the punishment and criminalization of racially minoritized youth. The authors presented an outline of the School to Prison Pipeline's contributions and limitations, which describe the ways in which various social practices within schools hinder the educational trajectory and wellness of racially minoritized youth through the various forms of exclusion and marginalization. Additionally, this chapter notes how the School-to Prison Nexus demonstrates how students are punished and criminalized in various spaces outside of the school setting, which is an important reminder for administrators and school counselors to be aware of the multiple challenges that students encounter in the various spaces they navigate. Considering the critical role of administrators and school counselors in dismantling racialized punitive policies and practices, it is imperative to note that they are also agents of prison nation (Annamma, 2018), as they can be active contributors of the policing that occurs in schools that punishes and criminalizes students of Color. Additionally, as various efforts exist at the local, state, and national level to remove and abolish school police, there is also an increase in promotion social-emotional learning

(SEL) in schools, as indicated by Carmagian and Cariaga (2021) who reminds us about the importance of being vigilant in how SEL can further reproduce harm as it centers on controlling and modifying student behavior, without any critique of the oppression that students and marginalized communities face.

Recognizing that administrators and school counselors can engage in carceral logics through various forms of policing, the theoretical framework of racialized organizations guides this study to situate the inequities that exist within schools that enroll a huge concentration of Black and Brown youth, as they are more likely to allocate resources in school police than counselors and other mental professionals that will attend to the care of students. Furthermore, within racialized space, such as schools, the ability for school counselors to exercise their agency and disrupt inequities through equity minded work often is hindered by administrators due the lack of support or awareness about the critical role of school counselors to be change agents. Thus, school districts and administrators have the power to redirect funds to school counselors who can support the mental wellness, academic, and college/career aspirations of racially minoritized youth. Yet, as Williams (2021) notes that while removing or reducing school police is important, the true objective is to abolish all forms of policing that takes place in school settings, as these acts can be carried out by school resource officers and even school counselors or social service providers.

Finally, in this chapter the authors have attempted to provide various examples to inform the practice of administrators and school counselors. The examples of possibilities of collaboration presented are a starting point, yet this work requires that BIYOC are provided with the resources and opportunities by administrators or school counselors to engage in justice work through relationship building and transforming conditions within their local context, as outlined by Turner III (2021). While, the authors recognize there might be more ways that administrators and school counselors are potentially engaging in this work already, this is an area that requires further attention to see in what ways they are supporting and building coalitions with BIYOC and community spaces. Furthermore, as BIYOC and community organizations have pushed for various school districts in California to terminate contracts with local school police departments and center an approach of care, research is needed to examine the roles and responsibilities of administrators and school counselors in these school districts. This will include examining how school counselors are maximizing their potential and truly supporting BIYOC in schools and not employing policing practices that have been persistently harmful. Finally, this will also center the narratives of BIYOC to learn how they are benefiting and utilizing school counselors or other mental health professionals to support their wellness and future aspirations.

REFERENCES

Allman, K. L., & Slate, J. R. (2011). School discipline in public education: A brief review of current practices. *The International Journal of Educational Leadership Preparation, 6*(2), n2.

American School Counselor Association. (2019b). *ASCA School Counselor Professional Standards & Competencies*. Author.

American School Counselor Association [ASCA]. (2018). *The School Counselor and Equity for All Students.* https://bit.ly/3rApCIg

American School Counselor Association [ASCA]. (2019a). *ASCA School Counselor Professional Standards & Competencies*. Author.

Annamma, S. A. (2018). *The pedagogy of pathologization: Dis/abled girls of color in the school-prison nexus*. Routledge.

Baćak, V., & Nowotny, K. M. (2020). Race and the association between police stops and depression among young adults: A research note. *Race and Justice, 10*(3), 363–375. doi:10.1177/2153368718799813

Bensimon, E. M., & Malcom, L. E. (2012). *Confronting equity issues on campus: Implementing the equity scorecard in theory and practice*. Stylus Publishing.

Black Lives Matter Long Beach. (2021, Oct 1). *BLM Long Beach Statement on Violence in our School District.* https://blmlbc.org/blm-long-beach-statement-on-violence-in-our-school-district/

Brint, S. (2017). *Schools and societies*. Stanford Social Sciences, an imprint of Stanford University Press. doi:10.1515/9781503601031

California Association for School Counselors. (2019). *Best practice: Guidelines for California school counselors.* Author. https://bit.ly/3pt5Rjc

Californians for Justice. (2021, Oct 1). *Black Lives Matter Long Beach Statement on Violence in Long Beach Unified School District.* https://caljustice.org/2021/10/01/black-lives-matter-long-beach-statement-on-

Camangian, P., & Cariaga, S. (2021). Social and emotional learning is hegemonic miseducation: Students deserve humanization instead. *Race, Ethnicity and Education.* Advance online publication. doi:10.1080/13613324.2020.1798374

Carter, R. T. (2007). Racism and psychological and emotional injury: Recognizing and assessing race-based traumatic stress. *The Counseling Psychologist, 35*(1), 13–105. https://doi.org/ftkw2v

Cisler, A., & Bruce, M. A. (2013). Principals: What are their roles and responsibilities? *Journal of School Counseling, 11*(10). http://www.jsc.montana.edu/articles/v11n10.pdf

Crawley, K., & Hirschfield, P. (2018). Examining the school-to-prison pipeline metaphor. In *Oxford Research Encyclopedia of Criminology and Criminal Justice.* doi:10.1093/acrefore/9780190264079.013.346

Dollarhide, C. T., Smith, A. T., & Lemberger, M. E. (2007). Critical incidents in the development of supportive principals: Facilitating school counselor-principal relationships. *Professional School Counseling, 10*, 360–369. https://doi.org/g8fz

Foucault, M. (1977). *Discipline and punish: The birth of the prison.* Pantheon Books.

Geiger, S. N., & Oehrtman, J. P. (2020). School counselors and the school leadership team. *Professional School Counseling, 23*(1), 1-9. doi:https://doi.org/g8fx

Geller, A. (2017). Policing America's children: Police contact and consequences among teens in fragile families. *IDEAS Work Pap Ser from RePEc*, 1-46.

Geller, A., Fagan, J., Tyler, T., & Link, B. G. (2014). Aggressive policing and the mental health of young urban men. *American Journal of Public Health, 104*(12), 2321–2327. https://doi.org/10.2105/ajph.2014.302046

Gon Ochi, N., Leung, V., Rodriguez, A., & Cobb, J. (2020). *Our rights to resources: School districts are cheating high-need students by funding law enforcement.* American Civil Liberties Union. https://www.aclusocal.org/sites/default/files/aclu_socal_right-to-resources.pdf

Goodman-Scott, E., Betters-Bubon, J., & Donohue, P. (2019). *The school counselor's guide to multi-tiered systems of support.* Routledge.

Gysbers, N. C. (2010). *Remembering the past, shaping the future: A history of school counseling.* American School Counselor Association.

Hatch, T., Duarte, D., & DeGregorio, L. K. (2018). *Hatching results for elementary school counseling: Implementing core curriculum and other tier one activities.* Corwin.

Hernandez, E., Espinoza, E., & Patterson, J. (2021). School counselors involvement and opportunities to advocate against racialized punitive practices. *Teaching and Supervision in Counseling, 3*(2), 10. doi:https://doi.org/g8fw

Howard, T. C. (2003). A tug of war for our minds: African American high school students' perceptions of their academic identities and college aspirations. *High School Journal, 87*(1), 4–17. https://doi.org/b9twt8

Howell, P. B., Thomas, S., Sweeney, D., & Vanderhaar, J. (2019). Moving beyond schedules, testing and other duties as deemed necessary by the principal: The school counselor's role in trauma informed practices. *Middle School Journal, 50*(4), 26–34. https://doi.org/g8ft

Jackson, D. B., Fahmy, C., Vaughn, M. G., & Testa, A. (2019). Police stops among at-risk youth: Repercussions for mental health. *The Journal of Adolescent Health, 65*(5), 627–632. https://doi.org/ghbhw4

Karatas, K., & Kaya, I. (2015). An investigation of the perceptions of school administrators towards the roles and duties of school counselors. *Eurasian Journal of Educational Research, 15*(61), 181-198. doi:https://doi.org/gg2z8s

Keels, M. (2020). Building racial equity through trauma-responsive discipline. *Educational Leadership, 78*(2), 40–45, 51. https://bit.ly/32FwCte

Keenan, H. B. (2021). Building classroom communities: A pedagogical reflection and syllabus excerpt. In Education for Liberation Network & Critical Resistance Editorial Collective (Eds.), Lessons in liberation: An abolitionist toolkit for educators (pp. 156-169). AK Press.

Kohli, R., & Solorzano, D. G. (2012). Teachers please learn our names! Racial microaggressions in the K-12 classroom. *Race, Ethnicity, and Education, 15*(4), 441-462. doi:https://doi.org/ggnsc2

Lane, J. J., Bohner, G. L., Hinck, A. M., & Kircher, R. L. (2020). Current administrative perceptions of school counselors: Kansas administrators' perceptions of school counselor duties. *Journal of School Counseling, 18*(2), n2. https://eric.ed.gov/?id=EJ1241840

Maschi, T., Hatcher, S. S., Schwalbe, C. S., & Rosato, N. S. (2008). Mapping the social service pathways of youth to and through the juvenile justice system: A comprehensive review. *Children and Youth Services Review, 30*(12), 1376–1385. https://doi.org/cqfjnq

McGrew, K. (2016). The dangers of pipeline thinking: How the school-to-prison pipeline metaphor squeezes out complexity. *Educational Theory, 66*(3), 341–367. https://doi.org/10.1111/edth.12173

Meiners, E. R. (2007). Right to Be Hostile: Schools, Prisons, and the Making of Public Enemies (1st ed.). Routledge. https://doi.org/10.4324/9780203936450.

Morris, M. (2016). *Pushout: The Criminalization of Black Girls in Schools*. New Press.

Ray, V. (2019). A theory of racialized organizations. *American Sociological Review*, *84*(1), 26–53. https://doi.org/gftw4h

Rios, V. M. (2011). *Punished: Policing the lives of Black and Latino boys*. New York University Press.

Saleem, F. T., Anderson, R. E., & Williams, M. (2020). Addressing the "myth" of racial trauma: Developmental and ecological considerations for youth of color. *Clinical Child and Family Psychology Review*, *23*(1), 1–14. https://doi.org/gg5fvw

Serrano, U. (2020). *Lessons learned from the Los Angeles Youth Movement against the Carceral State*. The Latinx Project at NYU. https://www.latinxproject.nyu.edu/intervenxions/lessons-learned-from-the-los-angeles-youth-movement-against-the-carceral-state

Shalaby, C. (2021). Imagining classroom management: as an abolitionist project. In Education for Liberation Network & Critical Resistance Editorial Collective (Eds.), Lessons in liberation: An abolitionist toolkit for educators (pp. 104-112). AK Press.

Shedd, C. (2015). *Unequal city: Race, schools, and perceptions of injustice*. Russel Sage.

Simon, J. (2009). *Governing through crime: How the war on crime transformed American democracy and created a culture of fear*. Oxford University Press.

Sink, C. A. (2016). Incorporating a multi-tiered system of supports into school counselor preparation. *The Professional Counselor*, *6*(3), 203–219. https://doi.org/dnn7

Skiba, R. J., Horner, R. H., Chung, C.-G., Rausch, M. K., May, S. L., & Tobin, T. (2011). Race is not neutral: A national investigation of African American and Latino dis- proportionality in school discipline. *School Psychology Review*, *40*(1), 85–107.

Smith, L. C., Garnett, B. R., Herbert, A., Grudev, N., Vogel, J., Keefner, W., Barnett, A., & Baker, T. (2017). The hand of professional school counseling meets the glove of restorative practices. *Professional School Counseling*, *21*(1). https://doi.org/gh3fst

Turner, D. C. III. (2021). The (good) trouble with Black boys: Organizing with Black boys and young men in George Floyd's America. *Theory Intro Practice, 60*(4), 422–433. doi:10.1080/00405841.2021.1983317

Welfare, L. E., Grimes, T. O., Lawson, G., Hori, K., & Asadi, G. (2021). The school to prison pipeline: Quantitative evidence to guide school counselor advocacy. *Journal of Counselor Leadership and Advocacy, 8*(1), 16–29. https://doi.org/10.1080/232 6716X.2020.1861490

Whitaker, A., Cobb, J., Leung, V., & Nelson, L. (2021). *No police in schools: A vision for safe and supportive schools in CA*. American Civil Liberties Union. https://bit.ly/3pvfkqb

Whitaker, A., Torres-Guillén, S., Morton, M., Jordan, H., Coyle, S., Mann, A., & Sun, W.-L. (2019). *Cops not counselors: How the lack of school mental health professionals is harming students*. American Civil Liberties Union. https://bit.ly/31vdBsX

Williams, E. M. (2021). Thinking beyond "counselors not cops": Imagining & decarcerating care in schools. In Education for Liberation Network & Critical Resistance Editorial Collective (Eds.), Lessons in liberation: An abolitionist toolkit for educators (pp. 318-327). AK Press.

Ziomek-Daigle, J., Goodman-Scott, E., Cavin, J., & Donohue, P. (2016). Integrating a multi-tiered system of supports with comprehensive school counseling programs. *The Professional Counselor, 6*(3), 220–232. https://doi.org/dnhw

Zyromski, B., & Mariani, M. (2016). *Facilitating evidence-based, data-driven school counseling: A manual for practice*. Corwin.

KEY TERMS AND DEFINITIONS

Carceral Logics: Refers to a punishment mindset, the ways in which our ideologies, practices and structures have been shaped by the idea and practice of imprisonment.

Co-Regulation: The interactive process of regulatory support that occurs within the context of caring relationships between adults and children, youth, or young adults that foster self-regulation development.

Culture of Care: Schools engage in love filled action tending to the psychological and emotional safety needs of students by valuing the whole child, prioritizing relationships, and recognizing that no child is disposable. Relationships are the center of the focus rather than curriculum, rules, and order.

Multi-Tiered Systems of Support: a proactive, comprehensive framework that focuses on aligning the entire system of initiatives, supports, and resources so that all students have access to high quality instruction and interventions.

Racialized Organization Theory: This theory argues that race is a constitutive part of American organizations. Race shapes the ways organizations distribute resources, how organizations treat their members, and even people's long-term life prospects.

School-to-Prison Nexus: A complex, multilayered existence of carceral logics within schools that positions Black and Brown bodies under constant observation and curtiny through policy, school culture, and educator practices.

School-to-Prison Pipeline: A metaphor used to describe the increasing pattern of contact students in the U.S. public school system have with law enforcement and the criminal justice system through discriminatory policies and practices at the federal, state, and local level.

Chapter 10
Building an Agenda for Restorative Justice Practices in Education:
Utilizing Public Relations Strategies to Influence Education Reform

Morgan D. Kirby
Texas Southern University, USA

ABSTRACT

Punitive disciplinary policies in schools have drastic effects on student performance and success among minority students. These disciplinary policies have a direct impact on the school-to-prison pipeline issue in America. In recent years, restorative justice practices have been implemented in schools to replace punitive disciplinary policies like the zero-tolerance policy. However, to truly see the benefits of restorative justice practices in schools, there needs to be an increased awareness of its principles and benefits. This study examines how restorative justice discourse on Twitter can build an agenda for increased awareness of restorative justice practices in schools and policy changes regarding punitive discipline practices.

INTRODUCTION

In recent years, enormous amounts of research have been conducted on issues concerning discipline practices within American school systems. Some disciplinary strategies, like zero-tolerance policies, strengthen the school-to-prison pipeline

DOI: 10.4018/978-1-6684-3359-1.ch010

(Heitzeg, 2009). These policies are known for aiding in increasing youth violence and embedding criminal characterizations of youth in communities of color. These policies undeniably affect drop-out rates and expulsion rates—while having little evidence proving they successfully increase school safety (Heitzeg, 2009).

Disciplinary actions such as suspension and expulsion have staggering implications on student performance in Black students. When students miss class, they are not able to receive necessary class time instruction (Bell & Puckett, 2020). Many teachers do not allow students to make up assignments, thus creating barriers to academic achievement (Bell & Puckett, 2020). Furthermore—in many urban cities, school suspension decreases achievement in subjects such as math and reading (Lacoe & Steinberg, 2019). Increased adoption of diverse methods of addressing discipline in schools is pertinent to the academic performance of minority students. One method to explore is restorative justice.

Restorative Justice

Restorative justice practices focus on repairing harm as opposed to focusing on the concept of punishment. This practice implements collaborative approaches that bring offenders, victims, and communities together to address the offender's offenses. Restorative justice holds students who misbehave accountable by addressing their offenses using various approaches (Mayworm et al., 2016). Some approaches are peacemaking circles, victim-offender mediation, and community conferencing (Mayworm et al., 2016).

Over the years, schools, communities, and lawmakers have rallied around the thought of turning disciplinary and behavioral violations into transformative learning experiences. This approach invites more significant opportunities to address disciplinary offenses in a less punitive manner. Brenda Morrison (2002) stated, "In broad terms restorative justice constitutes an innovative approach to both offending or challenging behaviour which puts repairing harm done to relationships and people over and above the need for assigning blame and dispensing punishment." School systems and local, state, and national governments should strongly consider adopting more policies that allow restorative justice practices to become widely utilized. One way to do this is through creating media campaigns that target understanding and adoption of restorative justice practices and programs.

The Role of Public Relations in Social Change

To change a system of governance is an act of social change. Social change movements have an interdependency on communication, media, and public relations. Movements like the civil rights movement, the women's suffrage movement, and the anti-war movement were all fueled by acts of public relations. Public relations and communication strategies used during social movements vary. Public protests, newspaper articles, magazine articles, television specials, and even music were carefully curated to help tell the stories and perspectives of many of the different social movements (Vliegenthart & Walgrave, 2012). The call to reform disciplinary policies in the American school system is an act of social change. This act of social change needs the help of communication, media, and public relations to achieve reform. A public relations campaign highlighting restorative justice will aggressively complement the work that has already been done—while gaining positive public opinion.

Theories

Agenda building theory and framing theory were used to examine raising awareness and participation in the discourse surrounding school systems' restorative justice programs and practices. Agenda building is a theory that suggests public opinion has the ability to drive which social issues become a part of the political agenda for lawmakers—while simultaneously becoming a part of local and national news agenda (Curtin, 1999). Agenda building theory is applicable in this study because it is imperative that individuals understand the role discriminatory school discipline policies play in feeding the school-to-prison pipeline and how this issue affects the criminal justice system, the economy, and many other social issues. Restorative justice programs are a way to create alternative methods to discipline and teach students. Creating media messages and public relations campaigns that focus on restorative justice can build positive public opinion, which can help school systems and governing bodies give greater consideration for restorative justice methods and practices (Zoch & Molleda, 2006).

Framing theory is important when examining strategic media messages and public relations campaigns. Framing theory suggests that media messages are created to guide viewers and readers to think about stories through the lens of the message curator (Snow et al., 2018). Framing theory speaks to the method by which message creators create a story or how a story is told. Public relations campaigns always communicate messages to encourage action from their audiences. Framing stories help create messages that result in action. In this case, the action is creating greater awareness and adoption of restorative justice practices.

BACKGROUND

Elements of Restorative Justice

Many scholars, policymakers, and community activists use varying verbiage to define restorative justice. Latimer et al. (2005) noted, "Despite the increased attention given to restorative justice, the concept still remains somewhat problematic to define as numerous responses to criminal behavior may fall under the so-called restorative umbrella. The term has been used interchangeably with such concepts as community justice, transformative justice, peacemaking criminology, and relational justice." Conceptually, restorative justice is considered to be the process of mediation between victims and offenders in efforts to confront, heal, and restore relationships during the aftermath of committed offenses (Latimer et al., 2005).

The concept of restorative justice is typically incorporated in conversations surrounding criminal justice reform. Policymakers and community activists consider restorative justice practices to be an emerging key component of practices concerning criminology; however, early scholars noted that restorative justice did not adhere to the academic theoretical framework of justice or crime (Miers et al., 2001). Restorative justice seeks to rehabilitate offenders without utilizing extremely punitive measures. Miers et al. (2001) states, "Its more particular purposes include the prevention of reoffending, the recognition of the victim's interest in the amelioration of and acceptance by the offender of the harm done, and of the community's interest in the longer-term rehabilitation of and support for the offender, and a reduction in criminal justice costs."

Miers et al. (2001) state:

The fundamental premise of the restorative justice paradigm is that crime is a violation of people and relationships (Zehr, 1990) rather than merely a violation of law. Therefore, the most appropriate response to criminal behavior is to repair the harm caused by the wrongful act (Law Commission, 2000). As such, the criminal justice system should provide those most closely affected by the crime (the victim, the offender, and the community) an opportunity to come together to discuss the event and attempt to arrive at some type of understanding about what can be done to provide appropriate reparation.

Llewellyn and Howse (1999) surmised that there were three key elements to restorative justice practices: participation, honesty, and face-to-face activities or encounters. Offenders need to participate willingly while being truthful about their criminal offenses and the harm they caused victims. All stakeholders should agree to meet in a safe environment conducive to repairing relationships between all parties involved.

Effectiveness of Restorative Justice Practices

Existing literature indicates that restorative justice programs are effective. In 2001, a meta-analysis of restorative justice literature was conducted to examine the validity of restorative justice literature. Latimer et al. (2001) noted:

Generally, compared to traditional nonrestorative approaches, restorative justice was found to be more successful at achieving each of its four major goals. In other words, based on the findings of the current meta-analysis, restorative justice programs are a more effective method of improving victim and/or offender satisfaction, increasing offender compliance with restitution, and decreasing the recidivism of offenders when compared to more traditional criminal justice responses (i.e., incarceration, probation, court-ordered restitution, etc.). In fact, restorative programs were significantly more effective than these approaches across all four outcomes (when the offender satisfaction outlier is excluded).

Public Relations and Media Campaigns

Public relations operate in a variety of ways. Campbell, Martin, and Fabos (2017) noted "public relations refers to the total communication strategy conducted by a person, government, or an organization attempting to reach and persuade an audience to adopt a point of view." Public relations is responsible for influencing people worldwide to adopt ideologies, economic practices, and other factors that shape public opinion. The cultural impact that public relations strategies have on public opinion is seen throughout the political and democratic process—from the election of political leaders to the adoption of public policies (Campbell et. al, 2017). Public relations and media campaigns are pivotal to increasing awareness about a given issue or topic. Rice and Atkin (2009) stated:

Public communication campaigns can be broadly defined as (1) purposive attempts (2) to inform, persuade, or motivate behavior changes (3) in a relatively well-defined and large audience, (4) generally for noncommercial benefits to the individuals and/ or society at large, (5) typically within a given time period, (6) by means of organized communication activities involving mass media, and (7) often complemented by interpersonal support

Public relations and media campaigns are powerful tools used to tell stories strategically and introduce ideas (Kopfman & Ruth-McSwain 2017). These purposefully constructed campaigns can entertain and inform while simultaneously influencing the behaviors of audience members and garner favorable opinions about a given issue (Singhal & Rogers, 2001). If a goal of social change and social justice is to transform society—media campaigns and aspects of public relations should be considered in the process (Ryan et al., 1998). Public relations and media campaigns can incorporate many media platforms. These platforms include radio, television, film, print, and social media. Expressly, public relations strategies can incorporate media convergence, traditional forms of media, social media, and modes of communication that incorporate none computer-mediated informational events and interpersonal communication.

News Consumption and Media Usage

In 2020, the Pew Research Center conducted a study that focused on the news consumption activity of Americans. In this study, it was noted that the digital era changed the ways in which Americans consume information. Media companies who are known for traditional forms of media, such as print and radio, are now forced to incorporate digital media in their dissemination of news. For example, newspapers are now available online, and broadcast news can now be streamed on social media applications (Barthel et al., 2020). These examples of how media converge illustrate the state of the digital media era.

The Pew Research Center also noted that while media convergence is on the rise and while many consumers are familiar with digital platforms, many media consumers do not prefer to use digital platforms like streaming services to consume news (Barthel et al., 2020). This is largely due to digital media literacy. Individuals who know how to navigate digital platforms may not find gratification in receiving news on digital platforms. Because of this, there is still a need to produce television broadcast news programming. While American consumers may not find the utilization of streaming services to consume news gratifying—studies show that social media platforms, such as Twitter, are becoming increasingly utilized for news consumption. According to a 2020 Pew Research Center study, 53% of Americans receive their news from social media (Shearer & Mitchell, 2021).

Not only are digital platforms like Twitter important for news consumption, but they also serve as digital environments for public discourse. In its origins, the internet was used to consume information; however, as technology advanced, the digital experience also advanced (Langmia, Tyree, O'brien & Sturgis, 2013). According to Boyd & Ellison (2007) social media creates a platform for people to interact with one another. Social media allows its users to share experiences, promote ideas, and create a sense of community. Because of this, social media is a huge component of contemporary information dissemination.

Public Relations Strategies, Social Media and Social Change

Public relations strategies can strategically promote propaganda for social change. Though some may view the term propaganda as a word that carries a negative connotation, it simply refers to communication that is strategically placed in media to create supportive public opinion about an idea, policy, or program (Campbell et al., 2017). In many cases, propaganda can produce social change. Social change needs the help of communication, media, and public relations to achieve reform. Public relations strategies that place heavy emphasis on semiotics and storytelling can assist in social change efforts.

Storytelling that highlights human interest stories can reach people in a sacred way that quantitative research is unable to accomplish on its own. In 1955, people all over the world heard about the horrors of racism. However, when the mother of Emmet Till, Mamie Till-Bradley, decided to invite journalists to her son's open casket funeral, many could see the evidence of the brutality that racism produces. The media image and story of Emmitt Till is considered to be one of the catalysts of the civil rights movement (Anderson, 2015).

Strategic storytelling was also a component of the work produced by Ida B. Wells-Barnett. Ida B. Wells-Barnett was a former educator who shifted her focus to creating a collection of writings that addressed the lynchings that took place in the southern region of the United States (Royster, 2016). She was able to raise awareness of the horrors of lynching that took place in the south. Her strategic storytelling abilities educated and helped in the fight for civil rights in the United States. Her work certainly incorporates propaganda used to influence social change through print journalism. Wells-Barnett and others helped trailblaze the practice of utilizing media to enhance the advocacy efforts of those seeking to achieve social change.

The contemporary practice of public relations adopts the use of media convergence and employing public relations strategies on social media platforms. This is especially true regarding the intersection of technology, public relations strategies, and social change (Guo & Saxton, 2014). Non-profit organizations that focus on social change rely heavily on social media because of its influence and cost-effectiveness. Social media-based public relations campaigns depend heavily on social media connections and social media messaging. In other words, emphasis is placed on how extensive an organization's social media network is, and the type of messages an organization disseminates (Guo & Saxton, 2014). Strategic messaging on social media typically includes hashtags, hyperlinks, reposting functions, and user mentions or profile tags.

These functions work together to create a digital discourse that can often result in social change.

Social media has become a necessary tool in the quest for social change. Movements like Black Lives Matter proved that social media allows users to consume information about injustices, reform ideas, and social media creates an opportunity for advocates to mobilize (Mundt et al., 2018). One of the most exciting aspects of using social media as a social change public relations strategy is that it allows people to become familiar with narratives that counter existing constructs. Social media has the ability to inform and inspire people to desire social change with less resistance from media gatekeepers who have historically silenced the voices of the oppressed (Mundt et al., 2018).

Regarding social media and education reform, research indicates that the social media platform Twitter is most used for public discourse that promotes reform rhetoric (Brewers & Wallis, 2015). Educational organizations like Teach for America utilized social media to promote its perspectives regarding education reform. According to Brewers & Wallis (2015), Teach for America utilized Twitter to engage with users to attempt to debunk myths about the organization and highlight some of their students, educators, and alumni—while simultaneously working to advocate for reform and public policy. However, it is essential to note that because social media apps like Twitter give its users the ability to speak freely, those with opposing views are given a platform. Brewers & Wallis noted, "it is unsettling that Twitter, as a form of media that has the potential to elevate and expand conversations, has seemingly become yet another mouthpiece to reinforce predetermined assumptions about education reform."

MAIN FOCUS OF CHAPTER

Identifying Communication Methods that Promote Social Change and Restorative Justice Programs

The researcher reviewed literature related to restorative justice, media usage, and the role of public relations in social movements. The researcher examined the ways restorative justice discourse is approached on the social media site, Twitter. Once literature was reviewed and media content was examined, the researcher identified public relations messages and strategies that restorative justice advocates can use in efforts to increase awareness, educate their various publics, and build a media agenda that will potentially increase positive public opinion, legislative support, and financial support for restorative justice programs (Ryan et al., 1998).

Methodology

This study used a critical discourse analysis (CDA) to investigate tweets and multimedia's role in advocacy and public opinion discourse about restorative justice in schools. It is important to evaluate and understand the perceptions people have surrounding restorative justice in schools and the social media messages that may influence perception and beliefs. An analysis of tweets was conducted to understand Twitter subscribers' thoughts and feelings regarding restorative justice in schools. Since public relations strategies aim to influence public opinion, it is crucial to understand the discourse surrounding restorative justice in schools. CDA is used when attempting to understand how various texts can contribute to the social construction of concepts and ideas. "Critical discourse analysis is a type of discourse analysis research that primarily studies the way social power abuse, dominance, and inequality are enacted, reproduced, and resisted by text and talk in social-political context" (Van Dijk, 2001).

CDA can also analyze text and discourse to promote and address social change (Scollon, 2001). CDA allowed the researcher to examine tweets to discover what common themes emerged from Twitter users' tweets about restorative justice in schools. This qualitative approach allowed the researcher to examine media messages and their ability to contribute to the construction of social change related to education reform. CDA seeks to challenge unjust institutionalized systems and seeks to achieve social equality, justice, and change. By utilizing CDA in the analysis of social media messages, the researcher was able to identify how Tweets challenged existing narratives about punitive discipline practices in schools. The analysis of Tweets identified social media messages that promoted misinformation surrounding restorative justice in schools. Lastly, the researcher extracted public relations strategies and strategic messaging that could aid in the increased adoption of restorative justice practices in schools.

Sample

To collect the sample for this research, the researcher used the hashtag #RestorativeJusticeInSchools to identify relevant tweets on the social media site Twitter. On the microblogging social media platform, Twitter, users can also use keyword searches to identify specific terminology tweets. As a result, the researcher searched "restorative justice in schools". The search function on Twitter allows users to search keywords by looking at the most recent tweets that incorporate specific terms or by looking at the "top" tweets that include keywords. The researcher chose to use the "top" tweets that were identified by using the hashtag #RestorativeJusticeinSchools and the keywords "restorative justice in schools." The tweets used in this sample were collected during 30 days. The sample consisted of 157 tweets.

RESTORATIVE JUSTICE ADVOCATE TWEETS

Most of the tweets in this sample were created by those who advocated for restorative justice practices in schools. Some of the advocates used their tweets to define aspects of restorative justice for their fellow Twitter users. For example, one Twitter user tweeted, "Restorative Justice in schools should focus on practices centered in community building, which is rooted in indigenous beliefs of interconnectedness. We do this through circles, identity building, empowerment, and healing. However, there are many practices that intersect with…" this Twitter user goes on to describe the components of restorative justice. "Storytelling telling -Collaborative problem solving -Trauma informed practices -Social emotional learning -Cognitive behavior therapy -Dialogue on social justice issues."

Restorative justice activists help other users understand the function of restorative justice by sharing perspectives about punitive approaches. One Twitter account tweeted, "[a community activist organization] advocates for restorative justice: "Zero-tolerance approaches to bullying don't give students or the school a chance to repair the harm or to create a new, positive, and supportive school environment in which these things don't happen. #WillfulDefiance." This Twitter account uses the zero-tolerance approach to bullying to discuss what punitive actions lack as it relates to solving issues within school environments. Through education on restorative justice, people begin to see that it may be a viable alternative to punitive approaches to school discipline. This is articulated in the following tweet "I'm reading more about Restorative Justice, specifically in schools to honor humanity and community. There's so much to learn and I think a lot about my ideas about rehabilitation, punishment, and how we operate as a society."

Another tweet used words, multimedia, and visual storytelling to share how a school implemented restorative justice practices "social-emotional learning and restorative justice are helping to educate the whole child, as well as create a more positive school climate with greater supports for our educators." This tweet included a video of students and teachers who illustrated what restorative justice practices looked like when used within teaching ideologies. The video illustrates how the proactive use of restorative justice can aid in developing empathy and accountability within students.

Not only did Twitter users contribute their understanding about restorative justice in schools, but some also linked restorative justice in schools to theories like Critical Race Theory (CRT) "Restorative Justice isn't a concept that is solely owned by CRT. It existed and does exist without that plus most kids don't get that complete or thoughtful of an education in k-12 I would have loved to [have] been at a school who even spends 10 minutes on that." This tweet was created in response to a conversation surrounding CRT rhetoric and how restorative justice could be a product of CRT. This particular Twitter user believes that restorative justice in schools is something that exists outside of CRT discourse.

Twitter restorative justice advocates share their thoughts on how local, state, and federal governments have repressed, suppressed, and oppressed conversations that challenge structural and institutional change. One Twitter user said, "Here in WI, our GOP-controlled legislature is trying to prohibit the use of certain words and phrases in schools. Restorative justice is one. Others include white supremacy, structural bias/racism, equity, multiculturalism, social justice, patriarchy and cultural awareness." This Twitter user believed that government officials who do not adopt policies that promote restorative justice in schools are also against promoting and engaging in discourse addressing race, equity, and inclusion issues. Twitter users also tweeted their sentiments regarding the changes they are seeing due to restorative justice policies "The discomfort comes from watching folks who have relied on the police in their classroom figure out what it looks like to be restorative instead of punitive, but it's a delicious discomfort."

Activists and those working with restorative justice programs use Twitter to promote restorative justice events. One tweet stated, "Yesterday, I presented for the [Twitter account for a school system] on Positive Behavioral Interventions and Supports, Conflict Resolution Tech, and Restorative Justice as part of the #4064 School-Based LE training." Another organization tweeted, "Our fall 2021 Liderazgo cohort is still having their classes [emoji] learning so much! In the October workshop, we talked about reimagining safety, restorative justice, and the school-to-prison pipeline. We are so happy to have these conversations with such a great group of people!" Another user tweeted, "Attending ABA panel on restorative justice and school-to-prison pipeline. Remarkable science showing how we perpetuate recidivism systemically, from the earliest ages, predominantly affecting black and brown communities, and communities in poverty. We know better & can do better!"

Activist organizations on Twitter tend to tweet resources and internet links to provide their followers with additional information regarding restorative justice. Because Twitter users can only create messages using 280 characters, activist organizations will often share a message and then provide their followers with resources that provide greater detail about a particular issue. This tweet demonstrates this "Restorative Justice practices are used by educators to create safe, supportive spaces in #schools. It is a more beneficial approach to discipline that all schools can use! Find out how Restorative Justice can benefit your school today. Call (xxx) xxx-xxx for more info." Another example is when a Twitter user tweeted, "For a lot of kids, system involvement starts at school. One thing districts can do to end the school-to-prison pipeline is to implement restorative justice practices. You can learn more about this issue in our report!" A report generated by this organization accompanied this tweet.

Tweets about Counternarratives of Restorative Justice

Unlike tweets created by advocates, restorative justice counternarrative tweets typically did not include additional resources that supported their opinions. Anti-restorative justice tweets in this sample did not include additional information that provided factual evidence of their claims. Many of the tweets linked restorative justice with a disdain for CRT. This Twitter user mentions CRT in their tweet about restorative justice "[lists Twitter handles of restorative justice supporters] Yur a fool. The tenets of CRT are 100% being taught in k-12 (at least where I'm at). Education/public policy also adopted tenets of CRT. This is why schools now perform largely worthless peace circles/restorative justice and Yur local alderman suggest the same when bullets fly."

Some Twitter users did not believe that restorative justice was practical and used their social media accounts to voice their opinions. One Twitter user posted an article about a school official whom a student attacked. The article was accompanied by this verbiage "My God! This is why restorative justice in schools is a failure." Another Twitter user believes that schools overuse restorative justice and find restorative justice to not be effective. Their opinion was articulated in the following tweet "Just found out that a lot of schools apparently obsessively use 'restorative justice'- including for racism, homophobia, etc. - to deal with bullying and just like...That's actively worse than the fat load of nothing that was done when I was in school."

Some Twitter users expressed a narrative that suggests restorative justice hides the wrongdoings of those who violate conduct policies. For example, one Twitter user would like to identify school board leaders who support restorative justice. They tweeted, "We need to expose every school board and superintendent across the country who covered up crimes committed against their students in the name of 'restorative justice' or any other trending terminology. All students should be safe at school." These tweets also spread the idea that restorative justice makes schools less safe.

Twitter users who promoted anti-restorative justice rhetoric typically believed restorative justice fails to hold people and students accountable for their actions. One Twitter user tweeted "Restorative justice" in action. Sacrificing innocent kids in service of ideology and "equity"…kids who bring knives to school get to say sorry and avoid detention." Another Twitter user tweeted, "These restorative justice (Utah) or promise programs (Fl) have infected every school policy. It is a delusional ideology, and making our schools dangerous. These policies Embolden the "criminals" and oppress the victims. Delusional. All in the name of safety."

There appeared to be a misunderstanding of the function of restorative justice among many of the anti-restorative justice Twitter users in this study. One tweet stated, "We talk about restorative justice and all this other bullshit in the school, yet we aren't doing anything to get to the root of serious issues." Restorative justice practices in schools are employed to address conflict's origins and help create meaningful resolutions.

Civic Engagement and Politics

Twitter users in this study used their tweets to encourage and promote civic engagement, political platforms and to highlight some of the work individuals are doing in restorative justice spaces in schools. A Twitter user tweeted their video testimonial to their school board "Schools. We desperately need major investments in counselors, restorative justice, conflict resolution. We took the first step by removing SROs, as research shows their presence harms some students and doesn't prevent violence."

Several Twitter users talked about the voting process and showed how they used their vote and voice to address restorative justice in schools. This tweet mentions restorative justice is one of the issues being voted on during the election cycle "I'm off to #Vote in my local city council and school board elections! Every election counts. City Councils can change zoning laws that expand affordable housing options. School Boards can choose to add solar or restorative justice. #Vote #EveryElection #EveryOffice #EveryTime." Another tweet thanked a candidate for running for public office and running a campaign that focused on restorative justice "Thank you @ MoreForD4 for running an unapologetic campaign for Boston city council! While last night wasn't the result we hoped for, we know that you will keep fighting for equity in education, restorative justice, and an end to the school-to-prison pipeline. The work continues."

One elected official called for constituents to hold them accountable for creating safer schools and taking action that affects the school-to-prison pipeline "Only 10% of schools have enough social workers and psychologists to meet guidelines. Safe schools invest in restorative justice and recognize the danger in creating a school-to-prison pipeline. Put the pressure on us." - @SenMurphyOffice #CounselingNotCriminalization." Other tweets share how elected officials are promoting restorative justice "On October 13th, 2021 Attorney General Nessel released a letter calling for educators to double down on Restorative Justice practices in schools and commit to "stamping out those disparities."

Tweets Sharing Articles and Other Media

Those who shared their opinion about restorative justice often did so by sharing articles. These articles were the most shared articles that addressed restorative justice in schools:

- "The Los Angeles Unified School District cut its police budget by $25 million and redirected the money to a $36.5 million Black Student Achievement Plan (BSAP) following months of student campaigning... @capitalandmain https://t.co/4A0CJa264Z"
- "In response to the George Floyd murder, #LAUSD cut its police budget by $25M in the summer of 2020 and redirected that money toward a $36.5-million Black Student Achievement Plan. https://t.co/aoLgjIaJmY#purposeinmotion #purpose"
- "Instead of allowing police back into schools as school resource officers. parents say the district should use funding to bring back restorative justice programs and invest in social work."
- "NYC, NY | "School safety officers will be transferred out of the police department and trained in restorative justice practices. But for some, 'retrofitting' the job isn't enough"

Tweets promoted virtual meetings to discuss restorative justice techniques in schools "Tuesday, Oct 5, at 6:30 pm via Zoom: Documentary/discussion about the restorative justice movement's progress in Santa Rosa, CA schools, the county judicial/probation system, and the lives of victims, offenders, teachers, students, volunteers and parents. https://t.co/g7QFPQ5HwF." Other tweets invited other Twitter users to watch restorative justice content on streaming services "Watched the "Explained" episode on apologies (on Netflix). Worth a watch. A lovely success story about Restorative Justice included in the episode. I'd like to see ALL school staff trained in #RestorativeJustice."

SOLUTIONS AND RECOMMENDATIONS

The collection and analysis of the data provided information that potentially aids in creating communication or public relation strategies for restorative justice in schools. These strategies could assist in the adoption of alternatives to punitive pressures to address discipline in schools. The data gave insight into public opinion and existing public relations strategies. Agenda building utilizes public-generated discourse to effect social change and policymaking. Social media sites, like Twitter, create unique opportunities to access public discourse and public opinion. The data suggests that Twitter users tweeted about restorative justice for four different reasons; as a result, public relations strategies should be focused on some of those factors. The factors are public opinion and discourse surrounding restorative justice in schools, information about restorative justice in schools, and political participation. The researcher recommends that education reform advocates utilize these factors when creating their education reform campaigns on restorative justice.

Research Public Opinion and Discourse Surrounding Restorative Justice in Schools

When creating media messages, it is essential to understand audiences (Drewniany & Jewlry, 2014). Understanding audience perspectives and their levels of understanding about restorative justice is necessary to creating media messages. Identifying public opinion informs content creators about what information they need to include in messages and how they should include them. By looking at the opinions of those who do not support restorative justice in schools, perspectives that articulate their reasoning behind their lack of support for restorative justice can be determined. As a result, communication that addresses this perspective can be formed and may correct instances of miseducation. Looking at public opinion and discourse about restorative justice can provide an analysis of how people discuss restorative justice in schools, and it can determine what strategies public relations campaigns can employ that will positively contribute to the discourse of restorative justice.

Information about Restorative Justice in Schools

To create a public relations strategy for restorative justice in schools, advocates need to incorporate informative materials and educational opportunities. Twitter users contributed to the discourse of restorative justice in schools by providing definitions, articles, and multimedia posts to broaden their audiences' perspectives of restorative justice practices in schools. Restorative justice advocates also shared information about programs and events that explored aspects of restorative justice that could not be addressed within a single tweet. Many of these tweets received a considerable amount of interaction and effectively created learning opportunities for Twitter followers. Users showed that exposure to educational research about restorative justice in schools helped shape their opinion about adopting restorative justice practices.

Political Participation

Public relations strategies should strive to incorporate communication that encourages action. Because restorative justice advocates want to see more institutions adopt restorative justice practices, they should incorporate communication that encourages participation in the political process. The tweets in this sample showed that Twitter users tweeted to encourage their followers to vote, talk to their elected officials, and read information about legislation that includes aspects of restorative justice practices in schools. Government officials who are supporters of restorative justice in schools should also take part in the discourse on social media. Tweets from the accounts of politicians talked about their initiatives that include restorative justice in schools; however, they need to improve on sharing reports and studies that give factual evidence about restorative justice in schools.

FUTURE RESEARCH DIRECTIONS

This chapter identified strategies that can be used to bring awareness and promote civic engagement related to restorative justice. This study also focused on how Twitter users utilize their platform to discuss restorative justice. Discourse on Twitter has been impactful to political and social change (Johnson & Goldwasser, 2016). Political strategists use Twitter to gauge their audiences about their sentiments regarding social and pollical issues. However, there needs to be further investigation related to how restorative justice in schools is discussed on other social media platforms. This will help create a more comprehensive approach to creating a public relations strategy to promoting restorative justice in schools.

It would also be helpful to examine the ways restorative justice advocates use other forms of media, like television and print, to raise awareness about restorative justice practices. Though media convergence allows news and communication organizations to publish stories on the internet and social media platforms, it is still helpful to examine restorative justice news stories and how media outlets communicate the restorative justice narrative. Not only would it be essential to examine how media outlets tell these stories, but researchers could gain greater insight into whether stories told by media outlets lead to increased support for restorative justice practices in schools.

CONCLUSION

Social movements and social change initiatives need communication and public relations strategies to accomplish goals effectively. Using communication and public relations tools are vital parts of influencing policy changes because effective public relations strategies have the power to impact thoughts and behaviors (Coombs & Holladay, 2013). The agenda building concept embodies the idea that public discourse incorporated with grassroots public relations strategies can influence and change public policy (Elder & Cobb, 1984). By identifying ways Twitter users engage in restorative justice discourse, restorative justice advocates can strategically create Twitter communication to build an agenda for policy changes, awareness, and an increase in the adoption of restorative justice practices in schools. Most importantly, building an agenda for policy reform allows advocates to speak truth to power.

This chapter illustrated how Twitter users engage in the discourse surrounding restorative justice in schools. Twitter users used their tweets to inform their followers about restorative justice in schools, share their opinions about restorative justice, and encourage civic engagement. This chapter also identified ways restorative justice advocates can use discourse to help promote restorative justice practices and inform Twitter users. Restorative justice advocates can form public relations strategies by (1) identifying problems related to discipline in schools and how restorative justice in schools is one potential remedy to the school-to-prison pipeline (2) developing an understanding of who audience members are and how they can be reached to receive information (3) creating content that educates, encourages public opinion, and inspires civic engagement.

REFERENCES

Anderson, D. S. (2015). *Emmett Till: The murder that shocked the world and propelled the civil rights movement.* Univ. Press of Mississippi.

Barthel, M., Mitchell, A., Asare-Marfo, D., Kennedy, C., & Worden, K. (2020). Measuring news consumption in a digital era. *Pew Research Center's Journalism Project, 8.*

Bell, C., & Puckett, T. (2020). I Want To Learn But They Won't Let Me: Exploring the Impact of School Discipline on Academic Achievement. *Urban Education.* doi:10.1177/0042085920968629

Boyd, D. M., & Ellison, N. B. (2007). Social Network Sites: Definition, History and Scholarship. *Journal of Computer-Mediated Communication, 13*(1), 210–230. doi:10.1111/j.1083-6101.2007.00393.x

Brewer, T. J., & Wallis, M. (2015). # TFA: The intersection of social media and education reform. *Critical Education, 6*(14).

Campbell, R., Martin, C., & Fabos, B. (2017). *Media & culture: Mass communication in a digital age*. Bedford/St. Martin's.

Coombs, W. T., & Holladay, S. J. (2013). *It's not just PR: Public relations in society*. John Wiley & Sons.

Curtin, P. A. (1999). Reevaluating public relations information subsidies: Market-driven journalism and agenda-building theory and practice. *Journal of Public Relations Research, 11*(1), 53–90. doi:10.12071532754xjprr1101_03

Drewniany, B., & Jewler, B. (2014). *Creative Strategy in Advertising*. Cengage.

Elder, C. D., & Cobb, R. W. (1984). Agenda-building and the politics of aging. *Policy Studies Journal: the Journal of the Policy Studies Organization, 13*(1), 115–129. doi:10.1111/j.1541-0072.1984.tb01704.x

Guo, C., & Saxton, G. D. (2014). Tweeting social change: How social media are changing non-profit advocacy. *Nonprofit and Voluntary Sector Quarterly, 43*(1), 57–79. doi:10.1177/0899764012471585

Heitzeg, N. A. (2009). Education or Incarceration: Zero Tolerance Policies and the School to Prison Pipeline. In Forum on public policy online (Vol. 2009, No. 2). Oxford Round Table.

Hopkins, B. (2002). Restorative justice in schools. *Support for Learning, 17*(3), 144–149. doi:10.1111/1467-9604.00254

Johnson, K., & Goldwasser, D. (2016). Identifying stance by analyzing political discourse on twitter. In *Proceedings of the First Workshop on NLP and Computational Social Science* (pp. 66-75). 10.18653/v1/W16-5609

Kopfman, J. E., & Ruth-McSwain, A. (2017). Public information campaigns. In *The practice of government public relations* (pp. 75–100). Routledge. doi:10.4324/9781315085524-6

Lacoe, J., & Steinberg, M. P. (2019). Do suspensions affect student outcomes? *Educational Evaluation and Policy Analysis, 41*(1), 34–62. doi:10.3102/0162373718794897

Lamia, K., Tyree, T., O'Brien, P., & Sturgis, I. (Eds.). (2013). *Social media: pedagogy and practice*. University Press of America.

Latimer, J., Dowden, C., & Muise, D. (2005). The effectiveness of restorative justice practices: A meta-analysis. *The Prison Journal, 85*(2), 127–144. doi:10.1177/0032885505276969

Llewellyn, J., & Howse, R. L. (1999). *Restorative justice: A conceptual framework.* Prepared for the Law Commission of Canada.

Mayworm, A. M., Sharkey, J. D., Hunnicutt, K. L., & Schiedel, K. C. (2016). Teacher consultation to enhance implementation of school-based restorative justice. *Journal of Educational & Psychological Consultation, 26*(4), 385–412. doi:10.1080/1047 4412.2016.1196364

Miers, D. R., Maguire, M., Goldie, S., Sharpe, K., Hale, C., Netten, A., ... Newburn, T. (2001). An exploratory evaluation of restorative justice schemes (No. 9). Home Office.

Mundt, M., Ross, K., & Burnett, C. M. (2018). Scaling social movements through social media: The case of Black Lives Matter. *Social Media + Society, 4*(4). doi:10.1177/2056305118807911

Oden Choi, J., Hammer, J., Royal, J., & Forlizzi, J. (2020, July). Moving for the Movement: Applying Viewpoints and Composition Techniques to the Design of Online Social Justice Campaigns. In *Proceedings of the 2020 ACM Designing Interactive Systems Conference* (pp. 75-86). 10.1145/3357236.3395435

Rice, R. E., & Atkin, C. K. (2009). Public communication campaigns: Theoretical principles and practical applications. In *Media effects* (pp. 452–484). Routledge.

Royster, J. J. (2016). *Southern Horrors and Other Writings: Anti-Lynching Campaign of Ida B. Wells, 1892-1900.* Macmillan Higher Education.

Ryan, C., Carragee, K. M., & Schwerner, C. (1998). *Media, movements, and the quest for social justice.* Academic Press.

Scollon, R. (2001). Action and text: towards an integrated understanding of the place of text in social (inter) action, mediated discourse analysis and the problem of social action. *Methods of Critical Discourse Analysis, 113*, 139-183.

Shearer, E., & Mitchell, A. (2021). *News use across social media platforms in 2020.* Academic Press.

Singhal, A., & Rogers, E. M. (2001). The entertainment-education strategy in communication campaigns. *Public Communication Campaigns, 3*, 343-356.

Snow, D. A., Vliegenthart, R., & Ketelaars, P. (2018). *The framing perspective on social movements: Its conceptual roots and architecture. In The Wiley Blackwell companion to social movements.* Wiley Blackwell. doi:10.1002/9781119168577

South African Law Commission. (2000). *Sentencing (a New Sentencing Framework): Report* (Vol. 82). The Commission.

Van Dijk, T. (2001). Critical Discourse Analysis. The Handbook of Discourse Analysis, 352-371.

Vliegenthart, R., & Walgrave, S. (2012). The interdependency of mass media and social movements. The Sage handbook of political communication, 387-397.

Zehr, H. (1990). *Changing lenses* (Vol. 114). Herald Press.

Zoch, L. M., & Molleda, J. C. (2006). Building a theoretical model of media relations using framing, information subsidies, and agenda-building. *Public Relations Theory II*, 279-309.

Chapter 11

From the Schoolhouse to the Prison Yard:
Discipline Disparities in K–12 Public Schools – A Call for Transformational Change

Mindy Brooks-Eaves
Kentucky State University, USA

ABSTRACT

This chapter is intended to help others seeking answers to the disciplinary disparities that limit opportunities for communities and students of color. The chapter begins with a grounding in the historical context, then identifies current issues in discipline disparities, and concludes with a call for transformational change in public education. Education significantly sets the path for individuals; likewise, it affects the course of society in crucial ways. Disparities in educational experiences have compounding effects. Discipline disparities in K-12 schools are particularly impactful.

Education is a lifeline for people and society.

Education significantly sets the path for individuals, and it affects the course of society in crucial ways. Disparities in educational experiences have compounding effects. Discipline disparities in K-12 schools are particularly impactful.

DOI: 10.4018/978-1-6684-3359-1.ch011

A historical, contextual analysis of public education and landmark court cases is necessary to fully understand present day disparities in discipline amongst Black and Brown groups. From the devastating Supreme Court cases of Plessy v. Ferguson in 1896 legalizing segregation and Cummings v. Richmond County Board of Education in 1899 that legalized closing Black schools for financial reasons while White schools remained open to the unfulfilled promises of Brown v. Board of Education, left public education for students of color in tatters.

In 1957, the "Little Rock Nine", the first group of Black students to attend a federally mandated desegregated school, endured virulent hatred from White communities displayed through verbal and physical assaults. The federal government, also, utilized resources such as armed troops to support the efforts to resist integration of public schools. Institutions mirror the attitude and values of dominant groups. A deeper examination of disciplinary practices of the public education system to determine values and attitudes indicates a lack of basic regard of students of color due to disparities in school discipline, which has widespread detrimental structural and individual implications.

The story of Little Rock is a microcosm of the United States and its troubled relationship with equality in all systems of society, including public education. In the United States, students of color are disproportionately suspended and for lengthier time periods than White students. Recent research indicates that the school to prison pipeline is a stark reality. The findings show that the school-to-prison pipeline is poses substantial risks for students, particularly for Black and Brown boys (Camera, 2021).

In a prescient warning in 1965, Clark in Dark Ghetto: Dilemmas of Social Power, admonished social scientists, teachers, and social workers for failing to engage and understand the conditions and experiences of poverty. Clark noted the lack of training for social scientists, teachers, or social workers to prepare them to understand and/or cope with or change the "normal chaos" of these marginalized populations. Clark cautioned that such a grave lack of preparation must be remedied, or dire consequences would be compounded.

To my knowledge, there is a present nothing in the vast literature of social science tree disease and textbooks and nothing in the practical and field training of graduates in social science to prepare them for the realities and complexities of this type of involvement in a real, dynamic, turbulent, and at times seemingly chaotic community. And what is more, nothing anywhere in the training of social scientist, teachers, or social workers now prepare them to understand, to cope with, or to change the normal chaos of ghetto communities. These are gray flex which must be remedied soon if these disciplines are to be calm relevant emphasis added to the stability in survival of our society (p. xxix)

This chapter is intended to help others seeking answers to the disciplinary disparities that limit opportunities for communities and students of color. The chapter begins with a grounding in the historical context, then identifies current issues in discipline disparities, and concludes with a call for transformational change in public education.

HISTORICAL CONTEXT

"We offer the research presented here to prompt additional scrutiny with respect to how and why educational agencies in the United States differently administered disciplinary actions especially when those actions are known to have dire consequences for the student. School suspension hinders academic growth" (Riddle and Sinclair, 2019, para 7).

After the Civil War ended, Black communities, churches, Black teachers, missionaries, and freed slaves organized to create schools (Anderson, 2016) as a necessary step to prosperity and equality. The South lacked a public education system, which gave rise to grassroots efforts to create schools that served people moving from chattel slavery. By the premature end of the Freedmen's Bureau in 1877, schools serving freed slaves existed throughout the South. Simultaneously, Southern states and municipalities passed Black Codes that enforced de facto slave laws and conditions (Anderson, 2016).

However, by the turn of the century, Jim Crow Laws and Supreme Court decisions gutted Black schools. In the landmark case, 1896 Plessy vs. Ferguson, the court set forth the separate but equal doctrine, i.e., legalized segregation. In Cummings v. Richmond County Board of Education (1899), the Supreme Court ruled that it was fair to shutter Black schools while White schools remained open—purportedly for financial reasons (Anderson, 2016). In 1947, Mendes v. Winchester, a federal circuit court in California ruled that segregation of school children was unconstitutional, which involved the segregation of Mexican American school children. The Ninth Circuit Court of Appeals' historic decision was critical to the Brown vs. Board of Education case. The Mendes case symbolized the important crossover between different ethnic and racial groups who came together to argue in favor of desegregation.

The 1954 Brown v. Board officially outlawed the longstanding separate but equal doctrine. Unfortunately, through several legal challenges, refusals by school boards and communities to integrate, and violence and intimidation, the effects of Brown were diminished to unfulfilled promises and shattered hopes for equitable outcomes for students of color. "Many interviewees of the Civil Rights History Project recount a long, painful struggle that scarred many students, teachers, and parents" (Library Congress, (n.d.). This active opposition and diminished impact has compounded effects.

Disparities in school discipline is one significant indicator of these unfulfilled promises and shattered hopes. Alarmingly, since the passage of the 1968 Civil Rights Act, suspensions for Black students increased 200% from 1972-1973 and 2009-2010 school years. Suspensions for White students increased by 1% (Losen & Martinez, 2013). Today, our nation's academic and discipline gaps can be seen as our nation's "educational debt" (Ladson-Billings, 2006). Educational debt the direct results of compounded economic, social, and political inequalities that have plagued the United States for centuries" (Carter et. al, 2016).

INEFFECTIVE DISCIPLINARY MEASURES: ZERO TOLERANCE AND EXPULSION

Zero-tolerance policies criminalize minor infractions of school rules, while police in schools lead to students being criminalized for behavior that should be handled inside the school. Students of color are especially vulnerable to push-out trends and the discriminatory application of discipline. (ACLU, 2021)

In the United States, teachers and administrators rely primarily on punitive rather than positive approaches in managing students' behavior, despite compelling evidence that such strategies are ineffective. Zero-tolerance are predetermined consequences, most often severe and punitive in nature, that are intended to be applied regardless of the gravity of the behavior, mitigating circumstances, or situational context. Zero tolerance policies continue to dominate public school disciplinary policies despite an absence of credible documentation to support their ineffectiveness for improving school safety or reducing problem behaviors (Krezmein, Leone, and Achilles, 2006).

Zero tolerance policies have the opposite effect. Zero tolerance policies related to discipline and order by school districts across the United States significantly *increase* the number of children who are being suspended and expelled from school (Norguera, 2003). In the 2013–2014 academic year, researchers estimated 2.6 million public school students received one or more out-of-school suspensions (U.S. Department of Education, 2019). Although Black students made up only 15% of the student population, they received as many as 39.3% of all out-of-school suspension. In the 2015–2016 academic year, in addition to out-of-school suspensions, Black students are more likely to be expelled or referred to law enforcement (Civil Rights Data Collection, 2017). Black males comprised 23% of expelled students in the 2015–2016 academic year, and Black females comprised 10%, despite each group making up just 8% of enrolled students (16% total).

In summarizing myriad reports, Lauren Camera reported that school suspension data shows glaring disparities and discipline by race. In the 2015 to 2016 school year 11 million instructional days were missed due to out of school suspensions given to Black and Latinx students. Notably, Camera further reported that districts with high rates of lost instruction days due to suspensions have higher numbers of security guards on campus.

School disciplinary practices appear to be vehicles for the myriad expressions of racial and class-based biases held by teachers and school administrators (Barrett, McEachin, Mills, & Valant, 2017). Teachers are using their subjective interpretations of what behavior is "inappropriate" and making referrals for discipline without further conversation with the student about the behavior. For example, a teacher tells a student to face the front of the classroom, the student feels something push the back of his chair, he turns around to see what it is, the teacher in turn tells the student to go to the office for insubordination.

RACIAL AND CULTURAL DIFFERENCES BETWEEN THE STUDENT AND TEACHER

As much as we seek to lock them from view, race and racism continue to color our interactions, including our disciplinary actions, on a daily, even moment by moment basis. (Carter, Skiba, Arredondo & Pollock, 2016).

Racial and cultural differences between the student and staff can result in unequal treatment. Discipline disparities is a result of social-cultural factors within the classroom and school setting that influence a teacher's decision to remove a student from the classroom. Often, the reasons given for referring students for "discipline" is based on subjective interpretations (e.g., being disrespectful, attitude problems, appearing threatening).

Implicit bias is the phenomenon in which such false perceptions shape experiences and influence decision-making without the individual being aware (Banaji, & Greenwald, 1995). Educator bias is associated with racial disparities in students' achievement and discipline. Teachers have been found to disproportionately refer Black students to school administrators for disciplinary actions (McFadden, et al as cited in Skiba, Michael, Nardo, & Peterson, 2002).

Research determined that Black students were referred for punitive measures more than twice as often as White students and for less severe infractions than White students. A study by American University and Johns Hopkins University found that non-Black teachers of Black students have significantly lower expectations in comparison to Black teachers. This was particularly the case for Black males and math teachers (Gershensen, Holt, Papageorge, 2015). The K-12 context is "ripe with suggestive, quasi-experimental evidence of pervasive implicit bias in the form of grading biases and student-teacher racial match effects," (Gershenson & Dee, 2017).

The Kirwan Institute (2014) identifies "cultural deficit thinking" as the primary cause. Such thinking leads educators to "harbor negative assumptions about the ability, aspirations, and work ethic of these students—especially poor students of color—based on the assumption that they and their families do not value education," (p. 8). Cultural deficit thinking is an example of explicit bias.

GIRLS OF COLOR MATTER: INTERSECTIONAL EXPERIENCES

Participants [girls of color] often mentioned that school police officers or other adults would tell them they "should have known better" or should attempt to modify the behavior of girls of color to follow more traditional White views of gender and sexuality, often suggesting that they should be more "ladylike". (LePage, 2021, para. 10).

Girls of color are also an at-risk student group due to racial and gender bias. Girls of color face some of the greatest barriers to educational opportunities and social emotional growth inside schools with poor school climates (Onyeka-Crawford, Patrick, and Chaudhry, 2017). Latina girls have high "pushout rates" (Lowman, 2017). Native girls experience disproportionate discipline on par with Black girls (Brown & Tillio, 2013). Black girls especially face scrutiny, often encountering rules, such as hair codes, that target their cultural climates (Onyeka-Crawford, Patrick, and Chaudhry, 2017). Black girls are referred to as too loud, too assertive, too sexually provocative, too defiant, and too adult-like. Professor Kimberlé Crenshaw coined the term intersectionality, which offers a way to explain oppression of Black girls (2010). Daily, girls of color must navigate through a landscape that reinforces multidimensional stereotypes and debilitating narratives that negatively impact school experience, connection, and performance.

Studies show that these differences in rates of suspensions are a result of policies and adult biases — not a result of differences in behavior (Bacher-Hicks, Billings, & Deming, 2019). Black and Native girls are not more likely to misbehave, but they are more likely to

be disciplined. An analysis of national U.S. Department of Education 2015-16 civil rights data found that Black girls are five times more likely than White girls to be suspended at least once and four times as likely as White girls to be arrested at school. Girls of color are over 50% of the U.S. girl population, it is imperative that

Figure 1.

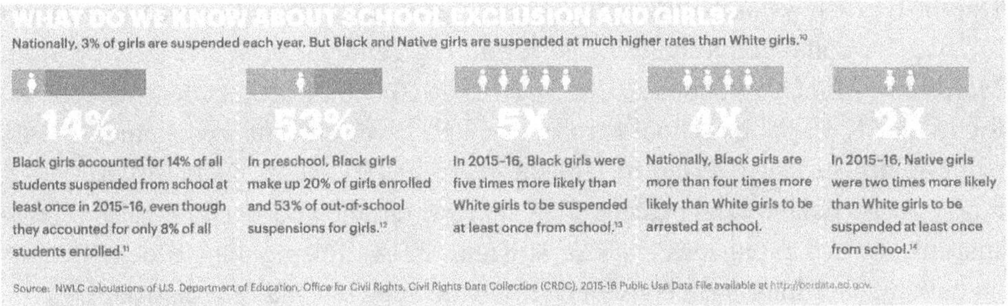

WHAT DO WE KNOW ABOUT SCHOOL EXCLUSION AND GIRLS?

Nationally, 3% of girls are suspended each year. But Black and Native girls are suspended at much higher rates than White girls.[10]

14% — Black girls accounted for 14% of all students suspended from school at least once in 2015–16, even though they accounted for only 8% of all students enrolled.[11]

53% — In preschool, Black girls make up 20% of girls enrolled and 53% of out-of-school suspensions for girls.[12]

5X — In 2015–16, Black girls were five times more likely than White girls to be suspended at least once from school.[13]

4X — Nationally, Black girls are more than four times more likely than White girls to be arrested at school.

2X — In 2015–16, Native girls were two times more likely than White girls to be suspended at least once from school.[14]

Source: NWLC calculations of U.S. Department of Education, Office for Civil Rights, Civil Rights Data Collection (CRDC), 2015-16 Public Use Data File available at http://ocrdata.ed.gov.

research about girls of color experiences that consider their intersectional experience and needs (Girls Leadership, 2021).

PUSHING OUT STUDENTS OF COLOR: ENTRENCHED DISPARITIES BY THE NUMBERS

On average, students who attend middle schools that rely heavily on suspensions are at greater risk of being arrested and incarcerated as young adults and less likely to graduate from high school and go to college. Further, these effects are most pronounced for Black and Hispanic males, who are dramatically underrepresented among college graduates and overrepresented in the nation's prison system (Bacher-Hicks, Billings, Deming, 2021).

Racial disproportionality in school disciplinary practices has a long history and continues today (Wallace, Goodkind, Wallace, Bachman, 2008). From 1972 to 2009, the U.S. Secondary School Suspension data reported that Black and Latino suspensions *increased 200%* [emphasis added] (Lowman, 2017). Bryan Stevenson, in *Teach Us All*, noted bleak statistics, 1 of 3 Black boys and 1 of 6 Latinx boys will be incarcerated (Lowman, 2017). In 2006, Krezmein, Leone & Achilles found that, although Black students comprise only 19.4% of the K-12 public school student population, they represented 56.7% of school suspensions. Furthermore, Black students more frequently have been subjected to harsh disciplinary measure such as corporal punishment, even when less obtrusive alternatives have been available (Drakeford, 2004). Black and Latinx students are susceptible are pushed out at alarming rates which increases the probability of going to prison by 400% (Lowen, 2017). Not only do Black students encounter school discipline earlier, but they are also expelled at greater proportions by the time they reach high school (Rausch & Skiba, 2004).

According to 2013-2014 data, The U.S. Department of Education reported that 18% of Black boys and 10% of Black girls received an out-of-school suspension in 2013-14, compared to only 5% of White boys and 2% of White girls (Barrett, McEachin, Mills, & Valant, 2017). In 2015-2016 data, Black students accounted for 15% of K-12 public school enrollment. Yet, Black students accounted for 26% of those arrested or referred to law enforcement (Sparks & Klein, 2018). Black boys only accounted for 8 percent of all students enrolled but accounted for 23% of suspensions and expulsions (Sparks & Klein, 2018). Suspensions and expulsions potentially have long-term consequences that extend beyond the classroom.

SCHOOL YARD TO THE PRISON YARD

"A suspension can be life altering. It is the number-one predictor— more than poverty—of whether children will drop out of school and walk down a road that includes greater likelihood of unemployment, reliance on social-welfare programs, and imprisonment." (Flannery, 2015, citing the National Education Association, para. 5).

This graph depicts the clear and consistent path from school discipline discrepancies to prison.

The school-to-prison pipeline is a disturbing national trend wherein children are funneled out of public schools and into the juvenile and criminal justice systems. Many students pushed out of public schools have a history of trauma, poverty, and learning disabilities. They would benefit greatly from educational and social interventions. Researchers from Boston University, the University of Colorado Boulder and Harvard University found a causal link between students who experience strict school discipline: suspensions, expulsions and being arrested or incarcerated as an adult (Bacher-Hicks, Billings & Deming, 2021). Addressing these deep-seated challenges requires serious accountability, resources, and social change (Ladson, Billings, 2021; Vaught & Castagno, 2008).

SOCIAL CHANGE THROUGH COLLECTIVE ACTION: TEACH US ALL

We have the schools we have because of the culture we have. The real answer resides in cultural transformation, a much more difficult and unpopular solution. But an absolute necessity to our stability and survival as a society. (Ladson-Billings, 2021, p.143)

Figure 2.

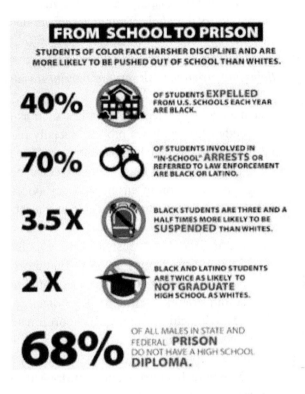

Public education is a lifeline for communities and students of color. Effectiveness requires a commitment to addressing the systemic inequities that students and communities face. Discipline disparities in education set a path for myriad unjust outcomes. Addressing these disparities creates powerful possibilities for transforming lives and communities. Discipline should be diagnostic, educative, restorative, community-building and resist criminal justice responses to student misconduct (Curren, 2020). Any solution to disciplinary disparities must address the cultural dynamics of oppression and power. Any solution must acknowledge the long-term structural and individual impacts that discipline disparities have on communities and students of color.

A multi-level solution strategy at the student/parent, school, district, state, and federal, levels are necessary to implement policies and practices with efficacy. On the federal level, President Biden signed Executive Order 13985, Advancing Racial Equity and Support for Underserved Communities Through the Federal Government. The order reads,

...advancing equity for all, including people of color and others who have been historically underserved, marginalized, and adversely affected by persistent poverty

and inequality. Affirmatively advancing equity, civil rights, racial justice, and equal opportunity is the responsibility of the whole of our government. Because advancing equity requires a systematic approach to embedding fairness in decision-making processes, executive departments and agencies must recognize and work to redress inequities in their policies and programs that serve as barriers to equal opportunity.

This executive order mandates that federal agencies, such as the Department of Education, evaluate whether their policies produce racially inequitable results and to make necessary changes to ensure equitable outcomes. For school districts, policy implementation at the school level must seriously consider resources such as space, staff, and program evaluation to ensure efficacy (Gordon, 2018). For example, a study in North Carolina found that students and teachers of the same race have improved disciplinary outcomes in that rates of exclusionary discipline (out-of-school suspensions, in-school suspensions, and expulsions) decreased (Lindsay & Hart, 2017). School districts may use such findings to inform robust partnerships and incentives such as tuition remission dedicated to increasing the number of educators and administrators of color. In San Francisco public schools, implementing an ethnic studies curriculum improved school climate and attendance and the Perspectives Experience Program intended to improve teacher bias reduced suspensions by half (Lepage, 2021).

Student led advocacy efforts have the collective power to transform their individual schools through collective action. States, districts, schools, and teachers may solicit student and parent input by involving student voice strategies that can meaningfully impact instruction, climate, and policies (Benner, Brown & Jeffrey, 2019; Toshalis & Nakkula, 2012). For example, in Teach Us All, the student advocacy efforts in a New York public school worked collectively with school administrators successfully improved school climate for students across lines of race (Lowen, 2017). The following strategies can influence discipline disparities:

- Hire, retain, and promote educators of color
- Encourage and elevate student led advocacy groups to involve student voice in decisions
- Teacher-facing interventions (affirmation, empathy, wise interventions)
- Implement culturally inclusive curriculum responsive teaching practices
- Enhance school environment to remove barriers
- Adopt social emotional learning standards
- Overhaul codes of conduct to remove punitive language and policies
- Implement restorative/transformative practices with program evaluation
- Fund support services such as social workers

Paulo Friere's transformation theory suggests that people interacting together in the learning environment stimulates reflection on their reality (2000). Teach Us All demonstrates powerful lessons from history within a timely context, emphasizing the need for unity and collective action to rectify the discipline disparities.

REFERENCES

Alexander, M. (2012). *The new Jim Crow: Mass incarceration in the age of colorblindness*. Pantheon Books.

American Civil Liberties Union. (2021). *School to Prison Pipeline*. Retrieved from https://www.aclu.org/issues/juvenile-justice/school-prison-pipeline/school-prison-pipeline-infographic

American Civil Liberties Union (ACLU). (2020). *Race and inequality in education*. Retrieved from https://www.aclu.org/issues/racial-justice/race-and-inequality-education

Bacher-Hicks, A., Billings, S. & Deming, D. (2019). *The school to prison pipeline: Long-run impacts of school suspensions on adult crime*. National Bureau of Economic Research No. w26257.

Barrett, N., McEachin, A., Mills, J., & Valant, J. (2017). *Disparities in student discipline by race and daily income*. Retrieved from https://educationresearchalliancenola.org/files/publications/010418-Barrett-McEachin-Mills-Valant-Disparities-in-Student-Discipline-by-Race-and-Family-Income.pdf

Black Lives Matter at Schools. (2020). *About: Zero-tolerance*. https://Blacklivesmatteratschool.com/about/

Brown, C. A., & Di Tillio, C. (2013). Discipline disproportionality among Hispanic and American Indian students: Expanding the discourse in U.S. research. *Journal of Education and Learning*, 2(4), 47–59. doi:10.5539/jel.v2n4p47

Camera, L. (2021). *Study confirms school-to-prison pipeline*. U.S. News & World Report. Retrieved from https://www.usnews.com/news/education-news/articles/2021-07-27/study-confirms-school-to-prison-pipeline

Carter, P. L., Skiba, R., Arredondo, M. I., & Pollock, M. (2017). You can't fix what you don't look at: Acknowledging race in addressing racial discipline disparities. *Urban Education*, 52(2), 207–235. doi:10.1177/0042085916660350

Civil Rights Act of 1964, Pub.L. 88-352, 78 Stat. 241 (1964).

Civil Rights Data Collection. (2017). *2015–16 state and national estimations.* Retrieved from https://ocrdata.ed.gov/StateNationalEstimations/Estimations_2015_16

Clark, K. B., & Myrdal, G. (1965). *Dark ghetto: Dilemmas of social power.* Harper & Row.

Crenshaw, K. W. (2010). Twenty years of critical race theory: Looking back to move forward. *Connecticut Law Review, 43,* 1253.

Curren, R. (2020). Punishment and motivation in a just school community. *Theory and Research in Education, 18*(1), 117–133. doi:10.1177/1477878520916089

Delgado, R., & Stefancic, J. (2000). *Critical race theory: The cutting edge.* Temple University Press.

Drakeford, W. (2004). *Racial disproportionality in school disciplinary practices.* National Center for Culturally Responsive Educational Systems. Retrieved from http://www.nkces.org/13891010914217070/lib/1398101091427170/DoES/Disproportionality/07_-_Disproportionality/_-_Displinary

Education National Women's Law Center & Education Trust. (2020). *How to create better safer learning environments for girls of color.* Retrieved from https://edtrust.org/wp-content/uploads/2014/09/And-they-cared_How-to-create-better-safer-learning-environments-for-girls-of-color_Aug-2020.pdf

Epstein, R., Blake, J., & González, T. (2017). *Girlhood interrupted: The erasure of Black girls' childhood.* Center on Poverty and Inequality, Georgetown Law.

Flannery, M. (2015). *The school-to-prison pipeline: Time to shut it down.* National Education Association.

Freire, P. (2000). *Pedagogy of freedom.* Rowman & Littlefield.

Girls Leadership. (2021). *Ready to lead: Leadership supports barriers for Black and latinx girls.* Retrieved from https://readytolead.girlsleadership.org

Gordon, N. (2018). Disproportionality in student discipline: Connecting policy to research. Brookings.

Krezmien, M., Leone, P., & Achilles, G. (2006). Suspension, race, and disability: Analysis of statewide practices and reporting. *Journal of Emotional and Behavioral Disorders, 14*(4), 217–226. doi:10.1177/10634266060140040501

Ladson-Billings, G. (2006). From the achievement gap to the education debt: Understanding achievement in U.S. schools. *Educational Researcher, 35*(7), 3–12. doi:10.3102/0013189X035007003

Ladson-Billings, G., & Tate, W. F. (2016). *Toward a critical race theory of education. In Critical race theory in education*. Routledge.

Lepage, B. (2021). In Schools, Black Girls Confront Both Racial and Gender Bias. *Future Ed*. Retrieved from https://www.future-ed.org/in-schools-black-girls-confront-both-racial-and-gender-bias/

Library of Congress. (n.d.). *Civil Rights History Project*. School Segregation & Integration. Retrieved from https://www.loc.gov/collections/civil-rights-history-project/articles-and-essays/school-segregation-and-integration/

Lindsay, C. & Hart. (2017). Exposure to same-race teachers and student disciplinary outcomes for black students in North Carolina. *Educational Evaluation & Policy Analysis, 39*(3). https://journals.sagepub.com/doi/abs/10.3102/0162373717693109

Losen, D., Martinez, T., & Okelola, V. (2014). *Keeping California's kids in school: Fewer students of color missing school for minor misbehavior*. The Center for Civil Rights Remedies at the Civil Rights Projects of UCLA.

Lowman, S. (2017). *Teach us all*. Lowell Milken Center for Unsung Heroes.

McFadden, A. C., Marsh, G. E., Prince, B. J., & Hwang, Y. (1992). A study of race and gender bias in the punishment of handicapped school children. *The Urban Review, 24*(4), 239–251. doi:10.1007/BF01108358

Noguera, P. (2003). Schools, prisons, and social implications of punishment: Rethinking disciplinary practices. *Theory into Practice, 42*(4), 341–350. doi:10.120715430421tip4204_12

Onyeka-Crawford, A., Patrick, K., & Chaudhry, N. (2017). *Let her learn: Stopping school pushout for girls of color*. National Women's Law Center.

Rausch, M. K., Skiba, R. (2004). Disproportionality in school discipline among minority students in Indiana: Description and analysis. *Center for Evaluation and Education Policy. Children left behind policy briefs supplementary analysis 2-A*.

Riddle, T., & Sinclair, St. (2019). Racial disparities in school-based disciplinary actions are associated with county-level rates of racial bias. *Proceedings of the National Academy of Sciences of the United States of America, 116*(17), 201808307. doi:10.1073/pnas.1808307116 PMID:30940747

Skiba, R., Horner, R., Chung, C., Rausch, M., May, S., & Tobin, T. (2011). Race is not neutral: A national investigation of african american and latino disproportionality in school discipline. *School Psychology Review, 40*(1), 85–107. doi:10.1080/0279 6015.2011.12087730

Skiba, R., Michael, R., Nardo, A., & Peterson, R. (2002). The color of discipline: Sources of racial and gender disproportionality in school punishment. *The Urban Review*, *34*(4), 317–342. doi:10.1023/A:1021320817372

Sparks, S., & Klein, A. (2018). Discipline disparities grow for students of color, new federal data show. *Education Week*. Retrieved from https://www.edweek. org/ew/arti- cles/2018/04/24/discipline-disparities-grow-for-students-of-color. html?cmp=soc-twitter- shr&print=1

Toshalis, E., & Nakkula, M. (2012). *Motivation, engagement, and student voice.* Jobs for the Future, Retrieved from http://www.studentsatthecenter.org/topics/motivation-

Townsend, B. (2000). The disproportionate discipline of African American learners: Reducing school suspensions and. *Exceptional Children*, *66*(3), 381–391. doi:10.1177/001440290006600308

Vaught, S., & Castagno, A. (2008). I don't think I'm a racist": Critical race theory, teacher attitudes, and structural racism. *Race, Ethnicity and Education*, *11*(2), 95–113. doi:10.1080/13613320802110217

Wallace, J., Goodkind, S., Wallace, C., & Bachman, J. (2008). Racial, Ethnic, and Gender Differences in School Discipline among U.S. High School Students: 1991-2005. *Negro Educational Review*, *59*(1-2), 47–62. PMID:19430541

West, C. (1995). *Critical race theory: The key writings that formed the movement.* The New Press.

Chapter 12

From Courageous to Unapologetic Conversations About School Discipline Disparities:
How Do We Stop the Hemorrhaging?

Anthony Troy Adams
Clark Atlanta University, USA

ABSTRACT

This chapter asserts that too much commentary has been given to school disciplinary disparities with few remedies for mitigating the problem. The time has come to move from courageous to unapologetic conversations about disciplinary disparities. Data furnished by the U.S. Department of Education, Office of Civil Rights, for the school year 2017-18 estimates that 11,205,797 youths missed school days from our nation's public schools due to out-of-school suspensions. The average school year is roughly 182 days. Thusly, 61,570 students per day missed invaluable instructional time due to out-of-school suspensions. Black/students of color, males, and students with special education identification are especially vulnerable. This chapter summarizes the extant literature; discusses the core issues, controversies, and problems; highlights the correlates associated with school disciplinary disparities; and proposes several unapologetic and radical recommendations for reducing disparities.

DOI: 10.4018/978-1-6684-3359-1.ch012

INTRODUCTION

Data furnished by the U.S. Department of Education, Office of Civil Rights, for the school year 2017-18 estimates that 11,205,797 million youths missed school days from our nation's schools public schools due to out-of-school suspensions. Taking into account that the average school year is roughly182 days, an average of 61,570 students per day missed invaluable instructional time due to out-of-school suspensions (U.S. Department of Education, 2021). Further, a United States Government Accountability Office (GAO) report (2018) maintains that "Black students, boys, and students with disabilities were disproportionately" suspended and/or expelled in K-12 schools (GAO, 2018). These findings are not new (Dunn, 1968). The time has come to move from courageous to unapologetic conversations about school discipline and to embrace radical approaches to ameliorating school disciplinary disparities. How Do We Stop the Hemorrhaging?

The author argues that we must move beyond courageous to unapologetic conversations about school discipline disparities. For over three decades the words courageous conversation has been linked to a broad swath of social issues, such as race, equity, and inclusion, social justice, LGBT equality, and interpersonal and gun violence to name a few.

The phrase Courageous Conversations has become an Internet sensation. A simple Google search using the tandem, "courageous conversation," unearthed over 10 million hits (August 14, 2021). Courageous conversations even has its own Website (Courageousconversations.com). The very notion of courageous conversations has become cliché. Courageous conversations are had through diverse mediums, including books (e.g., Singleton's 2015 *Courageous Conversations About Race: A Field Guide for Achieving Equity in Schools and More Courageous Conversations About Race,* Collins' (2021) *Mending Our Union: Healing Our Communities Through Courageous Conversations, and Delong's (2010)* Courageous conversations: The teaching and learning of pastoral supervision), guides, training seminars, Toolkits (e.g., "A Guide to Courageous Conversations for Principals," Feb. 7, 2020; "Courageous Conversations: Parents Say Policy Fails in Practice," Jan. 16, 2014; "Courageous Conversations Training – End Inequality in Schools," May 29, 2019; "Courageous Conversations and Discipline Audits," YouTube, March. 14, 2019; "Continuing Courageous Conversations Toolkit," August 8, 2017), listening sessions and professional conferences (e.g., Courageous Conversation Academy; Courageous Conversations Towards Racial Justice, a dialogue-centered initiative, Boston College; Courageous Community Conversations, A Series of Listening Session on Race, Racism, and Social Equity, Center for Racial and Social Justice, Shaw University; and, The State of the African American Male – Courageous Conversations, Eastern Michigan University, spring 2006).

The chapter's objectives are four-fold and include: (1) defining the concept of school discipline disproportionality and providing examples of conceptualization and measurement; (2) reviewing of the extant school discipline disproportionality literature and discussing some of the correlates of school discipline disproportionality; (3) describing the effects of school discipline disproportionality on the prison-to-pipeline and negative educational outcomes; and, (4) recommending alternatives for reducing and/or eliminating school discipline disparities. The use of leaderboards, augmented report cards, disciplinary policy augmentations, grassroots initiatives, and public social scientist and engaged scholars as potential social change influencers are also discussed.

Conceptualization of Disproportionality in School Discipline

What is disproportionality in school discipline? To answer this question one should consider two things, operationalization and measurement. First, the very nature of disproportionality refers to an unequal amount of something or an unbalanced share. In this context the unequal amount or unbalanced share pertains to school discipline penalties. Whereas school discipline (e.g., effect or outcome) refers to a system of sanctions or punishments. A list of school discipline outcomes or punishments include *in-school suspension* (e.g., implies that a student/s is/are removed from the classroom, located within the building or school campus, and possibly separated from other students), *out-of-school suspension* (e.g., short-term 1-5 days, long-term 6-10), *expulsion* (e.g., permanent removal of a student from the school district), or *disciplinary referral* to a school resources officer, law enforcement officer, or juvenile justice official.

Second, disproportionality is measured in a multitude of ways. This also contributes to researchers' variant conclusions about its incidence and prevalence. Girvan, McIntosh, and Smolkowski (2019), for example, elucidate five ways to measure school discipline disproportionality. These include (i) Risk Indices, (ii) Comparative Risk Metrics, (iii) Standardized Risk Differences, (iv) Raw Differential Representation, and (v) Discipline rate. Use of any of the aforementioned statistics provide theoretically useful ways for measuring the extent of school discipline proportionality. Each method has desirable aspects (e.g., ease of interpretation and theoretical applicability, convenience in making comparisons between target and reference groups, etc.) and limitations (e.g., results can vary widely and may interfere with reliability estimates, ratios can be unstable, and scale may not sufficiently assess target group).

Girvon et al. (2019) purport that best practices in assessing school discipline disproportionality should use at least three (3) metrics, including RDR, risk ratio, and discipline rate. They maintain that no single metric adequately captures the complexity of school discipline disproportionality. As space precludes a full examination of this topic, suffice it to say, disproportionality in school discipline measured variously can lead to strikingly different results. Researchers nor policy makers have reached an agreement. For a detailed discussion of school discipline disproportionality, readers are encouraged to survey Girvan et al. (2019).

BACKGROUND

What are the Correlates of School Discipline Disparities?

Explaining and understanding the complexities of school discipline disparities is no easy task. The antecedents of school discipline disparities are associated with individual-level, school-level/organizational, and extraneous factors. Complicating matters is that many of the correlates interact making this complex web even more challenging to disentangle and measure direct effects. Nonetheless the extant school discipline disparities literature identifies several contributing factors. These include sociodemographic (e.g., race/ethnicity, sex, age, and parent's education), individual-level (e.g., prior suspension history, special education identification, ESL), teacher-level (e.g., average educational level of teachers and years of experience), school-level (e.g., mean proportion of the school receiving free/reduced price lunch, mean GPA,), percentage of Black and other students of color), and extraneous factors (e.g., urban/rural dichotomy).

Effects of Race/Ethnicity, Low-Income, Special Education Identification, Building-Level Factors and School Climate

Race/ethnicity, low-income family background, and special education identification are variables implicated in school discipline disparities literature. Black students and students of color, students from low-income backgrounds, and those students identified with a disability designation are most likely to be suspended or expelled from our nation's public schools (Baker-Smith, 2018; Pyne, 2019; Kunesh & Noltemeyer, 2015; Mizel et al., 2016; Wright et. al, 2014; Wallace et. al 2008; Skiba et al., 2002). For example, Anyon, Lechuga, Ortega, Downing, and Simmons (2017) tested Critical Race Theory using cross-sectional data taken from over 9,000 K-12 students. Students in the sample experienced 1 or more discipline incidents (n=22,474), representing 185 schools, during the 2012-13 school year. There were more than 20,166 discipline incidents. Dependent variable was operationalized in terms of where offenses took place (e.g., Bus, cafeteria, gym, hallway, playground, etc.). Independent variables included student-level (race/ethnicity, gender, free reduced priced lunch, special Education, ESL) and School-level (Proportion students of color, racial composition, grades served, discipline outcomes). Authors concluded that racism is deeply embedded in US institutions and reproduced at all levels (e.g., micro to macro). Anyon et al. found that Black and students of color were not any more likely than white students to be involved in a discipline incident outside the classroom. However, the authors suggest attention should be refocused on systemic bias and colorblind policies that lead to disciplinary disparities, however.

Economic Disadvantage

The school discipline disproportionality literature has also shown consistent associations between exclusionary discipline and economic disadvantage. Students from low-income backgrounds have a greater risk of exclusion (Chu & Ready, 2018; Pyne, 2018; Skiba, Peterson, & Williams, 1997). Race and low-income background are enmeshed in this country. This raises at least two fundamental questions. Is the relationship between suspension and economic disadvantage a statistical artifact or a social reality? Are children from economically disadvantaged backgrounds predisposed to school misbehavior?

Special Education

Special education identification, race, low-income, and discipline disparities have a long convoluted history spanning over fifty years (Dunn, 1968). Black and low-income students have been identified special education and overly represented categorically (Tefera, 2020; Williams, 2017; Dunn, 1968). Black students with disabilities from low-income backgrounds are also more likely to be suspended or expelled from school. The literature on special education and discipline disparities is robust (Losen et al., 2015; Skiba et al., 2002). A U.S. Government Accountability Office report (2018), for instance, observed that Black students with disabilities were overrepresented in suspensions and expulsions, and while they represented 15.5 percent of all public school students, they represented 39 percent of the students suspended from school. This overrepresentation is approximately 23 percentage points (Nowicki, 2018, pp. 1-2) from the norm. The inextricable association between school discipline disproportionality, special education identification, race, and low income have been consistent in the literature.

Research conducted by Mendoza et al., (2020) found that after controlling for individual, school, and community characteristics, as well as race/ethnicity, previous year's discipline rate and student retention, that disproportionality was prevalent. The authors also noted that relationships among antecedents is complex. Compounding matters is the absence of consistently applied behavioral/emotional assessment protocols. Dever et al., (2016), for example, found that referrals typically lie with teachers' perceptions rather than data or clearly established screening protocols that assess behavioral and emotional risk. Using a nationally representative sample of over 4000 children they found that gender, race, and socioeconomic status are highly predictive of special education status. The authors recommend that data-driven methods for informing referral recommendations for special education placement should be a precursor to disciplinary referrals. This may reduce disproportionate placement of students of color and males in special education.

School-Level Contributions

Student conduct and individual characteristics are part of the equation, but the very nature of schooling also contributes to school discipline disparities. Teachers' attitudes, patience, tenure, and administrative style are also important factors associated with exclusion. Williams et al., (2020) found that teachers' perceptions and expectations of the students they serve impacts the likelihood of in-school and out-of-school suspensions. More, veteran teachers are more likely to be tolerant of students' varied attitudes and behaviors and demonstrate greater classroom management acumen lessoning the chances of exclusion (Williams, Johnson, Dangerfield-Persky, & Mayakis, 2020; Losen, 2015, p. 134). Teachers' experience level is closely related to school climate and may set the tone for whether students feel valued, safe, and secure.

School Climate

The school climate and discipline literature spans several decades (Fefer, 2020; Heilbrun, 2017; Voight, 2015; Gottfredson & Gottfredson, 1985). The effects of school climate is a driver in two ways. First, positive school climate can serve as protective armor and lesson the odds of student misbehavior and resultant suspension (Barnett, 2020). Positive school climate has been correlated with students' reports that teachers are generally more supportive, caring, and have their best interest in mind. Heilbrun, Cornell, and Konold (2017), for instance, examined the relationship between school suspension rates and authoritative school climate. A sample of Virginia 7th and 8th grade middle school students were examined (N=39,364) from the Authoritative School Climate Survey. The authors found that suspension rates were lowest in schools where students and teachers perceived school rules to be fair and applied consistently. Demographic factors including the level of school poverty and school size were also positively correlated with suspension rates. Accordingly, positive school climate is comprised of at least two elements: (a) structure, strict but fair discipline, and (b) support, students' perceptions of their teachers as caring and concerned about their welfare. There are consistent findings between the extant literature associating authoritative school climate and Baumrinds's (1968) theory of authoritative parenting. The authors also contend that parental discipline is most effective when it combines firm discipline with warm emotional support and schools that replicate parental-student rapport may experience fewer school infractions.

Second, negative school climate can exacerbate the frequency of student infractions and contribute to exclusion disparities by promoting a perceived hostile environment where students do not feel safe, secure, or trust teachers and other school officials (Fefer & Gordon, 2020). Further, surveys of students' attitudes about their experiences in schools reveal that lack of school trust, lowered sense of social belonging, and increased levels of external locus of control increase the odds of suspension (Pyne, 2019). Kunesh and Noltemeyer's (2015) research is consistent with the literature and supposition that implicit bias is a factor associated with school discipline disparities. They found that even among pre-service teachers, who are new to the profession, prevailing biases exist.

MAIN FOCUS OF THE CHAPTER

Issues, Controversies, Problems

Issues

School discipline disparities are not a new phenomenon. In fact, the problem has existed for over 50 years. Despite school discipline disparities' robust literature, utilizing both camps from quantitative to qualitative research methodologies, the problem prevails. Second, researchers cannot reach agreement upon a descriptive, operational definition, or common measures of disciplinary school discipline disparities. Thirdly, the conversations about reducing school disciplinary disparities run the gambit, but the resolutions for closing the discipline gap are bearish. In short, there is much talk and little resolve in over fifty years of research and social commentary.

Controversies

Race, special education identification, and low-income family background and their association with school discipline disparities are three of the most widely discussed and controversial issues. Race, for instance, has been theoretically and empirically implicated as an antecedent of school discipline disparities. Whether through implicit bias, institutional racism, or discrimination, Pandora's box remains open.

Second, the intersection between race and special education identification has not been untangled. Black and students of color designated as special education identification (e.g., intellectual disability, emotional disturbance, speech or language impairment, etc.) are three times more likely to be excluded from school and/or restrained (Tefera, 2020; Williams, 2017; Dunn, 1968). Does this suggest that some students are more likely to be excluded because of their race/ethnicity, and disability, a double jeopardy?

Third, whether it is a statistical artifact or a social reality, low-income status is highly correlated with school discipline disparities. This may be due to lack of agency and advocacy on the part of some parents to negotiate the administrative terrain and talk with school leaders about their children's disposition. In effect, parents' ability or inability to advocate for their children will impact disciplinary outcomes.

Problems

At least three problems ensconce the discussions on school discipline disparities. First, status quo practices, for example, zero tolerance policies exacerbate school discipline disparities. One-and-done policies have a tendency to adversely impact Black and minority students. These same students are more likely to be harshly disciplined for interpretative or discretionary offenses (e.g., insubordination, idleness, etc.).

Second, research has also linked students' experiencing exclusionary discipline (e.g., suspension and expulsion) with the school-to-prison pipeline (Dutil, 2020; Hullenaar, Kurpiel, & Ruback, 2021; Morgan, 2021; Novak & Fagan, 2021; Kim et. al, 2021; Welfare, Grimes, Lawson, Hori, and Asadi, 2021; Novak, 2019; Arredondo et. al., 2012; Gonzalez, 2012). Novak (2019) observed that students who were suspended by the age 12 reported involvement with the justice system by the age of 18, and the likelihood that these groups would come in contact with deviant peers during their youth increased. Increased exposure to aberrant behavior puts vulnerable youth at risk and increases chances for contact with the justice system. It is noteworthy to mention that innovative policies are on the horizon for reversing this trend. Reducing or eliminating school resources officers, placing caps on the number of low-level suspension infractions, and funding restorative justice models (Hughes, Raines, & Malone, 2020) may reduce students' interaction with the justice system.

Three, school discipline disparities are highly correlated with several negative educational outcomes. These outcomes can profoundly contribute to inequities in educational opportunity. Students regularly excluded from school (a) miss invaluable instructional time; (b) they are more likely to be retained in grade, (c) they are more likely to stop-out or drop-out of school; and, (d) their chances of college admission are diminished. Losen and Martinez's (2020) work, for instance, is one of the single most comprehensive reports on disparate school discipline and its consequences for inequities in educational opportunity. Readers are encouraged to peruse the nearly 100-page report. That said, Losen and Martinez describe disparities in exclusionary discipline standardizing data collected by U.S. Department of Education. Data have also been disaggregated and examine rates per one-hundred students. The report examines disproportionality among students with disabilities, school-level variation, district-level, race/ethnicity differences, state rankings by racial gap, and days lost of instruction for out-of-School suspensions for selected large cities, and more. Their report includes practical recommendations for reduction and elimination of out-of-school suspension at the state and local policy maker levels. This report is a must read for anyone embarking on the latest trends in school discipline disparities.

Losen and Martinez's report maintains that exclusionary discipline experienced through lost instructional days is a driver of exceptional inequities in educational opportunity. The storyline is even more discouraging when data have be disaggregated. Readers are invited to review an abridged summary of their report. At the secondary level, their report reveals that:

- Black students lost 103 days per 100 students, 82 more than days than the 21 days their White peers lost because of out-of-school suspensions;
- Hawaiian/Pacific Islanders had the second highest rate of 63 days lost per 100 students;
- Native Americans lost 54 days of school per 100 students enrolled;
- Students with disabilities at the secondary level lost 68 days of instruction per 100 students, twice as many secondary students without disabilities;
- Black boys lost 132 days of school per 100 students;
- Black girls had the second highest rate at 77 days of lost instructional time per 100 students, a rate of seven times that of White girls at the secondary level; and
- This is the first report showing students attending alternative schools experienced unprecedented disparate rates of lost instruction.

Further, Morris and Perry (2016) examined the relationship between exclusionary discipline and academic achievement. They examined data from the Kentucky School Discipline Study (n = 24,347). Academic achievement was the dependent variable. The authors assessed the correlates of exclusionary discipline (e.g., suspensions, expulsions, and referrals) on math and reading outcomes, controlling for race/ethnicity, gender, family structure (e.g., two or one parent), time, and SES. The results from this study support the supposition that school suspension contributes to inequalities in achievement. More directly, suspensions and achievement was negatively associated; students who have been suspended scored significantly lower on academic progress tests. Poor performance on progress tests was persistent across racial lines, with African Americans receiving significantly more suspensions, even after controlling for SES and other individual-level variables. These findings are consistent with the literature that exclusionary discipline contributes to the racial achievement gap and the reproduction of structured inequality.

SOLUTIONS AND RECOMMENDATIONS

Unapologetic and Radical Recommendations for Mitigating Disciplinary Disparities

This section describes several radical strategies for reducing dependencies on exclusionary discipline and potentially mitigating school disciplinary disparities. These strategies include the use of leaderboards, report cards, policy implementation, and grassroots movements. Although some of these strategies have been introduced in the literature on school discipline disparities, the author proposes augmentations to some of these approaches to strengthen their effectiveness.

Leaderboard

How do we slow the hemorrhaging and reduce the incidence and prevalence of school discipline disproportionality? Develop a real-time school discipline leaderboard accessible to students, teachers, building-level administrators, and the public at-large. In other words, frequency of suspensions, expulsions, and disciplinary referrals should be reported daily, weekly, or monthly and available on a school's Website twenty-four hours a day. This is beneficial for several reasons. First, the accessibility of leaderboards may bring greater exposure to the problem of school discipline disproportionality. Leaderboards create greater visibility to students, teachers, school personnel, policymakers, and stakeholders. Perhaps an unintended consequence will be that discipline outcomes become as important as other school outcomes, including graduation rates, attendance, positive school climate, and college admissions/attendance. The leaderboard can become a daily reminder for all constituents of both their singular and collective role in reducing disciplinary exclusion. The extrinsic and symbolic presence of the discipline leaderboard becomes normalized and a natural component of schools physical landscape.

Second, how can leaderboards be implemented? Leaderboards should be prominently displayed inside school buildings adjacent other symbols of school pride. Physically place school leaderboards near trophy cases celebrating sports and academic achievement awards, and other celebratory mementos. Leaderboards should be conspicuously visible to anyone inside the school, and anyone visiting the school campus and beyond. Third, what should the leaderboards reveal? In terms of leaderboard metrics, scores should highlight declining rates of suspension, expulsion, and disciplinary referrals. Postings should show rates over time and disaggregated by race/ethnicity, school level, grade level, and school. In other words, celebrate schools and units with lower suspension, expulsion, disciplinary referral leaderboard scores.

Finally, effective leaderboard messaging is imperative for continuing the discussion about the harmful effects of disciplinary exclusion. Make it part of the regular discussion among teachers and students and partial out time in small increments to highlight goals, progress, and confront new challenges for reducing exclusionary discipline. Challenge the school community to do better. Students can play a role in reducing the need for exclusion. Make reducing exclusion a collective value worthy of reduction.

Augmented Report Cards

Schools should adopt Discipline Report Cards. This informative mechanism would operate differently than conventional report cards adopted by some school districts. Augmented report cards go below the surface and would be available at several levels. Teachers are on the front lines. First, teachers would be given independent discipline report cards that chart their use of recommendations for suspension, expulsion, and disciplinary referrals. In other words, teachers, and because they operate at ground zero, would have readily available information concerning their use of discipline. Further, discipline report cards would give teachers comparative information. Each teacher could compare their frequency of discipline to that of other teachers in the school by subject, by unit, or between-district. The problem of indiscriminate use of discipline for highly subjective infractions (e.g., disobedience, disrespect, and defiance) may ultimately become self-correcting. Increasing teachers' awareness about their use of school discipline may ultimately limit reliance.

Use of augmented discipline report cards is practical for two reasons. First, teachers would be regularly informed about their reliance on, or use of particular disciplinary measures. The likelihood of change and systematic reduction in the use of exclusionary discipline is greater when teachers have substantive information that tracks their disciplinary referrals. Second, teachers can include discipline report cards as part of their dossiers and their efforts to reduce dependency upon exclusion and instead report positive disciplinary outcomes (e.g., infrequent use of exclusionary discipline, reduction in the use of exclusionary discipline over time). Teachers may also document their efforts to improve classroom climate and discuss intervention strategies deployed to reduce the odds of reliance on exclusionary discipline (McIntosh, 2020).

Further, for practical reasons comparisons among classroom disciplinary outcomes should be reviewed and outliers discussed. For example, if certain teachers/classrooms within a school building have significantly higher exclusionary discipline frequencies, this can become a talking point for administrators and teachers to examine and address, if necessary. In any event, teachers should be regularly informed of their exclusionary discipline tendencies. For example, frequency or use of exclusion that exceeds building-level and/or district level norms should alert teachers and administrators overusing exclusion. In other words, teachers' cognizance of their exceptional use of exclusion may influence them to seek additional in-service training, participate in classroom management exercises, experiment with alternative disciplinary practices, or consult with school staff or other professionals.

In terms of the administration of report cards, this author recommends that School discipline report cards be issued at the building level. Comparisons can be examined among high- and low-achieving schools with regards to school discipline outcomes. Schools can readily compare discipline outcomes and over time and potentially regress towards the average. This may become a powerful mechanism for sharing school discipline outcomes. School members and external constituents can increase dialogue and raise awareness about the incidence and prevalence of exclusionary discipline.

Building-level administrators can implement discipline report cards seamlessly. They can send weekly, bi-weekly or monthly discipline report cards to teachers. Report cards will quantify a teachers' frequency of suspensions, expulsions, and even disciplinary referrals. A school's average and range will also be reported for comparison purposes, and teachers can independently review and compare their reports to building norms. Further, schools can make comparisons by subject area (e.g., social sciences, physical sciences, etc.) to assess whether disaggregated data shows variation in the number of exclusions by subject area.

Discipline report cards should be part of a larger collaborative effort to reduce exclusion. Teachers and administrators should avail themselves for regular engaged and constructive dialogue about exclusion reduction. The dialogue should be as regular as the daily school bell. This is also a time for personal and collective reflection, leading to discovery on innovations to reduce exclusion. The end game is that teachers, administrators, and staff members will develop a free floating dialogue concerning exclusion, one that becomes part of regular conversation.

This author recommends four action steps for incorporating augmented disciplinary report cards. First, *buy-in* is an imperative. Teachers and administrators must agree that disciplinary report cards are in the best interest of the students they serve, and that it represents a coordinated effort to reduce exclusionary discipline. Principals and assistant principals, for example, can present the school's disciplinary data and engage teachers and other school officials in a fermented conversation. Buy-ins can take place in the form of a series of round-table discussions, unit meetings (e.g., specific academic departments), or even Town Hall meetings. Second, establish clearly articulated benchmarks for reducing exclusionary discipline based on a careful review of data disaggregated by teacher, classroom, unit, and school (e.g., long-term suspension, expulsions, and disciplinary referrals). Parties can agree to data-driven recommendations. Benchmarks for exclusionary discipline reduction should be reasonable and achievable. Third, individuals can determine a realistic timeline for implementation of the use of disciplinary report cards stressing a sense of urgency. Finally, do it! Initiate a process for sharing information/data and celebrate progress.

School Discipline Policy

Schools must invoke policies that have the potential to significantly reduce the use of exclusion that are not merely smokescreens. Suspension has not lived up to its promise of making schools safer, deterring future aberrant behavior (Hinze-Pifer and Sartain, 2018:229), improving educational outcomes (Morris, 2012; Skiba, 2000), reducing school violence (Williams, Bryant-Mallory, Coleman, Gotel, & Hall, 2017), or improving school climate (Voight, 2015).

Research on the effects of school policy changes and exclusion reduction shows some promise. Baker-Smith, for example, tested this assertion. Using data taken from NYC high schools first-time ninth grade students, between 2009 and 2014. Baker-Smith proposed the following research questions: (i) Does a policy rescinding the suspensions for low-level offenses (e.g., gambling, vulgar language, lying to school personnel, misusing school property, engaging in disruptive behavior on a bus, departing a school building without permission, etc.) affect suspension rates? (ii) Is heterogeneity in any change of suspension rates associated with students' race or gender? The dependent variable was students' likelihood of being suspended. Gender, race/ethnicity, free and/or reduced price lunch, English learner, special education identification, and over-age at grade nine were control variables. Baker-Smith found that overall suspension rates decreased when a policy on low-level offenses is restricted to a fewer number of designated outcomes, and diversity of the student population was unassociated with reductions in the likelihood of suspension. Baker-Smith's analysis also revealed that when a suspension policy rescinding certain offenses from its student code was invoked the number of suspensions declined generally, but a closer examination of the disaggregated data also showed that a minority of students were over-represented in the number of suspensions.

In addition, Hinze-Pifer and Sartain (2018) explored whether changing school disciplinary policy for more serious offenses in the Chicago Public Schools (CPS) would impact students' educational outcomes. They analyzed student-level data gleaned from the CPS administrative file, 2007-2008 to 2013-2014. Their sample included traditional schools with enrollments that exceeded thirty students. Students attending charter schools and selective schools (e.g., magnet schools) were excluded from the analyses. Results of the Hinze-Pifer and Sartain analysis indicated that the effects of policy changes have only minimal effects on test scores, attendance, and grades. Thusly indicating that changing policies on the use of exclusionary discipline may not be the panacea for improving educational outcomes or reducing disciplinary disparities. However, the study yielded positive outcomes associated with students' perceptions of school climate.

Summarily, the research on the impacts of school policy for reducing the use of exclusionary discipline and mitigating disparities provides a mixed bag of results. On the one hand, changes to disciplinary policy has brought greater discretion in the use of low-level infractions (e.g., disobedience, tardiness, etc.). On the other hand, more severe school infractions (e.g., fighting, weapons possession, etc.) are likely to result in long-term suspensions, or even expulsion. This suggests that teachers, school officials, and the at-large community should seek interventions that address root causes. For example, why has interpersonal violence increased? Do youths feel threatened? Does initiating fights increase street credibility among peers? Disaggregating data according to the type of offense/infraction may provide invaluable insights into root causes.

The author proposes a plan for moving policy forward. The approach is four-pronged and includes:

1. Parents, students, teachers, community ombudsman/woman, and the at-large community assemble a nimble group of three to seven (an odd number is preferred so that no ties result from voting.) members. They can be charged with preparing the mission and vision statements;
2. The group should decide on messaging (e.g., the group's vision and mission statements, and specific goals, reduce suspension, limit suspension to serious infractions, eliminate suspension within a reasonable time frame, etc.);
3. Orchestrate a grassroots assembly. Again, include parents and students, teachers and administrators, and members of the at-large community. An assembly reserved for (a) articulating and revising the mission, (b) establishing realistic benchmarks, (c) promoting the agenda (e.g., at the local school board level, city council, and the state board of education); and,
4. Include "school community" and local policymakers in discussions about exclusion. Meet state legislators and press for change and amendments to school discipline policies.

The Power of Grassroots Movements

Members of the *school community* (e.g., teachers, students and parents, administrators, and other constituents) have at their disposal the power of social change through organized movements. How can grassroots movements challenge school discipline policies and promote change? First, the school community can meet, discuss key issues, strategize and establish timelines for action, and implement their plans. Strategically, community members can publicize/broadcast information about time, date, and location for public forums/meetings about school discipline. Second, community members can begin drafting recommended school discipline ratifications/modifications to reverse exclusionary discipline disparities. In short, grassroots movements have a history in this country of reshaping politics and society. Affecting educational policies at the state and local levels is no different.

What follows are examples of grassroots efforts. There are other extraordinary grassroots efforts aimed directly at dismantling disciplinary disparities taking shape. A few are listed below and the number of grassroots movements are increasing exponentially.

These include:

- Dads on Duty (Harris, 2021) is an example of a grassroots movement mobilized to address a singular objective – stopping school violence. In response to over 20 student arrest for fighting within a three-day timespan at Shreveport Southwood High School, Shreveport, LA, Michael LaFitte and a group of approximately forty dads took matters into their own hands. The group led by LaFitte made daily rounds on the school's campus and since their arrival there have been no reported fights on-campus. Their demeanor has been one of "cool uncles" rather than stern dads. Dads on Duty illustrates the power and influence of both grassroots organizations and parental involvement. The evidence is convincing. Caring and supportive parents can reduce school violence and decrease reliance on exclusionary discipline, including suspension, expulsion, and disciplinary referrals.
- Racial Justice Now! This Dayton, Ohio grassroots movement won major victories in the fight to dismantle school discipline disparities by persuading policymakers to place a moratorium on pre-K to third-grade suspensions. The collective also fought to change the district's code of conduct chipping away at zero tolerance policies, and they implemented restorative justice alternative practices (https://rjnohio.org/).
- Dignity in Schools Campaign is offering opportunities to educate and train parents to advocate for policy change and inform parents about alternative models of student conduct codes (https://dignityinschools.org/).

- Alliance for Educational Justice (AEJ) consist of 30 intergenerational and youth-driven groups across the nation. AEJ works in conjunction policymakers to transform public education into a system ensuring equality for all students independent of race or socioeconomic status. (http://www. allianceforeducationaljustice.org/).

Without a doubt grassroots movements are part of the community apparatus capable of dismantling school discipline disproportionality. This will not happen overnight. Local movements will need to forge alliances and enlist entities at the local, regional, and national levels with common core interest (e.g., mission and vision) to mitigate or even eradicate the atrocities associated school discipline disparities. There is strength in numbers. Teachers, parents, empathetic administrators, and retired persons (e.g., American Association of Retired Persons) are needed to join the struggle for social justice through educational reform. Concerned individuals must remain vigilant as the struggle to combat school discipline disproportionality is a matter of national importance and essential to the promise of American democracy.

How Can Public Social Scientists an Engaged Scholars Help?

Public social scientists and engaged scholars should be solicited to embrace educational reform, generally, and school discipline disparities, more specifically. It is time to bridge a long overdue relationship between the Ivory Tower and communities (Hoffman, 2021). Institutions of higher education and their caretakers have a responsibility to use knowledge and tools of observation (e.g., quantitative, qualitative, etc.) to help communities. Social scientists and engaged scholars are emboldened with critical knowledge, including interpretation and use of theory and application of analytical techniques beneficial for social reform. Academics with a practice or applied orientation can help grassroots movements and communities advance school discipline reform. How? First, they can take the initiative by reaching out to grassroots entities with the aim of providing assistance. Second, applied social scientists and engaged scholars can commit in-kind services. Their expertise with examining social problems, framing strategies for public discourse, and public speaking acumen may help organized groups advance educational reform. Applied academicians can use their expertise in making sense of abstract empirical research in ways that are digestable to broad audiences. Efforts such as this can break down barriers and status quo disciplinary policies and unite grassroots efforts to dismantle exclusionary discipline.

Make disciplinary interventions a high priority by implementing alternative approaches and documenting their use. For example, Positive Behavior Interventions and Supports are being used in over thirty states. Empirical studies linking reductions in the use out-of-school and in-school suspensions shows promise (Cruz, Firestone, & Rodl, 2021; Baker-Smith, 2018). This school-wide strategy counters zero tolerance approaches and may addresses root factors related to student misbehavior and conduct. It has the potential to significantly reduce reliance on exclusionary discipline.

FUTURE RESEARCH DIRECTIONS

1. Develop best practices in research information on dissemination to the masses. This poses several questions, including: how can we spread research findings and results in real time? How can we share timely research results to individuals that will affect school disciplinary disparities? How can we conceptualize, measure, and package information for diffuse consumption? How can we create information pipelines directly to parents, policy makers, stakeholders, and local and national grassroots networks?

2. Conduct focus group studies of grassroots organizations that have assembled to promote social justice, particularly those that address school disciplinary disparities and fair discipline practices. This raises several important questions: how do local groups mobilize and garner resources (e.g., people, in-kind, financial) to affect school disciplinary policy change? What is the optimal number of grassroots members that bring about social change in a timely manner? What models of organization used by the grassroots organizations are the most effective?

3. Test and develop theories of discipline disparities. This raises several important questions: what are the prevalent theories utilized to describe, predict, or explain school disciplinary disparities? Do the theories help inform scholars and practitioners in ways that can reduce the use of exclusionary discipline? Have theories of school discipline disparities shown to be useful ...

4. Methodologically, increase use of meta-analyses to compare school discipline disparities measurement effects. Propose and test standardized measures. What can we learn from using standardized measures of school discipline disparities? How can we improve the quality of research and ensure robustness in the literature?

CONCLUSION

This chapter was divided into four sections. (1) The concept of school discipline disproportionality was defined, and conceptualization and measurement of the concept outlined. (2) A brief review of the extant literature was presented, and correlates of school discipline disproportionality at various theoretical levels was described. The chapter also explored the effects of school discipline disproportionality on the prison-to-pipeline and took a closer look at negative educational outcomes. (3) School discipline disproportionality has been negatively linked to grade retention, push-out and drop-outs, and decreased college attendance. (4) Lastly, this chapter discussed several radical and social change mechanisms for reducing or eliminating the use of exclusionary discipline. Leaderboards, report cards with a twist, status quo disciplinary polices, grassroots initiatives, and the potential role of public social scientist and engaged scholars as instruments of social change were explored.

REFERENCES

Amemiya, J., Mortenson, E., & Wang, M. T. (2020). Minor infraction are not minor: School infraction for minor misconduct may increase adolescents' defiant behavior and contribute to racial disparities in school discipline. *The American Psychologist*, *75*(1), 23–36. doi:10.1037/amp0000475 PMID:31081648

Anderson, K. P., & Ritter, G. W. (2020). Do school discipline policies treat students fairly? Evidence from Arkansas. *Educational Policy*, *34*(5), 707–734. doi:10.1177/0895904818802085

Anyon, Y., Lechuga, C., Ortega, D., Downing, B., Greer, E., & Simmons, J. (2017). An exploration of the relationships between student racial background and the school sub-contexts of office discipline referrals: A critical race theory analysis. *Race, Ethnicity and Education*, *21*(3), 390–406. doi:10.1080/13613324.2017.1328594

Arredondo, M., Williams, N., & Convey, M. (2012). The School-to-Prison Pipeline: Pathways from schools to juvenile justice. In *Discipline Disparities: A Research-to-Practice Collaborative*. The Equity Project at Indiana University.

Baker-Smith, C. E. (2018). Suspensions suspended: Do changes to high school suspension policies change suspension rates? *Peabody Journal of Education*, *93*(2), 190–206. doi:10.1080/0161956X.2018.1435043

Baumrind, D. (1968). Authoritarian vs. authoritative parental control. *Adolescence*, *3*(11), 255–272.

Chu, E. M., & Ready, D. D. (2018). Exclusion and urban public high schools: Short- and long-term consequences of school suspension. *American Journal of Education*, *124*(4), 479–509. doi:10.1086/698454

Collins, C. J. (2021). *Mending our union: Healing our communities through courageous conversations.* Authority Publishing.

Delong, W. R. (2010). *Courageous conversations: The teaching and learning of pastoral supervision.* University Press of America.

Dunn, L. M. (1968). Special education for the mildly retarded: Is much of it justifiable? *Exceptional Children, 35*(1), 5–22. doi:10.1177/001440296803500101 PMID:4234568

Dutil, S. (2020). Dismantling the school-to-prison pipeline: A trauma-informed, critical race perspective on school discipline. *Children & Schools, 42*(3), 171–178. doi:10.1093/cs/cdaa016

Fefer, S. A., & Gordon, K. (2020). Exploring perceptions of school climate among secondary students with varying discipline infractions. *International Journal of School & Educational Psychology, 8*(3), 174–183. doi:10.1080/21683603.2018.1541033

Girvan, E. J., McIntosh, K., & Smolkowski, K. (2019). Tail, tusk, and trunk: What different metrics reveal about racial disproportionality in school discipline. *Educational Psychologist, 54*(1), 40–59. doi:10.1080/00461520.2018.1537125

Gonzalez, T. (2012). Keeping kids in schools: Restorative justice, punitive Discipline, and the school to prison pipeline. *Journal of Law & Education, 41*(2), 281–335.

Gottfredson, G. D., & Gottfredson, D. C. (1985). *Victimization in schools.* Plenum Press. doi:10.1007/978-1-4684-4985-3

Harris, C. (2021, Oct 23). Dads on duty bring safety, tough love, and dad jokes to a Louisiana high school. They greet students as they arrive at school in the morning and "help maintain a positive environment for learning, rather than fighting, CBS reports. *Revolt.* https://www.revolt.tv/2021/10/23/22742377/dads-on-duty-bring-safety-tough-love-and-dad-jokes-to-a-louisiana-high-school

Heilbrun, A., Cornell, D., & Konold, T. (2017). Authoritative school climate and suspension rates in middle schools: Implications for reducing the racial disparity in school discipline. *Journal of School Violence, 17*(3), 324–338. doi:10.1080/15388220.2017.1368395

Hinze-Pifer, R., & Sartain, L. (2018). Rethinking universal suspension for severe student behavior. *Peabody Journal of Education, 93*(2), 228–243. doi:10.1080/0161956X.2018.1435051

Hoffman, A. J. (2021). *The engaged scholar: Expanding the impact of academic research in today's world.* Stanford University Press.

Hughes, T., Raines, T., & Malone, C. (2020). School pathways to the juvenile justice system. *Policy Insights from the Behavioral and Brain Sciences*, *7*(1), 72–79. doi:10.1177/2372732219897093

Hullenaar, K. L., Kurpiel, A., & Ruback, R. B. (2021). Youth violent offending in school and out: Reporting, arrest, and the school-to-prison pipeline. *Justice Quarterly*, *38*(7), 1319–1341. doi:10.1080/07418825.2021.1967426

Kim, B. K. E., Johnson, J., Rhinehart, L., Logan-Greene, P., Lomeli, J., & Nurius, P. S. (2021). The school-to-prison pipeline for probation youth with special education needs. *The American Journal of Orthopsychiatry*, *91*(3), 375–385. doi:10.1037/ort0000538 PMID:34138628

Kunesh, C. E., & Noltemeyer, A. (2015). Understanding disciplinary disproportionality: Stereotypes shape pre-service teachers' beliefs about black boys' behavior. *Urban Education*, *54*(4), 1–28. doi:10.1177/0042085915623337

Losen, D. J. (2015). *Closing the school discipline gap: Equitable remedies for excessive exclusion*. Teachers College Press.

Losen, D. J., & Martinez, P. (2020). *Lost opportunities: How disparate school discipline continues to drive differences in the opportunity to learn*. Learning Policy Institute, Center for Civil Rights Remedies at the Civil Rights Project, UCLA.

McIntosh, K., Smolkowski, K., Gion, C. M., Witherspoon, L., Bastable, E., & Girvan, E. G. (2020). Awareness is not enough: A double-blind randomized controlled trial of the effects of providing discipline disproportionality data reports to school administrators. *Educational Researcher*, *49*(7), 533–537. doi:10.3102/0013189X20939937

Mendoza, M., Blake, J. J., Marchbanks, M. P. III, & Ragan, K. (2020). Race, gender, and disability and the risk for juvenile justice contact. *The Journal of Special Education*, *53*(4), 226–235. doi:10.1177/0022466919845113

Mizel, M. L., Miles, J. N., Pedersen, E. R., Tucker, J. S., Ewing, B. A., & D'Amico, E. J. (2016). To educate or to incarcerate: Factors in disproportionality in school discipline. *Children and Youth Services Review*, *70*, 102–111. doi:10.1016/j.childyouth.2016.09.009 PMID:28503013

Morgan, H. (2021). Restorative justice and the school-to-prison pipeline: A review of existing literature. *Education Sciences*, *11*(4), 159. doi:10.3390/educsci11040159

Morris, E. W., & Perry, B. L. (2016). The punishment gap: School suspension and racial disparities in achievement. *Social Problems*, *63*(2), 68–86. doi:10.1093ocpropv026

Novak, A. (2019). The school-to-prison pipeline: An examination of the association between suspension and justice system involvement. *Criminal Justice and Behavior*, *46*(8), 1165–1180. doi:10.1177/0093854819846917

Novak, A., & Fagan, A. (2022). Expanding research on the school-to-prison pipeline: Examining the relationships between Suspension, expulsion, and recidivism among justice-involved youth. *Crime and Delinquency*, *68*(1), 3–27. doi:10.1177/0011128721999334

Nowicki, J. M. (2018). *K-12 education: Discipline disparities for black students, boys, and students with disabilities*. Report to Congressional Requesters. GAO-18-258. US Government Accountability Office.

Pyne, J. (2019). Suspended attitudes: Exclusion and emotional disengagement from School. *Sociology of Education*, *92*(1), 59–82. doi:10.1177/0038040718816684

Singleton, G. E. (2015). *Courageous conversations about race*. Corwin Press.

Skiba, R. J., Michael, R. S., Nardo, A. C., & Peterson, R. L. (2002). The color of discipline: Sources of racial and gender disproportionality in school punishment. *The Urban Review*, *34*(4), 317–338. doi:10.1023/A:1021320817372

Skiba, R. J., Peterson, R. L., & Williams, T. (1997). Office referrals and suspension: Disciplinary intervention in middle schools. *Education & Treatment of Children*, *20*(3), 295–315. https://www.jstor.org/stable/42900491

Tefera, A. A., & Fischman, G. E. (2020). How and why context matters in the study of racial disproportionality in special education: Toward a critical disability education policy approach. *Equity & Excellence in Education*, *53*(4), 434–449. doi:10.1080/10665684.2020.1791284

United States Government Accountability Office, Report to Congressional Request. (2018). *Discipline disparities for black students, boys, and students with disabilities*. Author.

U.S. Department of Education. (2014). *Rethinking school discipline*. Available from: http://www.2.ed.gov/policy/gen/guid/

Voight, A., Hanson, T., O'Malley, M., & Adekanye, L. (2015). The racial school climate gap: Within-school disparities in students' experiences of safety, support, and connectedness. *American Journal of Community Psychology*, *56*(3-4), 252–267. doi:10.100710464-015-9751-x PMID:26377419

Wallace, J., Goodkind, S., Wallace, C. M., & Bachman, J. G. (2008). Racial, ethnic, and gender differences in school discipline among U.S. high school students: 1991-2005. *Negro Educational Review*, *59*(1-2), 25–48. PMID:19430541

Welfare, L. E., Grimes, T. O., Lawson, G., Hori, K., & Asadi, G. (2021). The school to prison pipeline: Quantitative evidence to guide school counselor advocacy. *Journal of Counselor Leadership and Advocacy*, *8*(1), 16–29. doi:10.1080/23267 16X.2020.1861490

Williams, J. A., Johnson, J. N., Dangerfield-Persky, F., & Mayakis, C. G. (2020). Does employing more novice teachers predict higher suspensions for black students? A Hierarchical Multiple Regression Analysis. *The Journal of Negro Education*, *89*(4), 448–458. https://www.jstor.org/stable/10.7709/jnegroeducation.89.4.0448

Williams, J. A. III, Lewis, C., Starker Glass, T., Butler, B. R., & Hoon Lim, J. (2020). The discipline gatekeeper: Assistant principals' experiences with managing school discipline in urban middle schools. *Urban Education*. Advance online publication. doi:10.1177/0042085920908913

Williams, R. B., Bryant-Mallory, D., Coleman, K., Gotel, D., & Hall, C. (2017). An Evidence-Based Approach to Reducing Disproportionality in Special Education and Discipline Referrals. *Children & Schools*, *39*(4), 248–251. doi:10.1093/cs/cdx020

Wright, J. P., Morgan, M. A., Coyne, M. A., Beaver, K. M., & Barnes, J. C. (2014). Prior problem behavior accounts for the racial gap in school suspensions. *Journal of Criminal Justice*, *42*(3), 257–266. doi:10.1016/j.jcrimjus.2014.01.001

ADDITIONAL READING

Anderson, K. P., & Ritter, G. W. (2020). Do School Discipline Policies Treat Students Fairly? Evidence From Arkansas. *Educational Policy*, *34*(5), 707–734. doi:10.1177/0895904818802085

Borman, G. D., Pyne, J., Rozek, C. S., & Schmidt, A. (2022). A replicable identity-based intervention reduces the Black-White suspension gap at scale. *American Educational Research Journal*, *59*(2), 284–314. doi:10.3102/00028312211042251

Cruz, R. A., Firestone, A. R., & Rodl, J. E. (2021). Disproportionality reduction in exclusionary school discipline: A best-evidence synthesis. *Review of Educational Research*, *91*(3), 397–431. doi:10.3102/0034654321995255

Gion, C., McIntosh, K., & Falcon, S. (2022). Effects of a multifaceted classroom intervention on racial disproportionality. *School Psychology Review*, *51*(1), 67–83. doi:10.1080/2372966X.2020.1788906

Heidelburg, K., Rutherford, L., & Parks, T. W. (2022). A preliminary analysis assessing swpbis implementation fidelity in relation to disciplinary outcomes of black students in urban schools. *The Urban Review*, *54*(1), 138–154. doi:10.100711256-021-00609-y

Hines, E. M., Ford, D. Y., Fletcher, Jr, E. C., & Moore, III, J. L. (2022). All Eyez on Me: Disproportionality, Disciplined, and Disregarded While Black. *Theory Into Practice*.

Pullmann, M. D., Gaias, L. M., Duong, M. T., Gill, T., Curry, C., Cicchetti, C., Raviv, T., Kiche, S., & Cook, C. R. (2022). Reducing racial and ethnic disproportionality in school discipline through an assessment-to-intervention process: A framework and process. *Psychology in the Schools*, pits.22651. doi:10.1002/pits.22651

Rodriguez, L. A., & Welsh, R. O. (2022). The dimensions of school discipline: Toward a comprehensive framework for measuring discipline patterns and outcomes in schools. *AERA Open*, *8*. doi:10.1177/23328584221083669

Scott, T. M., & McIntosh, K. (2022). Considering disproportionality in school discipline: Promising practices and policy. *Preventing School Failure*, *66*(1), 64–65. doi:10.1080/1045988X.2021.1937028

KEY TERMS AND DEFINITIONS

Courageous Conversations: Strategic discussions concerning a litany of social or political concerns, including diversity, equity, inclusion, fragility, social justice, or environmental preservation.

Expulsion: A decision made by a local school board and district to remove a student from school that denies physical access to a school campus and where educational services are withdrawn.

Extraneous: A variable that contributes to school discipline disparities from outside the physical boundaries of a school.

Outcomes: Include academic, behavioral, and organizational changes such as grade distributions, retention rates, attendance, number of full-time equivalent faculty, and teacher and staffing separations and retirements.

School Climate: A complex term referring to a school's quality and nature where norms, values, goals, interpersonal relationships, teaching and learning, organizational structures, and leadership styles impact educational outcomes.

School Discipline: Refers to a violation of a school district's code of conduct. The code of conduct is a published document approved by the district's local school board.

School-Level Contributors: Includes such variables as number of support staff, ratio of students-to-teachers, Code of Conduct that may affect school disciplinary disparities.

Compilation of References

@ProPublica [@ProPublica]. (2021, October 10). *Three police officers went to an *elementary* school in Tennessee & arrested four Black girls* [Instagram photograph]. Retrieved from https://www.instagram.com/p/CUz7ZUILDcj/

AASA, & Children's Defense Fund. (2014). *School Discipline Data*. Retrieved 15 April 2020, from https://www.childrensdefense.org/wp-content/uploads/2018/06/school-discipline-data.pdf

Abramsky, S. (2011). *Hard Time Blues* [Ebook version]. Retrieved from https://www.google.com/books/edition/Hard_Time_Blues/dWVZkEDrLAgC

Acevedo, F. (2016). *Beyond Race: A Quantitative Study Of The Discipline Gap Among Predominantly Black High Schools In Chicago*. Retrieved 25 November 2020, from https://via.library.depaul.edu/cgi/viewcontent.cgi?article=1090&context=soe_etd

Achebe, C. (1958). *Things Fall Apart*. William Heinemann Ltd.

Agnew, R. (2005). *Why do criminals offend? A general theory of crime and delinquency*. Roxbury.

Agrawal, N. (2019). *California expands ban on 'willful defiance' suspensions in schools*. Retrieved 25 June 2021, from https://www.latimes.com/california/story/2019-09-10/school-suspension-willful-defiance-california

Alexander, M. (2010). *The new jim crow: Mass incarceration in the age of colorblindness*. The New Press.

Alexander, M. (2012). *The new Jim Crow: Mass incarceration in the age of colorblindness*. Pantheon Books.

Allen, Q., & White-Smith, K. A. (2014). *Just as Bad as Prisons": The Challenge of Dismantling the School-to-Prison Pipeline Through Teacher and Community Education*. Retrieved from Taylor & Francis https://www.tandfonline.com/doi/full/10.1080/10665684.2014.958961?src=recsys

Allman, K. L., & Slate, J. R. (2011). School discipline in public education: A brief review of current practices. *The International Journal of Educational Leadership Preparation, 6*(2), n2.

Amemiya, J., Mortenson, E., & Wang, M. T. (2020). Minor infraction are not minor: School infraction for minor misconduct may increase adolescents' defiant behavior and contribute to racial disparities in school discipline. *The American Psychologist, 75*(1), 23–36. doi:10.1037/amp0000475 PMID:31081648

American Academy of Child & Adolescent Psychiatry. (2014). *Corporal punishment in schools.* https://www.aacap.org/aacap/Policy_Statements/1988/Corporal_Punishment_in_Schools.aspx

American Association of School Administrators - AASA. (2004). *Using Data to Improve Schools: What's Working.* https://aasa.org/uploadedFiles/Policy_and_Advocacy/files/UsingDataToImproveSchools.pdf

American Civil Liberties Union (ACLU). (2020). *Race and inequality in education.* Retrieved from https://www.aclu.org/issues/racial-justice/race-and-inequality-education

American Civil Liberties Union and Human Rights Watch. (2010). *Corporal punishment in schools and its effect on academic success: Joint HRW/ACLU statement.* Retrieved from: https://www.hrw.org/news/2010/04/15/corporal-punishment-schools-and-its-effect-academic-success-jointhrw/aclu-statement

American Civil Liberties Union. (2021). *School to Prison Pipeline.* Retrieved from https://www.aclu.org/issues/juvenile-justice/school-prison-pipeline/school-prison-pipeline-infographic

American Psychological Association Services, Inc. (2019). *The Pathway from Exclusionary Discipline to the School to Prison Pipeline.* Retrieved October 21, 2021, from https://www.apa.org/advocacy/health-disparities/discipline-facts.pdf

American Psychological Association Zero Tolerance Task Force. (2008). Are zero tolerance policies effective in the schools? An eviden-tiary review and recommendations. *The American Psychologist, 63*(9), 852–862. doi:10.1037/0003-066X.63.9.852 PMID:19086747

American School Counselor Association [ASCA]. (2018). *The School Counselor and Equity for All Students.* https://bit.ly/3rApCIg

American School Counselor Association [ASCA]. (2019a). *ASCA School Counselor Professional Standards & Competencies.* Author.

American School Counselor Association. (2007). *Position statement: Corporal punishment the professional school counselor.* https://www.schoolcounselor.org/content.asp?contentid=199

American School Counselor Association. (2019b). *ASCA School Counselor Professional Standards & Competencies.* Author.

Anderson, K. P., & McKenzie, S. (2022). *Local Implementation of State-Level Discipline Policy: Administrator Perspectives and Contextual Factors Associated With Compliance.* AERA. https://journals.sagepub.com/doi/full/10.1177/23328584221075341

Anderson, D. S. (2015). *Emmett Till: The murder that shocked the world and propelled the civil rights movement.* Univ. Press of Mississippi.

Anderson, K. P., & Ritter, G. W. (2020). Do school discipline policies treat students fairly? Evidence from Arkansas. *Educational Policy, 34*(5), 707–734. doi:10.1177/0895904818802085

Angton, A. (2020). *Black girls and the discipline gap: Exploring the early stages of the school-to-prison pipeline.* Retrieved from https://lib.dr.iastate.edu/cgi/viewcontent.cgi?article=9280&context=etd

Annamma, S. A. (2018). *The pedagogy of pathologization: Dis/abled girls of color in the school-prison nexus.* Routledge.

Antoine, R. (2008). *Commonwealth Caribbean: law and legal systems* (2nd ed.). Routledge-Cavendish. doi:10.4324/9780203930397

Anyon, Y., Gregory, A., & Stone, S. (2016). *Restorative Interventions and School Discipline Sanctions in a Large Urban School District.* Retrieved 25 November 2020, from https://journals.sagepub.com/doi/full/10.3102/0002831216675719?casa_token=u2l0rK0EMegAAAAA%3Af U5CSDfSvnAp0qEd84SdNFkYOS6JZp6OVMurfn--x5yxy63I5ACEbgOmKggLsqL1Pjy8Yn YgB23w

Anyon, Y., Atteberry-Ash, B., Yang, J., Pauline, M., Wiley, K., Cash, D., Downing, B., Greer, E., & Pisciotta, L. (2018). It's all about the relationships: Educators' rationales and strategies for building connections with students to prevent exclusionary school discipline outcomes. *Children & Schools, 40*(4), 221–230. doi:10.1093/cs/cdy017

Anyon, Y., Lechuga, C., Ortega, D., Downing, B., Greer, E., & Simmons, J. (2017). An exploration of the relationships between student racial background and the school sub-contexts of office discipline referrals: A critical race theory analysis. *Race, Ethnicity and Education, 21*(3), 390–406. doi:10.1080/13613324.2017.1328594

Arcus, D. (2002). School shooting fatalities and school corporal punishment: A look at the states. *Aggressive Behavior, 28*(3), 173–183. https://psycnet.apa.org/doi/10.1002/ab.90020. doi:10.1002/ab.90020

Arredondo, M., Williams, N., & Convey, M. (2012). The School-to-Prison Pipeline: Pathways from schools to juvenile justice. In *Discipline Disparities: A Research-to-Practice Collaborative.* The Equity Project at Indiana University.

Athirathan, S. (2018). Corporal punishment and its effects on learning in Sri Lanka. *International Journal of Agriculture, 3,* 413–420. https://ijaeb.org/uploads2018/AEB_03_287.pdf

Autor, D., Figlio, D., Karbownik, K., Roth, J., & Wasserman, M. (2019). Family Disadvantage and the Gender Gap in Behavioral and Educational Outcomes. *American Economic Journal. Applied Economics, 11*(3), 338–381. doi:10.1257/app.20170571

Baćak, V., & Nowotny, K. M. (2020). Race and the association between police stops and depression among young adults: A research note. *Race and Justice, 10*(3), 363–375. doi:10.1177/2153368718799813

Bacher-Hicks, A., Billings, S. & Deming, D. (2019). *The school to prison pipeline: Long-run impacts of school suspensions on adult crime.* National Bureau of Economic Research No. w26257.

Bailey, C., Robinson, T., & Coore-Desai, C. (2014). Corporal punishment in the Caribbean: Attitudes and Practices. *Social and Economic Studies, 63*(3&4), 207–233.

Bakari, K. (2002). *The Hip Hop Generation.* BasicCivitas Books.

Baker-Smith, C. E. (2018). Suspensions suspended: Do changes to high school suspension policies change suspension rates? *Peabody Journal of Education, 93*(2), 190–206. doi:10.1080/0161956X.2018.1435043

Balfanz, R., Byrnes, V., & Fox, J. (2014) *Sent Home and Put Off-Track: The Antecedents, Disproportionalities, and Consequences of Being Suspended in the Ninth Grad.* Retrieved 5 July 2020, from https://digitalcommons.library.tmc.edu/cgi/viewcontent.cgi?referer=https://scholar.google.com/&httpsredir=1&article=1217&context=childrenatrisk

Balfanz, R., Byrnes, V., & Fox, J. (2012). *Sent Home and Put Off-Track: The Antecedents, Disproportionalities, and Consequences of Being Suspended in the Ninth Grade.* Johns Hopkins University School of Education Everyone Graduates Center.

Baptiste, D. A., Hardy, K. V., & Lewis, L. (1997). Clinical practice and Caribbean immigrant families in the United States: The intersection of emigration, immigration, culture, and race. In J. L. Roopnarine & J. Brown (Eds.), *Caribbean families: diversity among ethnic groups.* Ablex.

Barbee, B., & Blackburn, C. (2019). *SPLC Report: Corporal punishment in school disproportionately affects black students, students with disabilities.* Southern Poverty Law Center. Retrieved October 21, 2021, from https://www.splcenter.org/news/20190611/splc-report-corporal-punishment-in-school

Barrett, N., McEachin, A., Mills, J., & Valant, J. (2017). *Disparities in student discipline by race and daily income.* Retrieved from https://educationresearchalliancenola.org/files/publications/010418-Barrett-McEachin-Mills-Valant-Disparities-in-Student-Discipline-by-Race-and-Family-Income.pdf

Barron v. Baltimore, 32 U.S. 243 (1833).

Barthel, M., Mitchell, A., Asare-Marfo, D., Kennedy, C., & Worden, K. (2020). Measuring news consumption in a digital era. *Pew Research Center's Journalism Project, 8.*

Baumrind, D. (1968). Authoritarian vs. authoritative parental control. *Adolescence, 3*(11), 255–272.

Bell, C. (2020). "Maybe if they let us tell the story I wouldn't have gotten suspended": Understanding Black students' and parents' perceptions of school discipline. *Children and Youth Services Review, 110.* doi:10.1016/j.childyouth.2020.104757

Bell, C., & Puckett, T. (2020). I Want To Learn But They Won't Let Me: Exploring the Impact of School Discipline on Academic Achievement. *Urban Education.* doi:10.1177/0042085920968629

Bensimon, E. M., & Malcom, L. E. (2012). *Confronting equity issues on campus: Implementing the equity scorecard in theory and practice.* Stylus Publishing.

Bergland, C. (2017, May). Narrative Expressive Journaling Could Help Your Vagus Nerve. *Psychology Today.* https://www.psychologytoday.com/us/blog/the-athletes-way/201705/narrative-expressive-journaling-could-help-your-vagus-nerve

Berwick, C. (2016). *Ban school suspensions!* Retrieved 31 March 2020, from https://theweek.com/articles/640318/ban-school-suspensions

Besse, R., & Capatosto, K. (2018). *Ending Racial Inequity in Out of School Suspensions: Mapping the Policy Landscape and Equity Impact.* Retrieved October 27, 2020, from https://kirwaninstitute.osu.edu/implicit-bias-training/resources/OSS-racial-inequity-02.pdf

Bethel School District No 403 v. Fraser case, 478 U.S. 675 (1986).

Beyl, S. (2020). *Questioning the Rule: The Civic Implications of Positive Behavioral Interventions and Supports (PBIS) as a Pedagogy of Power* (Unpublished Education Studies capstone). Yale University, New Haven, CT.

Biblestudytools. (2022). *The New King James Version 1982.* https://www.biblestudytools.com/nkjv/proverbs/13.html

Black Lives Matter at Schools. (2020). *About: Zero-tolerance.* https://Blacklivesmatteratschool.com/about/

Black Lives Matter Long Beach. (2021, Oct 1). *BLM Long Beach Statement on Violence in our School District.* https://blmlbc.org/blm-long-beach-statement-on-violence-in-our-school-district/

Boeri, M. (2018, January 19). *Re-Criminalizing Cannabis Is Worse Than 1930s 'Refer Madness.'* The Conversation. https://theconversation.com/re-criminalizing-cannabis-is-worse-than-1930s-reefer-madness-89821

Bolling v. Sharpe, 347 US 497 (1954).

Bollmer, J., Bethel, J., Garrison-Mogren, R., & Brauen, M. (2007). Using the risk ratio to assess racial/ethnic disproportionality in special education at the school-district level. *The Journal of Special Education, 41*(3), 186–198. doi:10.1177/00224669070410030401

Boneshefski, M. J., & Runge, T. J. (2014). Addressing disproportionate discipline practices within a school-wide positive behavioral interventions and supports framework: A practical guide for calculating and using disproportionality rates. *Journal of Positive Behavior Interventions, 16*(3), 149–158. doi:10.1177/1098300713484064

Bouchrika, I. (2021, February). *Digital Storytelling: Benefits, Examples, Tools & Tips.* https://research.com/education/digital-storytelling#elements

Boudreau, E. (2020, August). Measuring implicit bias in schools: A Harvard study shows implicit bias affects discipline disparities. *Usable Knowledge*. https://www.gse.harvard.edu/news/uk/20/08/measuring-implicit-bias-schools

Bouillion, L. M., & Gomez, L. M. (2001). Connecting school and community with science learning: Real world problems and school–community partnerships as contextual scaffolds. *Journal of Research in Science Teaching: The Official Journal of the National Association for Research in Science Teaching, 38*(8), 878–898. doi:10.1002/tea.1037

Boyd, D. M., & Ellison, N. B. (2007). Social Network Sites: Definition, History and Scholarship. *Journal of Computer-Mediated Communication, 13*(1), 210–230. doi:10.1111/j.1083-6101.2007.00393.x

Bradshaw, C. P., Waasdorp, T. E., & Leaf, P. J. (2012). Effects of school-wide positive behavioral interventions and supports on child behavior problems. *Pediatrics, 130*(5), e1136–e1145. doi:10.1542/peds.2012-0243 PMID:23071207

Brady, K. (2002). Zero Tolerance or (In)Tolerance Policies? Weaponless School Violence, Due Process, and the Law of Student Suspensions and Expulsions: An Examination of Fuller v. Decatur Public School Board of Education School District. *BYU Educ. & L.J., 159*. Retrieved October 21, 2021, from https://digitalcommons.law.byu.edu/elj/vol2002/iss1/7

Brazil, B. (2022, Feb. 9). School discipline causes lasting, harmful impact on Black students, study finds. *Daily Pilot*. https://www.latimes.com/socal/daily-pilot/entertainment/story/2022-02-09/school-discipline-causes-lasting-harmful-impact-on-black-students-study-finds

Breay, C., & Harrison, J. (2014). *Magna Carta: An Introduction*. British Library. Retrieved October 21, 2021, from https://www.bl.uk/magna-carta/articles/magna-carta-an-introduction

Brewer, T. J., & Wallis, M. (2015). #TFA: The intersection of social media and education reform. *Critical Education, 6*(14).

Brint, S. (2017). *Schools and societies*. Stanford Social Sciences, an imprint of Stanford University Press. doi:10.1515/9781503601031

Brown v. Board of Education of Topeka, 347 U.S. 483 (1954).

Brown, C. A., & Di Tillio, C. (2013). Discipline disproportionality among Hispanic and American Indian students: Expanding the discourse in U.S. research. *Journal of Education and Learning, 2*(4), 47–59. doi:10.5539/jel.v2n4p47

Cabral, C., & Speek-Warnery, V. (Eds.). (2004). *Voices of children: Experiences with violence*. Report produced for Ministry of Labor, Human Services and Social Security, Red Thread Women's Development Programme, and UNICEF-Guyana. https://www.devnet.org.gy/sdnp/csoc/childviolreport.pdf

California Association for School Counselors. (2019). *Best practice: Guidelines for California school counselors*. Author. https://bit.ly/3pt5Rjc

Californians for Justice. (2021, Oct 1). *Black Lives Matter Long Beach Statement on Violence in Long Beach Unified School District.* https://caljustice.org/2021/10/01/black-lives-matter-long-beach-statement-on-

Camangian, P., & Cariaga, S. (2021). Social and emotional learning is hegemonic miseducation: Students deserve humanization instead. *Race, Ethnicity and Education.* Advance online publication. doi:10.1080/13613324.2020.1798374

Camera, L. (2021). *Study confirms school-to-prison pipeline.* U.S. News & World Report. Retrieved from https://www.usnews.com/news/education-news/articles/2021-07-27/study-confirms-school-to-prison-pipeline

Campbell, R., Martin, C., & Fabos, B. (2017). *Media & culture: Mass communication in a digital age.* Bedford/St. Martin's.

Carmichael, A. (2017, October 3). Student bleeds after 'wild cane' beating by teacher. *Guyana Times.* https://guyanatimesgy.com/student-bleeds-after-wild-cane-beating-by-teacher/

Caron, C. (2018, December 13). In 19 States, It's still legal to spank children in public schools. *The New York Times.* https://www.nytimes.com/2018/12/13/us/corporal-punishment-school-tennessee.html

Carter, P., Fine, M., & Russell, S. (2014). Discipline disparities series: Overview. *Discipline Disparities Series.* https://indrc.indiana.edu/tools-resources/pdf-disciplineseries/disparity_overview_040414.pdf

Carter, P. L., Skiba, R., Arredondo, M. I., & Pollock, M. (2017). You can't fix what you don't look at: Acknowledging race in addressing racial discipline disparities. *Urban Education, 52*(2), 207–235. doi:10.1177/0042085916660350

Carter, R. T. (2007). Racism and psychological and emotional injury: Recognizing and assessing race-based traumatic stress. *The Counseling Psychologist, 35*(1), 13–105. https://doi.org/ftkw2v

Carver, P. R., Lewis, L., & Tice, P. (2010). *Alternative schools and programs for public school students at risk of educational failure: 2007–08.* National Center for Education Statistics, Institute of Education Sciences, U.S. Dept. of Education.

Casa Palmera Staff. (2012, October 3). *The History of Illegal Drugs in America.* https://casapalmera.com/blog/the-history-of-illegal-drugs-in-america/

Center for Disease Control and Prevention. (2014). *Policy Strategies for Supporting Recess in Schools 2012-2013 School Update* [Brief]. Retrieved October 21, 2021, from https://www.cdc.gov/healthyschools/npao/pdf/LWP_Recess_Brief_2012_13.pdf

Center on PBIS. (2021). *Positive Behavioral Interventions and Supports.* www.pbis.org

Cerrone, K. (1999). The Gun-Free Schools Act of 1994: Zero Tolerance Takes Aim at Procedural Due Process. *Pace L. Rev., 20*(1), 131-188. Retrieved October 21, 2021, from https://digitalcommons.pace.edu/plr/vol20/iss1/7

Chen, G. (2020, February 14). *Teachers in 19 states allowed to physically punish students.* Public School Review. https://www.publicschoolreview.com/blog/teachers-in-19-states-allowed-to-physically-punish-students

Chen, E., Brody, G. H., Yu, T., Hoffer, L. C., Russak-Pribble, A., & Miller, G. E. (2021). Disproportionate School Punishment and Significant Life Outcomes: A Prospective Analysis of Black Youths. *Psychological Science, 32*(9), 1375–1390. doi:10.1177/0956797621998308 PMID:34387518

Christle, C. A., Jolivette, K., & Nelson, C. M. (2005, January 01). Breaking the School to Prison Pipeline: Identifying School Risk and Protective Factors for Youth Delinquency. *Exceptionality, 13*(2), 69–88. doi:10.120715327035ex1302_2

Chu, E. M., & Ready, D. D. (2018). Exclusion and urban public high schools: Short- and long-term consequences of school suspension. *American Journal of Education, 124*(4), 479–509. doi:10.1086/698454

Cisler, A., & Bruce, M. A. (2013). Principals: What are their roles and responsibilities? *Journal of School Counseling, 11*(10). http://www.jsc.montana.edu/articles/v11n10.pdf

Civil Rights Act of 1964, Pub.L. 88-352, 78 Stat. 241 (1964).

Civil Rights Data Collection. (2017). *2015–16 state and national estimations.* Retrieved from https://ocrdata.ed.gov/StateNationalEstimations/Estimations_2015_16

Clark, K. B., & Myrdal, G. (1965). *Dark ghetto: Dilemmas of social power.* Harper & Row.

CNN Editorial Research. (2021, August 19). *American Generation Fast Facts.* CNN. https://www.cnn.com/2013/11/06/us/baby-boomer-generation-fast-facts/index.html

Coleman, J. (1988). Social capital in the creation of human capital. *American Journal of Sociology, 94*, 195–120. doi:10.1086/228943

Collins, C. J. (2021). *Mending our union: Healing our communities through courageous conversations.* Authority Publishing.

Colombi, G., & Osher, D. (2015). *Advancing School Discipline Reform.* Retrieved 15 April 2020, from https://www.air.org/sites/default/files/downloads/report/Advancing-School-Discipline-Reform-Sept-2015.pdf

Conan, N. (Host). (2011, April 11). *Talk of The Nation* [Audio podcast]. NPR. https://www.npr.org/2011/04/27/135771115/ice-t-from-cop-killer-to-law-order

Conners-Burrow, N. A., Patrick, T., Kyzer, A., & McKelvey, L. (2017). A preliminary evaluation of REACH: Training early childhood teachers to support children's social and emotional development. *Early Childhood Education Journal, 45*(2), 187–199. doi:10.100710643-016-0781-2

Coombs, W. T., & Holladay, S. J. (2013). *It's not just PR: Public relations in society.* John Wiley & Sons.

Corcoran, B., & Ahrens, M. (2018). *Every kid has a story to tell.* https://www.edutopia.org/article/project-every-kid-has-story-tell

Cornel University Legal Information Institute. (n.d.a). *Intermediate Scrutiny.* Retrieved October 21, 2021, from https://www.law.cornell.edu/wex/intermediate_scrutiny

Cornel University Legal Information Institute. (n.d.b). *Procedural Due Process.* Retrieved October 21, 2021, from https://www.law.cornell.edu/wex/procedural_due_process

Cornel University Legal Information Institute. (n.d.c). *Rational Basis Test.* Retrieved October 21, 2021, from https://www.law.cornell.edu/wex/rational_basis_test

Cornel University Legal Information Institute. (n.d.d). *Strict Scrutiny.* Retrieved October 21, 2021, from https://www.law.cornell.edu/wex/strict_scrutiny

Cornel University Legal Information Institute. (n.d.e). *U.S. Constitution Fifth Amendment.* Retrieved October 21, 2021, from https://www.law.cornell.edu/constitution/fifth_amendment

Cornel University Legal Information Institute. (n.d.f). *U.S. Constitution Fourteenth Amendment.* Retrieved October 21, 2021, from https://www.law.cornell.edu/constitution/amendmentxiv

Cornell, D. G., & Mayer, M. J. (2010). Why do school order and safety matter? *Educational Researcher, 39*(1), 7–15. doi:10.3102/0013189X09357616

Countryreports.org. (2022). *Guyana facts and culture.* https://www.countryreports.org/country/Guyana.htm

Cramer, E. D., Gonzalez, L., & Pellegrini-Lafont, C. (2014, November 14). *From Classmates to Inmates: An Integrated Approach to Break the School-to-Prison Pipeline.* Retrieved from Taylor & Francis Online: https://www.tandfonline.com/doi/full/10.1080/10665684.2014.958962?src=recsys

Cramer, E. D., Gonzalez, L., & Pellegrini-Lafont, C. (2014). From classmates to inmates: An integrated approach to break the school-to-prison pipeline. *Equity & Excellence in Education, 47*(4), 461–475. doi:10.1080/10665684.2014.958962

Crawley, K., & Hirschfield, P. (2018). Examining the school-to-prison pipeline metaphor. In *Oxford Research Encyclopedia of Criminology and Criminal Justice.* doi:10.1093/acrefore/9780190264079.013.346

Crenshaw, K. W. (2010). Twenty years of critical race theory: Looking back to move forward. *Connecticut Law Review, 43,* 1253.

Crenshaw, K., Gotanda, N., Peller, G., & Thomas, K. (1996). *Critical Race Theory.* Academic Press.

Crenshaw, K., Ocen, P., & Nanda, J. (2015). *Black girls matter: Pushed out, overpoliced, and underprotected.* Center for Intersectionality and Social Policy Studies, Columbia University.

Cruz, R. A., Firestorne, A. R., & Rodl, J. E. (2021). Disproportionality reduction in exclusionary school discipline: A best-evidence synthesis. *Review of Educational Research, 91*(3), 397–431. doi:10.3102/0034654321995255

Cullen, F. T., Jonson, C. L., & Nagin, D. S. (2011). Prisons do not reduce recidivism: The high cost of ignoring science. *The Prison Journal, 91*(3), 48–65. doi:10.1177/0032885511415224

Curran, F. C. (2019). The law, policy, and portrayal of zero tolerance school discipline: Examining prevalence and characteristics across levels of governance and school districts. *Educational Policy, 33*(2), 319–349. doi:10.1177/0895904817691840

Curren, R. (2020). Punishment and motivation in a just school community. *Theory and Research in Education, 18*(1), 117–133. doi:10.1177/1477878520916089

Curtin, P. A. (1999). Reevaluating public relations information subsidies: Market-driven journalism and agenda-building theory and practice. *Journal of Public Relations Research, 11*(1), 53–90. doi:10.12071532754xjprr1101_03

Davis, C. J. (2016). *Teacher Beliefs Regarding Positive Behavior Support Programs in Mississippi Middle Schools*. Retrieved 15 July 2020, from https://aquila.usm.edu/cgi/viewcontent.cgi?article=1416&context=dissertations

Delgado, R., & Stefancic, J. (2000). *Critical race theory: The cutting edge*. Temple University Press.

Delong, W. R. (2010). *Courageous conversations: The teaching and learning of pastoral supervision*. University Press of America.

Devries, K. M., Knight, L., Child, J. C., Mirembe, A., Nakuti, J., Jones, R., Sturgess, J., Allen, E., Kyegombe, N., Parkes, J., Walakira, E., Elbourne, D., Watts, C., & Naker, D. (2015). The good school toolkit for reducing physical violence from school staff to primary school students: A cluster-randomised controlled trial in Uganda. *The Lancet. Global Health, 3*(7), E378–E386. doi:10.1016/S2214-109X(15)00060-1 PMID:26087985

Dhaliwal, T. K., Chin, M. J., Lovison, V. S., & Quinn, D. M. (2020, July 20). *Educator bias is associated with racial disparities in student achievement and discipline*. Brown Center Chalkboard. https://www.brookings.edu/blog/brown-center-chalkboard/2020/07/20/educator-bias-is-associated-with-racial-disparities-in-student-achievement-and-discipline/

Dingfelder, S. F. (2011). Our stories, ourselves. *Monitor on Psychology, 42*(1), 42.

Dollarhide, C. T., Smith, A. T., & Lemberger, M. E. (2007). Critical incidents in the development of supportive principals: Facilitating school counselor-principal relationships. *Professional School Counseling, 10*, 360–369. https://doi.org/g8fz

Doucleff, M., & Greenhalgh, J. (2019, March). *How Inuit parents teach kids to control their anger*. NPR. https://www.npr.org/sections/goatsandsoda/2019/03/13/685533353/a-playful-way-to-teach-kids-to-control-their-anger

Drakeford, W. (2004). *Racial disproportionality in school disciplinary practices*. National Center for Culturally Responsive Educational Systems. Retrieved from http://www.nkces.org/13891010914217070/lib/1398101091427170/DoES/Disproportionality/07_-_Disproportionality/_-_Displinary

Drewniany, B., & Jewler, B. (2014). *Creative Strategy in Advertising*. Cengage.

Drye, J. M. (n.d.). *Tort liability 101: When are teachers liable?* Education Resources. https://educator-resources.com/tort-liability101-when-are-teachers-liable/

Duffy, H. J. (2018). School Racial Composition and Discipline. Rice University's Kinder Institute for Urban Research. *Research Brief for the Houston Independent School District, 6*(4).

Duke Children's Law Clinic. (2015). *A Parents' Guide to Special Education in North Carolina*. Available at: https://law.duke.edu/childedlaw/docs/Parents%27_guide.pdf

Dunn, L. M. (1968). Special education for the mildly retarded: Is much of it justifiable? *Exceptional Children, 35*(1), 5–22. doi:10.1177/001440296803500101 PMID:4234568

Durkheim, E. (1961). *Moral education: A study in the theory and application of the sociology of education*. Free Press of Glencoe.

Dutil, S. (2020). Dismantling the school-to-prison pipeline: A trauma-informed, critical race perspective on school discipline. *Children & Schools, 42*(3), 171–178. doi:10.1093/cs/cdaa016

Eduardo, A. (2021, June 16). *Stop Telling Critical Race Theory's Critics We Don't Know What It Is | Opinion*. https://www.newsweek.com/stop-telling-critical-race-theorys-critics-we-dont-know-what-it-opinion-1600535

Education National Women's Law Center & Education Trust. (2020). *How to create better safer learning environments for girls of color*. Retrieved from https://edtrust.org/wp-content/uploads/2014/09/And-they-cared_How-to-create-better-safer-learning-environments-for-girls-of-color_Aug-2020.pdf

Edwards, L. (2016). Homogeneity and inequality: School discipline inequality and the role of racial composition. *Social Forces, 95*(1), 55–76. doi:10.1093fow038

Elder, C. D., & Cobb, R. W. (1984). Agenda-building and the politics of aging. *Policy Studies Journal: the Journal of the Policy Studies Organization, 13*(1), 115–129. doi:10.1111/j.1541-0072.1984.tb01704.x

Ellison, C. G., & Sherkat, D. (1993). Conservative Protestantism and support for corporal punishment. *American Sociological Review, 58*(1), 131–144. doi:10.2307/2096222

End Corporal Punishment. (2020). *Country report for Guyana, June 2020*. https://endcorporalpunishment.org/reports-on-every-state-and-territory/guyana/

End Corporal Punishment. (2021). *Country report for the USA*. https://endcorporalpunishment.org/reports-on-every-state-and-territory/usa/

End Corporal Punishment. (2022). https://endcorporalpunishment.org/

Epstein, R., Blake, J., & González, T. (2017). *Girlhood interrupted: The erasure of Black girls' childhood.* Center on Poverty and Inequality, Georgetown Law.

Fabelo, T., Thompson, M. D., Plotkin, M., Carmichael, D., Marchbanks, M. P., & Booth, E. A. (2011). *Breaking schools' rules: A statewide study of how school discipline relates to students' success and juvenile justice involvement.* Council of State Governments Justice Center.

Fabelo, T., Thompson, M. D., Plotkin, M., Carmichael, D., Marchbanks, M. P. III, & Booth, E. A. (2011). *Breaking Schools' Rules: A Statewide Study of How School Discipline Relates to Students' Success and Juvenile Justice Involvement.* Council of State Governments Justice Center.

Fabelo, T., Thompson, M. D., Plotkin, M., Carmichael, D., Marchbanks, M. P. III, & Booth, E. A. (2011). *Breaking schools' rules: A statewide study of how school discipline relates to students' success and juvenile justice involvement. New York, NY, and College Station.* Council of State Governments Justice Center and Texas A&M University Public Policy Research Institute. https://www.ojp.gov/ncjrs/virtual-library/abstracts/breaking-schools-rules-statewide-study-how-school-discipline-0

Fabelo, T., Thompson, M., Plotkin, M., Carmichael, D., Marchbanks, M. III, & Booth, E. (2011). Breaking Schools' Rules: A Statewide Study of How School Discipline Relates to Students' Success and Juvenile Justice Involvement. *Justice Center The Council of State Governments & Public Policy Research Institute.*, (July), 41–43.

Fallon, L. M., Veiga, M., & Sugai, G. (2021). Strengthening MTSS for Behavior (MTSS-B) to Promote Racial Equity. *School Psychology Review.* doi:10.1080/2372966X.2021.1972333

Fefer, S. A., & Gordon, K. (2020). Exploring perceptions of school climate among secondary students with varying discipline infractions. *International Journal of School & Educational Psychology*, *8*(3), 174–183. doi:10.1080/21683603.2018.1541033

Fenning, P. A., Pulaski, S., Gomez, M., Morello, M., Maciel, L., Maroney, E., Schmidt, A., Dahlvig, K., McArdle, L., Morello, T., Wilson, R., Horwitz, A., & Maltese, R. (2012). Call to action: A critical need for designing alternatives to suspension and expulsion. *Journal of School Violence*, *11*(2), 105–117. doi:10.1080/15388220.2011.646643

Fenning, P., & Jenkins, K. (2018). Racial and Ethnic Disparities in Exclusionary School Discipline: Implications for Administrators Leading Discipline Reform Efforts. *NASSP Bulletin*, *102*(4), 291–302. doi:10.1177/0192636518812699

FindLaw. (2021). *Find laws, legal information, and attorneys.* https://www.findlaw.com/

Flannagan, B. (1982). Kids Selling Heroin. *The Detroit News.* https://policing.umhistorylabs.lsa.umich.edu/s/crackdowndetroit/page/young-boys-incorporated

Flannery, K. B., Frank, J. L., Kato, M. M., Doren, B., & Fenning, P. (2013). Implementing school-wide positive behavior support in high school settings: Analysis of eight high schools. *High School Journal*, *96*(4), 267–282. doi:10.1353/hsj.2013.0015

Flannery, M. (2015). *The school-to-prison pipeline: Time to shut it down*. National Education Association.

Flynn, C. P. (1994). Regional differences in attitudes toward corporal punishment. *Journal of Marriage and Family*, *56*(2), 314–324. doi:10.2307/353102

Ford, T., Parker, C., Salim, J., Goodman, R., Logan, S., & Henley, W. (2017). The relationship between exclusion from school and mental health: A secondary analysis of the British Child and Adolescent Mental Health Surveys 2004 and 2007. *Psychological Medicine*, *48*(4), 629–641. doi:10.1017/S003329171700215X PMID:28838327

Forscher, P. S., Lai, C. K., Axt, J. R., Ebersole, C. R., Herman, M., Devine, P. G., & Nosek, B. A. (2019). A meta-analysis of procedures to change implicit measures. *Journal of Personality and Social Psychology*, *117*(3), 522–559. https://doi.org/10.1037/pspa0000160

Foucault, M. (1977). *Discipline and punish: The birth of the prison*. Pantheon Books.

Fowler, D. (2011, October 1). School Discipline Feeds the "Pipeline to Prison". *Phi Delta Kappan*, *93*(2), 14–19. doi:10.1177/003172171109300204

Freeman, J., Simonsen, B., McCoach, D. B., Sugai, G., Lombardi, A., & Homer, R. (2016). Relationship between school-wide positive behavior interventions and supports and academic, attendance and behavior outcomes in high schools. *Journal of Positive Behavior Interventions*, *18*(1), 41–51. doi:10.1177/1098300715580992

Freire, P. (2000). *Pedagogy of freedom*. Rowman & Littlefield.

Froelich, J. (2016, December 2) *Arkansas spanks: The natural state still practices public school corporal punishment*. Arkansas Public Media. https://www.arkansaspublicmedia.org/education/2016-12-02/arkansas-spanks-the-natural-state-still-practices-public-school-corporal-punishment

Fulwood, S. (2015, January 28). *When White Folks Catch a Cold, Black Folks Get Pneumonia*. Center for American Progress. https://www.americanprogress.org/article/when-whites-folks-catch-a-cold-black-folks-get-pneumonia/

Gaibiati, R. & Drago, F. (2018). *Deterrent effect of imprisonment*. doi:10.1007/978-1-4614-5690-2_407

Garbacz, S. A., McIntosh, K., Eagle, J. W., Dowd-Eagle, S. E., Hirano, K. A., & Ruppert, T. (2016). Family engagement within school wide positive behavioral interventions and supports. *Preventing School Failure*, *60*(1), 60–69. doi:10.1080/1045988X.2014.976809

Garman, J., & Walker, R. (2010). The Zero-Tolerance Discipline Plan and Due Process: Elements of a Model Resolving Conflicts Between Discipline and Fairness. *Faulkner Law Review*, *1*(3), 289–320.

Geiger, S. N., & Oehrtman, J. P. (2020). School counselors and the school leadership team. *Professional School Counseling*, *23*(1), 1-9. doi:https://doi.org/g8fx

Geller, A. (2017). Policing America's children: Police contact and consequences among teens in fragile families. *IDEAS Work Pap Ser from RePEc*, 1-46.

Geller, A., Fagan, J., Tyler, T., & Link, B. G. (2014). Aggressive policing and the mental health of young urban men. *American Journal of Public Health*, *104*(12), 2321–2327. https://doi.org/10.2105/ajph.2014.302046

Gerlinger, J., Viano, S., Gardella, J. H., Fisher, B. W., Chris Curran, F., & Higgins, E. M. (2021). Exclusionary School Discipline and Delinquent Outcomes: A Meta-Analysis. *Journal of Youth and Adolescence*, *50*(8), 1493–1509. doi:10.100710964-021-01459-3 PMID:34117607

Geronimo, I. (2011). Deconstructing the marginalization of "underclass" students: Disciplinary alternative education. *University of Toledo Law Review. University of Toledo. College of Law*, *42*(2), 429–465.

Gershoff, E. T. (2017). School corporal punishment in global perspective: Prevalence, outcomes, and efforts at intervention. *Psychology, Health & Medicine, 22*(sup1), 224–239. doi:10.1080/13548506.2016.1271955

Gershoff, E. T., & Font, S. A. (2016). Corporal Punishment in U.S. Public Schools: Prevalence, Disparities in Use, and Status in State and Federal Policy. *Social Policy Report, 30*(1), 1–26. doi:10.1002/j.2379-3988.2016.tb00086.x PMID:29333055

Gershoff, E. T., & Grogan-Kaylor, A. (2016). Spanking and child outcomes: Old controversies and new meta-analyses. *Journal of Family Psychology*, *30*(4), 453–469. doi:10.1037/fam0000191 PMID:27055181

Gershoff, E. T., Purtell, K. M., & Holas, I. (2015). *Corporal punishment in US public schools: Legal precedents, current practices, and future policy. 2015th Edition.* Springer Briefs in Psychology.

Gill-Marshall, B. I. (2000). *Child abuse in Guyana: A study of teacher abuse of children in secondary schools in Guyana* [Unpublished Master's thesis]. University of Guyana.

Girls Leadership. (2021). *Ready to lead: Leadership supports barriers for Black and latinx girls.* Retrieved from https://readytolead.girlsleadership.org

Girvan, E. J., McIntosh, K., & Smolkowski, K. (2019). Tail, tusk, and trunk: What different metrics reveal about racial disproportionality in school discipline. *Educational Psychologist*, *54*(1), 40–59. doi:10.1080/00461520.2018.1537125

Gon Ochi, N., Leung, V., Rodriguez, A., & Cobb, J. (2020). *Our rights to resources: School districts are cheating high-need students by funding law enforcement.* American Civil Liberties Union. https://www.aclusocal.org/sites/default/files/aclu_socal_right-to-resources.pdf

González, T. (2015). *Socializing schools: Addressing racial disparities in discipline through restorative justice.* Academic Press.

Gonzalez, T. (2012). Keeping kids in schools: Restorative justice, punitive Discipline, and the school to prison pipeline. *Journal of Law & Education*, *41*(2), 281–335.

Goodman-Scott, E., Betters-Bubon, J., & Donohue, P. (2019). *The school counselor's guide to multi-tiered systems of support*. Routledge.

Gordon, N. (2018). Disproportionality in student discipline: Connecting policy to research. Brookings.

Gordon, N. (2018). *Disproportionality in student discipline: Connecting policy to research*. Retrieved 25 November 2020, from https://www.brookings.edu/research/disproportionality-in-student-discipline-connecting-policy-to-research/

Gorski, P. (2018). *Reaching and teaching students in poverty: strategies for erasing the opportunity gap* (2nd ed.). Teachers College Press.

Goss v. Lopez, 419 U.S. 565 (1975).

Gottfredson, G. D., & Gottfredson, D. C. (1985). *Victimization in schools*. Plenum Press. doi:10.1007/978-1-4684-4985-3

Goyer, J. P., Cohen, G. L., Cook, J. E., Master, A., Apfel, N., Lee, W., Henderson, A. G., Reeves, S. L., Okonofua, J. A., & Walton, G. M. (2019). Targeted identity-safety interventions cause lasting reductions in discipline citations among negatively stereotyped boys. *Journal of Personality and Social Psychology*, *117*(2), 229–259. doi:10.1037/pspa0000152 PMID:30920278

Green, A. L., Hatton, H., Stegenga, S. M., Eliason, B., & Nese, R. N. T. (2021). Examining Commitment to Prevention, Equity, and Meaningful Engagement: A Review of School District Discipline Policies. *Journal of Positive Behavior Interventions*, *23*(3), 137–148. doi:10.1177/1098300720951940

Greenwald, A., & Hamilton Kreiger, L. (2006). Implicit Bias: Scientific Foundations. *California Law Review*, *94*(4), 946. doi:10.2307/20439056

Gregory, A., Allen, J. P., Mikami, A. Y., Hafen, C. A., & Pianta, R. C. (2014). The promise of a teacher professional development program in reducing racial disparity in classroom exclusionary discipline. *Closing the school discipline gap: Equitable remedies for excessive exclusion*, 166-179.

Gregory, A., Bell, J., & Pollock, M. (2014). How educators can eradicate disparities in school discipline: A briefing paper on school-based interventions. *Discipline Disparities Series*. https://indrc.indiana.edu/tools-resources/pdf-disciplineseries/disparity_intervention_full_040414.pdf

Gregory, A., Clawson, K., Davis, A., & Gerewitz, J. (2016). The promise of restorative practices to transform teacher-student relationships and achieve equity in school discipline. *Journal of Educational & Psychological Consultation*, *26*(4), 325–353. doi:10.1080/10474412.2014.929950

Gregory, A., Huang, F. L., Anyon, Y., Greer, E., & Downing, B. (2018). An examination of restorative interventions and racial equity in out-of-school suspensions. *School Psychology Review*, *47*(2), 167–182. doi:10.17105/SPR-2017-0073.V47-2

Gregory, A., Skiba, R. J., & Noguera, P. A. (2010). The achievement gap and the discipline gap: Two sides of the same coin? *Educational Researcher*, *39*(1), 59–68. doi:10.3102/0013189X09357621

Griffith, D., & Tyner, A. (2019). *Discipline Reform through the Eyes of Teachers*. Thomas B. Fordham Institute. Retrieved from https://eric.ed.gov/?id=ED597759

Griswold v. Connecticut, 381 U.S. 479 (1965).

Gross, J., Haines, S., Hill, C., Francis, G., Blue-Banning, M., & Turnbull, A. (2015). Strong School–Community Partnerships in Inclusive Schools Are "Part of the Fabric of the School…. We Count on Them". *School Community Journal, 25*, 9.

Guo, C., & Saxton, G. D. (2014). Tweeting social change: How social media are changing non-profit advocacy. *Nonprofit and Voluntary Sector Quarterly, 43*(1), 57–79. doi:10.1177/0899764012471585

Gysbers, N. C. (2010). *Remembering the past, shaping the future: A history of school counseling*. American School Counselor Association.

Hackett, A. (2018). *Black Students Are Disproportionately Disciplined in Public Schools*. Retrieved from https://psmag.com/education/Black-students-are-disproportionately-disciplined-in-public-schools

Haines, S. J., Gross, J. M., Blue-Banning, M., Francis, G. L., & Turnbull, A. P. (2015). Fostering family– school and community–school partnerships in inclusive schools: Using practice as a guide. *Research and Practice for Persons with Severe Disabilities, 40*(3), 227–239. doi:10.1177/1540796915594141

Hall, R., & Wallace, C. (1994). *Suicidal Thoughts. On Ready To Die* [CD]. Bad Boy Records.

Han, H. S. (2014). Supporting early childhood teachers to promote children's social competence: Components for best professional development practices. *Early Childhood Education Journal, 42*(3), 171–179. doi:10.100710643-013-0584-7

Hannon, L., DeFina, R., & Bruch, S. (2013). The Relationship Between Skin Tone and School Suspension for African Americans. *Race and Social Problems, 5*(4), 281–295. doi:10.100712552-013-9104-z

Hanson, A. (2005). Have Zero Tolerance School Discipline Policies Turned into a Nightmare? The American Dream's Promise of Equal Educational Opportunity Grounded in Brown v. Board of Education. *U.C. Davis Journal of Juvenile Law & Policy, 2*(9), 289-379.

Harding, D. J., Morenoff, J. D., Nguyen, A. P., Bushway, S. D., & Binswanger, I. A. (2019). A natural experiment study of the effects of imprisonment on violence in the community. *Nature Human Behaviour, 3*(7), 671–677. Advance online publication. doi:10.103841562-019-0604-8 PMID:31086334

Harris, C. (2021, Oct 23). Dads on duty bring safety, tough love, and dad jokes to a Louisiana high school. They greet students as they arrive at school in the morning and "help maintain a positive environment for learning, rather than fighting, CBS reports. *Revolt*. https://www.revolt.tv/2021/10/23/22742377/dads-on-duty-bring-safety-tough-love-and-dad-jokes-to-a-louisiana-high-school

Hatch, T., Duarte, D., & DeGregorio, L. K. (2018). *Hatching results for elementary school counseling: Implementing core curriculum and other tier one activities.* Corwin.

Heilbrun, A., Cornell, D., & Konold, T. (2017). Authoritative school climate and suspension rates in middle schools: Implications for reducing the racial disparity in school discipline. *Journal of School Violence, 17*(3), 324–338. doi:10.1080/15388220.2017.1368395

Heitzeg, N. A. (2009). Education or Incarceration: Zero Tolerance Policies and the School to Prison Pipeline. In Forum on public policy online (Vol. 2009, No. 2). Oxford Round Table.

Hernandez, E., Espinoza, E., & Patterson, J. (2021). School counselors involvement and opportunities to advocate against racialized punitive practices. *Teaching and Supervision in Counseling, 3*(2), 10. doi:https://doi.org/g8fw

Hinze-Pifer, R., & Sartain, L. (2018). Rethinking universal suspension for severe student behavior. *Peabody Journal of Education, 93*(2), 228–243. doi:10.1080/0161956X.2018.1435051

History Channel Editors. (2019). *Dred Scott Case.* The History Channel. Retrieved October 21, 2021, from https://www.history.com/topics/black-history/dred-scott-case

History.com Editors. (2018, August 21). *Cocaine.* https://www.history.com/topics/crime/history-of-cocaine

Hoffman, A. J. (2021). *The engaged scholar: Expanding the impact of academic research in today's world.* Stanford University Press.

Hopkins, B. (2002). Restorative justice in schools. *Support for Learning, 17*(3), 144–149. doi:10.1111/1467-9604.00254

Horn, I. B., Cheng, T., & Joseph, J. (2004). Discipline in the African American community: The impact of socioeconomic status on attitudes, beliefs, and practices. *Pediatrics, 113*(5), 1236–1241. doi:10.1542/peds.113.5.1236 PMID:15121935

House Media News Story. (2017, March 3). *Bill scaling back corporal punishment for students with disabilities.* Oklahoma State Legislature. https://www.okhouse.gov/Media/News_Story.aspx?NewsID=5218

Howard, T. C. (2003). A tug of war for our minds: African American high school students' perceptions of their academic identities and college aspirations. *High School Journal, 87*(1), 4–17. https://doi.org/b9twt8

Howell, P. B., Thomas, S., Sweeney, D., & Vanderhaar, J. (2019). Moving beyond schedules, testing and other duties as deemed necessary by the principal: The school counselor's role in trauma informed practices. *Middle School Journal, 50*(4), 26–34. https://doi.org/g8ft

Hudson, D. (2009). *Rap Music and The First Amendment.* The First Amendment Constitution. https://www.mtsu.edu/first-amendment/article/1582/rap-music-and-the-first-amendment

Hughes, T., Raines, T., & Malone, C. (2020). School pathways to the juvenile justice system. *Policy Insights from the Behavioral and Brain Sciences*, 7(1), 72–79. doi:10.1177/2372732219897093

Hullenaar, K. L., Kurpiel, A., & Ruback, R. B. (2021). Youth violent offending in school and out: Reporting, arrest, and the school-to-prison pipeline. *Justice Quarterly*, 38(7), 1319–1341. doi:10.1080/07418825.2021.1967426

Human Rights Watch and the ACLU. (2008). *A Violent Education: Corporal punishment in US Public Schools*. https://www.hrw.org/sites/default/files/reports/us0808_1.pdf

Ingraham v. Wright, 430 US 651 (1977).

Iselin, A.-M. (2011). *Research on School Suspension*. Retrieved 25 June 2021, from https://www.purdue.edu/hhs/hdfs/fii/wp-content/uploads/2015/07/s_ncfis06report.pdf

Jackson, D. B., Fahmy, C., Vaughn, M. G., & Testa, A. (2019). Police stops among at-risk youth: Repercussions for mental health. *The Journal of Adolescent Health*, 65(5), 627–632. https://doi.org/ghbhw4

James, A. G., Noltemeyer, A., Ritchie, R., Palmer, K., & University, M. (2019). Longitudinal disciplinary and achievement outcomes associated with school-wide PBIS implementation level. *Psychology in the Schools*, 56(9), 1512–1521. doi:10.1002/pits.22282

Jennings, M. (2020). *Excluded from Education: The Impact of Socioeconomic Status on Suspension Rates*. https://socialequity.duke.edu/wp-content/uploads/2021/07/Michael-Jennings.pdf

Johnson, K., & Goldwasser, D. (2016). Identifying stance by analyzing political discourse on twitter. In *Proceedings of the First Workshop on NLP and Computational Social Science* (pp. 66-75). 10.18653/v1/W16-5609

Kaieteur News. (2006, December 8). House defers debate on corporal punishment: AFC member optimistic government will change position. *Kaieteur News*. http://www.landofsixpeoples.com/news604/nk612082.html

Kamenetz, A. (2018). *Suspensions Are Down In U.S. Schools But Large Racial Gaps Remain*. Retrieved October 28, 2020, from https://www.npr.org/2018/12/17/677508707/suspensions-are-down-in-u-s-schools-but-large-racial-gaps-remain

Kang-Brown, J., Trone, J., Fratello, J., & Daftary-Kapur, T. (2013). *A generation later: What we've learned about zero tolerance in schools*. Vera Institute of Justice.

Karatas, K., & Kaya, I. (2015). An investigation of the perceptions of school administrators towards the roles and duties of school counselors. *Eurasian Journal of Educational Research*, 15(61), 181-198. doi:https://doi.org/gg2z8s

Keels, M. (2020). Building racial equity through trauma-responsive discipline. *Educational Leadership*, 78(2), 40–45, 51. https://bit.ly/32FwCte

Keenan, H. B. (2021). Building classroom communities: A pedagogical reflection and syllabus excerpt. In Education for Liberation Network & Critical Resistance Editorial Collective (Eds.), Lessons in liberation: An abolitionist toolkit for educators (pp. 156-169). AK Press.

Kennedy, B. L., Acosta, M. M., & Soutullo, O. (2019). Counternarratives of students' experiences returning to comprehensive schools from an involuntary disciplinary alternative school. *Race, Ethnicity and Education, 22*(1), 130–149. doi:10.1080/13613324.2017.1376634

Kim, B. K. E., Johnson, J., Rhinehart, L., Logan-Greene, P., Lomeli, J., & Nurius, P. S. (2021). The school-to-prison pipeline for probation youth with special education needs. *The American Journal of Orthopsychiatry, 91*(3), 375–385. doi:10.1037/ort0000538 PMID:34138628

Kinsler, J. (2011). Understanding the black-white school discipline gap. *Economics of Education Review, 30*(6), 1370–1383. doi:10.1016/j.econedurev.2011.07.004

Kirk, D. S., & Sampson, R. J. (2013). Juvenile arrest and collateral educational damage in the transition to adulthood. *Sociology of Education, 86*(1), 36–62. doi:10.1177/0038040712448862 PMID:25309003

Kline, D. (2016). *Can Restorative Practices Help to Reduce Disparities in School Discipline Data? A Review of the Literature.* Retrieved 25 November 2020, from https://www.tandfonline.com/doi/abs/10.1080/15210960.2016.1159099

Kohli, R., & Solorzano, D. G. (2012). Teachers please learn our names! Racial microaggressions in the K-12 classroom. *Race, Ethnicity, and Education, 15*(4), 441-462. doi:https://doi.org/ggnsc2

Kopfman, J. E., & Ruth-McSwain, A. (2017). Public information campaigns. In *The practice of government public relations* (pp. 75–100). Routledge. doi:10.4324/9781315085524-6

Korematsu v. United States, 323 US 214 (1944).

Krezmien, M., Leone, P., & Achilles, G. (2006). Suspension, race, and disability: Analysis of statewide practices and reporting. *Journal of Emotional and Behavioral Disorders, 14*(4), 217–226. doi:10.1177/10634266060140040501

Kunesh, C. E., & Noltemeyer, A. (2015). Understanding disciplinary disproportionality: Stereotypes shape pre-service teachers' beliefs about black boys' behavior. *Urban Education, 54*(4), 1–28. doi:10.1177/0042085915623337

Kupchik, A. (2016). *The real school safety problem: The long-term consequences of harsh school punishment.* Univ of California Press. doi:10.1525/california/9780520284197.001.0001

Kurtz, H. (1996, May 30). Benette Renews Attacks On Rap Lyrics. *The Washington Post.* https://www.washingtonpost.com/archive/lifestyle/1996/05/30/bennett-renews-attack-on-rap-lyrics/2bcb1b9e-a5d0-4564-acf3-b2fa7516d7e8/

Lacoe, J., & Steinberg, M. P. (2019) *Do Suspensions Affect Student Outcomes?* Educational Evaluation And Policy Analysis. Retrieved from https://journals.sagepub.com/doi/full/10.3102/0162373718794897

Lacoe, J., & Steinberg, M. P. (2019). Do suspensions affect student outcomes? *Educational Evaluation and Policy Analysis, 41*(1), 34–62. doi:10.3102/0162373718794897

Ladson-Billings, G. (2006). From the achievement gap to the education debt: Understanding achievement in U.S. schools. *Educational Researcher, 35*(7), 3–12. doi:10.3102/0013189X035007003

Ladson-Billings, G., & Tate, W. F. (2016). *Toward a critical race theory of education. In Critical race theory in education.* Routledge.

Lamia, K., Tyree, T., O'Brien, P., & Sturgis, I. (Eds.). (2013). *Social media: pedagogy and practice.* University Press of America.

Lane, J. J., Bohner, G. L., Hinck, A. M., & Kircher, R. L. (2020). Current administrative perceptions of school counselors: Kansas administrators' perceptions of school counselor duties. *Journal of School Counseling, 18*(2), n2. https://eric.ed.gov/?id=EJ1241840

Lansford, J. E., & Dodge, K. A. (2008). Cultural norms for adult corporal punishment of children and societal rates of endorsement and use of violence. *Parenting, Science and Practice, 8*(3), 257–270. doi:10.1080/15295190802204843 PMID:19898651

Latimer, J., Dowden, C., & Muise, D. (2005). The effectiveness of restorative justice practices: A meta-analysis. *The Prison Journal, 85*(2), 127–144. doi:10.1177/0032885505276969

Laursen, B., & Hafen, C. (2010). Future directions in the study of close relationships: Conflict is bad (except when it's not). *Social Development, 19*(4), 858–872. https://doi.org/10.1111/j.1467-9507.2009.00546.x

Laws of Guyana. (n.d.). *Chapter 8.01. Criminal Law (Offences) Act.* https://www.oas.org/juridico/spanish/mesicic2_guy_criminal_law_act.pdf

Lehr, C. A., Tan, C. S., & Ysseldyke, J. (2009). Alternative schools: A synthesis of state-level policy and research. *Remedial and Special Education, 30*(1), 19–32. doi:10.1177/0741932508315645

Lepage, B. (2021). In Schools, Black Girls Confront Both Racial and Gender Bias. *Future Ed.* Retrieved from https://www.future-ed.org/in-schools-black-girls-confront-both-racial-and-gender-bias/

Liberman, A. M., Kirk, D. S., & Kideuk, K. (2014). Labeling effects of first juvenile arrests: Secondary deviance and secondary sanctioning. *Criminology, 4*(3), 1–26. doi:10.1111/1745-9125.12039

Library of Congress. (n.d.). *Civil Rights History Project.* School Segregation & Integration. Retrieved from https://www.loc.gov/collections/civil-rights-history-project/articles-and-essays/school-segregation-and-integration/

Lindsay, C. & Hart. (2017). Exposure to same-race teachers and student disciplinary outcomes for black students in North Carolina. *Educational Evaluation & Policy Analysis, 39*(3). https://journals.sagepub.com/doi/abs/10.3102/0162373717693109

Lindsay, C., & Hart, C. (2017). Teacher race and school discipline: Are students suspended less often when they have a teacher of the same race? *Education Next*, *17*(1), 72–79. https://go.gale. com/ps/anonymous?id=GALE%7CA474717812&sid=googleScholar&v=2.1&it=r&linkacces s=abs&issn=15399664&p=AONE&sw=w

Llewellyn, J., & Howse, R. L. (1999). *Restorative justice: A conceptual framework*. Prepared for the Law Commission of Canada.

Losen, D. (2011). *Discipline policies, successful schools, and racial justice*. Retrieved 25 June 2021, from https://nepc.colorado.edu/publication/discipline-policies

Losen, D., & Skiba, R. (2011). *Suspended Education Urban Middle Schools in Crisis*. Retrieved 25 November 2020, from https://civilrightsproject.ucla.edu/research/k-12-education/school-discipline/suspended-education-urban-middle-schools-in-crisis/Suspended-Education_FINAL-2. pdf

Losen, D., Hodson, C., Keith, I. I. M., Morrison, K., & Belway, S. (2015). *Are we closing the school discipline gap?* Retrieved October 28, 2020, from https://www.civilrightsproject.ucla.edu/ resources/projects/center-for-civil-rights-remedies/school-to-prison-folder/federal-reports/are-we-closing-the-school-discipline-gap/AreWeClosingTheSchoolDisciplineGap_FINAL221.pdf

Losen, D. J. (2015). *Closing the school discipline gap: Equitable remedies for excessive exclusion*. Teachers College Press.

Losen, D. J., & Martinez, P. (2020). *Lost opportunities: How disparate school discipline continues to drive differences in the opportunity to learn*. Learning Policy Institute, Center for Civil Rights Remedies at the Civil Rights Project, UCLA.

Losen, D., Martinez, T., & Okelola, V. (2014). *Keeping California's kids in school: Fewer students of color missing school for minor misbehavior*. The Center for Civil Rights Remedies at the Civil Rights Projects of UCLA.

Losen, D., & Whitaker, A. (2018). *Eleven million days lost: Race, discipline, and safety at U. S Public Schools*. ACLU.

Louisiana State Legislature. (2021). *HB324*. https://www.legis.la.gov/legis/BillInfo.aspx?i=240209

Loveless, T. (2017). *2017 Brown Center Report on American Education: Race and school suspensions*. Retrieved October 28, 2020, from https://www.brookings.edu/research/2017-brown-center-report-part-iii-race-and-school-suspensions/

Loveless, T. (2017). How well are American students learning? With sections on the latest international test scores, foreign exchange students, and school suspensions. *The 2017 Brown Center Report on Education, 3*(6).

Lowman, S. (2017). *Teach us all*. Lowell Milken Center for Unsung Heroes.

Lundberg, I. (2020). *Exclusionary Discipline Disparities: A Case Study*. Retrieved 4 July 2020, from https://red.mnstate.edu/cgi/viewcontent.cgi?article=1366&context=thesis

Lurie, J., & Rios, E. (2016). *Black Kids Are 4 Times More Likely to Be Suspended Than White Kids*. Mother Jones. Available at: https://www.motherjones.com/politics/2016/06/department-education-rights-data-inequality-suspension-preschool/

Luster, S. (2018, July 19). *How Exclusionary Discipline Creates Disconnected Students*. Retrieved October 28, 2020, from https://www.nea.org/advocating-for-change/new-from-nea/how-exclusionary-discipline-creates-disconnected-students

Luster, S. (2018). *How Exclusionary Discipline Creates Disconnected Students*. National Education Association NEA Today.

Lustick, H. (2017). "Restorative Justice" or Restoring Order? Restorative School Discipline Practices in Urban Public Schools. *Urban Education*.

Marchbanks III, M. P., Blake, J. J., Booth, E. A., Carmichael, D., Seibert, A. L., & Fabelo, T. (2015). The economic effects of exclusionary discipline on grade retention and high school dropout. *Closing the school discipline gap: Equitable remedies for excessive exclusion*, 59-74.

Marchbanks, M., III, & Blake, J. (2018). *Assessing the Role of School Discipline in Disproportionate Minority Contact with the Juvenile Justice System: Final Technical Report*. Retrieved 25 November 2020, from https://www.ncjrs.gov/pdffiles1/ojjdp/grants/252059.pdf

Maschi, T., Hatcher, S. S., Schwalbe, C. S., & Rosato, N. S. (2008). Mapping the social service pathways of youth to and through the juvenile justice system: A comprehensive review. *Children and Youth Services Review*, *30*(12), 1376–1385. https://doi.org/cqfjnq

Mattison, E., & Aber, M. S. (2007). Closing the achievement gap: The association of racial climate with achievement and behavioral outcomes. *American Journal of Community Psychology*, *40*(1-2), 1–12. doi:10.100710464-007-9128-x PMID:17587175

Mayworm, A. M., Sharkey, J. D., Hunnicutt, K. L., & Schiedel, K. C. (2016). Teacher consultation to enhance implementation of school-based restorative justice. *Journal of Educational & Psychological Consultation*, *26*(4), 385–412. doi:10.1080/10474412.2016.1196364

McClure, T. E., & May, D. C. (2008). Dealing with misbehavior at schools in Kentucky: Theoretical and contextual predictors of use of corporal punishment. *Youth & Society*, *39*(3), 406–429. doi:10.1177/0044118X06296698

McCullum, M. M., Maldonado, N., & Baltes, B. (2014). Storytelling to teach cultural awareness: The right story at the right time. *LEARNing Landscapes*, *7*(2), 219–223. https://files.eric.ed.gov/fulltext/ED546872.pdf

McFadden, A. C., Marsh, G. E., Price, B. J., & Hwang, Y. (1992). A study of race and gender bias in the punishment of school children. *Education & Treatment of Children*, 140–146.

McFadden, A. C., Marsh, G. E., Prince, B. J., & Hwang, Y. (1992). A study of race and gender bias in the punishment of handicapped school children. *The Urban Review*, *24*(4), 239–251. doi:10.1007/BF01108358

McGrew, K. (2016). The dangers of pipeline thinking: How the school-to-prison pipeline metaphor squeezes out complexity. *Educational Theory, 66*(3), 341–367. https://doi.org/10.1111/edth.12173

McIntosh, K., Girvan, E. J., Horner, R. H., & Smolkowski, K. (2014). Education not Incarceration: A Conceptual Model for Reducing Racial and Ethnic Disproportionality in School Discipline. *The Journal of Applied Research on Children, 5*(2). https://digitalcommons.library.tmc.edu/childrenatrisk/vol5/iss2/4

McIntosh, K., Smolkowski, K., Gion, C. M., Witherspoon, L., Bastable, E., & Girvan, E. G. (2020). Awareness is not enough: A double-blind randomized controlled trial of the effects of providing discipline disproportionality data reports to school administrators. *Educational Researcher, 49*(7), 533–537. doi:10.3102/0013189X20939937

Meiners, E. R. (2007). Right to Be Hostile: Schools, Prisons, and the Making of Public Enemies (1st ed.). Routledge. https://doi.org/10.4324/9780203936450.

Mello, R. (2001). The power of storytelling: How oral narrative influences children's relationships in classrooms. *International Journal of Education & the Arts, 2*(1). http://www.ijea.org/v2n1/

Mendoza, M., Blake, J. J., Marchbanks, M. P. III, & Ragan, K. (2020). Race, gender, and disability and the risk for juvenile justice contact. *The Journal of Special Education, 53*(4), 226–235. doi:10.1177/0022466919845113

Merton, R. K. (1938). Social structure and anomie. *American Sociological Review, 3*(5), 672–682. doi:10.2307/2084686

Messner, S. E., & Rosenfeld, R. (2001). *Crime and the American dream*. Wadsworth-Thompson.

Michels, P. (2016). *Houston Schools Ban Suspensions in Early Grades*. Retrieved 25 June 2021, from https://www.texasobserver.org/houston-schools-ban-suspensions/

Michels, P., Beckner, A., Coronado, A., & Bova, G. (2016). *Houston Schools Ban Suspensions in Early Grades*. Retrieved 31 March 2020, from https://www.texasobserver.org/houston-schools-ban-suspensions/

Miers, D. R., Maguire, M., Goldie, S., Sharpe, K., Hale, C., Netten, A., . . . Newburn, T. (2001). An exploratory evaluation of restorative justice schemes (No. 9). Home Office.

Miller, R., Katrina Liu, K., & Ball, A. F. (2020, April). Critical Counter-Narrative as Transformative Methodology for Educational Equity. *Review of Research in Education, 44*(1), 269–300. https://doi.org/10.3102/0091732X20908501

Ministry of Education and Cultural Development. (1993). *Corporal punishment in Schools*. Circular No. 3/1993.

Ministry of Education, Guyana. (2022). *Digest of Education Statistics 2016-2017*. https://education.gov.gy/web2/index.php/or/digest-of-education-statistics

Ministry of Education. (2002). *Ministry of Education Manual of Guidelines for the Maintenance of Order and Discipline in schools.* https://www.education.gov.gy/web2/index.php/or/other-files/policy-documents/709-manual-of-guidelines-for-the-maintenance-of-order-and-discipline-in-schools/file

Ministry of Labor, Human Services and Social Security. (2006). *Assessment of procedural and physical standards in children's residential care institutions in Guyana. Summary and Recommendations.* https://bettercarenetwork.org/sites/default/files/attachments/Assessment%20of%20procedural%20and%20physical%20standards.pdf

Mississippi Legislature. (2019, July 1). *House bill 1182.* http://billstatus.ls.state.ms.us/2019/pdf/history/HB/HB1182.xml

Mississippi Legislature. (2021). *House bill 760.* http://billstatus.ls.state.ms.us/documents/2021/html/HB/0700-0799/HB0760IN.htm

Mitchell, C. (2010). Corporal punishment in the public schools: An analysis of federal constitutional claims. *Law and Contemporary Problems, 73*, 321–341.

Mizel, M. L., Miles, J. N., Pedersen, E. R., Tucker, J. S., Ewing, B. A., & D'Amico, E. J. (2016). To educate or to incarcerate: Factors in disproportionality in school discipline. *Children and Youth Services Review, 70*, 102–111. doi:10.1016/j.childyouth.2016.09.009 PMID:28503013

Monroe, C. R. (2005). *Understanding the discipline gap through a cultural lens: implications for the education of African American students.* Intercultural Education. Retrieved from https://www.tandfonline.com/doi/abs/10.1080/14675980500303795?src=recsys&journalCode=ceji20

Moore, E., Jr., & Ratchford, V. (2007). *Decreasing Discipline Referrals for African American Males in Middle School.* Retrieved 30 March 2020, from https://eric.ed.gov/?id=EJ831292

Morgan, H. (2021). Restorative justice and the school-to-prison pipeline: A review of existing literature. *Education Sciences, 11*(4), 159. doi:10.3390/educsci11040159

Morris, E. W., & Perry, B. L. (2016). The punishment gap: School suspension and racial disparities in achievement. *Social Problems, 63*(2), 68–86. doi:10.1093ocpropv026

Morris, M. (2016). *Pushout: The Criminalization of Black Girls in Schools.* New Press.

Morsy, L., & Rothstein, R. (2019) *Toxic stress and children's outcomes: African American children growing up poor are at greater risk of disrupted physiological functioning and depressed academic achievement.* Retrieved 9 July 2020, from https://www.epi.org/publication/toxic-stress-and-childrens-outcomes-african-american-children-growing-up-poor-are-at-greater-risk-of-disrupted-physiological-functioning-and-depressed-academic-achievement/

Mowen, T., & Brent, J. (2016). School Discipline as a Turning Point: The Cumulative Effect of Suspension on Arrest. *Sage Journals, 53*(5), 628–653. doi:10.1177/0022427816643135

Mundt, M., Ross, K., & Burnett, C. M. (2018). Scaling social movements through social media: The case of Black Lives Matter. *Social Media + Society, 4*(4). doi:10.1177/2056305118807911

My Teaching Partner Secondary Project. (2021). *Coaching Cycles*. https://www.secondarycoaching. org/mtps-model

Na, C., & Gottfredson, D. C. (2013). Police officers in schools: Effects on school crime and the processing of offending behaviors. *Justice Quarterly*, *30*(4), 619–650. doi:10.1080/07418825. 2011.615754

Nan. (2016). 10 Fast facts about Guyanese Immigrants in the US you should know. *News Americas*. https://guyaneseonline.net/2016/05/12/facts-about-guyanese-immigrants-in-the-us-you-should-know-newsamericas/

Nance, J. P. (2015). Students, police, and the school-to-prison pipeline. *Wash. UL Rev.*, *93*, 919.

National Association of State Boards of Education. (n.d.). *Corporal Punishment, Mississippi*. Retrieved from https://statepolicies.nasbe.org/health/categories/physical-environment/corporal-punishment/mississippi

National Center for Education Statistics. (2019). *Indicator 15: Retention, Suspension, and Expulsion*. Retrieved 9 July 2020, from https://nces.ed.gov/programs/raceindicators/indicator_RDA. asp#:~:text=A%20higher%20percentage%20of%20Black%20students%20(13.7%20percent)%20 than%20of,and%20Pacific%20Islander%20students%2C%203.4

National Center for Education Statistics. (2019). *Table 102.40. Poverty rates for all persons and poverty status of related children under age 18*. https://nces.ed.gov/programs/digest/d20/tables/ dt20_102.40.asp

National Center for Education Statistics. (2020). *Digest of education statistics 2020*. https://nces. ed.gov/fastfacts/display.asp?id=372

Nishioka, V. (2017). *School discipline data indicators: A guide for districts and schools (REL 2017–240)*. Washington, DC: U.S. Department of Education, Institute of Education Sciences, National Center for Education Evaluation and Regional Assistance, Regional Educational Laboratory Northwest. Retrieved from https://ies.ed.gov/ncee/edlabs

Nishioka, V. (2017). *School Discipline Data Indicators: A Guide for Districts and Schools. REL 2017-240*. Regional Educational Laboratory Northwest.

Noguera, P. A. (2010, June 24). *Schools, Prisons, and Social Implications of Punishment: Rethinking Disciplinary Practices*. Retrieved from Taylor & Francis Online: https://www.tandfonline.com/ doi/abs/10.1207/s15430421tip4204_12?src=recsys

Noguera, P. (2003). Schools, prisons, and social implications of punishment: Rethinking disciplinary practices. *Theory into Practice*, *42*(4), 341–350. doi:10.120715430421tip4204_12

Novak, A. (2019). The school-to-prison pipeline: An examination of the association between suspension and justice system involvement. *Criminal Justice and Behavior*, *46*(8), 1165–1180. doi:10.1177/0093854819846917

Novak, A., & Fagan, A. (2022). Expanding research on the school-to-prison pipeline: Examining the relationships between Suspension, expulsion, and recidivism among justice-involved youth. *Crime and Delinquency, 68*(1), 3–27. doi:10.1177/0011128721999334

Nowicki, J. M. (2018). *K-12 education: Discipline disparities for black students, boys, and students with disabilities.* Report to Congressional Requesters. GAO-18-258. US Government Accountability Office.

OCR. (2014). *U.S. Department of Education Office for Civil Rights.* Retrieved 9 July 2020, from https://ocrdata.ed.gov/Downloads/CRDC-School-Discipline-Snapshot.pdf

Oden Choi, J., Hammer, J., Royal, J., & Forlizzi, J. (2020, July). Moving for the Movement: Applying Viewpoints and Composition Techniques to the Design of Online Social Justice Campaigns. In *Proceedings of the 2020 ACM Designing Interactive Systems Conference* (pp. 75-86). 10.1145/3357236.3395435

Okri, B. (1997). *A way of being free.* W&N.

Onyeka-Crawford, A., Patrick, K., & Chaudhry, N. (2017). *Let her learn: Stopping school pushout for girls of color.* National Women's Law Center.

Orentlicher, D. (1992). Corporal punishment in schools. *Journal of the American Medical Association, 267*(23), 3205. doi:10.1001/jama.1992.03480230105036 PMID:1593744

OSEP Technical Assistance Center on Positive Behavioral Interventions and Supports. (2015). *PBIS Implementation Blueprint.* https://www.pbis.org/resource/pbis-implementation-blueprint

Osher, D., Fisher, D., Amos, L., Katz, J., Dwyer, K., Duffey, T., & Colombi, G. D. (2015). Addressing the root causes of disparities in school discipline: An educator's action planning guide. Washington, DC: National Center on Safe Supportive Learning Environments (Support and Collaboration with U.S. Department of Education).

Owen, J., Wettach, J., & Hoffman, K. C. (2015). *Instead of suspension: Alternative strategies for effective school discipline.* Duke Center for Child and Family Policy and Duke Law School.

Owens, J., & McLanahan, S. (2019, June 20). *Unpacking the Drivers of Racial Disparities in School Suspension and Expulsion.* Retrieved October 28, 2020, from https://academic.oup.com/sf/article-abstract/98/4/1548/5521044?redirectedFrom=fulltext

Owen, S. S. (2005). The relationship between social capital and corporal punishment in schools a theoretical inquiry. *Youth & Society, 37*(1), 85–112. doi:10.1177/0044118X04271027

Owens, J., & McLanahan, S. (2019). Unpacking the Drivers of Racial Disparities in School Suspension and Expulsion. *Social Forces, 98*(4), 1548–1577. doi:10.1093foz095 PMID:34017149

Owens, L., & Konkol, L. (2004). Transitioning from alternative to traditional school settings: A student perspective. *Reclaiming Children and Youth, 13*(3), 173–176.

Paintal, S. (2007). *Banning corporal punishment of children. A position paper*. Association for Childhood Education International. International Focus Issue 2007. Accessed 3/27/2008. http://www.stophitting.com/disathome/sureshrani.php

Parliament of the Co-operative Republic of Guyana. (2012). *Corporal punishment*. Speeches in the National Assembly. Speech delivered at: 28th Sitting - Tenth Parliament - August 9, 2012. Accessed January 13, 2022. https://parliament.gov.gy/media-centre/speeches/corporal-punishment1

Pas, E. T., Ryoo, J. H., Musci, R. J., & Bradshaw, C. P. (2019). A state-wide quasi-experimental effectiveness study of the scale-up of school-wide Positive Behavioral Interventions and Supports. *Journal of School Psychology*, *73*, 41–55. doi:10.1016/j.jsp.2019.03.001 PMID:30961880

Patrick Skahill, D., Watson, A., Thomas, J., Watson, A., Watson, A., & Thomas, J. (2019). *Students With "Emotional Disturbances" Face High Rate of Suspensions*. Retrieved 25 June 2021, from https://ctmirror.org/2019/05/20/students-with-emotional-disturbances-face-high-rate-of-suspensions/

Payne, A. A., & Welch, K. (2015). Restorative justice in schools: The influence of race on restorative discipline. *Youth & Society*, *47*(4), 539–564. doi:10.1177/0044118X12473125

Pearman, F. II. (2021). Gentrified Discipline: The Impact of Gentrification on Exclusionary Punishment in Public Schools. *Social Problems*, spab028. Advance online publication. doi:10.1093ocpropab028

Peden, J. (2001). Through A Glass Darkly: Educating with Zero Tolerance. *The Kansas Journal of Law & Public Policy*, *10*, 369–389.

Peguero, A. A., Bondy, J. M., & Shekarkhar, Z. (2017). Punishing latina/o youth: School justice, fairness, order, dropping out, and gender disparities. *Hispanic Journal of Behavioral Sciences*, *39*(1), 98–125. doi:10.1177/0739986316679633

Peguero, A. A., & Shekarkhar, Z. (2011). Latino/a student misbehavior and school punishment. *Hispanic Journal of Behavioral Sciences*, *33*(1), 54–70. doi:10.1177/0739986310388021

Perry, B. D., & Ablon, J. S. (2019). CPS as Neurodevelopmentally Sensitive and Trauma-Informed Approach. In A. R. Pollastri, J. S. Ablon, & M. J. G. Hone (Eds.), *Collaborative Problem Solving. An Evidence-Based Approach to Implementation and Practice* (pp. 122–138). Springer International Publishing.

Pierce v. Society of the Sisters of the Holy Names of Jesus and Mary, 268 U.S. 510 (1925)

Pierre, M. (2019). *The Push Out: A Disproportionality Study on Discipline in the State of Florida*. Retrieved from https://stars.library.ucf.edu/cgi/viewcontent.cgi?article=7725&context=etd

Pirani, F. (2017, August 11). 44 years ago, hip-hop was born – 7 things you never knew about hip-hop's history in America. *The Atlanta Journal Constitution*. https://www.ajc.com/news/national/years-ago-hip-hop-was-born-things-you-never-knew-about-hip-hop-history-america/8Hcx5Mbf6F3RANDUiIWMKJ/

Plessy v. Ferguson, 163 US 537 (1896).

Public Broadcast System. (n.d.). *Marijuana Timeline*. Frontline. https://www.pbs.org/wgbh/pages/frontline/shows/dope/etc/cron.html

Pushout Film. (2021). *About.* https://pushoutfilm.com/about

Pyne, J. (2019). Suspended attitudes: Exclusion and emotional disengagement from School. *Sociology of Education*, *92*(1), 59–82. doi:10.1177/0038040718816684

Rafa, A. (2022). *The Status of School Discipline in State Policy*. Education Commission of the States. https://www.ecs.org/wp-content/uploads/The-Status-of-School-Discipline-in-State-Policy.pdf

Raffaele Mendez, L. M., Knoff, H. M., & Ferron, J. M. (2002). *School Demographic Variables and Out-of-School Suspension Rates: A Quantitative and Qualitative Analysis of a Large Ethnically Diverse School District*. Retrieved 7 July 2020, from https://www.researchgate.net/profile/Linda_Mendez/publication/229731457_School_demographic_variables_and_out-of-school_suspension_rates_A_quantitative_and_qualitative_analysis_of_a_large_ethnically_diverse_school_district/links/5a7cc3200f7e9b9da8d6fee2/School-demographic-variables-and-out-of-school-suspension-rates-A-quantitative-and-qualitative-analysis-of-a-large-ethnically-diverse-school-district.pdf

Rathvon, N. (2008). *Effective school interventions: Evidence-based strategies for improving student outcomes*. Guilford Press.

Rausch, M. K., Skiba, R. (2004). Disproportionality in school discipline among minority students in Indiana: Description and analysis. *Center for Evaluation and Education Policy. Children left behind policy briefs supplementary analysis 2-A*.

Ray, V. (2019). A theory of racialized organizations. *American Sociological Review*, *84*(1), 26–53. https://doi.org/gftw4h

Reese, L. (2012). Storytelling in Mexican homes: Connections between oral and literacy practices. *Bilingual Research Journal, 35*(3). https:// doi:10.1080/15235882.2012.734006

Reinke, W. M., Herman, K. C., & Stormont, M. (2013). Classroom-level positive behavior supports in schools implementing SW-PBIS: Identifying areas for enhancement. *Journal of Positive Behavior Interventions, 15*(1), 39–50. doi:10.1177/1098007712459079

Rice, R. E., & Atkin, C. K. (2009). Public communication campaigns: Theoretical principles and practical applications. In *Media effects* (pp. 452–484). Routledge.

Rico, K. (2002). Excessive Exercise as Corporal Punishment in Moore v. Willis Independent School District - Has the Fifth Circuit Totally Isolated Itself in Its Position. *Jeffrey S. Moorad Sports L.J., 9*(2), 351-385. Retrieved October 21, 2021, from https://digitalcommons.law.villanova.edu/mslj/vol9/iss2/5

Riddle, T., & Sinclair, S. (2019). Racial disparities in school-based disciplinary actions are associated with county-level rates of racial bias. *Proceedings of the National Academy of Sciences of the United States of America*, *116*(17), 8255–8260. doi:10.1073/pnas.1808307116 PMID:30940747

Rios, E. (2018, April 25). *New data shows that America's schools are still disproportionately punishing students of color.* Retrieved October 28, 2020, from https://www.motherjones.com/politics/2018/04/new-data-america-schools-suspend-punish-arrest-black-students/

Rios, V. M. (2011). *Punished: Policing the lives of Black and Latino boys.* New York University Press.

Rios, V. M., & Vigil, J. D. (2017). *Human targets: Schools, police, and the criminalization of Latino youth.* University of Chicago Press. doi:10.7208/chicago/9780226091044.001.0001

Ripoll-Núñez, K. J., & Rohner, R. P. (2006). Corporal punishment in cross-cultural perspective: Directions for a research agenda. *The Journal of Cross-Cultural Research, 40*(3), 220–249. doi:10.1177/1069397105284395

Royster, J. J. (2016). *Southern Horrors and Other Writings: Anti-Lynching Campaign of Ida B. Wells, 1892-1900.* Macmillan Higher Education.

Russ, R., Donati, R., Rattigan, P., DiGrogorio, T., Abbadessa, E., & Richardson, K. (2009). *Physical activity used as punishment and/or behavior management* [Position statement]. National Association for Sport and Physical Education.

Ryan, C., Carragee, K. M., & Schwerner, C. (1998). *Media, movements, and the quest for social justice.* Academic Press.

Ryan, J., Sanders, S., Katsiyannis, A., & Yell, M. (2007). Using Time-Out Effectively in the Classroom. *Sage Journals, 39*(4), 60–67. Retrieved October 21, 2021, from. doi:10.1177/004005990703900407

Saleem, F. T., Anderson, R. E., & Williams, M. (2020). Addressing the "myth" of racial trauma: Developmental and ecological considerations for youth of color. *Clinical Child and Family Psychology Review, 23*(1), 1–14. https://doi.org/gg5fvw

Salmon, K. (2019). *Task Force on Student Discipline Regulations.* Retrieved 15 April 2020, from https://marylandpublicschools.org/stateboard/Documents/08272019/TaskForceStudentDisciplineRegulations082019.pdf

San Antonio ISD v. Rodriguez, 411 U.S. 1 (1973).

Scollon, R. (2001). Action and text: towards an integrated understanding of the place of text in social (inter) action, mediated discourse analysis and the problem of social action. *Methods of Critical Discourse Analysis, 113*, 139-183.

Sealey-Ruiz, Y. (2011, December 19). *Dismantling the School-to-Prison Pipeline Through Racial Literacy Development in Teacher Education.* Retrieved from Taylor & Francis Online: https://www.tandfonline.com/doi/full/10.1080/15505170.2011.624892?src=recsys

Selman, K. J. (2017). Imprisoning 'those' kids: Neoliberal logics and the disciplinary alternative school. *Youth Justice, 17*(3), 213–231. doi:10.1177/1473225417712607

Sentell, W. (2021). Louisiana House rejects bid to ban spanking in public schools. *The Advocate.* https://www.theadvocate.com/baton_rouge/news/politics/legislature/article_7e8c322c-ad15-11eb-a844-d783f3245d1c.html

Serrano, U. (2020). *Lessons learned from the Los Angeles Youth Movement against the Carceral State.* The Latinx Project at NYU. https://www.latinxproject.nyu.edu/intervenxions/lessons-learned-from-the-los-angeles-youth-movement-against-the-carceral-state

Shalaby, C. (2021). Imagining classroom management: as an abolitionist project. In Education for Liberation Network & Critical Resistance Editorial Collective (Eds.), Lessons in liberation: An abolitionist toolkit for educators (pp. 104-112). AK Press.

Shearer, E., & Mitchell, A. (2021). *News use across social media platforms in 2020.* Academic Press.

Shedd, C. (2015). *Unequal city: Race, schools, and perceptions of injustice.* Russel Sage.

Sheldon, S. B. (2007). Improving student attendance with school, family, and community partnerships. *The Journal of Educational Research, 100*(5), 267–275. doi:10.3200/JOER.100.5.267-275

Shollenberger, T. L. (2015). Racial disparities in school suspension and subsequent outcomes: Evidence from the National Longitudinal Study of Youth. In D. J. Losen (Ed.), *Closing the school discipline gap: Equitable remedies for excessive exclusion* (pp. 31–43). Teachers College Press.

Siegel, D., & Bryson, T. (2014, September 23). 'Time-Outs' Are Hurting Your Child. *Time Magazine.* https://time.com/3404701/discipline-time-out-is-not-good/

Siman, A. (2005). Challenging Zero Tolerance: Federal and State Legal Remedies for Students of Color. *Cornell Journal of Law and Public Policy, 14*(2), 337–364. Retrieved October 21, 2021, from https://scholarship.law.cornell.edu/cgi/viewcontent.cgi?article=1082&context=cjlpp

Simon, J. (2009). *Governing through crime: How the war on crime transformed American democracy and created a culture of fear.* Oxford University Press.

Simonsen, B., & Sugai, G. (2013). PBIS in alternative education settings: Positive support for youth with high-risk behavior. *Education & Treatment of Children, 36*(3), 3–14. doi:10.1353/etc.2013.0030

Singhal, A., & Rogers, E. M. (2001). The entertainment-education strategy in communication campaigns. *Public Communication Campaigns, 3,* 343-356.

Singleton, G. E. (2015). *Courageous conversations about race.* Corwin Press.

Sink, C. A. (2016). Incorporating a multi-tiered system of supports into school counselor preparation. *The Professional Counselor, 6*(3), 203–219. https://doi.org/dnn7

Skiba, R. J., Arredondo, M. I., & Rausch, M. K. (2014). New and developing research on disparities in discipline. *Discipline Disparities Series*. https://indrc.indiana.edu/tools-resources/pdf-disciplineseries/disparity_newresearch_full_040414.pdf

Skiba, R. J., Reynolds, C. R., Graham, S., Sheras, P., Conoley, J. C., & GarciaVazquez, E. (2006). *Are zero tolerance policies effective in the schools? An evidentiary review and recommendations.* A Report by the American Psychological Associate Zero Tolerance Task Force.

Skiba, R., Michael, R., Nardo, A., & Peterson, R. (2002). *The Color of Discipline: Sources of Racial and Gender Disproportionality in School Punishment.* Available at: https://www.indiana.edu/~equity/docs/ColorofDiscipline2002.pdf

Skiba, R. J. (2013). Reaching a critical juncture for our kids: The need to reassess school-justice practices. *Family Court Review*, *51*(3), 380–387. doi:10.1111/fcre.12034

Skiba, R. J. (2014). The failure of zero tolerance. *Reclaiming Children and Youth*, *22*(4), 27–33.

Skiba, R. J., Arredondo, M. I., & Williams, N. T. (2014). More than a metaphor: The contribution of exclusionary discipline to a school-to-prison pipeline. *Equity & Excellence in Education*, *47*(4), 546–564. doi:10.1080/10665684.2014.958965

Skiba, R. J., Horner, R. H., Chung, C. G., Rausch, M. K., May, S. L., & Tobin, T. (2011). Race is not neutral: A national investigation of African American and Latino disproportionality in school discipline. *School Psychology Review*, *40*(1), 85–108.

Skiba, R. J., Horner, R. H., Chung, C.-G., Rausch, M. K., May, S. L., & Tobin, T. (2011). Race is not neutral: A national investigation of African American and Latino dis- proportionality in school discipline. *School Psychology Review*, *40*(1), 85–107.

Skiba, R. J., & Knesting, K. (2001). Zero tolerance, zero evidence: An analysis of school disciplinary practice. *New Directions for Youth Development*, *2001*(92), 17–43. doi:10.1002/yd.23320019204 PMID:12170829

Skiba, R. J., & Losen, D. J. (2015). From reaction to prevention. *American Educator*, *39*(4), 4–46.

Skiba, R. J., & Peterson, R. (1999). The dark side of zero tolerance. *Phi Delta Kappan*, *80*(5), 372–376.

Skiba, R. J., Peterson, R. L., & Williams, T. (1997). Office referrals and suspension: Disciplinary intervention in middle schools. *Education & Treatment of Children*, 295–315.

Skiba, R., Horner, R., Chung, C., Rausch, M., May, S., & Tobin, T. (2011). Race is not neutral: A national investigation of african american and latino disproportionality in school discipline. *School Psychology Review*, *40*(1), 85–107. doi:10.1080/02796015.2011.12087730

Skiba, R., Michael, R., Nardo, A., & Peterson, R. (2002). The color of discipline: Sources of racial and gender disproportionality in school punishment. *The Urban Review*, *34*(4), 317–342. doi:10.1023/A:1021320817372

Skiba, R., & Sprague, J. (2008). Without suspensions. *Educational Leadership*, *66*(1), 38–43.

Smith, E. J., & Harper, S. R. (2015). *Disproportionate Impact Of K-12 School Suspension and Expulsion On Black Students In Southern States*. Retrieved from Penn GSE: https://web-app.usc.edu/web/rossier/publications/231/Smith%20and%20Harper%20(2015)-573.pdf

Smith, C., & Mbozi, J. (2008). *Removing corporal punishment corporal from schools: Integrating partner efforts*. Business Unlimited Consulting Services. https://www.hands.org.gy/files/Corporal%20Punishment%20Report%20-%202008.pdf

Smith, E. J., & Harper, S. R. (2015). *Disproportionate impact of K-12 school suspension and expulsion on Black students in southern states*. University of Pennsylvania, Center for the Study of Race and Equity in Education.

Smith, J. (2021). Racial Threat and Crime Control: Integrating Theory on Race and Extending its Application. *Critical Criminology*, *29*(2), 253–271. doi:10.100710612-019-09485-1

Smith, L. C., Garnett, B. R., Herbert, A., Grudev, N., Vogel, J., Keefner, W., Barnett, A., & Baker, T. (2017). The hand of professional school counseling meets the glove of restorative practices. *Professional School Counseling*, *21*(1). https://doi.org/gh3fst

Smyth, J. (2006). 'When students have power': Student engagement, student voice, and the possibilities for school reform around 'dropping out' of school. *International Journal of Leadership in Education, 9*(4), 285–298. https:// doi:10.1080/13603120600894232

Snow, D. A., Vliegenthart, R., & Ketelaars, P. (2018). *The framing perspective on social movements: Its conceptual roots and architecture. In The Wiley Blackwell companion to social movements*. Wiley Blackwell. doi:10.1002/9781119168577

South African Law Commission. (2000). *Sentencing (a New Sentencing Framework): Report* (Vol. 82). The Commission.

Sparks, S., & Klein, A. (2018). Discipline disparities grow for students of color, new federal data show. *Education Week*. Retrieved from https://www.edweek.org/ew/arti- cles/2018/04/24/discipline-disparities-grow-for-students-of-color.html?cmp=soc-twitter- shr&print=1

Spence, R. N. (2020). Saved by the bell: Reclaiming home court advantage for at-risk youth funneled into the school-to-prison pipeline. *Family Court Review*, *58*(1), 227–242. doi:10.1111/fcre.12464

Stabroek News. (2014). West Ruimveldt pupil severely whipped - Ministry probing headmistress. *Stabroek News* https://www.stabroeknews.com/2014/02/01/news/guyana/west-ruimveldt-pupil-severely-whipped/

Staff Reporter. (2015). Rupununi teachers charged for flogging female students –Ministry to intervene once action taken. *Guyana Chronicle*. https://guyanachronicle.com/2015/07/10/rupununi-teachers-charged-for-flogging-female-students-ministry-to-intervene-once-action-taken/

Staff Reporter. (2015, October 20). Corporal punishment to be totally banned soon – Dr. Roopnaraine …says alternative disciplinary measures being sought. *Guyana Chronicle.*

Staley, B., & Freeman, L. A. (2017). Digital storytelling as student-centred pedagogy: Empowering high school students to frame their futures. Research and Practice in Technology Enhanced *Learning, 12*(21). doi:10.1186/s41039-017-0061-9

Straus, M. A. (1994). *Beating the devil out of them: Corporal punishment in American families.* Jossey-Bass/Lexington Books.

Straus, M. A., & Donnelly, D. A. (2017). *Beating the devil out of them: Corporal punishment in American families and its effects on children* (1st ed.). Taylor & Francis Group. doi:10.4324/9781351314688

Straus, M. A., & Mouradian, V. E. (1998). Impulsive corporal punishment by mothers and antisocial behavior and impulsiveness of children. *Behavioral Sciences & the Law, 16*(3), 353–374. doi:10.1002/(SICI)1099-0798(199822)16:3<353::AID-BSL313>3.0.CO;2-O PMID:9768466

Sugai, G., Horner, R. H., Dunlap, G., Hieneman, M., Lewis, T. J., Nelson, C. M., Scott, T., Liaupsin, C., Sailor, W., Turnbull, A. P., Turnbull, H. R. III, Wickham, D., Wilcox, B., & Ruef, M. OSEP Center on Positive Behavioral Interventions. (2000). Applying positive behavior support and functional behavioral assessment in schools. *Journal of Positive Behavior Interventions, 2*(3), 131–143. doi:10.1177/109830070000200302

Sullivan, J. (2011, October 10). *Black America is Moving to The South–and to the 'Burbs. What it Means?* Colorline. https://www.colorlines.com/articles/black-america-moving-south-and-burbs-whats-it-mean

Suspension Stories. (2021). *About the Author.* https://www.suspensionstories.com/

Szalavitz, M. (2017, June 14). *One Hundred Years Ago, Prohibition Began in Earnest- And We're Still Paying For It.* https://psmag.com/social-justice/one-hundred-years-ago-prohibition-began-earnest-still-paying-97243

Tajalli, H., & Garba, H. (2014). Discipline or prejudice? Overrepresentation of minority students in disciplinary alternative education programs. *The Urban Review, 46*(4), 620–631. doi:10.100711256-014-0274-9

Tefera, A. A., & Fischman, G. E. (2020). How and why context matters in the study of racial disproportionality in special education: Toward a critical disability education policy approach. *Equity & Excellence in Education, 53*(4), 434–449. doi:10.1080/10665684.2020.1791284

Texans Care for Children. (2019). *Report: TX Schools Still Suspending Many Pre-k – 2nd Graders, But Out-of-School Suspensions Dropped Sharply — Texans Care for Children.* Retrieved 15 July 2020, from https://txchildren.org/posts/2019/8/27/report-tx-schools-still-suspending-many-pre-k-2nd-graders-but-out-of-school-suspensions-dropped-sharply

Texans Care for Children. (2021). *Keeping Kids in Class: Pre-K Through 2ⁿᵈ Grade Suspension in Texas and a Better Way Forward.* Retrieved 25 June 2021, from https://static1.squarespace.com/static/5728d34462cd94b84dc567ed/t/5b1ea6c270a6ad846fb7cbc9/1528735440357/keeping-kids-in-schools.pdf

Texas Compilation of School Discipline Law and Regulations. (2021). Retrieved from: https://safesupportivelearning.ed.gov/sites/default/files/discipline-compendium/Texas%20School%20Discipline%20Laws%20and%20Regulations.pdf

Texas Education Agency. (2018). *District Type Glossary of Terms.* Retrieved from: https://tea.texas.gov/reports-and-data/school-data/district-type-data-search/district-type-glossary-of-terms-2018-19

Texas Education Agency. (2020). *Comprehensive biennial report on Texas public schools.* https://tea.texas.gov/sites/default/files/comp_annual_biennial_2020.pdf

Texas Legislature Online. (2021, March 24). *Bill: SB 1595.* https://capitol.texas.gov/BillLookup/History.aspx?LegSess=87R&Bill=SB1595

The Florida Senate. (2021, July 7). *SB 858: Corporal punishment in public schools.* https://www.flsenate.gov/Session/Bill/2021/858

The National Archives. (n.d.a). *Bill of Rights: What Does It Say?* Retrieved October 21, 2021, from https://www.archives.gov/founding-docs/bill-of-rights/what-does-it-say

The National Archives. (n.d.b). *Constitution of the United States - A History.* Retrieved October 21, 2021, from https://www.archives.gov/founding-docs/more-perfect-union

The National Archives. (n.d.c). *The Declaration of Independence: A History.* Retrieved October 21, 2021, from https://www.archives.gov/founding-docs/declaration-history

The United Nations Educational, Scientific and Cultural Organization (UNESCO). (2017, January 19). Knocking out school violence and bullying. *Building peace in the minds of men and women.* https://en.unesco.org/

Tiegen, A. (2016, July). *Automatically Sealing or Expunging Juvenile Records.* National Conference of State Legislatures. https://www.ncsl.org/research/civil-and-criminal-justice/automatically-sealing-or-expunging-juvenile-records.aspx

Tinker v. Des Moines Independent Community School District, 393 U.S. 503 (1969)

Tomar, D. A. (2018). *Cops in Schools: Have we built a school-to-prison pipeline.* The Best Schools.

Toshalis, E., & Nakkula, M. (2012). *Motivation, engagement, and student voice.* Jobs for the Future, Retrieved from http://www.studentsatthecenter.org/topics/motivation-

Townsend, B. (2000). The disproportionate discipline of African American learners: Reducing school suspensions and. *Exceptional Children, 66*(3), 381–391. doi:10.1177/001440290006600308

Triplett, N., Allen, A., & Lewis, C. (2014). Zero Tolerance, School Shootings, and the Post-Brown Quest for Equity in Discipline Policy: An Examination of How Urban Minorities are Punished for White Suburban Violence. *The Journal of Negro Education*, *83*(3), 352–370. doi:10.7709/jnegroeducation.83.3.0352

Turner, D. C. III. (2021). The (good) trouble with Black boys: Organizing with Black boys and young men in George Floyd's America. *Theory Intro Practice*, *60*(4), 422–433. doi:10.1080/0 0405841.2021.1983317

U.S. Census Bureau. (2019). *Census Bureau Reports Nearly 77 Million Students Enrolled in U.S. Schools*. Retrieved from https://www.census.gov/newsroom/press-releases/2019/school-enrollment.html

U.S. Department of Education Office for Civil Rights. (2014). *Civil Rights Data Collection. Data Snap Shot: School Discipline. Brief No. 1*. Author.

U.S. Department of Education Office of Civil Rights. (2014). *Civil rights data collection data snapshot: School discipline*. Retrieved from https://www2.ed.gov/about/offices/list/ocr/docs/crdc-discipline-snapshot.pdf

U.S. Department of Education Office of Civil Rights. (2021). *An overview of exclusionary discipline practices in public school for the 2017-18 school year*. Retrieved from https:// www2. ed.gov/ about/offices/list/ocr/docs/crdc-exclusionary-school-discipline.pdf

U.S. Department of Education, Data, Civil Rights Collection Data. (2017). *School/District/State Comparison Report: At least one out-of-school suspension, Albuquerque, Bangor, Charlotte-Mecklenburg, Gahanna-Jefferson, Indian Prairie, Salt Lake City*. https://ocrdata.ed.gov/dataanalysistools/comparisongraphsanddatareport

U.S. Department of Education. (2014). *Rethinking school discipline*. Available from: http://www.2.ed.gov/policy/gen/guid/

UNICEF. (2019). *Study of social norms in Guyana as it pertains to sexual, physical and emotional violence against children*. Final Report. https://www.unicef.org/guyanasuriname/media/1166/file/Study%20of%20Social%20Norms%20on%20Violence%20against%20Children.pdf

United Nations (UN). (2004). *Committee on the Rights of the Child*. Thirty-fifth sessions consideration of reports submitted. UN.

United Nations Children's Fund (UNICEF). (1990). First *call for children*. World Declaration and Plan of Action from the World Summit for Children: Convention on the Rights of the Child. https://www.unicef.org/media/85571/file/WSC-declaration-first-call-for-children.pdf

United Nations Committee on the Rights of the Child (CRC) CRC General Comment No. 8. (2006). *The Right of the Child to Protection from Corporal Punishment and Other Cruel or Degrading forms of Punishment* (U.N. CRC/C/GC/8) 2007 Mar 2. Retrieved October 21, 2021, from https://www.refworld.org/docid/460bc7772.html

United States Commission on Civil Rights. (2019). *Beyond Suspensions*. Retrieved October 21, 2021, from https://www.usccr.gov/files/pubs/2019/07-23-Beyond-Suspensions.pdf

United States Department of Education. (n.d.). *A History of the Individuals With Disabilities Education Act*. Retrieved October 21, 2021, from https://sites.ed.gov/idea/IDEA-History#1950s-60s-70s

United States Department of Justice & United States Department of Education. (2014). *Joint Dear Colleague Letter: Nondiscriminatory Administration of School Discipline*. Retrieved October 21, 2021, from https://www2.ed.gov/about/offices/list/ocr/letters/colleague-201401-title-vi.html

United States Government Accountability Office, Report to Congressional Request. (2018). *Discipline disparities for black students, boys, and students with disabilities*. Author.

United States Government Accountability Office. (2018). *K-12 Education: Discipline Disparities for Black Students, Boys, and Students with Disabilities*. GAO-18-258. Author.

US Department of Education. (n.d.a). *Office for Civil Rights Data Collection, 2011-2012*. Available at http://ocrdata.ed.gov

US Department of Education. (n.d.b). *Office for Civil Rights Data Collection, 2013-14*. Available at http://ocrdata.ed.gov

US Department of Education. (n.d.c). *Office for Civil Rights Data Collection, 2015-16*. available at http://ocrdata.ed.gov

US Department of Education. (n.d.d). *Office for Civil Rights Data Collection, 2017-18*. available at http://ocrdata.ed.gov

Utley, O. (2008). Keeping the tradition of African storytelling alive. *Yale National Initiative*. https://teachers.yale.edu/curriculum/viewer/initiative_09.01.08_u

Van Dijk, T. (2001). Critical Discourse Analysis. The Handbook of Discourse Analysis, 352-371.

Vanden Poel, L., & Hermans, D. (2019). Narrative coherence and identity: Associations with psychological well-being and internalizing symptoms. *Frontiers in Psychology*. doi:10.3389/fpsyg.2019.01171

Varela, K. S., Peguero, A. A., Eason, J. M., Marchbanks, M. P. T. III, & Blake, J. (2018). School strictness and education: Investigating racial and ethnic educational inequalities associated with being pushed out. *Sociology of Race and Ethnicity (Thousand Oaks, Calif.)*, *4*(2), 261–280. doi:10.1177/2332649217730086

Vaught, S., & Castagno, A. (2008). I don't think I'm a racist": Critical race theory, teacher attitudes, and structural racism. *Race, Ethnicity and Education*, *11*(2), 95–113. doi:10.1080/13613320802110217

Velez, G., Hahn, M., Recchia, H., & Wainryb, C. (2020). Rethinking response to youth rebellion: Recent growth and development of restorative practices in schools. *Current Opinion in Psychology*, *35*, 36–40. doi:10.1016/j.copsyc.2020.02.011 PMID:32283520

Vliegenthart, R., & Walgrave, S. (2012). The interdependency of mass media and social movements. The Sage handbook of political communication, 387-397.

Voight, A., Hanson, T., O'Malley, M., & Adekanye, L. (2015). The racial school climate gap: Within-school disparities in students' experiences of safety, support, and connectedness. *American Journal of Community Psychology, 56*(3-4), 252–267. doi:10.100710464-015-9751-x PMID:26377419

Wake, D. G. (2012). Exploring Rural Contexts with Digital Storytelling. *Rural Educator, 33*(3), 23–37.

Walker, T. (2016). *Why are 19 states still allowing corporal punishment corporal in schools?* National Education Association (NEA). https://www.nea.org/advocating-for-change/new-from-nea/why-are-19-states-still-allowing-corporal-punishment-schools

Wallace, J., Goodkind, S., Wallace, C. M., & Bachman, J. G. (2008). Racial, ethnic, and gender differences in school discipline among U.S. high school students: 1991-2005. *Negro Educational Review, 59*(1-2), 25–48. PMID:19430541

Wallace, J. Jr, Goodkind, S., Wallace, C. M., & Bachman, J. G. (2008). Racial, Ethnic, and Gender Differences in School Discipline among U.S. High School Students: 1991-2005. *Negro Educational Review, 59*(1-2), 47. https://www.ncbi.nlm.nih.gov/pmc/articles/PMC2678799/ PMID:19430541

Washburn, D. (2018). *Countdown to expand ban on 'willful defiance' suspensions in California schools.* Retrieved 25 June 2021, from https://edsource.org/2018/youth-advocates-pushing-to-expand-californias-ban-on-willful-defiance-suspensions/593754

Weinstein, B. (2019). *Behavioral Data is as Important as Academic Data (maybe more).* Retrieved 25 November 2020, from https://blog.behaviorflip.com/behavioraldata/

Welfare, L. E., Grimes, T. O., Lawson, G., Hori, K., & Asadi, G. (2021). The school to prison pipeline: Quantitative evidence to guide school counselor advocacy. *Journal of Counselor Leadership and Advocacy, 8*(1), 16–29. https://doi.org/10.1080/2326716X.2020.1861490

Welsh, R. O., & Little, S. (2018). The School Discipline Dilemma: A Comprehensive Review of Disparities and Alternative Approaches. *Review of Educational Research, 88*(5), 752–794. doi:10.3102/0034654318791582

West, C. (1995). *Critical race theory: The key writings that formed the movement.* The New Press.

Wheeler, R. (2017). *Suspensions Don't Teach.* Retrieved from https://www.edutopia.org/article/suspensions-dont-teach

Whitaker, A., Cobb, J., Leung, V., & Nelson, L. (2021). *No police in schools: A vision for safe and supportive schools in CA.* American Civil Liberties Union. https://bit.ly/3pvfkqb

Whitaker, A., Torres-Guillén, S., Morton, M., Jordan, H., Coyle, S., Mann, A., & Sun, W.-L. (2019). *Cops not counselors: How the lack of school mental health professionals is harming students.* American Civil Liberties Union. https://bit.ly/31vdBsX

Whitaker, A., Torres-Guillen, S., Morton, M., Jordan, H., Coyle, S., Mann, A., & Wei-Ling, S. (2019). *Cops and no counselors: How the lack of school mental health is harming students.* American Civil Liberties Union.

Whitenton, K. (2017). *Narrative biases: When storytelling hurts user experience.* https://www.nngroup.com/articles/narrative-biases/

Wilkerson, K. L., Afacan, K., Yan, M.-C., Justin, W., & Datar, S. D. (2016). Academic remediation–focused alternative schools: Impact on student outcomes. *Remedial and Special Education, 37*(2), 67–77. doi:10.1177/0741932515620842

Williams, E. M. (2021). Thinking beyond "counselors not cops": Imagining & decarcerating care in schools. In Education for Liberation Network & Critical Resistance Editorial Collective (Eds.), Lessons in liberation: An abolitionist toolkit for educators (pp. 318-327). AK Press.

Williams, J. A. III, Lewis, C., Starker Glass, T., Butler, B. R., & Hoon Lim, J. (2020). The discipline gatekeeper: Assistant principals' experiences with managing school discipline in urban middle schools. *Urban Education.* Advance online publication. doi:10.1177/0042085920908913

Williams, J. A., Johnson, J. N., Dangerfield-Persky, F., & Mayakis, C. G. (2020). Does employing more novice teachers predict higher suspensions for black students? A Hierarchical Multiple Regression Analysis. *The Journal of Negro Education, 89*(4), 448–458. https://www.jstor.org/stable/10.7709/jnegroeducation.89.4.0448

Williams, R. B., Bryant-Mallory, D., Coleman, K., Gotel, D., & Hall, C. (2017). An Evidence-Based Approach to Reducing Disproportionality in Special Education and Discipline Referrals. *Children & Schools, 39*(4), 248–251. doi:10.1093/cs/cdx020

Winslade, J., & Monk, G. (2000). *Narrative mediation: A new approach to conflict resolution.* https://www.researchgate.net/publication/240132907

World Health Organization (WHO). (2016). *Global plan of action to strengthen the role of the health system within a national multisectoral response to address interpersonal violence, in particular against women and girls, and against children.* https://www.who.int/reproductivehealth/publications/violence/global-plan-of-action/en/

Wright, J. P., Morgan, M. A., Coyne, M. A., Beaver, K. M., & Barnes, J. C. (2014). Prior problem behavior accounts for the racial gap in school suspensions. *Journal of Criminal Justice, 42*(3), 257–266. doi:10.1016/j.jcrimjus.2014.01.001

Xu, X., Tung, Y., & Dunaway, R. G. (2000). Cultural, human, and social capital as determinants of corporal punishment: Toward an integrated theoretical model. *Journal of Interpersonal Violence, 15*(6), 603–630. doi:10.1177/088626000015006004

Young, D. B. (1983). Cesare Beccaria: Utilitarian or Retributivist? *Journal of Criminal Justice, 11*(4), 317–326. doi:10.1016/0047-2352(83)90071-5

Yuhas, D. (2018). *Restorative justice is about more than just reducing suspensions. The Hechinger Report.*

Compilation of References

Zak, P. J. (2013, October). How stories change the brain. *Greater Good Magazine*. https://greatergood.berkeley.edu/profile/paul_zak

Zehr, H. (1990). *Changing lenses* (Vol. 114). Herald Press.

Zelinski, A., & Bureau, A. (2019). *Texas banned out-of-school suspensions for most young children. 4,500 kids were suspended anyway*. Retrieved 25 June 2021, from https://www.houstonchronicle.com/politics/texas/article/Texas-banned-out-of-school-suspensions-for-most-14398476.php

Ziomek-Daigle, J., Goodman-Scott, E., Cavin, J., & Donohue, P. (2016). Integrating a multi-tiered system of supports with comprehensive school counseling programs. *The Professional Counselor*, 6(3), 220–232. https://doi.org/dnhw

Zoch, L. M., & Molleda, J. C. (2006). Building a theoretical model of media relations using framing, information subsidies, and agenda-building. *Public Relations Theory II*, 279-309.

Zyromski, B., & Mariani, M. (2016). *Facilitating evidence-based, data-driven school counseling: A manual for practice*. Corwin.

About the Contributors

Anthony Adams is a professor of sociology and chair of the Department of Sociology & Criminal Justice at Clark Atlanta University. He is also the former director of the Atwood Institute for Race, Education, and the Democratic Ideal at Kentucky State University in Frankfort, KY. Adams earned a doctorate (1990) and M.A. (1987) from the University of Michigan, Ann Arbor, Michigan. He earned a BS degree (1983) in criminal justice and criminology from Eastern Michigan University, Ypsilanti, MI. Adams' research interests have centered on secondary-level school violence, school discipline, and the medicalization of school discipline. He has published peer-reviewed articles in international, domestic, and regional journals. Adams' other research areas include service-learning education (middle/secondary/post-secondary level), and food deserts. More, his research has been funded by Michigan Campus Compact, the Office of Educational Research and Improvement, US Department of Education, the Bentley, and numerous fellowship and travel awards.

* * *

Jennifer Wyatt Bourgeois is a Center for Justice Research Postdoctoral Fellow. Her research focuses on race, class, and gender disparities within the criminal justice system. Jennifer holds a B.S. in Forensic Science from Baylor University, and a M.S. in Criminal Justice from Sam Houston State University. Dr. Bourgeois completed her doctoral studies in the Administration of Justice program, within the Barbara Jordan – Mickey Leland School of Public Affairs at Texas Southern University.

Mindy Brooks-Eaves, DSW, MSW, CSW, is Chair and Program Director of the School of Social Work at Kentucky State University, Kentucky's only public HBCU, a Whitney M. Young Scholar, Advisory Board Member of Continued, consultant for the Wellness Group ETC., and co-editor of The A to Z Self-Care Handbook for Social Workers and other Helping Professionals. Dr. BE has over 17 years of experience in the areas of social work, education, administration, and child welfare. She solely created the Ombuds Office for Jefferson County Public Schools. Her passion is equity, teaching, and sustainability of social workers with specific attention to disparity, blackness, identity, cultural inclusivity, and practicing radical self-care as a guiding principle. For the culture, Dr. BE regularly volunteers to support equity and democracy. Dr. BE earned her Doctor of Social Work (DSW) from the University of St. Thomas DSW program where teaching is practice. She is a proud member of Alpha Kappa Alpha Sorority Inc. and Phi Alpha Honor Society. She is a past recipient of the Cabinet for Health & Families Award for Excellence and Social Worker of the Year and Kentucky Court of Justice KLEO Award.

Thelma Laredo Clark is a doctoral candidate currently completing her dissertation regarding the overuse of exclusionary discipline on economically disadvantaged students.

Enrique Espinoza is a PhD candidate at the University of California, Riverside and a professional school counselor. His research is focused on racism in K-12 schools, particularly on the race-gendered experiences of male students of color. He also is interested in the role of school counselors in addressing racism and aiding the healing from racism-induced traumatic stress (racial trauma).

Brenda I. Gill, Ph.D., is a mixed-methods prepared family sociologist with a minor concentration in education. She serves as a Professor of Sociology and Associate Dean in the College of Liberal Arts and Social Sciences at Alabama State University. Dr. Gill received a Ph.D. in her field from Wayne State University, Detroit, Michigan, in 2009. Her national and internationally focused applied research centers on family issues such as multiculturalism, diversity, food insecurity, corporal punishment/family discipline, immigration, human trafficking, media, food insecurity, suicide, and violence. Her most recent publications include two collaborative chapters: Sex Trafficking of Girls: Focus on Latin American and The Caribbean; Sex Trafficking of Girls: The West African Quandary, published by Routledge and Springer, respectively, 2022. Her most recent journal article: Systemic Inequality, Sustainability and COVID 19 in the U.S. Prison System: Findings from two Sociological Garden/Sustainability Interventions, is published in the Research in Political Sociology, Vol 29, Emerald Publishing, 2022.

Howard Henderson is a professor of justice administration and director of the Center for Justice Research at Texas Southern University, where he focuses on issues of criminal injustice.

Edwin Hernandez is an Associate Professor and Coordinator of the Counseling Program in the College of Education at California State University, San Bernardino. His professional experiences as a school counselor in alternative schools prompted his research interest to examine the policies and practices that promote or hinder the educational experiences, opportunities, and success for racially minoritized youth who have been pushed out of traditional schools and consequently enrolled at alternative/continuation high schools. Another strand of his work examines the experiences and practices of school counselors in dismantling racialized punitive practices that harm racially minoritized youth.

Morgan D. Kirby is an Assistant Professor in the School of Communication at Texas Southern University. She serves in the Journalism Department where she teaches public relations and advertising courses. Dr. Kirby holds a B.A. in Public Relations from Hampton University, an M.A. in Government from Regent University, and a Ph.D. in Communication, Culture, and Media Studies from Howard University. Her research interests include strategic communication, social change, social justice, Black representation in media, and womanism.

Melissa Kwende is a Doctoral Candidate in the Administration of Justice department of the Barbara Jordan – Mickey Leland School of Public Affairs at Texas Southern University. Her research interests focus on African Criminology and the racial disparities in the American Criminal Justice System.

Caroline Lopez-Perry is an Associate Professor and program coordinator for the School Counseling program in the College of Education at California State University, Long Beach. Prior to her work in counselor education, she was a school counselor in the elementary and middle school setting. Her research and publications focus on school counselor leadership, specifically the school counselors' role in promoting equity in education through program design, service delivery, advocacy, and educational reform. Other areas of focus include group counseling, school counseling classroom instruction, career and college readiness, and the recruitment and retention of school counselors of color.

Herman R. Moncure, Jr., Esq., received his Juris Doctor from Western Michigan University Thomas M. Colley Law School in 2019. In November 2020 he became a member of the State Bar of Texas. He is a practicing estate planning attorney with Pyke & Associates, P.C. located in Dallas, Texas. He also earned both a Master of Science in Finance and a Master of Business Administration from Walsh College of Business and Accountancy in 2011 and 2014, respectively.

Elizabeth Anne Murray is a Postdoctoral Research and Clinical Fellow with Baylor University's Department of Curriculum and Instruction. As a fellow, she shares joint responsibilities working as a writing coordinator for students in the Learning and Organizational Change (LOC) doctorate and assisting with the LOC's program evaluation. Her research interests include difficult conversations in the ELA classroom and disruptive encounters with literature.

Brandi Ray is currently serving as graduate faculty and faculty advisor at Baylor University School of Education's Ed.D program in curriculum and instruction and organizational change. Her research includes leadership, media literacy, and teacher education.

Julian Scott is a professor of justice administration and an affiliated Research Fellow at the Center for Justice Research at Texas Southern University.

Wilsando Seegars has worked extensively in public education for over 20 years. He holds a Bachelor of Science Degree in Secondary English Education from Eastern Michigan University, Masters from Wayne State University in Education Leadership, and a Doctorates from The University of St Francis in Education leadership with extensive research on standardized assessment outcomes. He has been a classroom teacher, curriculum developer, reading and writing specialist, researcher, author, as well as the founder of the Scholars Group mentor program. He is currently an educator in IL that has served as a member of several committees geared towards discipline equity, cultural awareness, and enhancing academic outcomes.

Kisha Solomon is a writer, digital strategist, and data storyteller. A graduate of Clark Atlanta University, she has worked as a strategic advisor and enterprise leader at some of America's top companies, as an English-language educator in Spain's public school system, and as a freelance writer and essayist. Her passion for understanding how teams and organizations manage change in the context of building learning organizations has led her to contribute her unique perspective to this volume. Ms. Solomon maintains a permanent residence in Atlanta, Georgia.

Pamela Yeung is a science and technology consultant and a political activist for social justice. She is currently serving out her term as a school board member in Stafford County, Virginia. In November 2021, she was elected to represent her home district on the Board of Supervisors. She was raised in the Netherlands and speaks, read, and writes several languages. Her father was born in Curacao into a political family. Her mother was born in St. Maarten. Her parents met in Aruba, and both worked in tourism. She has six siblings and four children. Three of her four children graduated from prestigious universities, and one is currently enrolled. Pamela earned her baccalaureate degree in business and information technology from Howard University, a master's degree in science and technology from Johns Hopkins University and she is a doctoral candidate at Baylor University for leadership and organizational change. Pamela has a transformative worldview that drives her believe in self-empowerment, racial equality, and respect for one's civil rights. Pamela's worldview is rooted in her childhood experiences and her love for education and higher learning to improve Black and Brown student's chances of equal and equitable education. Pamela hopes to understand and reduce White teacher's implicit bias by using best practice strategies and looking through the lens of social justice to respond to educational disparities, reduce inequities and provide opportunities for better access to education to all students regardless of their zip code.

Index

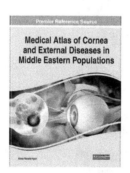
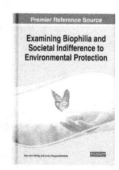
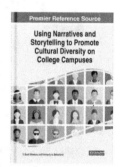

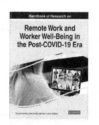

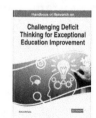

Printed in the USA
CPSIA information can be obtained
at www.ICGtesting.com
CBHW071226140124
3417CB00006B/123